MANY MORE LIVES OF THE BATMAN

EDITED BY

Roberta PEARSON, William URICCHIO, Will BROOKER

palgrave

A BFI book published by Palgrave

The Many Lives of the Batman published in 1991 by Routledge, an imprint of Routledge, Chapman and Hall, Inc., 29 West 35 Street, New York, NY 10001, USA
Published in Great Britain by BFI Publishing

First published in 2015 by
PALGRAVE

on behalf of the

BRITISH FILM INSTITUTE
21 Stephen Street, London W1T 1LN
www.bfi.org.uk

There's more to discover about film and television through the BFI. Our world-renowned archive, cinemas, festivals, films, publications and learning resources are here to inspire you.

PALGRAVE in the UK is an imprint of Macmillan Publishers Limited, registered in England, company number 785998, of 4 Crinan Street, London N1 9XW. Palgrave Macmillan in the US is a division of St Martin's Press LLC, 175 Fifth Avenue, New York, NY 10010. Palgrave is a global imprint of the above companies and is represented throughout the world. Palgrave® and Macmillan® are registered trademarks in the United States, the United Kingdom, Europe and other countries.

Cover artwork: Clay Rodery

Set by couch
Printed in China

This book is printed on paper suitable for recycling and made from fully managed and sustained forest sources. Logging, pulping and manufacturing processes are expected to conform to the environmental regulations of the country of origin.

British Library Cataloguing-in-Publication Data
A catalogue record for this book is available from the British Library
A catalog record for this book is available from the Library of Congress

ISBN 978–1–84457–764–4 (pb)
ISBN 978–1–84457–765–1 (hb)

CONTENTS

ACKNOWLEDGMENTS

Roberta Pearson and William Uricchio would again like to thank Dennis O'Neil for taking the time to share the secrets of the Batcave with us, for his generosity with his scripts and the Batbible, and for his interest in the project. Thanks to Denny and to Frank Miller for allowing their interviews to be reprinted in this volume and to contributors Henry Jenkins, Lynn Spigel, Jim Collins and Eileen Meehan for providing postscripts to their chapters. We are also grateful to Anthony N. Smith for consultations concerning the update to our chapter. Will Brooker would specifically like to thank Grant Morrison and Kristan Morrison for their generosity and time, and Roberta and William for, respectively, supervising and examining his PhD on Batman in 1999. Thanks also to Phillip Bevin, who has just completed his PhD at Kingston University on Superman, for the inspiring and provocative tutorials over the last four years.

NOTES ON CONTRIBUTORS

PHILLIP BEVIN completed his PhD on the cultural and political history of Superman at Kingston University, Surrey, and is an assistant editor of *Cinema Journal*.

WILL BROOKER is Professor of Film and Cultural Studies at Kingston University and editor of *Cinema Journal*. He is the author of several books on popular culture, including *Batman Unmasked* and *Hunting the Dark Knight*.

JIM COLLINS is a Professor at the University of Notre Dame where he teaches courses in digital culture and postmodern studies. His most recent book is *Bring on the Books for Everybody: How Literary Culture Became Popular Culture*.

MARK GALLAGHER is Associate Professor of Film and Television Studies at the University of Nottingham. He is the author of *Another Steven Soderbergh Experience: Authorship and Contemporary Hollywood* and *Action Figures: Men, Action Films and Contemporary Adventure Narratives*, and co-editor of *East Asian Film Noir*.

HENRY JENKINS is Provost's Professor of Communication, Journalism, Cinematic Arts and Education at the USC Annenberg School for Communication and the USC School of Cinematic Arts. His many books include *Convergence Culture: Where Old and New Media Collide*, *Textual Poachers: Television Fans and Participatory Culture* and *What Made Pistachio Nuts?: Early Sound Comedy and the Vaudeville Aesthetic*.

PAUL LEVITZ is a comic fan (*The Comic Reader*), editor (*Batman*, among many titles), writer (*Legion of Super-Heroes*, including two *New York Times* best-sellers), executive (thirty years at DC, ending as President & Publisher), historian (*75 Years of DC Comics: The Art of Modern Myth-Making*) and educator (including the American Graphic Novel at Columbia University). His many awards include Comic-Con International's Inkpot Award and the prestigious Bob Clampett Humanitarian Award.

EILEEN R. MEEHAN is a Professor in the Department of Radio, Television and Digital Media at Southern Illinois University. Her research has addressed the commodity audience, corporate synergy, gendered economics and, most recently, *Dog the Bounty Hunter*.

ROBERTA PEARSON is Professor of Film and Television Studies at the University of Nottingham. She is one of the editors of *The Many Lives of the Batman*. Among her many other books are *Star Trek and American Television* (co-authored with Máire Messenger Davies) and the edited collection *Storytelling in the Media Convergence Age: Exploring Screen Narratives* (co-edited with Anthony N. Smith).

CHRISTOPHER SHARRETT is Professor of Communication and Film Studies at Seton Hall University. He is author of *The Rifleman* and editor of *Crisis Cinema: The Apocalyptic Idea in Postmodern Narrative Film, Mythologies of Violence in Postmodern Media* and co-editor of *Planks of Reason: Essays on the Horror Film*, the first academic collection on the horror film

ANTHONY N. SMITH is Lecturer in Television Theory at the University of Salford. He has published articles in the journals *Television and New Media* and *Critical Studies in Television* and is co-editor of the forthcoming anthology *Storytelling in the Media Convergence Age: Exploring Screen Narratives.*

IAIN ROBERT SMITH is Senior Lecturer in Film Studies at the University of Roehampton, London. He is author of *The Hollywood Meme: Transnational Adaptations of American Film and Television* and co-chair of the SCMS Transnational Cinemas Scholarly Interest Group.

LYNN SPIGEL is the Frances E. Willard Professor of Screen Cultures at the School of Communication at Northwestern University. Her books include *TV by Design: Modern Art and the Rise of Modern Television, Welcome to the Dreamhouse: Popular Media and Postwar Suburbs* and *Make Room for TV: Television and the Family Ideal in Postwar America.*

WILLIAM URICCHIO is Professor of Comparative Media Studies at the Massachusetts Institute of Technology where he is Principal Investigator for the MIT Open Documentary Lab. He is also Professor of Comparative Media History at Utrecht University in the Netherlands. He has published extensively on the history of old media when they were new.

INTRODUCTION
REVISITING THE BATMAN
Roberta Pearson, William Uricchio and Will Brooker

On 26 July 2014, fans at the San Diego Comic-Con watched the first teaser trailer for a new Batman movie. A pumped-up, armour-clad Dark Knight, his eyes glowing under a bulky helmet, turned on the Bat-signal: the beam of light found Superman, hovering mid-air, his eyes burning with crimson heat-vision. This brief preview of *Batman v Superman*, scheduled for release in March 2016, is clearly indebted to the final chapter of Frank Miller's *The Dark Knight Returns* (1986), from its concept and tone to the specifics of its visual design; meanwhile, the hype around the movie and the excited fan reception to every clip, costume and publicity photo recall the buzz that preceded Tim Burton's *Batman* of 1989. Those two versions of the character were, with hindsight, the primary focus of and the prompt behind the original book, published in 1991. Despite its detailed engagement with other aspects of the character's then fifty-year history – most notably, the television show of the late 1960s – *The Many Lives of the Batman* would not have been conceived or published without Miller's 1986 graphic novel and the Tim Burton blockbuster that followed it.

The existence of this sequel suggests that there is more to say; that we have moved on in the last twenty-five years, between the Batman's fiftieth and seventy-fifth anniversaries, and have not simply returned to the same place. Of course, that is the case. Despite the powerful echoes of the late-1980s Batman in the Comic-Con teaser trailer, the character has changed, as have his cultural and industrial contexts. At the publication of *The Many Lives of the Batman*, two official Batmen, that of the film and that of the comic books, dominated the media, although the campy Batman of the 1960s TV show still occupied a prominent position in cultural memory, as documented by Lynn Spigel's and Henry Jenkins's chapter reprinted in this volume. In 2015, multiple Batmen, in multiple timelines, universes and media, compete for attention. The original book appeared at the end of the relative stability of the decades-long Cold War; this sequel is published amidst a worldwide chaos that as yet has no name beyond the increasingly inaccurate 'post-9/11'. If the international scene has transformed almost beyond recognition, so has the domestic situation. The original appeared during the final term of Bush 41; the sequel is published during the final term of the first African-American president. The mediascape exhibits both continuities and disjunctures with that of the early 1990s. International conglomerates such as Warner Bros. continue to dominate production and distribution, but now take advantage of new technologies and new regulations (or lack thereof) to extend their power and their reach. The Batman is now distributed and publicised across platforms as yet unimagined in 1991, from digital comics to Twitter. As Alan Moore wrote in his Introduction to Miller's *Dark Knight Returns*, 'Everything is exactly the same, except for the fact that it's all totally different.'[1]

The Batman's changing industrial contexts

The original book appeared at a time before the DVD helped users to redefine their relationship to the moving image, the World Wide Web went public, YouTube offered a platform for fan-produced texts, and before the US Telecommunications Act of 1996 permitted cross-media ownership and opened the door for new rounds of industry concentration. 'Permitted' is a loaded word in this context, as Eileen Meehan showed in her chapter on the political economy of Warner Communications Inc. and Time Warner in *The Many Lives of the Batman*, reprinted in this volume. The 1970s and 80s witnessed a frenzy of trans-industry mergers, and with them, textual strategies designed to maximise production efficiencies and financial return. The Telecom Act essentially endorsed the facts on the ground, cleared remaining regulatory hurdles and encouraged a redoubling of mergers, acquisitions and media concentration. The logics of commodity production mapped out by Meehan and exemplified by the multimedia surround that accompanied Warner's 1989 box-office blockbuster *Batman* would only intensify over the coming decades.

A look back at the *locus classicus* of the Batman – the comic book – tells the tale in vivid terms. From National Allied Publications to Detective Comics to National Comics to National Periodical Publications, the entity eventually known as DC Comics spent its first forty years changing hands within the small world of pulp magazine publishers and distributors. ABC's *Batman* series (1966–8) and Kinney National Company's 1967 takeover of National Periodical Publications and 1968 acquisition of Warner Bros.–Seven Arts changed all that. Call it coincidence, but just as the *Batman* TV series accompanied the merger of DC Comics and Warner Bros., so too did the 1989 *Batman* film accompany the merger of Warner Communications and Time Inc. The corporate platform for the Batman's migration across media was in place, and by 2009, when DC Comics was folded into DC Entertainment Inc., a Warner Communications subsidiary, the Batman was truly media-agnostic. Marvel Comics, DC's 'archrival', has followed a similar trajectory, beginning in the publishing world in the late 1930s and surviving numerous reorganisations until its 2009 takeover by the Walt Disney Company. Its IP-protected characters, like DC's, have learned to move like synchronised swimmers across screens large and small, gaming platforms, the printed page and just about anything capable of bearing a logo. And they have by now swum across most of the planet.

If the terms of media ownership and control have changed since the 1991 publication of *The Many Lives of the Batman*, so too have the conditions for transnational exchange. In part signalled by the formation of the World Trade Organization in 1995 (effectively replacing the General Agreement on Tariffs and Trade), the global flow of products accelerated at the same time that the control of intellectual property tightened. 'Globalisation' – with a history as old as human culture – emerged as a new buzzword in academic and policy circles where it was put to use variously as descriptor, cause and effect. Whereas nearly one-third of the 1989 *Batman*'s box-office income was generated outside of North America, *The Dark Knight* (2008) earned almost half of its $1 billion overseas. Although exceptional in breaking box-office records in each of their respective years, these two films, as data points, exemplify Hollywood's steadily growing reliance on global distribution and income. As Mark Gallagher's chapter in this collection shows, however, whatever globalisation may be, it is not monolithic. While global markets constitute a clearly defined target for the various Bat-films, factors such as running time, narrative complexity, level of melodramatic emplotment, alignment with local tastes and politics, and even the 'otherness' of superheroes can undercut the producers' best laid plans.

Fans have been the most vocal – and most studied – of audiences, and offer another crucial counterweight to the dynamics of media concentration, cross-platform marketing and globalisation. Just as these dynamics have intensified since the initial publication of *The Many Lives of the Batman*, so too has a key enabling condition for fandom: the internet. According to the World Bank, the United States had 1.2 internet users per 100 people in 1991, in contrast to 84.2 users per 100 in 2013. Given that the Batman films and games now earn much more revenue and reach many more people than the comics, diehard comic book fans have, then, become a specialist, niche audience at this point in the Batman's history; but they can express themselves far more easily, more widely and more vocally than they could in 1989. Readers who were unhappy with the casting of Michael Keaton in Tim Burton's film could write to a magazine or newspaper in protest, and hope that their letter might be selected for publication.[2] When Ben Affleck's casting as the next Batman was announced in August 2013, fans were able to express their disapproval within moments on Twitter, and every subsequent pre-production image of the actor in costume was swiftly photoshopped and circulated, often as satirical memes such as 'Sad Batman'. Developments in digital technology and social media now mean that fan-made videos can look as professional as – and sometimes prove more popular than – official trailers, while the fact that the *Batman v Superman* teaser was available online as shaky camera-phone footage immediately after the preview screening (removed by Warner Bros. from some websites, only to reappear on others) is suggestive of the current dynamic between fans and producers (and fan-producers).

Bat-fandom has taken many forms over the years, some expressed in letters to the Batman comic book editors, some in costumes, collections, convocations, fan-created comics and mash-ups. But experiencing and aggregating these far-flung expressions, similar to those captured by Henry Jenkins in his 1992 *Textual Poachers*, posed real challenges in the days before widespread internet connectivity. For example, although our initial collection was thoroughly researched, we only later discovered *Batman Aukene!* (*Batman Revealed!*), published in 1988 by the Finnish Bat-Instituutti.[3] A heavily illustrated compendium of essays by a collective that included some of Finland's leading media scholars, *Batman Aukene!* documents an impressive array of fan engagements in the course of its exploration of the Batman and his many cultural forms.[4]

Today, those engagements have taken on new life. YouTube has tens of thousands of fan-produced videos, from machinima based on the various Bat-games, to 'Ultimate Fan Fights' pitting the Batman against Captain America, mash-ups of films and trailers, Lego-productions and highly polished fan shorts. All these declare themselves to be fan productions, based on a character created by Bob Kane but not for profit in any way, shape or form.[5] Some, like the French fan production *Mad Wolf: Robin Origins* (2013), stray far outside the pages of the Batbible, with a Black Batman, French-accented Albert and new Robin origin story.[6] (More surprising is the film's array of sponsors, including Ducati, and ancillary sales, including comic books – times have indeed changed!) Batman fan fiction sites with dozens of subgenres, Nolan fan forums, Dark Knight art sites, Batman-hate sites ... the list is endless and access only a click away. The power of aggregated fandom, evident in these examples, manifests itself most prominently in Kickstarter campaigns. From the $54,820 raised in 2013 for the *Legends of the Knight* documentary ($31,850 requested) to £242 raised in the same year for *Lego Batman: Zombie Genesis Series* (£125 requested), fans have pitched in financially to support productions.[7] The networking affordances of the internet have complicated Moore's suggestion that 'Everything is exactly the same, except for the fact that it's all totally different.' The ability to connect, to cluster, to engage in a global dialogue has arguably exploded the number of alternative universes and empowered fans in ways unimaginable when we edited the earlier book.[8]

The myriad contextual changes seen since the early 1990s, including the further empowerment of media conglomerates at the same time as the internet's empowerment of fandom, have all worked to the character's advantage. Despite his ongoing reconfigurations, the Batman retains his prominence in the mediascape and popular culture as signalled by the near-simultaneous releases of the first *Batman v Superman* trailer and the new TV series *Gotham* (Fox, 2014–). As Paul Levitz reminds us in this volume, 'three times in forty years the Batman became a dominant cultural symbol in America, each time propelled by the power of mass media, with the continually evolving comics providing a wide variety of rich depictions as source material ...' Those previous triumphs took place in different historical moments, relied on different media constellations and, of course, played out in different cultural registers. But how did one character manage both to retain a core identity yet exhibit sufficient flexibility to work across such different historical, media and cultural contexts? A closer look at the character's undulations and multiplicities, particularly from where *The Many Lives of the Batman* left off, can help to frame an answer.

The Batman's changing textual incarnations

The Batman, a multiple figure almost since his earliest incarnation – even by 1940, he had transformed from his 1939 look and persona, and by 1943 he was a cross-platform cultural icon, appearing in two comics, a newspaper strip and a film serial – has multiplied further in the last twenty-five years. Within his own fictional universe, there are now far more Batmen than existed in the late 1980s. While 1986 had seen the release of Miller's possible-future Dark Knight, it also witnessed a DC Comics crossover event, the 'Crisis on Infinite Earths', which aimed to simplify continuity by rebooting superhero history and wiping the crazier, campier stories out of existence. *The Dark Knight Returns* was swiftly followed by Miller's *Year One* (1987), a gritty, street-level retelling that established a new official origin for the character. From that point onwards, every more speculative and more fantastical Batman story – in which, for instance, the Batman meets Jack the Ripper, Houdini, Hitler or Dracula – was released under the 'Elseworlds' imprint and designated as an imaginary tale, outside the canon.

While these new rules held firm, reinforcing the sense of a 'darker', more 'realistic' narrative world, there was only one Batman within present-day DC Comics continuity. However, a series of subsequent cross-universe events – from *Zero Hour* (1994) and *The Kingdom* (1999) through *Infinite Crisis* (2005) and *Final Crisis* (2008) to the most recent *Flashpoint* (2011) – progressively unsettled the system, loosening it up and allowing more variation. In 2014, Scott Snyder's *Zero Year* – a colourful science-fiction romp with a young Bruce Wayne facing the Riddler – has replaced Miller's *Year One* as the official origin story, while Grant Morrison's *Multiversity* (2014) explores a range of alternative worlds within the DC Comics universe. One of those worlds, Earth-31, houses the Batman of Frank Miller's stories; Earth-43 is home to the vampire Batman of *Red Rain* (1991), and Earth-19 the steampunk Victorian Batman of *Gotham by Gaslight* (1989). All these Batmen, ruled out of continuity for years, have now been officially invited back into the mainstream universe.

Before he re-entered DC's 'multiverse' of alternate earths, Morrison had already introduced several global Batman variants into official continuity, during his run on the flagship title between 2006 and 2011. *Batman Incorporated* revisited a concept from 1955 – the 'Batmen of all nations' – and had Bruce Wayne recruiting crime-fighters from around the world, including The Gaucho (Argentina), Nightrunner (Paris), Batwing (North Africa) and Black Bat (Japan). In another Morrison storyline, the Batman travelled not geographically but chronologically, shot back in time and progressing forward through various historical incarnations, from Palaeolithic through pirate, concluding with adventures in the Wild West and noir genres. Within comics continuity alone, then, there are far more Batmen at large now than there were in the late 1980s.

Morrison explored the Batman as a brand within the fictional universe, deliber-ately echoing the character's real-world status as a commercial property. In 2011, DC Comics' list included not just *Batman* itself, but also *Detective Comics*, *Batman and Robin*, *Red Robin*, *Nightwing*, *Red Hood and the Outlaws*, *Catwoman*, *Batgirl*, *The Dark Knight* and *Batman Incorporated*. Beyond the comic books, 'Batman' could also refer to Christopher Nolan's hugely successful film trilogy (2005–12), the *Arkham* video game franchise and a range of cartoon versions including the child-friendly *Batman: The Brave and the Bold* (2008–11) and the full-length animated adaptations of *Batman: Year One* (2011) and *The Dark Knight Returns* (2013). Compared to Warner Bros./DC's cautious corporate stance in 1989, when the producers narrowed their focus to two main lines of merchandise – the comic book character and the Michael Keaton/Jack Nicholson movie incarnations –

the current situation suggests a complex dialogic network, a Batman matrix, rather than a single figure. The *Gotham* TV show, which claims no direct relationship with the now-completed Nolan franchise, the forthcoming Zach Snyder *Batman v Superman* movie (and its probable sequels) and the other contemporary TV shows based on DC Comics properties, such as *Arrow* (CW, 2012–) and *The Flash* (CW, 2014–) and *Constantine* (NBC, 2014–), create further complexities in this already intricate network.

The current range of Batman cross-media texts has broader implications in terms of how we currently experience and engage with superhero narratives. Nolan's *The Dark Knight* grossed over $1 billion worldwide.[9] As noted, Scott Snyder's *Batman*, during its popular 'Zero Year' storyline of 2014, was the top-selling comic book distributed by any company; it typically sold just over 100,000 copies per month.[10] Clearly, the Batman of comic books and graphic novels is dwarfed, in terms of audience figures, by the Batman of blockbuster movies, and in turn, fans of the Batman in his original medium constitute a tiny minority of those who pay to watch Batman films worldwide. Perhaps more surprisingly, the video game market also vastly outnumbers the comic book readership; *Arkham City* (2011) sold two million units in its first week of release, and six million within its first four months.[11]

The rise of video games as a market and as a medium – *Batman* computer and video games existed in 1989, of course, but on a far more limited scale – has led to a corresponding field of study. Justin Mack and Benjamin Beil, for instance, consider *Arkham Asylum* (2009) in relation to the Batman's comic book history and the recent Nolan film franchise, employing a range of approaches from transmedia convergence to an analysis of game mechanics and an aesthetic interpretation of virtual 'shot' types, adapted from film studies.[12] As Grant Morrison enthusiastically admitted in 2014 (see interview in this volume), this new form enables an entirely different relationship with the character, where we are invited not just to observe, root for or even identify with him in a more traditional (cinematic and literary) sense, but to become the Batman.

One further change could hardly have been foreseen by the editors of the previous edition when they commissioned *The Many Lives of the Batman* at the end of the 1980s; that collection played a part in changing the way we study the Batman, superheroes and comic books more broadly. While comic book scholarship still struggles for respectability and credibility in some traditional circles, there is no doubt that the field has become far more established in the last twenty-five years, and academic work on superheroes has also flourished. The last three years alone have seen the publication of Marc DiPaolo's *War, Politics and Superheroes*, Dan Hassler-Forrest's *Capitalist Superheroes*, Robin S. Rosenberg and Peter Coogan's edited collection *What Is a Superhero?*, Charles Hatfield, Jeet Heer and Kent Worcester's *The Superhero Reader*, James N. Gilmore and Matthias Stork's *Superhero Synergies* and, more specifically yet, Will Brooker's *Hunting the Dark Knight*, Liam Burke's anthology *Fan Phenomena: Batman* and Matt Yockey's 'TV Milestones' volume on *Batman*.[13] *The Many Lives of the Batman* was in some ways a bold, brave venture within a new field; *Many More Lives of the Batman* returns to that earlier scene to find it far more crowded and to survey the changes.

From *The Many Lives of the Batman* to *Many More Lives of the Batman*

With an additional editor and much new material, *Many More Lives of the Batman* is a sequel to rather than a second edition of *The Many Lives of the Batman*. Since the original has for many years been available only through libraries and exorbitantly priced second-hand copies, this volume reprints original contributions, both interviews and scholarly analyses, that have been repeatedly cited in subsequent research on the comics and media industries. These chapters serve a historical purpose, providing snapshots of both industrial configurations and industry scholarship in the last decade of the twentieth century; at the same time they remain relevant to current concerns, and will continue, as they have for the past two decades, to provide the underpinnings for further research. This volume also includes new chapters that address the character's creation, circulation and meanings in the second decade of the twenty-first century and bring the original book's multi-perspectival analyses of the Batman up to date. As did the original, the sequel analyses the Batman phenomenon both from industrial and academic perspectives. It contains several contributions from comics practitioners in the form of a chapter penned by Paul Levitz, former DC publisher and writer, and interviews with three writers crucial to the Batman's history. The book's academic contributions include four chapters from the original publication, supplemented by newly written postscripts from their authors that reflect upon the many changes in the comics and media industries since 1991. Five new chapters, authored by both established and early career researchers, deal with the Batman's contemporary incarnations.

Taken together, the book's chapters provide a comprehensive overview of the Batman's past and present. The book's first section, 'Creating the Batman', focuses on the comic book industry, its practitioners and its narratives. The second section, 'Circulating the Batman', documents the distribution of both authorised and non-authorised Bat-texts. In the third section, 'Reading the Batman', academics interrogate the Batman's relationship to ideology and to popular culture and memory. Finally, the fourth section, 'Multiplying the Batman', reprints the original editors' chapter on the many competing versions of the Batman seen in 1989.

Section One, 'Creating the Batman', kicks off with Paul Levitz's chapter 'Man, Myth and Cultural Icon'. Levitz provides an overview of the Batman's history as he seeks to explain why the character is the most protean of all superheroes, capable of resonating with ever-changing audiences and in ever-changing cultural contexts across his seventy-five-year history. Chapter 2, 'Notes from The Batcave: An Interview with Dennis O'Neil', is reprinted from *The Many Lives of the Batman*. In his interview, O'Neil, at that time editor of *Batman* and *Detective Comics*, shares his take on the Batman and discusses in illuminating detail the creative processes that gave rise to the character. Chapter 3, 'Batman and the Twilight of the Idols: An Interview with Frank Miller', is also reprinted from the original. Frank Miller, the writer most associated with the Batman's Dark Knight incarnation, discusses his involvement with the character, his earlier and at the time future work, the state of the comics industry in the 1990s and the meaning of the superhero as a symbol of our times. Chapter 4, 'Fifth-Dimensional

Batman: An Interview with Grant Morrison', is a new one, expressly commissioned for this volume. Between 2006 and 2011, Morrison wrote multiple Batman titles and has had a profound influence upon the character's current comic book configuration. In Chapter 5, from another new contributor, Anthony N. Smith addresses the relationship between DC's industrial and narrative strategies, detailing the ways in which attempts to appeal to different audience segments have resulted in different continuity strategies. Smith's chapter demonstrates how industry data, such as the interviews with practitioners in the previous chapters, can further our understanding of textual representations of the Batman.

'Circulating the Batman' begins with Eileen Meehan's now-classic essay reprinted from *The Many Lives of the Batman*, 'Holy Commodity Fetish, Batman!: The Political Economy of a Commercial Intertext'. Meehan's discussion of the emergence of Warner Communications Inc. as a media conglomerate powerhouse and of the corporation's strategies for publicising the 1989 film touches on many of the concerns that have since become paramount in media studies, among them industrial convergence/synergy and transmedia storytelling. When Meehan wrote her chapter, however, globalisation was not yet one of those paramount concerns and she says nothing about the global market which, as we noted above, accounted for half the profits of the first film in the Nolan trilogy. In Chapter 7, 'Batman in East Asia', Mark Gallagher discusses one of the most important of those global markets and attempts to account for the discrepancies in box office and reception in China, Korea and Japan. In Chapter 8, 'Batsploitation: Parodies, Fan Films and Remakes', Iain Robert Smith extends the analysis of the Batman's screen circulation to include the unauthorised texts – from fan films to porn parodies – that proliferate without Warner's blessing. Together these two chapters augment Meehan's perspective, showing that ownership of the IP in no way guarantees Warner's control of the character or of the revenues that he generates.

Chapter 9, 'Batman Versus Superman: A Conversation', begins the next section. Phillip Bevin's discussion of DC's reworking of the Batman–Superman relationship echoes the previous section's concern with the Batman's industrial underpinnings. Bevin argues that the contrast emphasised in post-1986 comics between the Batman's Dark Knight and Superman's 'white knight' results not from an essential opposition between the two cultural icons, but from DC's desire to compete with Marvel by emulating the new company's more edgy characters. In Chapter 10, 'Batgirl: Continuity, Crisis and Feminism', Will Brooker reclaims Batgirl for women's history. He argues that the character, who originally reflected the gender turmoil of the 1960s and 70s, has, since the 80s, been reconfigured to suppress her initial ideological meanings. Chapters 11 and 12, both reprinted from the original book, connect iterations of the Batman to larger trends within the popular culture of the 1960s and the 80s. In 'Batman: The Movie, Narrative – The Hyperconscious', Jim Collins takes the Batman character as emblematic of a 'distinguishing feature of recent popular narrative, namely its increasing hyperconsciousness about both the history of popular culture and the shifting status of popular culture in the current context'. As Collins's postscript argues, this hyperconsciousness and the dense web of intertextuality in which it results have now become commonplace in popular entertainment. In 'Same Bat Channel, Different Bat Times: Mass Culture and Popular Memory', Lynn Spigel and Henry Jenkins first relate the reception of the Batman television show by critics and audiences to then current debates about television. Then, using oral history data, they delineate how the show features in adults' reconstructions of their childhood memories and histories, revealing that *Batman*'s initial reception differs from long-term memories of the programme. As a whole, this section's chapters demonstrate that a full understanding of Batman texts requires accounting for the character's industrial, reception and cultural contexts.

The final section, 'Multiplying the Batman', consists of just one chapter reprinted from the original volume: '"I'm Not Fooled by That Cheap Disguise"'. That volume's editors, Roberta Pearson and William Uricchio, discuss the tensions in the Batman's identity, which has fluctuated over time and across media as multiple authors and fan communities have competed over his definition. They conclude by speculating that the fragmentation of this identity seen in 1989 might undermine the character's continued commercial viability. Their postscript situates the chapter within the evolution of the comic book's industry of multiplicity strategy that they were among the first to document.

The Many Lives of the Batman played a part in changing the way we study the Batman and superheroes, as well as providing insights into the operations of the comics and media industries that subsequent generations of scholars have followed up on. The book proved to be as resilient as the character at the core of its collected essays, with generations of informed Batman fans and university students and researchers turning to it for methods, insights and interviews. We hope that this sequel will have an equal impact upon fans and scholars and an equally long life.

Notes

1. Alan Moore, 'The Mark of Batman: An Introduction', in Frank Miller with Klaus Janson and Lynn Varley (eds), *Batman: The Dark Knight Returns* (London: Titan Books, 1986), p. 3.
2. See Will Brooker, *Batman Unmasked* (London: Continuum, 2000), pp. 280–3.
3. Thanks to Edward Buscombe for bringing this to our attention. Bat-Instituutti, *Batman Aukene!* (Turku: Lieke Kustannus, 1988).
4. The Bat-Instituutti included among its members now prominent media academics and critics such as Erkki Huhtamo, Anu Koivunen, Kimmo Laine and Hannu Salmi.
5. Kane's role in the creation of the Batman and the surrounding mythos has long been debated, and a campaign to give collaborator Bill Finger appropriate credit – with Finger's granddaughter, Athena, as its patron – is rapidly gaining momentum in 2015.
6. <http://en.madwolf-lefilm.com/>.
7. <http://www.wearebatman.com/> and <https://www.kickstarter.com/projects /1288486598/lego-batman-zombie-genesis-series>.
8. DC's multi-pathed, multi-ending initiatives such as *Batman: Arkham Origins – A DC^2 Multiverse Graphic Novel* can be read as a response to this increasingly unstable narrative universe.

9. <http://boxofficemojo.com/movies/?id=darkknight.htm>.

10. <http://www.comicbookresources.com/?page=article&id=52018>.

11. <http://en.wikipedia.org/wiki/Batman:_Arkham_City#cite_note-SalesFeb2012-175>.

12. Justin Mack, 'The Dark Knight Levels Up: *Batman: Arkham Asylum* and the Convergent Superhero Franchise', and Benjamin Beil, 'The Fears of a Superhero: *Batman Begins* and *Batman: Arkham Asylum*', in James N. Gilmore and Matthias Stork (eds), *Superhero Synergies* (Lanham, MD: Rowman & Littlefield, 2014), pp. 137–54, 155–72.

13. In addition to Gilmore and Stork, *Superhero Synergies*, see Marc DiPaolo, *War, Politics and Superheroes: Ethics and Propaganda in Comics and Film* (Jefferson, NC: McFarland, 2011); Dan Hassler-Forrest, *Capitalist Superheroes: Caped Crusaders in the Neoliberal Age* (Hants.: Zero Books, 2012); Robin S. Rosenberg and Peter Coogan (eds), *What Is a Superhero?* (New York: Oxford University Press, 2013); Charles Hatfield, Jeet Heer and Kent Worcester (eds), *The Superhero Reader* (Jackson: University Press of Mississippi, 2013); Will Brooker, *Hunting the Dark Knight* (London: I. B. Tauris, 2012); Liam Burke (ed.), *Fan Phenomena: Batman* (Chicago: Intellect, 2013); Matt Yockey, *TV Milestones*: Batman (Detroit: Wayne State University Press, 2014).

CREATING THE BATMAN

1

MAN, MYTH AND CULTURAL ICON

Paul Levitz

Of the pantheon of superheroes who became world cultural figures, Batman stands out as the character whose portrayal is somehow the most elastic or protean, capable of capturing the gestalt in several very different tones and depictions, the many lives from which this volume and its 1991 predecessor take their titles. There is no provable answer to the question of why this has been the case, in part because scholarly examination of comics (or even documented introspection by comics creators) is a comparatively new phenomenon, and so the record of why people responded so powerfully to certain incarnations of Batman is disproportionately thinner than the evidence of the depth of the response itself, as measured by the success of those versions. But we can consider the way those lives of Batman differed from each other since the original DC comics of 1939 by Bob Kane and Bill Finger, and theorise why he had the potential to connect with the public imagination in such varied guises – from the camp humour of the 1960s *Batman* (ABC, 1966–8) television hit to the darker (yet very different from each other) films of directors Tim Burton and Christopher Nolan.

Superman may be justly considered the most important of the superheroes, having embodied the concept first in 1938 by combining the dual identity of Baroness Orczy's Scarlet Pimpernel with the agenda of pulp heroes like Doc Savage, the pseudo-logic of science-fiction protagonists from Edgar Rice Burroughs's John Carter of Mars and Philip Wylie's *Gladiator* (1930) with the skin-tight leotard of the Phantom – each element being taken up to the next level of evolution or exaggeration. Superman's instant success made DC and the entire comic book industry viable, brought the very term 'superhero' into the lexicon, and inspired a host of imitators and potential competitors, the most significant of which ultimately proved to be Batman. Yet Superman, with his vast array of extraordinary powers, has lacked one critical ability that the nominally human Batman possesses in full: the ability to thrive in very different creative executions. With one important exception, each of the most culturally significant expressions of the Superman story since the original comics by Jerry Siegel and Joe Shuster have shared fundamental tonal characteristics: a dramatic through line for the hero's adventures, tempered by a touch of romantic comedy centred on the triangle between his two identities and the woman he loves. Following a 'no tights, no flights' motto, the writers of the decade-long *Smallville* (WB/CW, 2001–11) launched the television series with a major departure by focusing on a maturing young Clark Kent and no Lois Lane. But even that incarnation ultimately brought Lois into the story and, while avoiding the full use of a costumed identity, mimicked many of the tonal aspects of a fully fledged Superman dramatic series. It's even possible to cut together frames of the many different Superman films, television series and cartoons to continuously illustrate the original 'Look up in the sky' narration that introduced the Superman radio show, without any apparent jarring other than the anachronistic levels of visual production.

The other two great heroes of the first wave to emerge from comic books in the 1940s each faced even greater limitations in transcending their original interpretations. Wonder Woman, originally created by William Moulton Marston and H. G. Peter, became a beloved figure, and even a mascot of sorts to the women's liberation movement with her appearances on MS. Magazine covers from its very first issue to a fortieth anniversary celebration, but never achieved the same level of appeal in other media, or the sizeable audiences of her two male companions in the DC stable. The one superhero who did outsell Superman and Batman in this period was Captain Marvel, developed by Bill Parker and C. C. Beck for Fawcett. But the unique blend of humour that tempered his adventures has proven difficult to replicate, and none of the hero's productions in any medium since he was revived in 1972 after almost twenty years' hibernation have returned him to his original levels of prominence.

The enormous impact of the superheroes of the second wave to emerge from comic books into mass culture is even narrower in their stylistic approaches than their predecessors. Created in the 1960s for Marvel Comics by the collaboration of writer/editor Stan Lee with artists Steve Ditko and Jack Kirby, their translations to other media have generally been the most successful when they captured the tone of the original stories (Lee's wisecracking dialogue, Ditko's sympathetic portrait of the tortured young Spider-Man and Kirby's immeasurable energy and giant canvas), and when all the heroes, enacting a shared soap opera theme, discover that their superpowers are not sufficient to solve their personal problems.

So then, why is Batman different?

Let's first look at potential factors that can be judged objectively. The level of craft and experience of the original creators is not determinative. If it were, either the older team of Marston and Peter (at publication, aged about forty-eight and sixty-one respectively) would have built the more versatile folk tale, or the deeply experienced team of Lee, Ditko and Kirby might have infused a folk-tale quality into one of their creations (the trio had produced literally hundreds of comics, and Kirby had two decades earlier co-created Captain America, a plausible next candidate for the first-wave pantheon if we had explored it any more deeply).

Similarly, the amount of preparatory development and forethought doesn't weigh in Batman's favour. While many of the great comic book superheroes were developed on the run, Superman had the benefit of several years of Siegel and Shuster's collaborative thought while they were trying to sell the strip, and Wonder Woman and Spider-Man each have well-documented stages in pre-publication evolution (a different name for Wonder Woman, and a very different collaborator and origin for Spider-

Man). Batman is simultaneously the shortest debut of any of these at six pages, apparently produced very rapidly in response to an editorially initiated opportunity, and the one that most overtly borrowed previously existing material from the pulps and film.

As the story goes, artist Bob Kane responded to his editor's request for a contribution to *Detective Comics* that could capture Superman's sales momentum with a sketch of a Bat-Man figure, inspired in part by Leonardo da Vinci's drawing of a man in a flying mechanism. Kane engaged ghostwriter Bill Finger, the visuals were further refined and story elements built around it. Could it be, then, that part of the protean nature of Batman is simply built on a purely visual icon, which has proved to be remarkably reinterpretable?

Of the great comic book superheroes, Batman alone does not have his origin story disclosed in his first appearance. In fact, it isn't revealed at all until six months into his career, and then is essentially ignored for almost a decade. In several of his translations to other media, this dynamic repeats itself: there is no origin story in the 1960s television series, nor is it touched on in the long-running *Super Friends* (1973–86) cartoons until their very end. The origins of the other heroes have direct links to their villains in most cases, or the clear parallelism of the early Spider-Man villains, who also mimic the abilities of the eponymous creatures. It isn't until fifty years into Batman's existence that his origin was tied to that of his greatest villain, the Joker, by Tim Burton – a linkage rejected by subsequent incarnations as non-canonical and unnecessary.

So perhaps part of Batman's transformability may be that, unlike his peers, he is less linked to, and less dependent on, his origin. And, less objectively, we can consider the fact that he was born, shall we say, more impulsively or spontaneously as at least a possible factor in his protean nature. But perhaps there is another reason why his birth process is relevant to his versatility: the fact that he was born as a sketch, loosely drawn and even more loosely defined. Let us examine some of his more interesting (and audience-pleasing) variations, and how they came to be, and then we shall return to his beginnings.

Kane and Finger's hero, with considerable contributions from an early stage by others working directly for Kane or for DC (most notably the young but immensely talented Jerry Robinson), adopted most of the tropes of the pulp magazines: a flamboyant playboy secret identity (with occasional women more as decoration than as sustained romantic interests), a police commissioner ally and a succession of opponents with murderous, but basically criminal, schemes. The villains were colourful characters, probably influenced by those in the *Dick Tracy* comic strip by Chester Gould, yet quickly surpassing them in their hold on the public's imagination. This hold was cemented by the fact that they were visually more extreme and outrageous than the original *Tracy* villains, who were more plausibly distorted human beings. Opponents such as Catwoman, the Penguin and, most durable of all, the Joker were introduced as exaggerated archetypes that would enjoy sustained lives in every medium that Batman invaded in the next seven decades. Even the series' most precedent-shattering departure – making Batman's sidekick in detection a young boy – was fundamentally a visual decision as well as a solution to the classic problem of giving the hero someone who will admire his brilliance and to whom he can elucidate his deductions. Robin was a surprising visual counterpoint to Batman, with his bold red vest – a look that a later, more cynical generation would tag 'Robin, the Boy Target'.

Like most of the hero comics of the 1940s and 50s, the adventures of Batman grew lighter in tone and less dangerous, less pulp-influenced, as the audience was perceived to be composed more exclusively of young children. Relatively few of the heroes made this transition successfully (only Superman, supported by the popular early television series *The Adventures of Superman* [syndicated, 1952–8], appeared in more titles in the mid-1950s than in the 40s), but Batman endured, losing only a short-lived Robin spin-off series. However, this transformation cannot be offered in support of the protean theory, simply because it reflected a change that was affecting the entire genre at once, and survival should not be confused with cultural success.

Still, we should note the addition of enduring new elements to the Batman lore during this time: the use and progressively refined image of a Batmobile, Batcopter and the summoning Bat-signal in the sky. Other heroes from the pulps onwards had autogyros and fast cars, but the convention of branding each of his devices with his name and the dark blue scallops of his iconic cape was a distinctive innovation for Batman. Once more, the power of the visual branding of the iconic original figure made a distinct statement.

This period of Batman's chronicles was followed by a decade of material from the mid-1950s to the early 60s of which the less said, the better. The kindest thing we can say about this time, in which the hero's adventures were shifted to either mimic the popular science-fiction/monster movies of the period or the far better-selling Superman titles, is that Batman managed to survive as a continuously published property, unlike all of his pulp progenitors and all but two of his contemporary superhero fellows.

Batman's downward commercial and creative trajectory was arrested in the early 1960s as editor Julie Schwartz introduced the fondly recalled 'New Look', a general improvement in the artwork led by the sleek appearance of Carmine Infantino's visual interpretation of the hero and marked by Schwartz's improbable addition of a bright yellow oval around Batman's emblem, mimicking the Bat-signal in the sky. The stories included more episodes with a genuine element of detection, but the period might have been forgettable if not for an evening at the Playboy Mansion, where Hugh Hefner's audience for a screening of the Batman movie serials of the 1940s included a Hollywood producer named William Dozier. The serials were, even by the standards of a form whose limited budgets were matched by their limited creative ambitions, pretty terrible, especially when viewed two decades later. But Dozier found inspiration in them.

Coming almost at the moment when writer Susan Sontag was defining 'camp' and pop art was exploding as a new style, with Roy Lichtenstein finding inspiration in the comic book panels he transformed, Dozier saw the potential for reinterpreting Batman through these new cultural lenses for television. Giant comics-style sound effects helped open the show, and the exaggerated seriousness of actor Adam West and a cast that included dozens of film and television stars having fun playing the villain of the week made for a tone that perfectly captured the moment. In-the-know adults got the joke, and felt on the cutting edge; younger kids clustered around the television saw what could be considered a comic book come to life and were enthralled. ABC, weakest of the three competing broadcast networks of the time, had a hit on its hands as soon as *Batman* launched in January 1966.

Describing *Batman* as a hit, however, understates its significance. This was an era of fads that had startling cultural hegemony: if Davy Crockett had every child wearing a coonskin cap, or the Hula Hoop danced around every waist, so *Batman* made an impact impossible now in our era of hundreds of channels and thousands of accessible websites. The hero, transformed in tone and style through Dozier's camp lens, captured the spirit of the moment and was rewarded with a phenomenal rush of licensing revenues from toys and other products, and the compliment of imitations in every medium. A *Batman* movie was rushed into production, using the television cast and props (and modest budget), and released even before a second season of the programme launched. It had been decades since any comic book character had assumed such a powerful presence in the economy, and never before had one achieved that feat based on a transformation that took its style so far from the source material.

But while this version of Batman was tonally utterly different from its predecessors, it was constructed with the same building blocks: the characters, their relationships, their props were all taken from the comics. Even the costumes were rendered as faithfully as the transition from a drawn line to fabric made possible, which perhaps added to the absurdity. The figure of Batman dancing the Bat-usi (parodying the then popular Watusi) was the iconic drawing come to life, but strictly for laughs. Notable differences, however, included the way that his body language and even 'combat' were acted out, and how the exaggeration was played for camp humour.

The explosive success of the television series immediately fed back into the comics, which took visual cues from it even more than tonal ones. The comics never quite descended into comedy throughout, but the covers took the extreme sound effects and poses from the show, and occasionally adopted the humour as well, all to massively increased sales. It was a glorious period for Batman, after three decades of solid but unspectacular performance. It was also, unfortunately, brief. Fads by their very nature tend to burn hot and fast – and burn out as swiftly as they ignite. The television show was out of production in three years, and out of fashion as well.

The camp influence on Batman persisted longer in the television cartoon series. Adam West's continuing presence as the voice of the hero helped, providing a cue for how to interpret his actions, even when the scripts and visuals were relatively straightforward. But the comics' sales plummeted back to pre-fad levels, and the search for a defining style resumed.

With Infantino having moved on to a series of executive positions, editor Schwartz tried out a number of talents before settling on the team whose version of Batman would endure. Writer Denny O'Neil and artist Neal Adams went back to the dramatic pulp roots of the character, but decidedly made him the Dark Knight Detective. His adventures now took place almost exclusively at night and the physicality of the hero changed: he perched atop buildings or on ramparts and gargoyles, he disappeared when Commissioner Gordon turned to look at him, and he swung across the city like a dark shadow eclipsing the moon. Adams's work was also a strong influence on the colouring style that combined with his placement of solid black shadows to create a darker sense of 'lighting', an aesthetic that would carry over to later film versions. Because comic book scripts aren't generally published, the degree to which the 'acting' and movement of characters emerges from an alchemical collaboration between writers and artists is rarely studied. O'Neil and Adams, separately important voices in the field from the 1970s onwards, forged a style for Batman that was influential on both their comics successors and film producers. Again, the identities of the characters and elements remained the same, but the dramatic lens through which they were viewed meant that the presentation differed more radically than many other comics following a change in their creative teams.

Of the comics that demonstrate Batman's protean quality, perhaps none is as important as the 1986 classic by a young writer/artist who had worked closely with both O'Neil and Adams and then went on to break every contemporary boundary of mainstream comics: Frank Miller's *The Dark Knight Returns*. Introducing layered storytelling, more complex political and social overtones, and an aged and battered hero, Miller's Batman was a totally different depiction – built entirely on the fundamental structures of the underlying character and his world. He keyed into the iconic power of the superhero with a simple first cover, a stark black Batman silhouette against a white lightning bolt cracking a dark blue night sky. Not until the comic was opened would the reader realise how much Batman had changed.

Miller's work on *The Dark Knight Returns* and a reworking of Batman's origin as *Batman:Year One*, with David Mazzucchelli's illustrations, were significant influences on the *Batman* film that was developed through most of the 1980s, and finally realised by director Tim Burton. Miller's work attracted a degree of critical acclaim outside the narrow comics community that was largely unprecedented for a superhero story, a recognition of its literary qualities that far exceeded anything Stan Lee's P. T. Barnum-like publicising of his Marvel characters had achieved. A serious *Batman* now seemed possible and the visually brilliant Tim Burton took on the challenge.

Burton worked with designer Anton Furst to create a Gotham City that was towering, menacing and a palpable presence in his film; a setting where an Adams-like Batman could perch atop a gargoyle impossibly high in the skyline or an overwhelming Batmobile could smash through walls. His depiction was a synthesis of many previous influences on the property, plus his own distinctive artistic sensibility. The key elements were stripped down to their pulp roots, reeking of melodrama and overly broad visual scale, then reclad in materials that made them darker and menacing, like the rubberised armour that became the Batman costume.

Curiously, as production and marketing on Burton's film moved forward, an improbable combination of circumstances sparked a new Batman fad. The 1960s television series began airing in Britain to great ratings, and the first trailers for the new film stoked the fire. By the time the film was released, it was virtually impossible to buy black T-shirts in America not emblazoned with the Bat-symbol, as every bit of black-dyed cotton was running through a licensee's screen-print factory. Again, a simple iconic depiction proved to be the essence of Batman in the consumers' mind.

Burton's film was the top grossing picture of 1989 in America by a massive 27 per cent margin, and his very dark portrayal of Batman became a cultural fad of similar proportion to the light, campy incarnation of two decades before. It was extraordinary for a creative property to return to that kind of cultural prominence, and still more unusual for it to do so in a style vastly different from its initial peak. Along with the first two *Superman* films of a decade earlier that had established the visual style for depicting superpowers, Burton's *Batman* would provide the blueprint for virtually all succeeding superhero films for years to follow.

Echoing the transformation of the Burton film, a new series of Batman cartoons was launched for television, developed by Bruce Timm and Eric Radomski. Timm and Radomski made the visuals much darker than any previous television cartoon series, and focused on using the power of animation to depict the hero's movements – a dark presence, appearing out of nowhere and returning to the shadows. Because the medium of animation is based on movement, the body language and acting of the characters were vital and the visual stylisation was far more complex than had been attempted before. Their work set the style for a long list of comic book-based cartoons to follow.

With comic books' increasing sophistication, the ensuing decades saw more varied depictions of Batman, including a noteworthy series of collaborations between writer Jeph Loeb and artist Tim Sale, with Sale's visualisation of Batman drawing on a stark cartoon style that often depicted him as a dark silhouette. Sale's Batman moved unlike any previous version and provided a specific inspiration to the next great director to make Batman a film hit.

Christopher Nolan's trilogy of *Batman* films were more centred on the human tragedy of Bruce Wayne's life than any previous look at the character, visualised within a noir sensibility. While the initial outing, *Batman Begins* (2005), was a solid performer (number eight of the year's top grossing films), it was the middle episode, *The Dark Knight* (2008), that reignited the Batman phenomenon. Sparked in part by the real-world tragedy of Heath Ledger's death following his remarkable performance as the Joker, *The Dark Knight* was 2008's top film by an amazing 75 per cent. Once again, Batman products flew off shelves and clothing racks at fad-level speeds – and once again, the essential elements of the hero's life remained the same, albeit depicted stylistically in a very different way. Nolan emphasised the reality of the world in which Batman operated, and tried to show the hero as little as possible – shrouded in darkness and silhouetted so that he could more plausibly be a part of that realistic world.

Three times in forty years Batman became a dominant cultural symbol in America, each time propelled by the power of mass media, with the continually evolving comics providing a wide variety of rich depictions as source material and occasionally lesser but still important penetrations of the overall gestalt. Catchphrases became part of the vernacular each time, despite being as diverse as 'Same Bat-time, Same Bat-channel' (in a melodramatic narrator's voice), 'Where does he get those wonderful toys?' (as only Jack Nicholson's Joker could have intoned) or 'Why so serious?' (in Heath Ledger's Joker tones). Each reiteration is very different, centring on camp humour, dark melodrama and then noir tragedy. It is difficult to make the case for any other creative property reaching such repeated peaks of success over a similar period, with depictions whose styles varied as greatly.

So then, why is Batman different?

It is a reasonable hypothesis that the birth of Batman as a simple iconic image contributed to his protean nature. Perhaps the inspired incompleteness of his inception has allowed generations of talented, creative people to find their own meaning in that icon and to manipulate the structured parts of the mythology that has grown up around it in their own styles, even taking it to extremes that fit the zeitgeist. The imagery that made a wide range of vehicles – be it the Batmobile, unmistakable even when as different as the elongated 1950s model or the 'tumbler' from the Nolan films, or the Bat-symbol, instantly recognisable across the world whether in round or oval shape – all stem from those first sketchy drawings produced by Kane and Finger.

Scott McCloud, in his seminal *Understanding Comics*, posited that the simplicity of a cartoon image allows us to shape the character in our minds, associating with it more powerfully than with the photographic image of a stranger.[1] In interviews and conversations, many of the creative talents who have shaped Batman have described their process as returning the character to his roots. It is possible that each simply looked into the stories and identified in the core iconography a reflection of their own creative potential and of the cultural zeitgeist as they saw it. Dozier recognised the absurdity, Burton the visual melodrama and Nolan the tragedy; each was able to incorporate echoes of what so many talented writers and artists had seen before them.

Maybe more carefully constructed heroes just can't match the simple inspiration that happened one day in 1939? Or maybe, as Miller showed in his classic cover, some things just happen in the split second that it takes lightning to illuminate an iconic image that we can each see through our own eyes.

Notes

1. Scott McCloud, *Understanding Comics* (New York: Harper Perennial, 1993).

2

NOTES FROM THE BATCAVE
AN INTERVIEW WITH DENNIS O'NEIL
Roberta Pearson and William Uricchio

At the time of the initial publication of this interview in 1991, Dennis O'Neil, one of the most prominent figures in the comics industry, had been an editor at both Marvel and DC, where, since 1986, he edited *Batman* and *Detective Comics*. He started his professional life as a journalist but began writing comics in 1965 at Marvel. He worked on several long-standing titles at DC and Marvel, breathing new life into old characters, such as Superman, Green Lantern and Captain Marvel. His Green Lantern and Green Arrow series in the early 1970s were among the first comic books to deal with social problems. His collaborations with Neal Adams and Dick Giordano in the late 1960s and early 70s transformed Batman from the campy comedian of the mid-60s back to the Dark Knight Detective. Aside from his editorial duties, O'Neil carried on writing: he scripted the first five issues of the third Batman title, *Legends of the Dark Knight*, and continued to do another DC book, *The Question*. He also wrote teleplays, short stories, novels, film criticism and hundreds of book reviews. He is now retired from the comics industry.

Roberta Pearson/William Uricchio: *When you first started to write Batman, did you bring a new perspective to the character?*

Dennis O'Neil: My brilliant idea was simply to take it back to where it started. I went to the DC library and read some of the early stories. I tried to get a sense of what Kane and Finger were after. With the benefit of twenty years of sophistication in storytelling techniques and twenty years of learning from our predecessors, Neal Adams and I did the story 'The Secret of the Waiting Graves'. Batman was kind of my assignment from then on. It was a different system in that writers or artists were not assigned to characters as they are today. I showed up once a week with a finished script and got another assignment, and it just so happened for several years that that assignment was Batman – plus other things. You certainly couldn't survive writing one comic book a month then, but you would do okay if you could write four.

RP/WU: *What was your vision of the Batman?*

DO: The basic story is that he is an obsessed loner. Not crazy, not psychotic. There is a big difference between obsession and psychosis. Batman knows who he is and knows what drives him and he chooses not to fight it. He permits his obsession to be the meaning of his life because he cannot think of anything better. He is also rife with natural gifts. He is possibly the only person in the world who could do what he is doing. But he is not for one second ignorant of *why* he is doing it and even what is unhealthy about it, nor is he ever out of control. That is why I have to edit the writers who have Batman kill somebody. I think this is not something he does. The trauma that made him Batman had to do with a wanton waste of life. That same trauma that makes him go catch criminals will forbid his ever taking a life. He is not Dirty Harry. He is not Judge Dredd. He is, God knows, not Rambo, though some people want to make him that. I said this a couple of months ago to an audience in London and got the one spontaneous burst of applause I ever got in my life, which did my heart good. It shows there are some liberal humanists left out there.

RP/WU: *What kind of changes do you think the character has been through in the twenty years that you have been involved with him?*

DO: I started editing Batman about four years ago. I gather I got the job because I had written what people kindly considered to be something close to the definitive version of the character. Therefore, presumably, I would be able to edit the character. In the twenty years that I have been around Batman he has been pretty much the obsessed loner. However, there was a time right before I took over as Batman editor when he seemed to be much closer to a family man, much closer to a nice guy. He seemed to have a love life and he seemed to be very paternal towards Robin. My version is a lot nastier than that. He has a lot more edge to him. I think of Frank Miller's and my Batman as the same person. I think that Frank may have taken the concept further than I did, but we were both working with the same material. Steve Englehart did a nicer version of the same guy who was nowhere near as obsessed as mine. I have to emphasise that none of these are wrong – they are just different.

Batman started off as a first cousin to the mystery men of the pulps in '39 and '40. He held that persona in varying degrees until the 1950s when he became a sort of ebullient scout master for a while. He was a bright, sunny fellow who would walk down the street in the middle of the day and people would say, 'Hey, Batman, hi, how's it going?' He could also be very science fictiony. Very light. The science fiction was really fantasy, only with a rocket ship instead of a magic carpet. He stayed like that until the 1960s when he effectively became a comedian or a perpetrator of camp, which I think is a one-line joke.

RP/WU: *How do you think Robin functions with Batman?*

DO: Robin, as far as I can tell, serves as a counterbalance. He has been a bright, cheerful, sunny presence in an otherwise grim world in the times when we have been playing Batman darkly. He is the equivalent of the comic-relief scenes in Shakespeare's plays. This is not to say he is specifically there to introduce yucks, but he does bring a kind of light tone into all of this grimness and also effectively humanises Batman. If Batman were a real person, Robin probably would be keeping him from crossing the line into nuttiness. It gets hard talking about these things, because I don't have the critical vocabulary to differentiate between the character within the story and the character that is contrived for story purposes by a writer. But Robin functions in both areas. In the made-up universe of the stories, he is what keeps Batman and Bruce Wayne from going too far. In terms of the purpose he serves for writers, he allows the story to lighten up from time to time. When I was writing my *Legends of the Dark Knight*, which was without Robin, I found that I had to make Alfred a bit wittier than he usually is for exactly that purpose. I needed some lightness. I needed some humour in the story and it would have been out of character for Bruce Wayne and Batman to supply it, so it fell to Alfred. Robin also serves the old hero sidekick role in allowing Batman to talk and explain things and therefore explain them to the reader. He allows for another dimension of human interest to come in. He has his functions both in Bruce Wayne's life and in the life of those of us who have to write about Bruce Wayne.

RP/WU: *Since Robin seems so necessary, why did Dick Grayson abandon his Robin role and become Nightwing?*

DO: I imagine the writers wanted to do *Teen Titans* and began to look around for popular teen characters. Robin was certainly the most popular of them and certainly the oldest teenage character in our little universe. Robin was simply a logical character to put in *Teen Titans* and he couldn't be Robin anymore, so they made him Nightwing. These decisions are seldom made with any long-range plans. It's usually more like, 'Hey, it seems like a good idea now.' Superman became God over the years because guys said, 'Wouldn't it be neat if he could freeze things with his breath? Okay, let's write that in.' Not realising that they were stuck with that for ever. Many of the writers I know now, having learned from our predecessors' experience, *do* worry about those things. We are not going to give a character a power that is going to make it impossible to plot future stories.

RP/WU: *When did the new Robin come in? Was that while you were editor?*

DO: No. It was 1983, I believe. He was invented by Gerry Conway in an origin that is a virtual duplication of Dick Grayson's Robin origin. I doubt that they were worried about creating a new character. I think they thought, 'We've got to have a Robin in the series, so let's go with the tried and true. This Robin has worked for so many years, so let's do him again.'

RP/WU: *Why did everyone hate him so much? Why did he get killed?*

DO: Boy, that's a good question. They *did* hate him. I don't know if it was fan craziness – maybe they saw him as usurping Dick Grayson's position. Some of the mail response indicated that this was at least on some people's minds. I think this is taking the whole thing entirely too seriously. It may be that something was working in the writers' minds, probably on a subconscious level. They made the little brat a little bit more disagreeable than his predecessor had been. He did become unlikeable and that was not any doing of mine. But we became aware that he was not very popular. Once we became aware of that, of course, we began playing to it.

RP/WU: *And this decision was influenced by the fan letters you were getting?*

DO: Yeah. The general response. The fan letters and then being a comic book editor, artist and writer in the 1980s means you go out and meet the fans a lot. What we get in the way of verbal response and mail is certainly not definitive, but it is probably as informative as the television ratings. It's sort of an informal sampling. I think that once writers became aware that fans didn't like Jason Todd, they began to make him bratty. I toned some of it down. If I had to do it again, I would tone it down more. But you make these decisions from hour to hour and sometimes not under the best conditions. So we did a story, for example, in which it was left vague as to whether or not Jason pushed someone off a balcony. The writer, Jim Starlin, thought he did – I thought he didn't, but we let the reader decide. There was certainly no doubt that throughout much of the story he wanted to push this guy off of the balcony. And then when we were building up to the death of Robin we made him rebellious – he ran away, and in a way he got what he was asking for. He disobeyed Batman twice and that's what led to his demise.

RP/WU: *How did you decide to come up with the device of the phone-in poll as to whether he was going to live or not?*

DO: We were sitting around brainstorming at an editorial retreat. I mentioned the 900 number that had been used by *Saturday Night Live* and one or two other places, and Jenette [Kahn] thought it was an interesting idea. We began to discuss how we could use it. I guess I came up with killing somebody and the logical candidate to be in peril was Jason, because we had reason to believe that he wasn't that popular anyway. It was a big enough stunt that we couldn't do it with a minor character. If we were going to do it, it had to be a big, significant change. I don't think it would have had the impact we wanted if we had created a character and built him up and then put him in danger. It had to be something dramatic. This was the first time we were going to have real reader participation in comic books. Then, I confess, it seemed like a great caper. It had that value to us. Like wow, what a neat thing to do.

RP/WU: *Well, it worked. You got a lot of publicity out of it.*

DO: Much, much more than we anticipated. I thought it would get us some ink here and there and maybe a couple of radio interviews. I had no idea – nor did anyone else – it would have the effect it did. I spent three days doing nothing but talking on the radio. Peggy [May], our publicity person, finally just said, 'Stop, no more, we can't do any-more', or I would probably still be talking. She also nixed any television appearances. At the time, I wondered about that, but now I am very glad she did, because there was a nasty backlash and I came to be very grateful that people could not associate my face with the guy who killed Robin. I got phone calls that ranged from 'You bastard', to tearful grandmothers saying, 'My grandchild loved Robin and now I don't know what to tell him.' That broke my heart.

I also forgot that there are John Hinkleys out there. A lot of us have gotten death threats. Miller got one when he killed Elektra. I got kind of a death threat when I made Tony Stark an alcoholic character over at Marvel. Chris Clairmont got one when he killed Phoenix, a popular X-Men character. Every once in a while, I run into guys at signings that I think might be a potential danger. There are guys out there that don't seem to be able to grasp the difference between a story and reality. I call them the hov-erers. They get a book signed and they stand back about six to ten feet from you and then they will dash up again when there is a break in the conversation. They often ask about violence. 'Why doesn't Batman kill him? I just want him to kill him.' I say, 'Come on, it's just a story.' And they just keep on saying, 'I would kill all the criminals if I were Batman.' Keep an eye on that guy! Nothing has ever happened, but it's scary, because I keep thinking it might.

The 'death of Robin' caper also made me realise that all this goes a lot deeper in people's consciousnesses than I thought. All these years, I've considered myself to just be writing stories. I now know that that's wrong. That Batman and Robin are part of our folklore. Even though only a tiny fraction of the population reads the comics, everyone knows about them the way everybody knows about Paul Bunyan, Abe Lincoln and so on. Batman and Robin are the post-industrial equivalent of folk figures. They are much deeper in our collective psyches than I had thought. Because these characters have been around for fifty years, everybody in the country knows about them. They have some of the effect on people that mythology used to, and if you get into that you can't avoid the question of religion.

RP/WU: *When you've got a character who has been around as many years as Batman and who, as you say, has a prominent place in the nation's psyche, how do you control character consistency across different titles?*

DO: Well, back in the old days, you didn't. Julie Schwartz did a Batman in *Batman* and *Detective* and Murray Boltinoff did a Batman in the *Brave and Bold*, and apart from the costume, they bore very little resemblance to each other. Julie and Murray did not coordinate their efforts, did not pretend to, did not want to, were not asked to. Continuity was not important in those days. Now it has become very important, which is decidedly a mixed blessing. I sometimes want to say to these people who insist on continuity, 'Hey, it is just a story. This is not real life. Don't get upset.' Also, I think it's the idea of Batman that's important, the folklore/mythological roots of the character rather than the foolish consistency which, Emerson said, is the hobgoblin of little minds. Nonetheless, continuity is something our audience demands.

RP/WU: *Why more now than before?*

DO: I don't know. I think maybe the audience is more cohesive. Comic books are not read on a hit-or-miss basis anymore. They are read by fewer people than they were in the 1940s but the current fans read a great deal more intently and with a great deal of care. Also, thanks to the direct market, it is now possible to get every issue of everything. Back in the old days, it was sort of news-stand roulette and fans couldn't worry about consistency, because they didn't have all the stories. Also, letter columns did not exist back then, so there was no arena to exchange opinions, nor were there conventions and all those other places where fans can get together and compare notes. Now, I keep coming back to the point that the Batman phenomenon has certain things in common with religion in that it is built around a mythology or pseudo-mythology, and maybe that explains the concern with continuity. Anyway, for whatever reason, continuity and consistency have become important, so DC has a guy like me to watch over things. Anything that has Bats in it I have to approve, therefore presumably I am the quality control. I am the guy who keeps the character consistent and says, 'You may or may not do this with him.'

RP/WU: *How do you go about making sure all your writers and artists are dealing with essentially the same character?*

DO: By giving people a bible which sets limits and by looking at the material. If Bats is doing something totally out of character, then the writer will be asked to rewrite the story. It's as simple as that. It's more or less true of the other characters also. If we are going to do anything with Superman, Mike [Carlin] has to see it. If we are going to do anything with Wonder Woman, Karen Berger has to see it. We have lists of what characters are assigned to which editors. Obviously, Batman is a lot more important than the rest because of all of the brouhaha attending the character at the moment. But, two years from now, Superman may be the big deal and Mike will have to do all this reading of other people's scripts.

RP/WU: *Is the obsessive return to the origin story for reasons of character continuity or is it just because of a turnover in readership?*

DO: The origin is the engine that drives Batman. The reason we didn't meddle with the origin when we were meddling with a lot of origins four years ago is that it's perfect. When the question of changing it came up, I said, 'How are you going to improve on this?' It simply in one incident explains everything that anybody will ever need to know about the character. Why he does what he does and why he is who he is. The times I have written it, it just seemed organic to the story. In the old days, we would have repeated it every three years, because the assumption was that the readership turned over every three years. This may have been true back then. The origin story has appeared a little too often recently. When I did it in *Legends of the Dark Knight*, I felt it needed to be there but I made it a dream and made the characters snowmen to at least make it a little different. I have put out one of my ban memos saying that nobody gets to do the origin for at least one year. I put one out about the Joker six months ago saying no Joker stories for at least one year, because we have done him too much.

RP/WU: *Could we talk a little bit about the production process? Could you tell us on a very basic level what is the relationship among the editor, writer, penciller, inker, letterist, colourist and how does everybody work together?*

DO: Anything I tell you will be a broad generalisation. One of the things that makes the job interesting is that there is no right way to do it. Every editor I have ever met, every editor I worked for, does it a different way and I do it a different way from day to day or hour to hour. Basically, in very broad general terms, a writer is given an assignment – it may be that he is assigned a series, it may be one issue or it may be that he comes in with an idea for a series. At any rate, he ends up with an assignment and meets with the editor, by phone, for lunch or in the office, and talks about his story. The writer and editor agree on what the story is going to be about. That is pretty basic. From there on it can go a lot of different ways. My preferred way of working as a writer is to write a script, which looks very much like a television script. It's a format that I have developed over the years. There are panel and page numbers and descriptions of the visuals and dialogue and captions. The other method is that the writer does a plot. This has become known as the Marvel way of working, since it was developed by Stan Lee. The plot can be anything from a paragraph, as it was in the early 1960s with Stan, to something that is as long as a final script. Okay, the penciller pencils the story and at that point it comes back to the writer and the writer adds copy, and if the writer is doing his job, he also does balloon placement.

RP/WU: *And how much dialogue do you usually put in a panel?*

DO: Depends on how big the panel is and what the needs of the story are. The rule I learned when I was starting out a quarter of a century ago was thirty-five words per panel. This is not a bad rule of thumb, though depending on the composition of the frame, it might accommodate fifty words, and if it is a half-page, it might accommodate a hundred words. The idea is not to kill the artwork. Don't have so much copy that you lose the picture.

Then the letterer does the panel borders, puts in the lettering and puts in the balloons working from the guideline he is given. Lettering is a great unacknowledged art form. It can make an immense amount of difference in how a job is perceived. The minimum requirement is that the lettering should be neat and very legible, but we are getting sophisticated to the point that we actually use it as part of the story. We'll use upper and lower case or italics or bold and also what I designate on scripts as spooky lettering. That can be anything the letterer wants to make it, provided it is really different. It adds visual texture and I think in your mind you hear it differently. At least I do.

From the letterer it goes to the inker. At its crudest, his job is just going over the pencil with ink so it will photograph. But, like the letterer, an inker can make an immense amount of difference. He can do anything from redrawing and correcting the artist's mistakes, to adding textures, to giving depth to the picture by his placement of blacks, by his placement of sepia tone, by highlights. The best inkers are always intensely conscious of where the light source is in the panel. A good inker can take a mediocre pencil job and make it great, and, conversely, a bad inker can take a pretty good pencil job and make it look awful. The guys who do this work tell me that it is a very different mindset to pencilling. A really good inker chooses to be an inker but probably could make his living as a penciller.

RP/WU: *But not many people do pencilling and inking, do they?*

DO: No, they don't. The reason that pencilling and inking are separate jobs is just an accident of historical evolution. In the 1940s, comic books were mass-produced and it was a lot faster if one guy did the pencilling and another guy did the inking. Now that is no longer true, but for most guys it's a matter of choice.

When all of the writing, pencilling and lettering is done, the editor has pages photographically reduced to a 6" x 9" comic book size. Those are given to the colourist. Until six months ago, I would have told you that colourists work with a palette of sixty-four colours. They are aniline dyes, which is a kind of watercolour. The colourist goes through, colours the job and, if he or she is conscientious, makes notations – for instance, 'R2 B2', which means 25 per cent red, 25 per cent blue. This is a notation to the separator for a specific dot pattern. Now, we are working with computer colours and the palette is a lot larger. On the upscale books, for example on *Digital Justice*, we have a sixteen million colour palette. We aren't going to use that many. But we will probably use 500 of those. The letterpress books, which are half of our stuff, are not sophisticated enough to handle that many variations, but they will probably be able to handle well above sixty-four colours.

Colouring is another unacknowledged art form. The basic task in comic book colouring is to give depth to the picture. The easiest way to do that is dark colours come forward, pastels recede, so make the backgrounds pastel. When people are designing superhero costumes, they tend to do them in primary colours, which simplifies the process. If a colourist wants to get a bit more sophisticated, he or she can emphasise story elements. The colourist can be part of the storytelling process. If the vase in the corner is going to be very important to the story, they will colour the panel in such a way to subtly emphasise that vase without a little arrow pointing to it saying 'important clue'. The very best colourists think in those terms. The worst of them just think in colouring-book terms and they usually don't get much work. The colourist, like everybody else in the process, has to think of himself as one of the storytellers. The process of colouring is far harder than you would imagine, because with superheroes, you have certain givens. Batman's costume is not going to change. That gives the artists real headaches in terms of what they can do in backgrounds. For example, how to handle the colour of the clothing of the people around Batman, particularly since they move from place to place in the context of the story. It is really far more complicated than dabbing colours on the page.

RP/WU: *We want to talk about the business side of the industry and ask if you see really significant changes in the relationship between creative types and the company over the past few years.*

DO: Oh Lord, yes. My timing stinks. When I started out, the editor was God, because it didn't make any difference who was doing the books, not a bit. Batman sold regardless of who the creative team was. So if a writer was giving you trouble, the hell with him. Get out your Rolodex, call the next warm body. Up till about ten years ago that is the way it worked. Then DC in particular began to emphasise the creators. The audience became sophisticated and began to demand a certain quality level. Now it is a very complicated relationship between the company, particularly as represented by the editor, and the creative people. Creative people have a lot more say in what goes down. We consult with them constantly about everything. In the old days, if there was going to be any kind of major change, the writer could find out about it the same time the readers did. I have been fired off books and didn't know it until I suddenly realised I hadn't done a Wonder Woman for four months and found out there had been six issues done in that time. We wouldn't dare do that now. If we are going to have any major change in policy, we call the creators.

RP/WU: *The artist and writers also started getting royalties a few years ago. Is that right?*

DO: Yes. That was seven or eight years ago. The probable reason was the rise of the direct market. I've heard that the business people here at DC were coming to believe that the direct market was the wave of the future and that this would create a body of knowledgeable readers. In the old days, when sales were all through the news-stands, quality didn't matter a lot, much less the names attached to that quality, because it was virtually impossible to be sure of reaching the readers who would care about good material and would notice bylines. With the direct-sales shops, that isn't true. Those are precisely the readers you do reach through the comics shops, and if that's the case, it's just good business to reward the creators who produce higher sales. You want to keep them working on your titles. A system of royalties was the obvious answer.

Finally, Paul Levitz came up with a royalty plan. When DC's plan was announced, Jim Shooter came up with a counterplan for Marvel, which had also rejected the royalty idea up to this point. Jim claims he had proposed it two years earlier and had been rejected by his bosses. Anyway, DC's original royalty plan has been modified several times, always to the benefit of the creative people. One of the things we have done, for example, is reduce the break-even point from 100,000 to 75,000 copies, which means that on a news-stand book, after your first 75,000 copies are sold, you start making additional money. On our direct-only books, the break-even point is 40,000. But if you created the character, the break-even point is around 20,000, depending on the price of the book.

RP/WU: *Does this mean that people can write fewer titles?*

DO: Absolutely. Because of the sale of the five issues of *Legends of the Dark Knight*, if I were freelance, I would consider taking next year off. I wouldn't have to do a lick of work to live at my present standard because of the totally phenomenal and crazy sale of that one book. And Frank Miller coming off of *Dark Knight* probably didn't have to work for a couple of years at least. So if you were Miller or John Byrne, you could do a lot less work. Certainly, gone are the days when a top creator had to produce six stories per month. Of course, some of us would choose to do that. One of the realisa-tions I came to a few years ago is that there are people who are prolific and there are people who are not prolific. Quality doesn't have very much to do with it. There are some people that just are not happy unless they are producing a large volume of work. Somebody like John Byrne, if he doesn't have quite enough comic book work, will look for something outside comics to do.

RP/WU: *How do the recent changes in distribution of the books affect the way you tell stories, particularly in terms of serial versus individual issues?*

DO: You used to have to tell one-issue stories because news-stand distribution was irregular and your audience could not be certain if they bought *Batman* #28 of being able to buy *Batman* #29. You could have serial stories but you had to work in a flash-back or exposition in each issue. I did that until about two years ago just as a matter of writing technique, even with the direct market. I gradually became aware writing *The Question* that while its fans are not numerous, they are very loyal and they are going to buy everything. I have chosen to do a lot of one-issue stories, because that is what I felt like doing. But if I wanted to do a three-issue story, any reference to the backstory would be organic and help to propel some present-tense piece of action in the same way that a novel will refer in Chapter 20 to what happened in Chapter 1, because it will be natural for the characters to make those references. You don't reach and twist and contrive to get backstory exposition in. In *Legends of the Dark Knight*, I went full out and treated it as if I was writing a 125-page novel. The concession I made to the fact that it's episodic was to put a hook at the end of each episode, some reason why you will want to see where the story goes from there.

RP/WU: *Have you been reading Dickens lately?*

DO: I was going to say that novelists do that anyway. Particularly people who write suspense fiction. Even if they are just writing a book, they will put those hooks in from time to time. Stephen King is great at it. It helps pull you through the story. But I am assuming that anybody who read issue 1 of *Legends of the Dark Knight* will read issues 2, 3, 4 and 5. On the other hand, this may not be true, because I would guess that half of the people who bought issue 1 bought it because it was issue 1. It looks like issue 2 will sell considerably less.

RP/WU: *A lot of people are probably expecting issue 1 to appreciate in value.*

DO: Oh sure. And then we did that sort of sneaky stunt of bringing it out with four different coloured outer covers. I was in California signing copies last week and I signed a lot of sets. People felt that they had to buy all four versions of the first issue.

RP/WU: *We have been talking a lot about the readers and fans. We wanted to ask you a few questions about that. The letter columns seem to reflect an articulate readership and we were wondering if the letters you print are representative of what you receive?*

DO: Well, there is a bottom part of our mail where the letters are illiterate and we don't print them. Sometimes they are illiterate because they are from seven-year-olds, who are probably very intelligent seven-year-olds, but they are seven-year-olds. We may occasionally print one of those and clean up the grammar and spelling. But we try to make the letters representative. It's that sampling of fan opinion again. If 75 per cent of our mail hated a story, we will reflect that in the letter column. Most of our readership is articulate. If you go out to schools, as I do, you will find that the kids who read comic books are the bright kids, the verbal kids. And then our marketing information shows that our average reader is twenty-four and male and very literate, so it is not surprising that we get a pretty high percentage of articulate, literary letters. That is one of the changes that has come about. I no longer feel very much need to write down to anybody when I am doing a comic book. I feel a very large, persistent need to honour the tradition out of which I am working, but I don't have to worry about using big words anymore or even big concepts.

RP/WU: *So you think that your twenty-four-year-old males are pretty consistent readers, then? The three- to four-year readership turnover has stopped?*

DO: The conventional wisdom about the turnover was that comic books were being read by children and when they got to the age of twelve they got into something else and they stopped reading comic books. We now know that they probably begin to seriously get interested in them at about that age.

RP/WU: *Do you think that the marketing of graphic novels like* The Killing Joke *and* The Dark Knight *in bookstores and even by the Quality Paperback Book Club have pulled in a new readership for you?*

DO: Sure, because people may have liked the form but felt the stories were too simplistic for them. Not interesting enough. Maybe the very crude version of superheroes, which is basically the male macho fantasy trip, *was* a little too crude for a lot of our potential readers. But, something like *Watchmen* or *The Killing Joke* is sophisticated and it gives the new readers the form they like with a content that is acceptable to them.

RP/WU: *Do you think a lot of women read Batman and, if not, how would you go about attracting a larger female readership?*

DO: I wish I knew. We have talked about this for at least fifteen years. We know that women are very much a minority of our readers, though it is a minority that is growing. It may be because, through one of those historical accidents, comic books have been about strong guys who vanquish evil. This is not a subject that a lot of little girls have a consuming interest in, so there is nothing in them to attract this readership. When we did try and attract them, the stories were done by middle-aged men, who didn't have a handle on what a girl might really like. As I said, this is changing.

RP/WU: *Do you have plans to try to attract more female readers?*

DO: Yeah. I think the current version of Wonder Woman appeals to women – in fact, it may be too feminist for some people's taste. It's edited by a woman and written by a man who is certainly very sympathetic to feminist concerns.

RP/WU: *And what about Batman?*

DO: I don't know. I could guess that the movie will attract some women, but I think it's going to be a slow process, because historically the character has not appealed to women. Women are going to have to discover comics on their own and then decide what they like and what they don't like.

RP/WU: *The industry seems to be unique in that a lot of creative people have started out as fans. What do you think the impact of this is? The pluses and minuses?*

DO: The pluses are that they are familiar with the material and with the vocabulary and the visual conventions of the medium. The downside is that they may become a little too concerned about repeating the stuff that they just absolutely loved when they first discovered comics. The good comic book writers who came up as fans at some point in their lives got interested in a lot of other stuff. Those who stay only interested in comics cripple their potential development as writers. Some of them are bright, talented guys but the medium has moved beyond what they loved when they were twelve years old.

RP/WU: *What do you think the difference is between somebody like yourself who comes out of a journalistic background and wasn't heavily into comics and the writers who were fans, in terms of the different approaches to a character?*

DO: People with diverse backgrounds bring ideas and even fictional techniques from outside comics. In that way they push the envelope, they expand the possibilities, both in terms of subject matter and in terms of storytelling technique. They bring cinema to it. They bring novels to it. I think that Alan Moore, for example, has the instincts of a novelist – he has read a lot of novels and loved them. I think Frank Miller is, in his soul, a visual writer, a very good one; he comes to it with the instincts of a moviemaker. But the point is that they are both bringing to it something from outside comics. If you grew up only being interested in comics, you are probably only going to regurgitate, both in terms of content and in terms of technique, what has already been done. You can't get too radical and violate the medium, but you can expand it. It has to be a gradual thing. The Green Lantern stories I did in the 1970s that got a lot of publicity at the time came about because I was a journalist and I brought a journalist's curiosity and social concerns to comic books. It wouldn't have happened if I had just been a comic book writer.

RP/WU: *When we talked to you the last time, you were using a lot of cinematic terms to describe artwork. Is that something a lot of people tend to do?*

DO: No, that's something pretty much only I do. It's just because I found it's the easiest way to do it. If I am in the middle of a story and I am really cooking and it's 3 a.m., hey watch out. It's a lot easier for me to write 'ECU Myra' than 'We see Myra's face close up'. The nice thing about writing screenplays is that the language is such a nice, economical shorthand. It's almost music notation. I have written two television shows in the last six months and I find it easy work, because you don't have to work on transitions. You write 'cut to' and the cameraman accomplishes the transition for you. It seems like a good thing to borrow from cinema insofar as we do a lot of the same things.

RP/WU: *But most writers don't use this cinematic shorthand?*

DO: No. Take Alan Moore, for example. His description for the first panel of *The Killing Joke*, one-ninth of a page, is two and a half single-space pages. It took me a day to read the script of *The Killing Joke*. It was a pretty good day though, I enjoyed it.

RP/WU: *How did Brian Bolland feel about the lengthy descriptions?*

DO: Alan will give you this incredibly detailed description of not only what is in the panel but why it's there, and what happened twenty years ago, and what the character had for breakfast this morning and what the kids were doing. Then at the end he'll say, 'You could ignore all that and do whatever you want.' So I think Brian basically followed what Alan indicated. At one point we thought about publishing Alan's script, because it is so entertaining in itself and then ultimately decided that that would be a little bit like being invited backstage to a magic show.

RP/WU: *We saved one of the things we are most interested in for last, which is the relationship between comics and films. What similarities and differences do you see between the two?*

DO: Well, there is an awful lot that is similar but you can carry the analogy too far. Basically, if a comic book works, you will be able to get the broad story by looking at the pictures. But comic books are meant to be read. Reading requires more participation from the audience than cinema, where if you are just passive you can still get it. You have to bring your brain cells to reading. I think that there is that interaction between the part of you that perceives images and the part of you that translates the very abstract stuff that is language. If you like comics, I think it's because of some kind of chemical process in your brain. Those two messages entering your consciousness at the same time through the same sense organ are very pleasing to you. If you are looking at a movie or television show, it's a different experience. You don't have to use your imagination as much, the language is coming in through the ear, the visual information is coming in through your eye. That's what you experience everyday in your life, it's not special in the way of perceiving a comic book.

3

BATMAN AND THE TWILIGHT OF THE IDOLS
AN INTERVIEW WITH FRANK MILLER
Christopher Sharrett

If there is a single artist most identified with the resurgence in popularity of Batman it is without question Frank Miller. His 1986 graphic novel *Batman: The Dark Knight Returns* not only made Bob Kane's 1939 creation once again the most popular comic book hero, but played no small role in the incredible burgeoning of the comics industry in the 1980s. Inked and coloured by Klaus Janson and Lynn Varley, *Dark Knight* offered a troubled, suicidal, alcoholic Bruce Wayne in his mid-fifties who tries to repress the urge to again don his Batman persona after a ten-year retirement. The worsening scene (Gotham City totally corrupt, the world on the brink of nuclear war, the Joker released from a mental institution) forces Batman into one last go-round that for Miller is the 'Great American Superhero story', a four-part 'opera' about the fall of the hero in a world that has rendered him obsolete. This book and a follow-up, *Batman: Year One* (1987) (a very grim retelling of Batman's origins), aside from recasting Batman and the other mainstay DC Comics superheroes, became part of a general re-evaluation of hero worship in comic book narrative. Alan Moore and Dave Gibbons's mammoth 1986 graphic novel *Watchmen* (about a 1980s US very similar to our own where superheroes are an accepted part of the landscape, with disastrous results), and Moore's *Miracleman* and *V for Vendetta*, use the superhero as a vehicle for challenging received notions of charismatic authority and leadership, among the driving strategies within the comic book renaissance.

Decidedly more romantic than Moore's superheroes, Miller's Batman is nonetheless offered as a radical opponent to the status quo and an obsessed and brooding personality infinitely more three-dimensional than the type generally offered by the narrow moral universe of the comics industry. The renewed interest in Batman caused by *Dark Knight* and its successors far outstripped Batman's principal rival in pop fiction, Superman (described by a character in *Dark Knight* as 'that big blue schoolboy'), and spurred not only new Batmania but the impetus for bringing Batman to the screen after various scripts remained Hollywood back-burner projects for over a decade.

Aside from his Batman work, Miller has produced a number of other provocative titles in the superhero genre, including the graphic novel *Elektra: Assassin* (1986–7) and a celebrated run on Marvel Comics' popular *Daredevil* series, another character Miller virtually reinvented. As Miller's Batman books were enjoying great success and tremendous notoriety, Alan Moore made the field even richer with his own Batman novel (drawn by Brian Bolland) *The Killing Joke* (1988), a melancholy meditation on the psychological relationship of Batman to his arch-rival the Joker. In 1987, at the height of one of the comics industry's most creative and productive periods, a new wave of censorship and a war over the industry's control of artists' work caused Miller, Moore and a number of top creators to part company with DC and Marvel Comics. Miller has since written the screenplay for *RoboCop II* (1990) and developed new characters for independent comics publishers.

In what follows, Miller discusses his involvement with Batman, his earlier and future work, the state of the comics industry and the meaning of the superhero as a symbol of our times.

Christopher Sharrett: *There is a perception that* Dark Knight *almost single-handedly started the new renaissance in comic books.*

Frank Miller: *Dark Knight* got a lot of immediate attention because it was Batman and everyone recalls that character from the old TV show. But *Dark Knight* was only one of several things going on in the field that showed what comics could really do. Spiegelman's *Maus* got similar attention, perhaps from a slightly different audience.

CS: *But Maus and Raw and such seem to be somewhere in the avant-garde. They still haven't gained the notoriety of a Dark Knight. Is it because Batman is simply such a strong popular icon?*

FM: Well, I'd love to say that the success of *Dark Knight* was based solely on the talents of myself and my collaborators, but Batman after all is a major American folk hero who was due for a revival. About every ten or twenty years or so you see renovations of Superman or Batman, and in this case I was lucky enough to have almost complete autonomy and produce something that for me was ultimately very personal.

CS: *You don't think that at least part of the interest was involved in the rather panicked search for heroes in 1980s culture? The incredible popularity of the work of Joseph Campbell also seems involved in a new phase of hero worship.*

FM: Anytime a hero is done even reasonably well, there's a *tremendous* popular response. Modern art and literature have so diminished the idea of the hero, at least up until a few years back, that there was a crying need.

CS: *I want to come back to this idea of hero worship. Could you speak for a moment to the influence of* Dark Knight *on the image of Batman? We see constant references to the 'Dark Knight' in the comics, but are the current Batman stories showing the type of complex character you created in the book? Some suggest that while Batman has become a 'darker' character, more substantive ideas from* Dark Knight *have been dropped.*

FM: The comics industry is dominated by two publishers, who don't believe in or even understand what comics can be. They shrink from censors whenever they appear. They have historically depended on a sweatshop atmosphere, even to survive. Since *Dark Knight*, very cynical editors have hired artists to trace off pages of *Dark Knight* and they've hired writers to repeat what they think they understand about *Dark Knight*, which essentially is that it is very brutal, and that it includes little TV panels. Of course, all this misses the point of the whole thing, so what we're seeing are a lot of third-rate imitations. I don't like saying this, really. It's pretty embarrassing. The same publisher that bought Superman and Batman and totally corrupted them got a shot in the arm with *Dark Knight* and *Watchmen* and a few other things. And look what they've done with it.

CS: *Are there any Batman books or miniseries which interest you and seem close to your sensibility? We've seen* Batman: The Cult, Batman: Year Two, Killing Joke, A Death in the Family *and quite a few other major Batman projects.*

FM: *A Death in the Family* should be singled out as the most cynical thing that particular publisher has ever done. An actual toll-free number where fans can call in to put the axe to a little boy's head. On the other hand, *Killing Joke* was a very fine piece of work that came out at about the same time.

CS: *Some of the Batman stories seem the very opposite of* Dark Knight *with their one-dimensional moral simplicity. I'm thinking of* Ten Nights of the Beast *with the KGB supervillain.*

FM: You're getting beyond me here. I haven't read that.

CS: *It's not worth talking about. It's basically another example of turning back the clock on the whole genre.*

FM: What offended me most was seeing the tracing off of David Mazzucchelli's drawings in the *Catwoman* series and also seeing my own drawings traced off in *The Cult*. I really would have thought better of them. I would have thought the artists involved in those projects would do better than that.

CS: *We've mentioned* The Killing Joke. *How close is Alan Moore's sensibility to your own in terms of the conception of Batman and his world, particularly to the image of the Joker?*

FM: I disagreed completely with everything he did in that book, but Alan did it all so beautifully I couldn't argue. And Brian Bolland's illustrations were gorgeous, some of his best work. You've got to understand that when I'm involved with these characters the involvement is total: I have to believe in them. Alan's view of the Joker was very humanistic. My Joker was more evil than troubled; Alan's was more troubled than evil.

CS: *It does seem that* Dark Knight *contains a very metaphysical notion of evil, while in* Watchmen *and* Killing Joke, *evil is produced by social forces.*

FM: There is a wonderful line in *Killing Joke* about 'one bad day'.

CS: *Yeah, that is a great line. Let's stay with Batman and the Joker. In the current conceptions of Batman, including the movie, we have this idea of Batman as rather insane, with the Joker as a kind of doppelgänger.*

FM: The Batman folklore is full of doppelgängers for Batman. The Joker is one of them. The more accurate one, although a less interesting villain, is Two-Face. Two-Face is identical to Batman in that he's controlled by savage urges, which he keeps in check, in his case, with the flip of a coin. He's very much like Batman. The Joker is not so much a doppelgänger as an antithesis, a force for chaos. Batman imposes his order on the world; he is an absolute control freak. The Joker is Batman's most maddening opponent. He represents the chaos Batman despises, the chaos that killed his parents.

CS: *So it's control versus the loss of control.*

FM: Yeah. What really makes it so tantalising is the sexual aspect of the whole thing.

CS: *In terms of the Joker?*

FM: In terms of the Joker and Batman. In a way, the Joker is a homophobic nightmare.

CS: *Can you develop this a bit?*

FM: In *Dark Knight*, the Joker says he never keeps count of all the hundreds of people he's killed, but he knows Batman does and he loves him for it. To Batman, who's not asexual but really the essence of sublimation, this character represents every single thing he despises. It gets pretty weird.

CS: *In* Dark Knight, *the Joker seems more overtly gay than in other Batman narratives. In Chapter 3, his henchman Bruno seems to be a transsexual.*

FM: Bruno is a woman. I have a hard time expressing the ways I initially conceived some of these rather bizarre characters without sounding like a psychopath. Anyway, Bruno was a woman, a cohort of the Joker. He never had sex with her, because sex is death to him. Put more accurately, death is sex.

CS: *There seem to be so many gay aspects to the Joker in* Dark Knight. *The make-up man at the TV studio taunts him about lipstick. The Joker actually wears lipstick. He calls Batman 'Darling'. A lot of gay signifiers there.*

FM: I don't want to sound simplistic, but it seemed like a good idea at the time I was working on the character. I know we live in very rough times in terms of persecution of gays and gay stereotyping, but I wasn't trying to address this as much as portray this villain in a way I felt to be sensible and interesting.

CS: *Of course, an issue here is that the Joker is the only gay character in the book. There is no counterbalancing force in terms of a gay character who's more heroic. This is apparently one reason why* Dark Knight *was criticised.*

FM: I've had flak from almost every group. I can only say that when I write my stories I honestly try to avoid targeting anyone. Working in Hollywood recently, I've come to realise how many prohibitions there really are against even touching one group or another, to a point where the villain can't be female, can't be gay, can't be black. I understand this, but I still don't like the limitations placed on how you can go about creating characters. Anyway, yeah, the homophobic nightmare is very much part of the Batman/Joker mythos. It's always been there, I just spelled it out a little more plainly.

CS: *If we can stay with the sexual theme for a minute, it seems that this has been developed increasingly after decades of repression, especially with Fredric Wertham's attack on the Batman/Robin relationship as gay.* Watchmen *insisted on superhero sexuality. Some readers have suggested that your Robin, Carrie Kelly, finally allows Batman to express his sexual feelings for Robin, since the character is suddenly female. It's a subtle expression of his gayness.*

FM: Come on. It's a father/child relationship. It's clearly defined as such. This is where this stuff gets preposterous. When he says 'Good soldier' to her, he's holding this little girl. He's confronting his limitations as a human being. Batman isn't gay. His sexual urges are so drastically sublimated into crime-fighting that there's no room for any other emotional activity. Notice how insipid are the stories where Batman has a girlfriend or some sort of romance. It's not because he's gay, but because he's borderline pathological, he's obsessive. He'd be *much* healthier if he were gay.

CS: *I'd like to touch on* Dark Knight's *politics. You're probably familiar with the* Village Voice *review that called the book 'Rambo in a cape'.*

FM: It gets pretty silly. The book is what it is. In that *Village Voice* attack they also said that the Mutant dialect was a disguised black dialect, but it was taken almost word for word from a suburban white dialect that Lynn [Varley] brought to it. Lynn co-wrote all the dialogue with Robin and the Mutants, because it's all based on a dialect in her home town, a predominantly white suburb, a real 'Leave It to Beaver' land. You check that place and you won't find it a centre for much urban black culture. The *Village Voice* reaction, along with a few others, was a reaction based on the fact that *Dark Knight* did not offer a didactic left-wing perspective. I was having great fun with parody, and I've never been able to give up on the idea of superheroes. I couldn't have done Batman and have been politically correct at the same time, because the politically correct contingent won't allow for any character with a larger-than-life status. Also, of course, violence is out, and Batman is an extremely violent character.

CS: *Another criticism is that* Dark Knight, Watchmen, Batman: Year One, Miracleman *and the works that re-evaluate the superhero are essentially pessimistic. There is this apocalyptic vision throughout these works.*

FM: I don't know how I could write a superhero story and be pessimistic. To go into history for a moment, what made the whole superhero idea impotent was censorship. With fear on from pressure groups, the industry adopted a self-censoring code. The code through which most comics still pass insists on a benevolent world where authority is always right, policemen never take bribes, our elected officials always serve our best interests, and parents are always good and sound people. They don't even make mistakes. The world we live in does not resemble the world of the censors. I simply put Batman, this unearthly force, into a world that's closer to the one I know. And the world I know is terrifying. I don't think *Dark Knight* is pessimistic, because the good guy wins.

CS: *But it seems that your hero finally loses at the end of* Dark Knight. *Moreover, it seems like these god-like characters are made irrelevant in the operatic atmosphere you create, with the nuclear backdrop and the contempt for superheroes expressed by the world at large. At the end, Bruce Wayne immolates his Batman persona.*

FM: For me, that was a hopeful ending. He's looking forward to his next adventure after realising that the methods of the past are no longer appropriate. The book starts with Bruce Wayne contemplating suicide; at the end, he's found a reason to live. He's adjusted to the times.

CS: *He's not going to be carrying on as a romantic superhero?*

FM: The sequel I had in mind was as preposterous as the original. He would be much more direct in his actions, much more willing to mess with the order of things. He wouldn't be going after the poor bastards who are muggers. He'd be going after the people who make them muggers.

CS: *So he would operate as Bruce Wayne, going after politicians and businessmen?*

FM: Oh, I would have thrown all kinds of capes and cowls into it too, because that's the stuff of it. The key transition would be his recognition that he's no longer part of authority. That's really the transition at the end of *Dark Knight*, this knowledge that he's no longer on the side of the powers that be anymore, because the powers that be are wrong.

CS: *So in that sense, then, the book is very radical, with Batman representing an anti-`Establishment image.*

FM: Sure. And that's what I think these books can offer. Go back to the origins of Superman, before World War II. He was dragging generals to the front of battles. He was fighting corrupt landlords. He was *not* the symbol of the status quo he's since become.

CS: *He was a real FDR/New Deal character.*

FM: Yeah, in a sense.

CS: *So in the conservative 1980s, superheroes again represent very firmly the standing order, except for your work,* Watchmen *and a few others.*

FM: There's tremendous pressure in the field, at the two major publishers, to do that. When Jerry Falwell and his ilk were riding high, there was this edict down at Marvel Comics not to use words like 'God', or 'damn', or 'Good Lord', or anything else that might by chance offend pseudo-Christians. You really have to keep in mind that Marvel and DC are scared chickens. If you can generate five letters, they'll do what you say. And the characters reflect their publishers' fearfulness, so we have a Superman who's starting to spread around the middle and might have lunch with Nancy Reagan next week, and Batman has turned into a real jerk. Luckily, there was a time when there was a little opening up, and Alan Moore and Dave Gibbons and Lynn Varley and myself and a few others were allowed the opportunity to paint our own portraits of these heroes.

CS: *What's your feeling about the Batman movie? It seems that it couldn't have come into being without* Dark Knight *paving the way.*

FM: I didn't enjoy it. I disagreed with almost everything in it. I get locked into my visions of these characters and become resistant to other interpretations. I'm the last person who should attempt to review anything with Batman in it.

CS: *OK. What about the constant use of the term 'Dark Knight' in every Batman narrative?*

FM: Well, I didn't make it up. It wasn't used very commonly in Batman folklore, it's true. Now DC is milking the idea for all it's worth. That's just the way they work. To me, the whole killing of Robin thing was probably the ugliest thing I've seen in comics, and the most cynical.

CS: *Has there been anything in the superhero genre lately that has really interested you?*

FM: There's *Watchmen*. Back when we were doing *Dark Knight* and *Watchmen*, there was a feeling among a few of us that we were re-entering adolescence in working on this form. Now I feel that this has become true generally, with people going into this retrograde adolescence along several different directions. There's really no form of entertainment where the idea of the hero has been more fully explored than in comics, and now that public attention has grown, there is a retreat to a more juvenile outlook. Marvel and DC are retreating to the styles of the 1960s while keeping some of the trappings of the 80s. There's a little more violence, there's an occasional bare breast or whatever, but basically it's a retreat to the same material of the early 1960s. Alan and I and a few others are trying to go our own way. I'm writing more stories about heroes. I'm not through with them yet.

CS: *What's coming up?*

FM: There are a few projects due later this year. One is called *Hard Boiled*, a kind of futuristic tough-guy series. The other is *Give Me Liberty*, drawn by Dave Gibbons, which is a future history with a female lead. Geof Darrow is drawing *Hard Boiled*. I finished an *Elektra* book with Lynn Varley.

CS: *You said* Watchmen *is the only book that interests you. That's now almost three years old and part of a time when you and Alan Moore were helping to change the industry. There's nothing else out there lately?*

FM: Quality comes and goes, of course. I haven't been keeping up with the field. Someone may pop up with something amazing. You have to consider also what Alan and I were working on. I was working on a revivification of a folk hero, but I was also reaping all the benefits of fifty years of the hero's history. It's true also with Alan, because you couldn't really approach *Watchmen* without growing up with the Justice League of America. Now I'm on much less steady ground, because I'm creating characters out of whole cloth. I'm trying to build walls to push against. With Batman that's easy, because you know the rules of the game. If things are a bit fallow or bland right now, it may be natural enough, because there was an earthquake a few years back. I've seen things happening in the field, but not with superheroes. *Love and Rockets* is delightful; Spiegelman's work is of great value. Have you seen the new *Raw*? Excellent stuff. I'm especially interested in some imports – it's great to finally be able to read one of Milo Manara's books.

CS: *Some fans suggest that after* Dark Knight *and* Watchmen, *there isn't very much more to be said about superheroes.*

FM: I heard that *before* those books came out. It's the old idea that there are only two or three stories that can be told about a character. It's just talk. There's plenty more work to be done.

CS: *Does the sweatshop atmosphere of the publishers simply kill imagination?*

FM: It's a combination of things. For one thing, you might notice that people's time at these publishers tends to be shorter and shorter. I spent a lot less time at DC than Neal Adams, for example, and certainly less than Gardner Fox did. You can't own your own work, or even a piece of it. You cannot control your work as you produce it. It's a condition intolerable enough to drive me and Alan and a number of other people away from those companies and therefore away from these essential folk heroes. So you have to figure what your options are if you want to work with the idea of the superhero. You can't just come up with an imitation Superman – that would be cheap and silly and not as good as the original. So for my part, since I can't let go of these heroes, I'm trying to come up with new ones without ripping off the old ones.

CS: *I'd like to backtrack for a moment to some of the themes in* Dark Knight. *In that book and* Watchmen, *there is a strong apocalyptic current. In* Dark Knight, *there is a kind of near-miss nuclear attack that sets up a very bleak landscape for Batman to take a role in. In* Watchmen, *a superhero causes a holocaust in order to usher in utopia. Most of the major superhero re-evaluations seem intimately tied to an apocalyptic impulse in mass culture.*

FM: Things don't look good right now. The environment is collapsing. That crisis may well be the next major theme in entertainment. I think it's finally sinking in that the planet is on its way to dying. Whether or not we decide to do something may be irrelevant. When we were doing those books, nuclear terror was definitely in everyone's minds. It was obvious that everything could end very fast. *Dark Knight* and *Watchmen* were both an attempt to weave the superhero into that terror. That was sort of the basic backdrop. It was a bit of a stretch to weave Batman into it, but it seemed necessary, and it seemed to be good material.

CS: *Some fans were let down that there weren't full-scale disasters at the end of* Dark Knight *and* Watchmen, *since you and Alan seemed to be building towards them and the end of the world seemed to be the culmination you were preparing us for.*

FM: And these are the people who call us pessimists!

CS: *Yeah, it's interesting. But obviously there's tremendous interest in these* Mad Max-*style narratives about a post-nuclear wasteland out of which something new develops.*

FM: Yes, well, science says that stuff is all wrong. I've never done a post-apocalypse story. I just don't believe it. If that exchange ever happened, there just wouldn't be any humans left alive. The planet might survive but there wouldn't be any people on it. *Mad Max* movies present the most reassuring fantasy of all, that we would somehow survive the catastrophe. As far as the interest in catastrophe in fiction, I suppose I tried to deal with this a bit with the Mutant gang. There is a suicidal, or rather geno-cidal, fantasy that all our problems will go away if we just get it over with and drop the bomb. It's also a sociopathic fantasy that we can just wipe everything clean instead of dealing with the much more difficult problem of how to manoeuvre our way out of it all. It's lessening a bit for the moment anyway with *perestroika*, but we still have a Republican in the White House, so who knows where it will go. But the nuclear terror isn't quite so pronounced right now. I perceive the nuclear terror thing as a bit of a shill for some real problems in front of us, some of the deeper terrors going on in the planet. It's hideous. How we are going to write stories where superheroes deal with environmental issues is going to be a real bitch.

CS: *That brings me back to the basic issue of superheroes. You seem to think that we need them, that strong, charismatic individuals are basic to history.* Watchmen *says the opposite. That book suggests that heroes can take you into hell and that each of us must take responsi-bility for history's direction.*

FM: Like so many things Alan says, I would like to talk with him about this for about three hours, and I have. I just disagree completely with this particular idea *Watchmen* brings up. I don't believe that governments or committees or political movements accomplish much. I believe people do, individually. I'm in love with heroes, not because I think there are that many, or that there is any one individual who could do what Batman does or what Superman does, but because I think we're at our best when we're autonomous.

CS: *I think one of Alan Moore's points is somewhat similar to Frank Herbert's argument in the* Dune *books, in that we tend to project too much onto individual charismatic father figures. No matter how well meaning the hero might be, this abrogation of the will always poses disaster for society.*

FM: When I create a story, I take a very small thing and make it very big. It just hap-pens to be the way I make my fiction. Someone mugs me and I make a Batman comic, to put it in the crudest possible terms. While there is room for political parody and while there is political meaning in all of this, presenting a hero is not presenting a case for political power. I don't want Batman as president, and I don't think the book says that at all. There's a tendency to see everything as a polemic, as a screed, when after all, these are adventure stories. They can have a lot of ramifications, they can bring in an awful lot of other material, but anyone who really believes that a story about a guy who wears a cape and punches out criminals is a presentation of a political viewpoint, and a presentation of a programme for how we should live our lives under a political system, is living in a dream world.

CS: *But it's possible to see a character like Ozymandias in* Watchmen *as a powerful metaphor for specific political attitudes.*

FM: Absolutely. That's part of Alan's brilliance. He did that wonderfully, but I'm just coming at this whole thing with a different attitude.

CS: *But your Batman can also be seen as an image of a certain type of power.*

FM: Everyone from Alexander to Hitler. But mostly Zorro. Batman doesn't work when he's a figure of authority. He would be a tyrant. Anyone who professes an absolute ideological point of view is a would-be tyrant. Batman doesn't do this. Heroes have to work in the society around them, and Batman works best in a society that's gone to hell. That's the only way he's ever worked. He was created when the world was going to hell, and *Dark Knight* came out when the world went to hell.

CS: *Yeah. When Bob Kane created him, the war was beginning.*

FM: Sure. But he's also a dionysian figure, a force for anarchy that imposes an individual order. He's never been an authority figure except in some of the comics of the 1960s that actually initiated the TV show, where Batman begins to wear a badge and whatever. But *Dark Knight* didn't end with Batman wanting to take over the US.

CS: *That last panel of the book suggests he's become a kind of Jim Jones figure, creating a new cult out of the Mutants and whoever else he can pull together.*

FM: That's what's fascinating about the character, the way he pulls together all these sinister urges. At the end, Bruce Wayne is looking to the next stage, the next phase of his life.

CS: *One of the problems with perceiving Batman as a dionysian, anarchical figure is the fact that he's a privileged person. Bruce Wayne is a rich man who seems self-satisfied despite his supposed trauma. We are asked to accept this man as a force for the common good.*

FM: Anyone can be a victim. This is exactly what makes him a good character. It's how one uses the evil inside. It's how we use our rage, our venom. One of the things that makes Batman so strangely hip and unhip at the same time is that modern liberalism has totally divorced the forceful, violent aspect of the will from other aspects of personality. There is this view that this forceful aspect of individual will is just plain wrong and shouldn't exist in any form. You can see the kind of censorship in children's entertainment. There is no sense of individual will, let alone violent individual will. We're not simple creatures. We all have God and the devil in us. Batman makes his devils work for the common good.

CS: *There seems to be an attitude now that the Joker is at least as appealing as Batman in terms of the dark forces he represents. His kind of madness seems associated with the Ted Bundys of society, who seem to hold a powerful fascination for people in the 1980s and 90s. An issue of* Film Threat *magazine calls mass murderers the 'heroes of the '80s'.*

FM: It's fantasy. One of the big mistakes of modern times is to assume fantasy should be some kind of behavioural modification device. Fantasy is where we vent our spleens. Freddy Krueger – he's a child molester for Christ's sake! It all gets back to the term 'role model' that castrates every hero or villain who falls under the sway of the censors. The Joker is popular right now because a charismatic actor played him, and because he represents doing whatever the hell you want to anybody at any time, any way. It's the horror comics of the 1950s. It's harmless. To think that our own fantasy lives must be censored is just crazy.

CS: *Concerning your plans for the future, do you intend to stay with superheroes?*

FM: Yes. I still have some things to say about superheroes, but I have some other projects I want to get into.

CS: *For me, what's more bothersome is the tendency of DC to cultivate this 'adult market' with projects like Piranha Press. They drop terms like 'expressionism'. The whole thing is so mannered and forced.*

FM: Oh God, isn't it awful? That stuff is about as painful as going to the dentist. I went to a comic book store recently and spent about a hundred bucks just to see what's going on after a period of being a bit out of touch and feeling that things were rather barren right now. I'm very disturbed by the way that Marvel and DC looked at *Watchmen* and *Dark Knight*. All they got from them is that they were naughtier and a bit more brutal than other comics. They're interpreting stuff that was admittedly violent, but they're making it all vicious and very small. When Alan and Dave were working on *Watchmen* and I was working on *Dark Knight*, we were coming at the superhero from two different directions. I'm a real romantic. Alan's approach towards heroes, at least intellectually, is much more detached and sceptical. But when I saw that book, I was absolutely knocked out. It was some of the most amazing stuff I've ever seen in the medium. It was so well thought out and so carefully crafted. But you have to take one position or the other.

CS: *Alan commented in an interview with me that* Watchmen *was a political and moral fable that happened to contain superheroes, and* Dark Knight *was a superhero adventure that contained political and moral ideas.*

FM: Alan and I have had *many* conversations on the subject. My main comment was that I saw *Dark Knight* as profoundly American and *Watchmen* profoundly British. In *Watchmen*, you can't help but see American icons reworked from a very European point of view. It's very hard to miss the whole British flavour.

CS: *A couple of final things. Any thoughts on the current wave of Batmania?*

FM: America is primed for a fad. It's been about twenty years since that thing happened. It just seems time for a good fad.

CS: *I'm thinking how Superman's anniversary fell flat in comparison with what's going on right now with the tons of Batman paraphernalia. Is there something more primal about Batman imagery?*

FM: What better image for a time of despair?

CS: *Since Batman indeed speaks to a very bleak attitude towards the future?*

FM: Sad to say, a very accurate one right now. We live in very dark times. It fits that this would be our hero.

4

FIFTH-DIMENSIONAL BATMAN
AN INTERVIEW WITH GRANT MORRISON
Will Brooker

Grant Morrison first came to prominence in 1987 with 'Zenith', the first superhero story in British science-fiction comic *2000AD*. He was subsequently recruited to DC Comics, writing the ongoing series *Animal Man* (1988–90) and *Doom Patrol* (1989–93) and the Batman graphic novel *Arkham Asylum* (1989), followed by *Batman: Gothic* in 1990.

A practising magician – as detailed in his 2011 autobiography, *Supergods* – Morrison typically explores alternate earths, altered realities and multiple identities in his work. These themes emerged in his popular superhero series, such as *JLA* (1997–2000) and *All-Star Superman* (2005–8) for DC Comics, as well as his more challenging, personal and politically engaged *The Invisibles* (1994–2000) and *The Filth* (2002) for Vertigo. After a period writing *X-Men* and other titles for Marvel, Morrison was brought back to DC

Grant Morrison and Dave McKean, *Batman: Arkham Asylum* (New York: DC Comics, 1989); Grant Morrison and Klaus Janson, *Batman: Gothic* (New York: DC Comics, 1990)

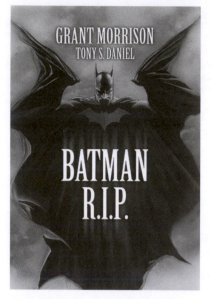

Grant Morrison and Tony Daniel, *Batman: R.I.P.* (New York: DC Comics, 2008)

in the mid-2000s to revamp a range of minor characters in *7 Soldiers* (2005–6) and coordinate a major cross-universe event in *Final Crisis* (2008–9). These series integrated Morrison's experimental approaches to storytelling and character within the mainstream superhero genre, to the frustration of some readers.

From 2006 to 2011, Morrison wrote multiple *Batman* titles, introducing new characters and concepts such as Damian Wayne – son of Bruce and Talia Al-Ghul – and the global organisation Batman Incorporated. His underlying concept – that every event in Batman's continuity had happened within Bruce Wayne's incredibly eventful lifetime – was disrupted by the introduction of DC's 'New 52' reboot, and while Morrison's storyline continued, concluding soon after the death of Damian, Scott Snyder has been writing and managing the main Batman narrative since September 2011.

In June 2014, Morrison took part in a panel with Will Brooker, Sarah Zaidan and Warren Ellis as part of the British Library's 'Comics Unmasked' exhibition. That panel led to this interview.

Will Brooker: *What is the story, in a fundamental sense, of your run on Batman through* Batman & Son *and* Batman RIP *to* The Return of Bruce Wayne, Batman and Robin, Batman Incorporated? *Not in a literal sense, but on a more archetypal, deep-rooted mythical level, what story is being explored and expressed here?*

Grant Morrison: That's for my readers to decide in the end. For me, it was simply the story of a man who, instead of fearing or succumbing to the darkness and horror in his life, used it to inspire him to greatness.

WB: *Was your run on Batman intended to produce a specific magical effect in the reader? Do you see it as adding up to a massive, connected sigil [a sign charged with an often magical meaning] with a specific purpose?*

GM: There's always some 'magical' – where magic means a willed and intentional desire to create specific and instructional states of altered consciousness – element in everything I write. The idea of the hole in things, of that ultimate refusal of reality to be explained, became paramount in Batman and suggested the direction for a lot of my subsequent work, particularly the *Annihilator* book I'm doing with Frazer Irving. That's what I've been trying to write about at least since I started on Batman, and it's in Batman you can see me crystallising my take on that idea of the dynamic Coriolis swirl of event and idea around a hole big enough to contain everything. The emptiness we strive to fill with meaning. Death. The Void.

The fact that Batman inhabits that boundary and draws his strength from the ferment of our darkest fears of abandonment, loss and meaninglessness became key to my approach. Batman says 'No' to our terrors and gives us a powerful, low-culture image of defiant humanity at its peak. At his best, Batman encourages us to use our resources in service to our community and our best ideals. He brings gold out of darkness, like bat's piss.

WB: *Was that purpose compromised or undermined in any way by the introduction of* The New 52, *which disrupted the final stage of* Batman Incorporated *and changed its relationship to continuity?*

GM: I tried to roll with it. The New 52 also changed the relationship to 'continuity' of every Batman story ever, including those written and drawn by the character's creators, so I don't feel singled out. My approach to Batman was an attempt to include everything that came before me and even some parts of what came after. That history can't be erased from the memories of its readers, so I'm assuming the version of Batman I created with my artistic collaborators will endure as some kind of auteuristic summation of that entire history.

WB: *When writing* The Invisibles, *you inhabited lead character King Mob and vice versa. Did you do anything comparable with Batman during the recent series? You channel his voice, but did you also live like him, think like him in any way?*

GM: I put much more effort into my fitness regime – and yoga, meditation and martial arts – while I was writing Batman stories, and I tried very hard to imagine what a good capitalist oligarch might feel like. Since I stopped working on Batman, I've gained almost a stone in weight! I need to start writing the Flash.

WB: All-Star Superman *was inspired in part by a cosplayer who seemed to inhabit the role of Superman. If you didn't meet a similar figure before writing your recent Batman, where did you gain the sense of who he is and how he responds to situations, what his relationship is like with other characters?*

GM: I've known Batman all my life, and by combining every version of the character I'm familiar with I have a fairly strong impression of how he might sound and move. I came to my specific approach by reading every Batman story in my so-called comic book collection, from Bill Finger's earliest efforts to the most recent work – at the time – by James Robinson.

Applying a small degree of in-story 'realism' to the character's history meant that I had to deal honestly with the idea of a man who had studied and mastered every known martial art and meditation method. That kind of training would kick out a lot of emotional bugs and I felt he couldn't have come through it all as the rage-driven, paranoid loner he was becoming in many stories prior to my tenure. I didn't want to ignore that portrayal either, but I was able to rationalise that period of his life as the result of his having lived through all the grim, dark stories of the 1980s and 90s. Ultimately, I wanted to deal with a Batman who was the Optimum Man. I wanted to think up to his level rather than imagining him as a neurotic and tortured man who could only feel normal by beating the crap out of junkies and burglars and who constantly seemed to be yelling 'This is MY CITY!' like a petulant child fighting over a stuffed toy.

WB: *How does Joker speak, in your head? What is your sense of him?*

GM: The Joker is well read and super-media literate; all lateral thinking, rapid-fire allusions and correspondences. He puts on voices all the time. He's theatrical and mercurial. His body language changes constantly. He's the terrifying creepy man who sits near you on the train and makes everyone feel uncomfortable. My Joker stands slightly outside the text, which gives him a kind of sardonic aerial perspective. The Joker is also the diseased, sleazy, fashion-y, piss-taking European decadent opposed to the muscular, can-do American Bruce Wayne. My version of the Joker is influenced by David Bowie conceptually and Johnny Rotten physically, and incorporates a strong performance aspect. In that sense, these are two drag acts in a pantomime war.

WB: *You said at the British Library panel that Batman in JLA was a Loki figure. How is this Batman different from the ones you wrote in* Gothic, Arkham Asylum *and the* Batman & Son–Batman Incorporated *series? Has your conception and articulation of who Batman is changed since you first wrote him, decades ago?*

GM: It was actually Warren Ellis who said Batman was a Loki/Trickster figure in *JLA*. I'm not sure I agree, and Warren could probably articulate this idea better than I could. For me, it was Plastic Man who played the Trickster figure in the *JLA*'s modern pantheon, while Batman was more of a Hadean, Plutonic underworld figure. It was not my goal to create realistic superhero stories which might conceivably be possible within limits of physics, so I felt free to treat Batman as the best humanity had to offer and therefore the equal of the gods – Batman in *JLA* was man as god. The Bat-God, as this approach came to be known.

WB: *If your recent Batman is a man who's had a fascinating life, in which the 1960s were a drug-fuelled attempt to capture the 40s, where does* Arkham Asylum *fall in that man's life? How old was he when he went through his late-1980s phase, and how does he now feel about that particular adventure?*

GM: I always saw *Arkham Asylum* as a glimpse into the darkest corners of Batman's interior life. It's a dream story, so it could fit almost anywhere. In my own personal attempt to create a timeline capable of incorporating if not all of Batman's adventures, then at least the flavour of every different era, while keeping him at the optimum age of thirty-five or thirty-six, I worked out that a fifteen-year career would just about make things work, so the 1980s Batman would be somewhere around twenty-seven or twenty-eight years old.

WB: *The New 52 has explicitly tried to contain and compress this mosaic Batman, for whom everything happened, into a simpler figure who has only been active for five years. How long do you think this containment can last before the mosaic, 'prismatic' Batman explodes out again?*

GM: It can, as we've seen before, last for a long time. The new Batman could last a generation or be replaced in six months by a new continuity. I imagine his rich comic book history is the least interesting feature of Batman's mercantile value to his corporate owners, except as a source of antagonists for games, cartoons and movies.

WB: *If Batman can be a variety of different forms and figures, what (if anything) are the key elements that make him Batman? What never changes, from one Batman to another? What could you not take away, without taking away the essence and framework of Batman?*

GM: It's hard to say – someone might always come along with a way of doing Batman that eschews all of the familiar gimmicks and still works. Look at Dave McKean's Batman in *Arkham Asylum* and extrapolate from that, for instance. A monstrous, expressionistic, abstract Bat-motif might be used to tell as powerful a story as a nuanced, emotional, layered examination of Batman's human needs and relationships. Batman is at the point where the Bat-symbol alone is sufficient to trigger a flood of associations, meanings and emotions, so maybe that distinctive Bat-sigil – and all its equally distinctive prior variants! – is all he needs.

WB: *Your characters, including Batman, are written from an affectionate, expert knowledge of the DC Universe and comic book history and continuity in general. How do you feel about your characters, or your versions of characters, being returned, or taken, from your personal writing back into the collective ownership of DC?*

GM: I don't mind. If I sign on to do work for hire, I know that my work will be 'owned' by the corporation for as long as the terms of copyright law endure, by which time I will be dead. I have no particular proprietary feelings about work I create for hire and which helps sustain a fictional reality I think is worth preserving – i.e. the DC Comics universe. Otherwise, I own a substantial portfolio of my own creations or intellectual properties, so this is work I do because it's fun and rewarding not because I need to.

WB: *As a specific example, how do you feel about other writers using Damian Wayne? Do you feel possessive about your creation, or do you feel you created him and let him loose into this jointly authored, mythical playground where others can do what they like?*

GM: When I read the character written badly, I feel possessive in the sense that I can hardly believe anyone could find it difficult to replicate Damian Wayne's very distinctive voice. I've observed that what tends to go first is his sense of aristocratic entitlement and the clipped precision of his language and movements, usually replaced by a kind of West Coast rich-kid brattishness, which only proves that Americans will never ever grasp the nuances of the European post-feudal class system. God bless them.

WB: *You own (some of) your characters legally, but do you feel you own them artistically? Crazy Jane from* Doom Patrol, *for instance, is your creation, but also a contemporary articulation of an archetype (or multiple archetypes), and arguably returns as Ragged Robin in* The Invisibles. *Are you curating these myths, rather than creating them? Would you feel happy with the idea of someone else writing your characters in 2114?*

GM: The prospect of any living thing remembering my name, my work or my characters in 2114 is a ludicrous one. As a thought experiment, however, I'm fine with anyone revisiting characters I've created. I inserted them into DC Comics continuity in the hope that they'd be reused. It's rarely happened in the past but Scott Snyder and others have been kind enough to keep characters like Professor Pyg and Scorpiana in circulation, so maybe there's hope.

The literally hundreds of characters I've created for DC were specifically developed as work for hire. In the highly unlikely event of anyone using, say, Mr Nobody or the Scissormen from *Doom Patrol* in a film, I get some small amount of compensation for having created those characters.

I enjoy making things up. I do it all the time. The characters I wanted to retain legally, I did and still do, along with my artistic collaborators. Other characters were specifically invented to inhabit the ongoing quilt of many hands that is the DC Universe. The idea of corporations owning characters, like owning slaves, is an idea I hope will one day be seen as insane and objectionable.

Ultimately, my name is on the books I wrote. My Batman is my version of Batman, not Denny O'Neil's version, or Frank Miller's or Scott Snyder's.

WB: *As a 'superstar' author, you now hold a position of creative authority whereby your stories set the rules for other, less-established writers. If you decide Bruce Wayne is in the past, after the events of* Final Crisis, *other writers and artists are now unable to use him until you bring him back. If you create Earth-5 in a comic book, that world is now established and its rules set for other creators, because of your status. Doesn't that make you a boss, a manager, rather than the rebel that you used to be?*

GM: I used to be young. I used to shit in a plastic potty. I used to have hair. I used to have a mum and dad who were alive. At the age of fifty-four, I'd be a bit disappointed if all I'd ever been permitted to be in my life was a 'rebel'. When do *I* get to be the Establishment, daddy? Joking aside, the answer to your question above is yes, it probably does to a certain extent, although that has more to do with an editorially driven attempt to maintain consistency between titles than it does with any desire of mine to tell people how to do their jobs.

Having said that, Paul Dini's Batman stories, written at the same time as my own, owed nothing to me, or to my approach, so clearly my take on Batman didn't impinge too harshly on Paul's own very highly developed view of the character. In addition, I too must bow to the pressure of events and revisions occurring in the DCU.

I've never imposed my 'version' of Batman on my fellow writers. I've always encouraged everyone to tell their own best version of the Batman story. To a large extent, the 'prismatic' approach you clearly discern in my writing precludes any such Napoleonic attempts to take control of the narrative.

WB: *Could it be said that you're setting the structures and the boundaries for other people?*

GM: It could be said. In fact, you just said it! There's the implication here that setting boundaries is essentially pernicious, but had I not been set boundaries by Bill Finger, Denny O'Neil, Frank Miller or any of the Batman creators who came before me, my Batman stories wouldn't exist. As I've said in the past, we can think of the idea of Batman as a twelve-bar blues. The unimaginative might see that structure as a demoralising constraint, but compare a twelve-bar blues played by Bill Haley to the same structure as expressed by the Rolling Stones, the Velvet Underground, Status Quo, Led Zeppelin or Jimi Hendrix and you may come to an understanding of the fractal freedom of expression made possible within simple formal frameworks.

Everything in our world is multidimensional; the opposite of a great truth is also a great truth. In order to comprehend things in their full majesty, we need to accommodate as many different viewpoints and perspectives as we can. Only by seeing all the possible interpretations can we hope to begin to grasp what any given 'thing' actually means. That's what the 'prismatic' approach implies, to me anyway.

Those 'other people' you mention are in exactly the same position I'm in when it comes to dealing with long-running fictional characters. If you choose to engage with Batman, you are deliberately engaging with corporate interests and a certain degree of stricture. Amazingly, the potential for personal expression is still enormous.

WB: *How do you feel about that role? Are you subverting the structures from your position inside, opening them up for others to play in?*

GM: My role is not that of a reformer. I'm simply in a position to tell the kinds of stories I like to read, using these characters. Having applied my abilities and intelligence to the history of Batman, that's what I came up with. By accepting into the canon every Batman story, even the most ridiculous and unfashionable, I felt I'd uncovered a character that was rich, dynamic, contradictory and, dare I say it, more 'human' than I'd suspected.

WB: *What is your relationship with the Batman Group Editor and other roles in Editorial, like Dan DiDio and Jim Lee? Can they tell you what to do with a character or a storyline?*

GM: They can but they never have. I assume they hire me because they have faith in my ability to do the kind of work that sells superhero comics. In corporate terms, I am a proven asset. As a reward for fulfilling my part of that contract, I get to reshape Batman or Superman to suit the needs of my personal agendas while serving corporate interests.

WB: *If you're writing Wonder Woman or Green Lantern, do you have to negotiate with a different editor in charge of that character, in terms of what they can and cannot do in the story? [This was the case in the 1980s and 90s under Denny O'Neil.]*

GM: There is a degree of negotiation. My editors on *JLA* – Ruben Diaz and Dan Raspler – tended to protect me from the worst of the dogmatic edicts emerging from the Batman office in the 1990s. I certainly wouldn't insist on any one interpretation of Batman, especially one which tried to make him 'realistic' or 'plausible', but that was what O'Neil tried to do in the 1990s. I maintain that Batman can safely handle any and all interpretations; each one only makes the idea stronger. The proof being that my inclusion of a teleport device in the Batcave didn't damage Batman as a property in the slightest. In fact, he's stronger now than ever.

WB: *If Scott Snyder now wrote an overarching Batman storyline that affected one of the titles you were writing, would you be given parameters within which you had to work, to fit his larger story?*

GM: Certainly, if I were to write Batman into an 'in-continuity' story now, it would be with the understanding that I was working in collaboration with Scott's revision of the character and his history. My job as a commercial writer of Batman comics would be to work within those constraints to tell the kind of story I wanted to tell.

WB: *To what extent is your freedom to do what you want within DC the consequence of your established status? How would it be different for a new writer, on his or her first superhero title?*

GM: It would be very different. Over decades, I've become a trusted, proven commodity who sells comic books. The three best-selling comic book writers in the world are, I'm told, Stan Lee, Alan Moore and me, so hiring me tends to be a guarantee of increased sales on any comic book. Obviously, I'm treated very differently from anyone else in the business, just as U2 is treated differently from a newly signed band.

Thinking again about the question, there may be a case for presenting Scott Snyder as a fairly obvious exception to that rule. Scott was a fairly new writer when he came aboard the Batman books but he's been given carte blanche to reinvent the character's entire history.

Both answers are therefore true!

WB: *In pragmatic, layperson's terms, how did you go about pitching the story of Batman from Batman & Son to Batman Incorporated? Was it locked down under contract from 2006 – not just in your head, but agreed with DC Editorial that this is how things would pan out for the next seven years?*

GM: No. There was no sense that my Batman run would last as long as it did. My original plan was for somewhere around fifteen issues culminating in what was then only a version of the story that eventually became *Batman RIP*. On the way, I got more entangled with the character than I'd anticipated and stayed with him for a few years longer than planned. Intriguing story threads kept suggesting themselves and I kept on following them until they ran out.

WB: *Did everyone know and agree that it would result in* Batman and Robin, Batman Incorporated – *did they know when you started Batman & Son that* The New 52 *would disrupt that saga by its end?*

GM: Not at all. Both *Batman and Robin* and *Batman Incorporated* arose naturally as a result of plot threads that took on lives of their own. Given the success of my work on Batman, DC Editorial was happy to allow me to continue.

The New 52 only came about as a result of the departure of Paul Levitz from the position of President and Publisher at DC. When Paul left, the new regime was able to put its own stamp on the material and the process of modernisation and revision was initiated almost immediately, resulting in the minor disruption you mention.

WB: *Is Batman inherently 'queer' and strange, a figure of carnival? How do you see his relationship with the queer elements in his life, such as Joker and (arguably) the gay overtones between himself and Dick Grayson? Is he a repressed figure?*

GM: As I've said before, Batman has no sexuality other than what we see on the page – he is a figure of pen and ink and meaning, and so far, he has been shown to be heterosexual. Nor do I see him as repressed. My take on Bruce Wayne is that he does whatever he feels will make his body and his mission more effective. If he feels a macrobiotic diet will make him stronger, that's what he'll eat. If he thinks sex will make him less uptight and more flexible, he'll have sex and be as good at fucking as he is at everything else. The stories have established a succession of girlfriends since Julie Madison in the 1930s and we must presume he wasn't just giving them a chaste peck on the cheek or his reputation as a playboy would have been shot down in flames by the media fairly early on. The inference is that Bruce has sex, and with women, lots of women. What he clearly lacks is any real emotional attachment to these women and any sense of commitment to anything other than his mission as Batman and whatever it takes to facilitate that. He's not repressed, but he's detached.

Having said that and when I started on the book, I was almost overwhelmed by the sense of an intrinsic homoerotic queerness at the heart of the Batman universe, with all the boy companions and buried passions and whatnot. My first few issues are, I think, an attempt to rationalise and reframe this element – from the first pole-dancing appearance of Robin to the fruity relationship between Alfred and Bruce and the weird psychosexual desire of Damian to replace the jealous Tim Drake as the object of daddy's affections. To be honest, I was quite surprised by how camp it all was and tried hard to broaden the possibilities of Batman beyond that seductive – if reductive – reading.

This is why I've always intimated that a gay version of Batman would work incredibly well. A kind of *Queer as Folk* interpretation, where the often casual nature of gay sex among young men, with its high turnover of partners, would naturally suit Bruce's psychology and protect him from commitment. It should be remembered, however, that the main focus of Batman stories will always be crime-fighting, not sex.

WB: *You've written at least one text story about Batman [Batman #633, April 2007]. Is Batman best suited to the specific form of comic books, rather than cinema, video games, prose or (for instance) poetry?*

GM: I've written two in fact – *The Stalking* for the UK *Batman Annual* in 1986 was my first professional Batman story. Otherwise, Batman is well developed enough to survive interpretation in any form. Check out Adrian Mitchell's 'Batpoem'. Or the lyrics to the punk classic 'Batman in the Launderette' by The Shapes. As a slightly pointless aside, the music fanzine I produced with my bandmates from The Mixers in 1982 was entitled 'Bombs Away, Batman!'

WB: *You incorporate the Batman stories of the past in your own work. Are you also influenced at all by the Batman stories being told at the same time, such as Nolan's movie trilogy, the video games, the various animated series?*

GM: Absolutely. *Batman: The Return* was fairly obviously coloured by the Nolan trilogy. And I loved the first video game in the *Arkham* series. I was very inspired by the sense it gave me of Batman's physicality and dogged relentlessness.

WB: *As a visual artist, is it frustrating sometimes when you write a story and see it drawn in a way that doesn't match either your own imagination, or the way you would have drawn it?*

GM: Yes, but as I've said before, doing monthly comics is like playing live music and there's little time for reflection or second drafts. Playing live is an exhilarating, life-affirming experience but very often it's raw and sometimes the guitarist is out of tune, or the singer hits a few bum notes. You just have to get on with it. I've been lucky to work with some great artists on Batman.

WB: *What are your thoughts about being able to control Batman as an avatar in a video game? How does that change our relationship with him? Does it work?*

GM: Speaking for myself, I thought it worked spectacularly well in the first game – I sat up all night to complete it in one sitting. I felt completely absorbed in the experience of being Batman and of effortlessly performing kung fu moves to take down multiple assailants, solving simple clues and soaring through night skies with a dreamlike, effortless ease my training had already taken care of.

I got bored about a third of the way through both subsequent *Arkham* games. Gave up on the second game with the Mr Freeze boss battle, then gave up on the next one when he was fighting Deathstroke, and I really couldn't be arsed anymore. The first one was a genuine state-of-the-art masterpiece.

WB: *People discuss the influence of British culture on DC superhero comics. What about your Scottishness, or specifically Glaswegian-ness? Does that come across in, or shape, your writing of these American myths?*

GM: It's in there somewhere, I'm sure. Glasgow, with its ghastly diet, its rampant alcohol and drug abuse, its violence and humour, its poor health and early-death statistics, is probably some kind of template for the monstrous, glamorous Gotham of my imagination.

WB: *You've often returned to also-rans, B-listers, forgotten heroes – from* Doom Patrol *to the people in Limbo from* Animal Man *and* Final Crisis. *If Superman represents the best we can be, our sun god, what do these forgotten, sometimes pathetic figures like Speed Freak, the Gay Ghost and Sunshine Superman represent?*

GM: They represent all those selves we created when we were young as attempts to frame or even engender something resembling a personality. To me, they have the poignancy of old clothes, photographs and haircuts. They possibly represent ideas which seemed gaudy and demonstrative at the time but which now look infantile or laughable. They represent the freaks and outsiders, the not good enough but still hopeful – a group I tended to count myself among when I was young and have a great deal of sympathy for.

WB: *What and where do you think Batman will be in seventy-five years?*

GM: The distinctions between what is real and what is not real will, by that time, have become so thoroughly shredded that I expect Batman to have evolved into some sort of 5-D crime-fighting Omni-President of the Earth-Media Gestalt.

5

HISTORY LEFT UNSAID
IMPLIED CONTINUITY IN BATMAN'S CONTEMPORARY COMIC BOOK NARRATIVES

Anthony M. Smith

In 2011, DC comics significantly revamped its large line of comic books, resetting the issue numbering of long-enduring superhero titles and streamlining the narrative continuity – the interconnected backstory – that the characters had accumulated and shared over decades.[1] The new line – dubbed 'The New 52' – was intended in part to attract new readers to the DC Universe.[2] As the company's Co-Publisher (and fan-favourite artist) Jim Lee explained, the line's high issue numbers (*Detective Comics* had reached #881 prior to the reset) and complicated character biographies 'made the world of comic books a little more daunting to jump into'. The changes, the company hoped, would enable 'new readers' to 'jump in and understand what's going on from the very first issue'.[3] The Batman backstory, however, was exempted from the simplification process that DC's wider narrative universe underwent.[4] As Batman writer Scott Snyder stressed shortly after the comic book line reboot, in contrast to the likes of Superman, many of the significant events that the Caped Crusader had experienced within the prior universe would remain part of DC's newly created continuity. But Snyder, who took charge of the *Batman* title as part of The New 52 launch, nevertheless ensured that his storytelling approach complemented DC's aim of appealing to new audiences. With the relaunched title, he elected to avoid obvious references to recent and significant storyworld incidents – such as Bruce Wayne's death/resurrection – so that 'new fans' would not 'trip over' such potentially confusing material.[5]

While being careful not to confuse an intended new readership, however, Snyder – together with illustrator Greg Capullo – nevertheless adopted storytelling techniques that emphasised to existing readers the narrative links between his *Batman* story arcs and Batman-related comic book narrative published prior to the reboot. A large panel occupying the second and third pages of *Batman* #1 (November 2011), for example, depicts a host of menacing villains lined up to confront the book's titular hero within Arkham Asylum. This host includes various staple characters – such as Two-Face, Scarecrow and Killer Croc – that will likely register with new readers familiar with Batman's incarnations in film, television and video games. Yet standing shoulder to shoulder with these enduring villains is the relatively obscure figure of Professor Pyg, a deranged, snout-faced adversary specific to DC's comic book continuity prior to The New 52 reboot, having been introduced by the writer Grant Morrison two years previously.[6] Another less renowned villain, also specific to pre-New 52 continuity, appears within a subsequent sequence in which Batman trades blows with foes at the asylum. A small panel within this sequence depicts the serial killer James Gordon Jr, whom Snyder had introduced as part of his *Detective Comics* run in the previous year; the murderer lies on his cell bunk reading, apparently unperturbed by the brawl outside his door.[7] Pyg and Gordon have seemingly little narrative import to the sequence: neither is attributed dialogue; neither is identified via caption. Their minor appearances in the opening scene are unlikely therefore to 'trip up' new readers, since many faces familiar to first-time readers have more prominence. Yet the pair's presence in the sequence sends a message to loyal readers, who typically derive pleasure from the persistence and expansion of narrative continuity, subtly reassuring them that these particular characters, and by implication the narrative events in which they participated, will remain part of Batman's fictional chronology despite DC's reboot.

The above is just one example from a range of narrative techniques upon which the contemporary comic book industry relies to service a loyal, dedicated readership while simultaneously addressing a potential wider audience. Using contemporary Batman narrative as a case study, this chapter analyses this comic book storytelling strategy, linking its emergence to significant industrial shifts that have occurred since the mid-1990s. The increased pressure on publishers to attract a wider audience while also retaining the core readership has required rethinking continuity: writers still reference the Caped Crusader's complex and extended backstory but use techniques far subtler than those deployed prior to the emphasis on new readers. By implying Batman continuity as opposed to explicitly flagging it up, writers appease a core following of dedicated readers while not confusing and/or irritating a broader audience unfamiliar with the minutiae of Batman's biography. In identifying and accounting for this change in storytelling techniques, this chapter augments scholarship concerned with the connections between narrative practices and industrial contexts in the US comic book industry. Scholars have explained how the comic book marketplace in the 1980s and 90s brought about an intensification of continuity and serial narrative practices in superhero storytelling; this chapter expands upon this work by illustrating how these practices altered as marketplace conditions once more transformed.[8] The chapter first outlines the industrial changes that have motivated the shift towards techniques of what I refer to as *implied continuity* – that is, writers' referencing of an overarching storyworld in ways that satisfy dedicated readers without baffling new and/or casual readers ignorant of prior events.[9] The chapter then moves on to explore this storytelling mode in more detail through textual analysis of specific Batman narratives.

Continuity in context

Prior to the 1960s, superhero comic book series did little to suggest that the storyline of an individual issue contributed to a wider unified fictional history – that is, a narrative continuity. As Umberto Eco (writing in 1962) suggested of the *Superman* series, each of its issues' storylines represents 'a virtual beginning, ignoring where the preceding event left off. ... The very structure of time falls apart [as a consequence of this narrative mode] ... that is, the notion of time that ties one episode to another.'[10] Certain historical factors contributed to the absence of narrative continuity within super-hero comic books during this industrial phase. Most significantly, because children/adolescents represented the primary target audience in this period, the market experienced a general customer turnover every three years.[11] This constant change of readership provided little incentive for editors to ensure narrative connections to prior storylines with which its fast-changing audience would likely be unfamiliar. In addition, due to the perception of comic books as disposable entertainment, there was an absence of back issues within reading cultures, meaning there was also little available prior narrative within circulation to which readers might refer.[12] Superman did not recall events that had (at least in terms of publication) occurred years earlier for the simple reason that his readers could not recall events of which they were ignorant.

In the 1960s, however, an important transition in audience activity induced an editorial turn towards narrative continuity techniques. Whereas comic books had previously been regarded as ephemeral artefacts to be discarded, traded or just handed around from friend to friend, the decade saw the origin of a niche of dedicated readers seeking to collect and preserve back issues.[13] This trend was due in part to the emergence of an audience of older comic book consumers wanting to celebrate their favourite books from earlier decades.[14] To appeal to the segment of the readership that had begun to accumulate and revisit its own collection of comic book experiences, publishers – particularly Marvel, but to a lesser extent DC also – began to forge an explicit and consistent memory within fictional universes during this period. Narratives began to regularly and explicitly reference events in other series and from earlier storylines, suggesting that a publisher's collection of superhero titles operated as a single, coherent storyworld.[15]

A significant industrial shift in the following decade linked to the preferences and activities of this highly dedicated readership would prove key to an intensification of narrative continuity practices. The continued growth of comic book collecting, combined with a simultaneous decline in news-stand sales (via which comic books had traditionally been marketed), influenced publishers in the late 1970s to shift towards the direct-market method of distribution. Speciality comic book stores, opened by dedicated comic book readers to meet the growing demand for back issues, began to replace traditional retail outlets as the primary venue for new comic books.[16] By the late 1980s, most comic books were being sold through speciality comic book stores, leading publishers to prioritise narrative modes appropriate for the highly concentrated group of dedicated readers that have typically comprised the consumer base of this retail channel.[17]

Such modes include the implementation of long-running serialised storylines that journey through many issues and between multiple different series and that require readers to purchase many comics to consume the entire narrative. One example of this would be the Batman 'Knightfall' saga (1993–4), which spans more than sixty issues published across a number of different Batman-related series. But stories from this period also typically emphasise narrative continuity within long-running series and between different series (outside of the auspices of distinct serialised story arcs), which speaks to the importance that the direct-market readership has typically placed on the establishing of storylines within a wider fictional framework. As Matthew J. Pustz observes, narrative continuity is central to this audience's engagement with superhero comic books: 'Information based on continuity becomes the source of discussion, jokes and arguments, making it the raw material for the interactive glue that holds comic-book culture together.'[18]

Reflecting a context in which publishers regarded these dedicated consumers as their primary readership, the evoking of continuity within comic book narratives – a chief source of pleasure for these readers – is not only frequent but also highly explicit. This is the case, for example, in the single-issue storyline 'Transition', from New Titans #55 (June 1989), which functions as an amplification to Batman #428 (December 1988), in which DC's second Robin, Jason Todd, is killed. As part of the New Titans storyline, Dick Grayson, the first Robin, learns of Jason's death. The angst-ridden Dick visits Bruce Wayne (Batman), and the pair row, each betraying their guilt about Jason's demise and making myriad unambiguous references to significant incidents within their shared history.[19] A further example occurs within Batman #494 (June 1993) after Batman has rescued Commissioner Gordon from the killer Cornelius Stirk. As Batman explains to Gordon's wife that her 'husband was the target', an angry Sarah Essen-Gordon retorts, 'Just as he was in the Headhunter incident – when I told you to leave us alone', thus drawing a parallel between the issue and a prior storyline in which the assassin Headhunter targeted the Commissioner.[20] Each of these examples foregrounds narrative continuity via character dialogue that clearly cites specific incidents from previously published storylines; this storytelling technique unequivocally addresses the requirements of a readership that favours an emphasis on narrative continuity.

However, another significant industrial transition in the 1990s – in the form of a rapid decline of the direct-market audience – ultimately curtailed publishers' prioritisation of their highly dedicated readership; as a consequence, writers and illustrators have recalibrated their approaches to the evocation of narrative continuity. Strategies foregrounding continuity had enabled publishers to nurture and engage an isolated niche of highly committed consumers who consistently purchased multiple comic books every week. But the danger of an overriding dependence on this 'precariously narrow' consumer base was exposed, notes Bradford W. Wright, in the mid-1990s.[21] The direct-market system had enabled year-on-year increases in sales through the 1980s and early 90s, leading industry sales to reach $1 billion in 1993, but – due to the collapse of an artificially inflated collector/speculator market – revenues had declined to $450 million by 1996.[22]

By the beginning of the twenty-first century, the industry – chiefly in the form of its two leading publishers, Marvel and DC – had realised that to survive they must appeal to an audience beyond the contracted direct market. Publishers therefore sought to better address new readers generally, but they also more specifically looked to court a more casual consumer type; that is, the type of consumer that might be open to reading comic books, but who doesn't relish the prospect of going to specialist stores once a week to purchase a wide range of titles. In the hopes of luring these potential readers, publishers began to develop alternative formats and distribution channels.

In the first instance, publishers sought to maximise the commercial possibilities of the collected edition (a graphic-novel format that compiles previously published comic book issues).[23] DC, in particular, had already helped to establish a nascent graphic-novel market in the 1980s and 90s through its reformatting of select adult-oriented material, including *Watchmen* (1987), *Batman: The Dark Knight Returns* (1986) and various titles published under the company's edgy Vertigo imprint. By marketing such content through mass-market bookstores, publishers had by the end of the century established a new retail conduit capable of reaching consumers outside of direct-market culture.[24] However, by 2001, the graphic-novel market's revenues ($43 million via comic book stores, $32 million via mass market) were still dwarfed by direct-market periodical sales.[25] But, since publishers regarded the collected edition format as the ideal product to address new and/or casual consumers, they began to greatly increase the production and distribution of these titles via both direct-market and mass-market channels (such as Amazon and Barnes & Noble).[26] By 2013, annual North American sales of graphic novels had massively expanded ($170 million via comic book stores, $245 million via mass market), easily exceeding those of print periodical comic books ($345 million).[27]

Having developed one market sector better suited to a wider audience of new and/or casual consumers, publishers have more recently moved to rapidly grow another – the digital comics market. Publishers distribute monthly comic book issues (primarily intended for print) in digital form via online platforms such as Comixology and Marvel Unlimited. The format and its distribution mode therefore enables a new and/or casual readership to conveniently consume such content via tablets, computers and smartphones, and avoid the more intensive consumption practices of direct-market culture. Publishers have focused resources on digitally reproducing back issues, releasing digital versions of their collected editions and ensuring that the digital version of any new issue is published simultaneously with its print incarnation. The digital market has grown rapidly, with North American revenues escalating from a mere estimated $1 million in 2009 to $70 million in 2013.[28] As the publishers intended, the format has proved especially attractive to new and casual readers.[29]

Parallel to the developing of formats and distribution channels better suited to new and/or casual readers, publishers have also reconfigured their narratives for this intended audience. While the foregrounding of complicated storyworld continuity in 1990s superhero comics helped cultivate dedicated, high-spending consumers, as Pustz observes, the impenetrability of these narratives proved a barrier of entry to a wider group of readers.[30] The narrative practice of implied continuity has therefore evolved in order to simultaneously appeal to not only dedicated readers, but new and/or casual consumers also. The separate issues of a distinct story arc continue to foreground serial connections that bind the instalments together, but explicit referencing of a wider narrative continuity is often reduced. New readers can begin following a new story arc without requiring extensive knowledge of storyworld material published previously or simultaneously (in separate but related series). This approach to narrative coherence also permits casual readers to easily consume a story arc as a single discrete text following its reformatting as a collected edition. At the same time, however, implied continuity unobtrusively connects new story arcs to the larger structure of the overarching storyworld. In this manner, implied continuity addresses new and/or casual readers' desire for coherent narratives not dependent upon any prior knowledge while also catering for dedicated readers' preferences for a complex narrative continuity that references the wider storyworld. Both new/casual readers and dedicated readers must still purchase all the instalments of a particular story arc, either individually or together as part of a collected edition, but while the former can delight in the serial pleasures of that arc's narrative enigma and resolution, the latter can also relish the arc's implied connections to the broader fictional universe with which they are familiar.

Snyder and Capullo's 'Death of the Family' story arc (*Batman* #13–17, October 2012–February 2013), which concerns the Joker's campaign against Batman's allies, is one example of this strategy of dual appeal. Together, its five issues operate explicitly as a serial storyline – with a given issue's causal chain of events directly leading to the next (via such devices as cliffhangers). In line with DC's audience-targeting strategies, Snyder has ensured that the story arc, which has since been published as a single collected edition in both print and digital formats, does not obviously rely on wider continuity and functions as a discrete narrative. As he stressed while promoting the story arc's first issue, 'I don't want you to feel that you have to read anything else to understand what's happening within' his *Batman* run. 'I would never write a story that's dependent on another story', he added.[31] The story arc is therefore very well suited to the requirements of a new and/or casual readership. But, as this chapter's following case study sections go on to demonstrate, while this story arc forgoes the storytelling practice characteristic of the late 1980s/90s of overtly referencing events published previously, it nevertheless acknowledges a wider narrative framework via techniques of implied continuity. Such techniques neither threaten the apparent narrative independence of the story arc nor alert new and/or casual consumers to their ignorance of prior events, yet they address dedicated readers familiar with those events, rewarding them for their investment of time and money.

The following two sections explore in detail the range of implied continuity techniques that practitioners have adopted to suit the requirements of the contemporary comic book industry. Using recent Batman comic book story arcs as case study material, these sections focus in particular on the works of the two writers who have dominated creative control over Batman-related comic book titles in recent years: namely, Grant Morrison and Scott Snyder.[32] The first section focuses on the distinct ways in which these writers utilise the storyworld ingredients of props, settings and character dialogue to discreetly establish connections between their story arcs and earlier storylines along what Robert C. Allen refers to as a 'syntagmatic' axis of the narrative.[33] This means that, in such cases, the connective tissue between these writers' contemporary Batman narratives and storylines published years previously forms a single chronological sequence of fictional events – that is, the seriality of the overarching storyworld rather than that of a discrete narrative arc within the story-world. The second section, by contrast, demonstrates how these writers also subtly imply narrative continuity across what Allen refers to as the 'paradigmatic' narrative axis, wherein associations between distinct storylines are not tied to a chronology of depicted events, but are instead dependent on an inferred thematic parallelism.[34]

Implied syntagmatic connectivity in Batman continuity

Storytellers across media are able to imply – as opposed to explicitly punch up – syntagmatic continuity through the use of evocative storyworld settings. As Karen Lury observes of soap opera, for example, recurrent storyworld locations 'can, for the long-term viewer, become imbued with a series of visually inspired memories of dif-ferent characters and plot lines', emphasising the continuity that these storyworld components share.[35] Morrison – together with illustrator Frank Quitely – relies on the resonating power of storyworld settings in the maiden story arc of his *Batman and Robin* run, weakly linking it to the characters' history by setting it in a location signifi-cant to Batman mythology. In 'Batman Reborn' (#1–3, August–September 2009), the Caped Crusader battles the aforementioned Professor Pyg, who is holed up at a dilap-idated amusement park. This arc represents Pyg's first appearance in DC narrative and also Dick Grayson's first outing under the Bat cowl (after having replaced a temporarily deceased Bruce Wayne). But contrasting with the newness of both this Batman and his opponent, the amusement park setting is resurrected from the 1988 original graphic novel *Batman: The Killing Joke*. In this earlier narrative, by Alan Moore (writer) and Brian Bolland (illustrator), the Joker acquires an amusement park, subsequently utilising its ghost train as part of his elaborate torture of Commissioner Gordon. The events of 'Batman Reborn' bear little obvious relation to those of *The Killing Joke* but Morrison and Quitely's choice of setting suggests that the two storylines are linked by a vast chronology of events that separate them. Quitely's depictions of the amusement park environment, which are sometimes almost identical to those of *The Killing Joke* (his near-recreation of Bolland's ghost train signage being a case in point), strongly empha-sise this link for those readers familiar with both narratives.

The final issue of 'Batman Reborn' (#3) further evokes the implied connection with *The Killing Joke*. Following Batman and Robin's defeat of Pyg and his menacing circus troupe, Commissioner Gordon oversees the police round-up of Pyg's henchmen at the amusement park. In a dialogue exchange with Batman, Gordon mutters in an aside, 'I hate this place', referring to his earlier ordeal. This oblique nod to continuity sits in stark contrast to the explicit referencing to prior narrative typically found within char-acter dialogue in the late 1980s/90s (such as Sarah Essen-Gordon's citation of the Headhunter incident). For the new and/or casual reader unfamiliar with Gordon's biography, the Commissioner's unremarked upon comment might be slightly baffling, but it is unlikely to raise awareness of their own ignorance of prior storyworld material; for the dedicated consumer, Gordon's comment accentuates the continuity shared between the more recent story arc and *The Killing Joke*. *Batman and Robin*'s subtle allusion to Moore and Bolland's earlier narrative through the use of environmental backdrop and brief, elliptical dialogue reflects Morrison's philosophies regarding continuity, which he suggests should merely operate as 'background window dressing' within a story that will not turn off newcomers.[36]

Similar to Morrison's 'Batman Reborn', Snyder's 'Death of the Family' story arc also subtly signals its connection to a famous Batman comic book narrative published in the 1980s; in this case, the earlier story is 'A Death in the Family' (*Batman* #426–9, December 1988–January 1989), which the title of Snyder's story arc clearly pays homage to. Rather than use an evocative location to suggest this continuity, however, 'Death of the Family' instead relies on a distinctive prop. Snyder's story arc concerns the Joker's plot to kill the Dark Knight's 'family' of close associates – Alfred, Robin, Nightwing, Batgirl, Red Hood, Red Robin and Commissioner Gordon. In issue #16 (January 2013), Batman confronts the Joker at Arkham Asylum, which the Clown Prince of Crime has taken over. Within the asylum's walls, the hero is met by a bizarre piece of Joker handiwork suspended from a ceiling: a macabre makeshift canvas comprised of many still-breathing humans. The canvas has been painted with a collection of various scenes involving Batman and the Joker (Joker: 'The live flesh makes the colours pop, no?'). The scenes include Batman carrying a limp Robin, the Joker carrying a small child and the Joker kicking a bound Batman.

The Joker implies that this exhibit – 'a royal tapestry', as he refers to it – chronicles prior conflicts between the two. As a sequence of panels provides close-ups of the illustrations on the canvas, the Joker remarks, 'It's like yesterday, isn't it? Our adventures! The times we've had! The laughter!' The new and/or casual reader, unfamiliar with Batman comic book narratives published decades previously, is able to interpret the canvas's juxtaposed scenes in the way the Joker's dialogue seems to intend: that is, as a totality of shared moments – 'the times we've had'. Yet, while the fact is unlikely to concern new and/or casual readers, the scenes depicted on the canvas can also each be interpreted as symbolising a specific moment within Batman continuity. They therefore prompt dedicated readers to consider the relationship between each depicted scene and the 'Death of the Family' story arc. For dedicated readers, the scene of Batman carrying Robin will likely carry particular resonance, as it evokes the earlier 'A Death in the Family' story arc; the cover art for the graphic-novel version of 'A Death in the Family' features a similar image of Batman holding a limp Robin in his arms. In this earlier story arc, the Joker captures and murders the second Robin, Jason Todd. The elaborate prop's evocation of 'A Death in the Family' thus subtly reminds dedicated readers of a previous event that relates strongly to the Joker's efforts to kill Batman's associates in Snyder's story arc.

Just as Morrison had with 'Batman Reborn', Snyder also uses a highly furtive reference via character dialogue to reaffirm the connections between 'A Death in the Family' and his own story arc. In *Batman* #17 (April 2013), the Joker holds court with his captives, Nightwing, Batgirl, Red Robin and Red Hood (the current guise of Jason Todd), espousing his thesis as to why he has been able to capture Batman's allies. 'You want to know …

why I get to creep in … [*speaking directly to Red Robin*] to get you, [*to Robin*] and you, [*to Red Hood*] and you (again), [*to Nightwing*] and you, [*to Batgirl*] and you?' By having Joker briefly and vaguely signal (via the 'again') that he has been able to capture Todd previously, Snyder further hints at the key incident of 'A Death in the Family'.

In the examples discussed so far, the connections that writers establish between new story arcs and storyworld material produced decades previously are clearly syntagmatic, forming chronological sequences of related fictional events in a chain of cause and effect. Commissioner Gordon's display of antipathy towards Gotham's condemned fairground is subsequent to and a consequence of his prior suffering there. The Joker's knowing referencing of 'A Death in the Family' is contingent upon his own integral involvement in this earlier story arc. But, as the following section explores, contemporary writers also subtly convey narrative continuity across a paradigmatic narrative axis by implying thematic associations between distinct storylines.

Implied paradigmatic connectivity in Batman continuity

In Chapter 11 in this volume, Jim Collins observes that the 'distinguishing feature of recent popular narrative' is 'its increasing hyperconsciousness about … the history of popular culture', leading to 'popular texts construct[ing] quite elaborate intertextual arenas'. Analysing Warner Bros.' 1989 *Batman* film, Collins notes that while its plot – concerning the hero's conflict with the Joker – connects along the narrative's syntagmatic axis, its frequent use of 'motifs' from 'comic books, Hollywood films, nineteenth century novels [and] medieval architecture' simultaneously establishes links with many antecedent texts along a paradigmatic axis. Collins attributes the prevalence of this mode of 'intertextual narration' within popular texts to an increased general awareness and interest in the history of pop culture among producers and audiences. Yet, specifically within contemporary comic book production, this narrative mode has also been absorbed as part of writers' and illustrators' wider strategy to complement publishers' audience-targeting aims. Writers and illustrators often deploy intertextual allusions that imply to dedicated readers the presence of continuity – in this case, thematic continuity – within a vast storyworld; less dedicated readers are unlikely to pick up on these allusions.

This practice is evidenced, for example, by the connections established between Morrison's *Batman and Robin* run and DC's 'Blackest Night' crossover event (2009–10). In the latter narrative, Green Lantern and his allies defend the universe from a possessed legion of heroes and villains resurrected from their graves. In the sixth issue of the eight-part *Blackest Night* miniseries, published February 2010, (a deceased) Bruce Wayne rises to join the undead's fold in Coast City, California. The first issue of Morrison's slyly titled 'Blackest Knight' arc on *Batman and Robin* (#7–9) landed in stores the following month. Within that issue, Batman (Dick Grayson) attempts to bring a deceased Bruce Wayne clone back to life courtesy of a 'Lazarus pit' located in a Northumbrian mine. In the subsequent issue, the reanimated Wayne-clone proves to be a demented zombie, resulting in Batman having to quell the threat. According to Morrison, his arc was designed to complement 'Blackest Night'. But, 'rather than tie directly into the main event', he recalls, 'we chose to reflect it in a more thematic way with this story of a walking dead man'.[37]

While the events of the 'Blackest Knight' story arc don't directly link to those of the 'Blackest Night' plot via the syntagmatic axis, their shared similarities in story-world theme encourage dedicated DC readers to detect an association between the two different storylines along the paradigmatic axis. The coincidence in publication times of the respective periodicals further encouraged this paradigmatic linking. So too did Frank Quitely's cover art for the first issue of the *Batman and Robin* arc, which features a detailed portrait of the eerie, undead Batman. But, crucially, due to the nature of Morrison's allusions to wider continuity, the new and/or casual *Batman and Robin* reader can enjoy the 'Blackest Knight' storyline as a self-contained dramatic conflict without having to be aware of the Green Lantern's battles with raised corpses in *Blackest Night*. Morrison's technique contradicts the traditional direct-market practice, which developed out of an aim to attract highly committed readers, of explicitly connecting a publisher's range of books via the syntagmatic axis of a major crossover event narrative. Yet this new technique meets the requirements of dedicated consumers, while simultaneously serving the needs of a wider audience, in keeping with DC's twenty-first-century consumer-targeting strategies.

For 'The Court of Owls' (#1–12, November 2011–October 2012), the first *Batman* story arc of The New 52 era, Snyder also opted to engage dedicated readers through the establishing of thematic connections with antecedent DC narratives. The story arc concerns Batman's battle with the Court of Owls, a secret criminal society that includes a cadre of deadly assassins – dubbed 'Talons' – within its membership. While the Court – a Snyder creation – is revealed to have manipulated Gotham for centuries, this story arc marks its debut within DC fiction. Yet 'The Court of Owls' was nonetheless strongly inspired by previous storylines concerning owl-themed characterisations scattered throughout Batman's prior history. 'Everything is a re-imagining of the elements that went into Owl villains [and other characters] in Batman', notes Snyder; 'the whole story, honestly, came flowing out of that'.[38]

Early in 'The Court of Owls', for example, Batman discovers (misleading) evidence suggesting that Dick Grayson (since returned to his Nightwing role) was a former Talon. This plot point evokes the theme of a *Batman* issue storyline published decades previously (#107, April 1957) in which a young Dick temporarily adopts the persona of 'Owlman'. As Snyder acknowledges, this type of intertextual referencing is deliberately intended to engage and reward the dedicated reader:

> Within the story itself, the history of Gotham is brought against the heroes of the present … And then for readers of *Batman* and lovers of Batman and the Bat-mythology, there are story elements that feel that way on a meta-level, you know? It's like, 'Hey, I remember that issue where Robin was Owlman. Look at this, now Dick was supposed to have been a Talon.'[39]

But by relying on subtle evocations of thematic continuity – which are unlikely to even register with a new/casual readership – as a means to address loyal and knowledge-able consumers, Snyder is still able to meet his objective of crafting coherent, self-contained story arcs. He ensures, therefore, that his narratives are also appropriate for those readers less committed to DC's highly complex fictional universe.

Conclusion

Expanding upon previous scholarship linking US comic book production contexts in the 1980s and 90s to prevalent narrative modes of the period, this chapter demonstrates how subsequent industrial transitions have influenced shifts in storytelling strategy. It shows how publishers, faced with the direct market's decreased revenues, have in recent years adjusted formatting and distribution practices to complement their recalibrated audience-targeting aims. Using Batman narratives as a case study, it reveals how writers and illustrators have complemented these aims via the development of a range of implied continuity techniques intended to address the contrasting requirements of two distinct audience groups. The chapter thus speaks to this book's broad concern with Batman and his media, highlighting the contingency of Batman narrative on specific – and highly changeable – conditions of production within a given medium.

While this focus on techniques of evoking continuity within superhero narratives has been (due to the necessarily limited scope of a single chapter) a narrow one, the recent reconfiguration of the US comic book industry in terms of its audience-targeting strategies has had a wider influence on its storytelling. As I demonstrate elsewhere, for example, publishers' aims this century to appeal to a potential wider audience of consumers mostly familiar with superheroes via their appearances in Hollywood blockbusters have had a significant impact on comic book narrative; for instance, certain comic book story arcs have been consciously conceived to resonate with particular superhero movie storylines, while comic book visual style during this period often emulates modern action film-making.[40] As the US comic book industry continues to evolve – as it, for example, turns increasingly to the nascent digital comics form as a means to broaden its readership – it will be useful to further trace connections between publishers' priorities in the marketplace and the narratives these companies disseminate.

Notes

1. The company had carried out a less comprehensive simplification of continuity in 1986.
2. The New 52 moniker reflects the number of #1 books DC simultaneously launched as part of the initiative.
3. Melissa Block, 'Several DC Comics Go Back to Issue No. 1', NPR, 31 August 2011. Available at: <http://www.npr.org/2011/08/31/140093549/several-dc-comics-go-back-to-issue-no-1>.
4. In the case of Superman, for example, the only significant backstory material that remained following The New 52 continuity reboot was a version of his standard origin story.

5. Admin1, 'CBR TV @ NYCC: Scott Snyder on "Batman," "Severed" and Bat-Continuity',
    Comic Book Resources, 16 October 2011. Available at:
    <http://video.comicbookresources.com/cbrtv/2011/cbr-tv-nycc-scott-snyder-on
    -batman-severed-and-bat-continuity/>.
6. See *Batman and Robin* #1 (2009).
7. See *Detective Comics* #871–81 (2010–11).
8. Bradford W. Wright, *Comic Book Nation* (Baltimore, MD: Johns Hopkins University Press,
    2001); Matthew J. Pustz, *Comic Book Culture: Fanboys and True Believers* (Jackson:
    University Press of Mississippi, 1999).
9. The term is adapted from Matt Hills's 'implied story arc', which he uses to describe
    the subtle connections made between individual episodes of *Doctor Who* during Russell
    T. Davies's tenure as executive producer on the television series. Matt Hills, 'Absent
    Epic, Implied Story Arcs, and Variation on a Narrative Theme: *Doctor Who* (2005–8) as
    Cult/Mainstream Television', in Pat Harrigan and Noah Wardrip-Fruin (eds), *Third
    Person: Authoring and Exploring Vast Narratives* (Cambridge, MA: MIT Press, 2009),
    pp. 333–42.
10. Umberto Eco, *The Role of the Reader: Explorations in the Semiotic in Texts* (London:
    Hutchinson, 1981), pp. 113–14, 117. Despite this tendency, there are a few exceptional
    instances of continuity being established within early superhero comic books. For
    Batman-related examples, see Pat, 'Some Golden Age Continuity Examples', *Nothing
    but Batman*, 22 December 2009. Available at: <http://nothingbutbatman.blogspot.co.uk
    /2009/12/some-golden-age-continuity-examples.html>.
11. See 'Notes from the Batcave: An Interview with Dennis O'Neil', in this volume, p. 26.
12. On the transitory status of comic books pre-1960, see Pustz, *Comic Book Culture*, p. 15.
13. By the mid-1960s, some bookstores began to sate this demand by specialising in the
    sale of back-issues. Ibid.
14. Paul Lopes, *Demanding Respect: The Evolution of the American Comic Book* (Philadelphia,
    PA: Temple University Press, 2009), p. 93.
15. For example, while DC had launched new versions of The Flash and Green Lantern in
    the late 1950s, in the 60s it developed continuity between these new identities and
    prior versions of the same heroes by suggesting that the latter continued to exist
    within a parallel reality.
16. Wright, *Comic Book Nation*, pp. 260–2; Pustz, *Comic Book Culture*, p. 15; Chuck Rozanski,
    'Evolution of the Direct Market: Part One', *Mile High Comics*, November 2003. Available
    at: <http://www.milehighcomics.com/tales/cbg95.html>.
17. Wright, *Comic Book Nation*, pp. 260–2.
18. Pustz, *Comic Book Culture*, p. 134.
19. The pair cite prior events within continuity, including instances of Dick's
    impetuousness and ill discipline (Bruce: 'When *you* didn't listen to me, *your* injuries
    weren't fatal'), Bruce's removal of Dick from the Robin role (Bruce: 'I would have had
    to *fire him* [Jason] as I did you') and Dick's chagrin at Bruce having adopted Jason
    (Bruce: 'You told me you resented it that I had adopted *him* and not you').
20. See Batman #487 (December 1992).

21. Wright, *Comic Book Nation*, p. 280.

22. Ibid., p. 283.

23. The term 'graphic novel' is popularly used to denote a comics publication that is distinguished from standard periodical comic books by its greater bulk and its card or hardback cover.

24. For more on the emergence of the graphic-novel market, see Charles Hatfield, *Alternative Comics: An Emerging Literature* (Jackson: University Press of Mississippi, 2005), and William Uricchio and Roberta Pearson, '"I'm Not Fooled by That Cheap Disguise"', Chapter 13 in this volume.

25. Anon., 'Graphic Novels by the Numbers', *Publishers Weekly*, 3 March 2007. Available at: <http://www.publishersweekly.com/pw/print/20070305/4192-graphic-novels-by-the -numbers.html>. The dollar sales for the top 300 comic books from each month distributed to speciality stores in 2001 totalled $186.98 million. John Jackson Miller, 'Comic Book Sales by Year', *Comichron*. Available at: <http://www.comichron.com/year lycomicssales.html>.

26. Regarding DC and Marvel's perception of the collected edition as the best format with which to address casual consumers, see Milton Griepp, '20 Questions: Paul Levitz, Part II: DC's Executive VP Talks about the Comic Business', *ICv2*, 3 October 2001. Available at: <http://www.icv2.com/articles/indepth/759.html>. Owen Vaughan, 'An Interview with Spider-Man's Boss, Marvel Chief Joe Quesada', *The Times*, 21 March 2009. Available at: <http://www.thetimes.co.uk/tto/arts/books/article2454472.ece>. As an example of increased collected edition production, Marvel's backlist of in-print titles grew from approximately 250 in 2001 to upwards of 1,100 in 2011. 'Marvel Ratchets up Book Production', *ICv2*, 12 March 2001. Available at: <http://www.icv2.com/articles /news/220.html>; John Rhett Thomas, *Marvel Backlist Chronology* (New York: Marvel, 2011).

27. John Jackson Miller, 'Comics and Graphic Novel Market Reaches $870 Million in 2013', *Comichron*, 15 July 2014. Available at: <http://blog.comichron.com/2014/07/comics-and -graphic-novel-market-reaches.html>.

28. Seth Rosenblatt, 'Digital Comics Successful Sidekick to Print, Say Publishers', *CNET*, 20 July 2013. Available at: <http://www.cnet.com/uk/news/digital-comics-successful-side kick-to-print-say-publishers/>; Miller, 'Comics and Graphic Novel Market'.

29. Heidi MacDonald, 'DC's Rood Breaks down Reader Survey', *Publishers Weekly*, 14 February 2012. Available at: <http://www.publishersweekly.com/pw/by -topic/booknews/comics/article/50633-dc-s-rood-breaks-down-reader-survey.html>.

30. Pustz, *Comic Book Culture*, p. 134. This was a perspective taken by key publisher personnel in the late 1990s/2000s, such as former DC Publisher and President Paul Levitz. See Griepp, '20 Questions'.

31. Tony 'G Man' Guerrero, 'Interview: Scott Snyder Talks "Return of the Joker: Death of the Family"', *Comic Vine*, 9 July 2012. Available at: <http://www.comicvine.com/articles/interview-scott-snyder-talks-return-of-the-joker -d/1100-144917/>.

32. Morrison's (intermittent) run on *Batman* stretches from 2006 to 2011; he also launched the ongoing series *Batman and Robin* (in 2009) and *Batman Incorporated* (in 2011). Snyder

began writing *Detective Comics* in 2010 before taking charge of *Batman* in 2011 (where, at the time of writing, he remains).

33. Robert C. Allen, *Speaking of Soap Operas* (Chapel Hill: University of North Carolina Press, 1985), p. 69.

34. Ibid., pp. 69–71.

35. Karen Lury, *Interpreting Television* (London: Hodder Arnold, 2005), p. 14.

36. Grant Morrison, 'Morrison Manifesto', in *New X-Men*, Ultimate Collection Vol. 3 (New York: Marvel, 2008), n. p.

37. Grant Morrison, Cameron Stewart and Andy Clarke, *Batman & Robin: Batman vs. Robin* (New York: DC Comics, 2010), p. 154.

38. Vaneta Rogers, 'Scott Snyder on BATMAN #10 & You-Know-Who [SPOILERS]', *Newsarama*, 14 June 2012. Available at: <http://www.newsarama.com/9671-spoiler -sport-scott-snyder-on-batman-10-you-know-who.html>.

39. Ibid.

40. Anthony N. Smith, 'Media Contexts of Narrative Design: *Dimensions of Specificity* within Storytelling Industries', PhD dissertation (University of Nottingham, 2013). Derek Johnson similarly considers the influence of superhero blockbusters on comic book storytelling with regards to articulations of familiar characters; see Derek Johnson, 'Will the Real Wolverine Please Stand Up? Marvel's Mutation from Monthlies to Movies', in Ian Gordon, Mark Jancovich and Matthew McAllister (eds), *Film and Comic Books* (Jackson: University Press of Mississippi, 2007), pp. 64–85.

CIRCULATING THE BATMAN

6

'HOLY COMMODITY FETISH, BATMAN!'
THE POLITICAL ECONOMY OF A COMMERCIAL INTERTEXT
Eileen R. Meehan

Batman took the United States by storm in the spring and summer of 1989. T-shirts, posters, key chains, jewellery, buttons, books, watches, magazines, trading cards, audiotaped books, video games, records, cups and numerous other items flooded malls across the United States with images of Batman, his new logo and his old enemy the Joker.[1] Presaged by a much pirated trailer, *Batman* the film drew unprecedented crowds to theatre chains, of which the two largest (United Artist Theater Circuits and American Multi-Cinema) distributed four to five million brochures for mail-order Bat-materials.[2] *Batman*'s premiere on the big screen was matched by appearances on the small screen. Film clips were packaged as advertisements and free promotional materials for the interview and movie review circuits on both broadcast and cable television; Prince's 'Batdance' video played in heavy rotation on MTV. Over the radio,

Batman (1989)

'Batdance' and other cuts from Prince's *Batman* album got strong play on rock stations and 'crossed over' for similarly strong play on black radio stations. Subsequently, retail outlets filled with Bat-costumes and Joker make-up kits for Halloween; Ertl Batmobiles and ToyBiz Batcaves and Batwings were being deployed for Christmas shoppers. In the speciality stores serving comics fandom, the *Advance Comics Special Batlist* offered 214 items ranging from $576 to $2 in price.[3] And in grocery stores, special Bat-displays offered children a choice between Batman colouring books, Batman trace-and-colour books, and Batman magic plates. It would seem that Batman and his paraphernalia transcend age, gender and race.

This deluge of material has generated a complex web of cross-references as the major text, *Batman*, ricochets back in cultural memory to Bob Kane's original vision of a caped vigilante, then up to the more recent dystopian *Dark Knight Returns*, with ironic reference to the camp crusader of television and all the intervening Bat-texts. This web of cross-references creates an intertext into which we position ourselves to construct different readings of the film, and position the film and its intertext to suit our own particular purposes. When a text like *Batman* generates such a rich and complex inter-text – in short, when Batmania takes the nation by storm – cultural critics are naturally drawn to analyse the text and intertext in order to discover why that text resonates with so many people, why it activates such widespread participation in the intertext.

If the prevalence of Bat-paraphernalia in the stores and the ubiquity of the Bat-logo on the streets are indicators, then indeed *Batman* has struck a chord deep in the American psyche. Certainly, the temptation to speculate on the larger significance of *Batman* is strong given the irony of this dark, yet ultimately hopeful, film being released at a time when the mythic Gotham of *The Dark Knight Returns* and the mythos of the American Imperium both seem to crack under the strains of social injustice and personal irresponsibility.

This speculation, however tempting, is not quite fair to us or to the film. Such speculation requires an assumptive leap that reduces consciousness, culture and media to reflections of each other. It assumes that the American psyche can be read off the film, which reflects American culture that determines how we see the world and how the film is constructed. This old and much criticised error retains its emotional force, despite the articulation of more careful theories about media texts and intertexts, about reception and reinterpretation of those materials by active viewers, as illustrated by the other essays in this volume. In this essay, however, I will argue that another dimension must be added to our analyses of media generally and of *Batman* specifically. Namely, economics must be considered if we are fully to understand the texts and intertexts of American mass culture. Most cultural production in the United States is done by private, for-profit corporations. These corporations comprise the entertainment/information sector of the American economy and encompass the industries of publishing, television, film, music, cable and radio. Significantly, American capitalism organises the creation of cultural artefacts as a process of mass production carried out by profit-oriented businesses operating in an industrial context. Profit, not culture, drives show business: no business means no show.

For much of American culture, corporate imperatives operate as the primary constraints shaping the narratives and iconography of the text as well as the manufacture and licensing of the intertextual materials necessary for a 'mania' to sweep the country. This is not a claim that evil moguls force us to buy Bat-chains: such reductionism is as vulgar and untenable as the assumptive leap from a film to the national psyche. Rather, the claim here is that mass-produced culture is a business, governed by corporate drives for profit, market control and transindustrial integration. While movies may (and do) flop, the decision to create a film is a business decision about the potential profitability of a cinematic product. Further, as film studios have been either acquired by companies outside the industry or have themselves acquired companies in other entertainment/information industries, decisions about movies are increasingly focused on the potential profitability of a wide range of products. The film per se becomes only one component in a product line that extends beyond the theatre, even beyond our contact with mass media, to penetrate the markets for toys, bedding, trinkets, cups and the other minutiae comprising one's everyday life inside a commoditised, consumerised culture.

To understand *Batman*, then, requires that our analyses of the text and intertext, and of fandom and other audiences, be supplemented by an economic analysis of corporate structure, market structures and interpenetrating industries. These conditions of production select, frame and shape both *Batman* as a commercial text and the product line that constitutes its commercial intertext. We begin, then, with *Batman*'s owner, Warner Communications Incorporated (WCI).

WCI: structures and industries

Warner Communications Inc. traces its history to the founding of Warner Brothers Studio in 1918. The four founding brothers have been the object of considerable scholarship, as has their studio and its products, which include sound film, social realist films, TV Westerns and cartoons.[4] Less well studied is the modern structure of Warner as Warner Communications Inc., a transindustrial media conglomerate. While much discussion has surrounded WCI's merger with Time Inc., that debate included little analysis on the impact of corporate structure on the content of cultural production. To see how that structure constrains content, we will trace the ways that WCI's external business pressures and internal markets shaped *Batman* as text and intertext. After sketching the emerging structure of Time Warner, we will examine conditions at WCI from 1982 to 1989 and analyse the commercial intertext as a response to economic conditions.

WCI is now half of the newly merged, transindustrial Time Warner. The combined holdings of Time and WCI in book publishing, cable channels, song publishing, cable systems, recorded music, television production, magazine/comics publishing, film production, television stations and licensing make Time Warner the predominant media conglomerate in the world. The Time-Warner merger signals a further concentration in the ownership of outlets, distribution systems and content production across multiple media industries by a single company.[5]

Significantly, the major difference between the independent WCI and the new Time Warner is a difference in size, not in kind. Prior to the 1989 merger, WCI had assumed the aggressive, expansionist pose typical of the 1970s and 80s.[6] By the 1980s, the company had joint ventures with American Express in cable operations, satellite distribution, pay cable channels and basic cable channels (QUBE; Warner Amex Satellite; Showtime and The Movie Channel; MTV Networks comprised by MTV, NIK and VH1). These rounded out WCI's wholly owned operations in film and television production, recorded music, cartoons and comic books, magazines, books, video cassettes and licensing of characters. But WCI had pushed beyond these interests to purchase the Franklin Mint (collectibles by subscription), Atari (computers and home video games), Warner Cosmetics, Knickerbocker Toy, Gadgets restaurant chain and other non-media firms. Throughout this expansion, revenues from WCI's core media companies remained strong.

However, the economic burdens of expansion almost capsized WCI when the home video game market collapsed in 1983[7] and when American Express moved to discontinue the joint ventures in 1985.[8] Only the willingness of the Chris-Craft Industries to expand its holdings of WCI stock saved WCI from a takeover attempt by Rupert Murdoch in 1983.[9] Having lost $420 million despite sales of $3.4 billion, WCI began selling assets both unprofitable (Atari) and profitable (MTV Networks to Viacom for cash and stock in Viacom) in an apparent attempt to both right itself and buy out American Express.[10] I say 'apparent attempt' only because of its willingness to accept stock in Viacom as partial payment along with much-needed cash. This suggests that WCI tried to solve its short-term crisis without sacrificing its long-term interest in retaining some influence over MTV Networks, the primary television outlet used to promote records. Despite its prodigious losses in 1983, WCI's film and television production units earned revenues of $109 million, while the publishing division enjoyed $43.3 million in revenues. By refocusing on its profitable media operations, the company began rebuilding profits, with earnings spiralling up to $693 million by October 1986.[11] With these revenues, WCI was poised for another round of acquisitions in December 1986.

This time, however, WCI focused its efforts more narrowly, absorbing and investing in companies that operated in the entertainment/information industries. Beginning with investment as a white knight in the Cannon Group (film production, home video, European theatre chains), WCI went on to acquire such firms as Lorimar Telepictures (film and television production, home video, television stations, television series including *Dallas* [1978–91] and *Alf* [1986–90], licensing), Cinema Venture (theatre chain co-owned by Gulf and Western) and Chappell Music Publishing before the culminating merger with Time Inc.[12]

In economic terms, the initial diversification helped trigger a crisis that forced WCI to shed its non-media acquisitions and to sell off some of its profitable media operations. Because of continued profitability in film, television, publishing and music, the company soon found itself poised for re-expansion. However, this time WCI adopted a more restrained approach to expansion, emphasising acquisition of media companies to achieve further integration in industries where it was already strong.

The merger with Time marks an intensification in the extent to which operations in different media industries are subordinated under the aegis of WCI (now Time Warner). WCI's recovery and retrenchment transformed the Warner of 1982, a diversified conglomerate with strong media interests, into the pre-merger Warner of 1989, a highly concentrated and integrated media conglomerate.

Financing recovery: recycling

While WCI's retrenchment required that its media companies remained profitable, its re-emergence as a major media conglomerate and subsequent expansion required increases in revenues and profits. This fostered greater cost efficiencies in film production as more profit was required from each project, whether directly from box-office revenues or indirectly by repackaging sections of the film for recycling through WCI's non-film outlets. For instance, film soundtracks became much more important as a source of possible revenues, since WCI could repackage soundtracks as records and music videos. For the film *Against All Odds* (1984), this meant that two sequences were simply lifted out of the film, soundtrack intact, and intercut with shots of WCI artist Phil Collins lip-syncing the words. Both videos were played in heavy rotation on MTV and on the daily show *NIK ROCKS* on Nickelodeon, thereby advertising both the film and the album. These videos for 'One More Night' and 'Against All Odds' were next recycled as part of the Phil Collins video album *No Jacket Required* (1985). *Against All Odds* fed not only WCI's film operations but also its music publishing, MTV Networks, recorded music and video cassette operations.

Similarly, WCI's distribution of Prince's independently made *Purple Rain* (1984) included an album, multiple music videos and publishing materials. Perhaps the company's reluctance to finance the film project may explain why *Purple Rain* looks like a half-dozen videos stitched together by a loose narrative. In contrast, *Against All Odds* looks like a movie with two videos embedded in it. In any case, both projects not only earned revenues for WCI but also filled its multiple outlets with product to which the company had first claim. Thus, WCI created an internal market where product for one unit could be recycled to provide product for multiple units. This reduced operation costs by decreasing the total cost of obtaining product for all media units. It also increased potential profitability per product, since repackaging and recycling allow a product's component parts to earn multiple revenues. Thus, the potential for repackaging and recycling become criteria for judging proposed projects.

The impact of these criteria on the finished product can literally be seen in *Against All Odds* and *Purple Rain*. Interestingly, such increasing cost efficiency in cultural production may ultimately decrease diversity of output. In any case, repackaging and recycling have the immediate effect of encouraging media conglomerates both to mine their stock of owned materials for new spin-offs and to view every project as a multimedia product line. WCI and Prince seem to have pioneered an intensified recycling of content.

Unlike *Against All Odds* and *Purple Rain*, the Bat-project began with a tried and true product that was already earning revenues for WCI: Batman, the only 'normal' adult

Superman (1978)

in DC Comics' stable of superheroes. When DC was acquired by WCI in 1971, it was evidently viewed by the chair of WCI's publishing division (William Sarnoff) as a source of licensing revenues and movie materials.[13] However, both licensing and book sales were decreasing across the comics industry due to problems in distribution, an exodus of production personnel, and a perceptible drop in the quality of narratives, portrayals of characters and artwork. Compounding this was the phenomena of underground comix (sic) with their explicit portrayals of drugs, sex, violence, political corruption and the ills of capitalism. Although underground comix never achieved the mass circulation enjoyed by Superman or Batman, the undergrounds opened the way for a fully commercial line of comics aimed at adults. Often mixing neoconservative ideologies with vigilantes, victims of child abuse and explicit violence, these comix became the centrepiece of speciality comics stores, which served as the major retail outlet for all comics by 1984. Further, the clientele of these stores was mainly adults; buying by children continued to drop.[14]

To compete in its own industry, then, DC and its comics had to be reorganised. From 1976 to 1981, DC struggled to rebuild revenues, achieving profitability with one-third of its revenues from comics sales, one-third from licensing and one-third from other sources. Obviously movies helped, as Superman proved a box-office smash in 1978, to be followed by three sequels (1979, 1983 and 1987) and one spin-off (Supergirl in 1984), all distributed by WCI. After six months of negotiating, DC granted rights for a Batman film to independent producers Peter Guber and Jon Peters, whose films have all been released through WCI. With WCI's decision to bankroll as well as distribute the film, Batman achieved the status of an in-house blockbuster production on which vast sums would be lavished. Hence, it is notable that the film's director, Tim Burton, enjoyed a track record with WCI, having directed PeeWee's Big Adventure (1985) at a cost of $7 million with box-office revenues of $40 million, as well as directing Michael Keaton in Beetlejuice (1988) at a cost of $13 million with box-office revenues of $80 million. The latter film was credited by WCI as the keystone of the film division's second-quarter earnings of $51.5 million in 1988.[15] With WCI risking $30 million with *Batman* in 1988, some assurances were necessary; hence the selection of producers, directors and stars with solid track records at the box office. But the company had other ways to build assurances given its internal markets, and the decision to release the film on *Batman*'s fiftieth birthday.

Internal markets and Batman

The mid-1980s marked the beginning of a process in which WCI both tested the waters and began building towards the release of *Batman*.[16] By issuing *The Dark Knight Returns* in comic form, WCI essentially test-marketed a dark reinterpretation of Batman with an adult readership whose experience with the character would include the camp crusader of the 1960s. The four issues comprising the *The Dark Knight Returns* sold out, prompting DC to establish a recurring title and Warner Publishing to repackage the original series as a book. Priced at $12.95, the book sold 85,000 copies in bookstores to a general reading public. Besides earning revenues twice from *The Dark Knight Returns*, WCI tapped different systems of distribution, placing the *Dark Knight* in different kinds of retail outlets, tapping the markets of fandom and general readers to determine if the grim version of Batman could gain acceptance from both specialised and generalised consumers.

The *Dark Knight*'s success prompted DC's repackaging of classic superheroes in a forty-eight-page anthology *Action Comics Weekly*, selling at $1.50 per issue, and the Warner Books publication of *Batman: Year One*.

Also, circulation figures for the Batman comic began rising as the Dark Knight's success rubbed off on the younger, less dystopian version of the character. The process of building an audience for the Batman film was thus started. It was intensified in 1988 when WCI let readers vote (via a 900 telephone number) on whether Robin should survive or not. With 5,343 nays versus 5,271 ayes, Robin was duly killed in 'A Death in the Family', which not surprisingly sold out. From comics sales of 89,747 copies in 1988, *Batman* sold 193,000 in 1988, as rumours abounded that Robin's cape would be taken up by a young woman. The entire incident was labelled a publicity stunt by both the *Comics Buyers Guide* and the *New York Times*.

Be that as it may, filming started in 1988 with the revenues from *Beetlejuice* safely in hand. Negative reactions from fans to casting decisions made the first page of the *Wall Street*

Frank Miller followed the speculative future of *The Dark Knight Returns* with a hardboiled origin story, *Batman: Year One* (New York: DC Comics, 1987)

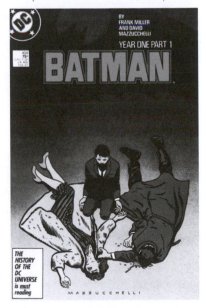

Journal, with claims by the *Journal* that WCI would modify content in order to ensure fan attendance.[17] From the use of its publishing division, WCI already had market measures that fans and the general public were willing to buy a darker interpretation of a lone vigilante. Just as important, WCI had information on the identity of fans from an industry survey funded by DC's main rival Marvel, which described the average reader as a twenty-year-old male spending $10 a week on comics. As a male-oriented action film, *Batman* would rely on the public personae of Jack Nicholson and Michael Keaton to widen the audience. Similarly, WCI would rely on the film to feed its internal markets in both the short and long run.

The $30 million sunk into *Batman* is not entirely the cost of a single film. Rather, it includes the root costs of a film series. The construction of sets, development of props, total investment and plot presume that sequels will be shot. In the long run, WCI's investment in plant for *Batman* can be spread out across two or four other films. While revenues per sequel can be expected to decrease as the number of Bat-movies increase, the major cost of sets for each sequel was largely included in WCI's original $30 million budget. The costs of recurring cast members would seem fairly manageable, although the initial expense of Nicholson's Joker probably precludes that character's resurrection. Keaton is the only necessarily recurring cost in the cast; should contract negotiations take an unacceptable turn, off-screen tragedies can easily explain the absence of either Vicki Vale or Alfred. WCI will probably use casting to build talk about the sequels just as it used the original casting of Nicholson and Keaton to create news stories about *Batman* and thereby gain free advertising for the film. Similarly, with the principal themes established in the orchestral soundtrack, new scoring can be limited largely to themes for villains and sidekicks, leaving WCI another chance to showcase one of its recording artists in the sequels (à la Prince on the first soundtrack). Similarly, the sequels should provide the raw materials for novelisations and comic books. Over the long run, then, WCI's $30 million investment in *Batman* has built the basic infrastructure necessary for manufacturing a line of films, albums, sheet music, comics and novelisations.

In the short run, this investment served as the seed money for a line of Bat-media to be distributed through WCI's non-film media outlets. The script for the film was adapted to both novel and comic book forms. The novel retells the film with only minor differences; the comic's visuals reproduce the shots of the film with slight variation in plot and pictorials. Thus, both the plot and the movie's visuals were broken out to earn income. Similarly, the soundtrack was broken out as two products: an album by Prince with songs from the soundtrack and songs inspired by the film (with the album going double platinum), plus an orchestral album by Danny Elfman, which surpassed the usual sales for orchestral scores with sales around 150,000.[18] Both album jackets featured the Bat-logo, differentiated only by decals stuck to the wrappers, thereby realising a slight cost efficiency in album production, although perhaps at the risk of some confusion among purchasers. In a departure from previous practice, Prince's video of his album's lead song, 'Batdance', featured no footage from the film. Instead, 'Batdance' broke out dialogue from the film, using the actors' lines as the basis for rap elements in Prince's funk sound.[19] The video played with Prince's usual themes of sexuality, androgyny and punishment. 'Batdance' was frequently featured on MTV, the music channel targeted primarily at middle-class whites from youth to middle age.[20] The use of a rap-funk style secured airplay on radio stations targeted at black audiences. This was a rather significant extension of Prince's audience, which WCI had pegged as white females in their late twenties to middle thirties. The crossover had the effect of cultivating black audiences, and Bat-logos began to crop up on black male performers featured on MTV's rap segments. But if rap elements generalised the appeal of 'Batdance', Prince's performance in the video replayed the themes that endeared him to his long-time fans and made *Purple Rain* a hit at the box office and in the record store. In this way, the decision to showcase Prince as a musical guest on the soundtrack promoted the film to an audience atypical of comics fans (white women); the style of Prince's musical performance promoted *Batman* in terms of black culture to black youth despite the minimal role of black actors (including Billy Dee Williams) in the film. All this had the effect of widening the pool of potential ticket-buyers for *Batman*.

This also earned revenues for WCI. Both albums represented extra income from an integral part of *Batman*: musical score and dialogue. Similarly, the sheet music from the score and from Prince's songs inspired by the film provided fodder for WCI's song publishing operation. This had recently expanded to become the largest song publisher in the world with WCI's acquisition of Chappell, thereby also enlarging WCI's need for music to publish. And with sequels in the planning, *Batman* promises to feed WCI's interests in comics, books, albums, sheet music, film production, music videos, MTV Networks, film distribution, theatres and home video cassettes for quite some time.

The relative swiftness of those sequels is suggested by WCI's video cassette release of *Batman* on 15 November 1989, less than six months after the film's premiere. Taking the trade press by surprise, this decision should serve to hasten *Batman* into the tertiary distribution circuits of pay cable and home video, cutting short the film's booking in second-run theatres. This promises to feed product to WCI's home video operations as well as Time Warner's HBO/Cinemax pay channels and WCI's pay-per-view channels on QUBE. Eventual distribution to basic cable raises suspicions that Time Warner's 17 per cent interest in TBS may shape Time Warner's selection of a basic cable channel. However, regardless of which major cable channel carries *Batman*, one can expect wide distribution of the film over Time Warner's ATC cable systems. The final distribution of the film on network television may even earn revenues for Time Warner's television stations. Each redistribution means more income from the basic product; repackaging means more distribution through more outlets to earn more revenues. Further, each step promotes the entire product line by getting the logo and characters before the potential consumer in yet another setting.

WCI's use of the Batman product line to feed its internal markets for media products indicates how media conglomerates bring together media industries that were once distinct and separate. The interpenetration of the music, film, print and video industries does not arise in response to demand from moviegoers, record buyers or comics subscribers. Rather, this interpenetration is orchestrated by the conglomerate in its search for more profitable and cost-efficient ways to manufacture culture.

But internal markets, corporate structure and interpenetrating industries are not the total sum of economic structures that constrain cultural production. External markets are also important in show business. Earning profits from shows means working in two very different external markets. The first is the market for licensing, a closed market in which a limited number of corporations secure exclusive rights over copyrighted materials. The second is an open market where real people go to movies, listen to favourite songs, read murder mysteries, change channels and rent videos. After feeding internal markets, media conglomerates sometimes turn to external markets and negotiate licensing agreements with firms whose concerns lie outside the pale of the licensor's operations. By granting exclusive use of copyrighted materials for use in the manufacture of particular product categories (e.g. toy figures, key chains, etc.), the licensor guarantees a secondary source of income from images, logos and characters from the original media product. Since licensing is both a form of promotion and a source of income, we turn next to a discussion of WCI's expenditures for advertising and arrangements for income from promotion. Since internal markets shape deals in the closed market, we'll begin by analysing that market and *Batman*.

External markets and Batmania

The extent to which WCI could make *Batman* a 'must see' film depended on promotion, comprised by advertising and licensing. While the former is a cost, the latter is a source of revenues. However, the $10 million WCI spent on advertising would not be a complete loss even if the film did poorly at the box office. Under US tax law, advertising is an ordinary cost of doing business and deductible as such. When advertising is accompanied by licensing in a promotional campaign, the producing company has the opportunity of earning revenues from licences to toy companies, clothes manufacturers, fast-food chains, etc. even if the film flops. Licensing is increasingly used, then, to augment revenues, and licensed products are used to augment advertising for the film.

Because of WCI's cartoon properties, licensing has always played a role in the company's revenues. For *Batman*, WCI licenses two different properties: *Batman* the movie or Batman of comics and television fame. Potential licensees could opt for the film's logo or the traditional logo; for the Dark Knight or the Dynamic Duo; for Keaton's body armour or Adam West's costume; for Nicholson's Joker or DC's Joker, Riddler, Penguin and Catwoman. This mix-or-match approach gave WCI's 100 licensed manufacturers considerable latitude in devising merchandising campaigns to cash in both on the company's ad campaign for the film and on Batman's anniversary. Manufacturers could license images appropriate to their targeted consumers: children as traditional consumers of Batman; young adult males and bookstore patrons as consumers of the Dark Knight; the forty million people estimated as the viewership for reruns of the syndicated Batman television show; ticket-buyers for films rated PG13/Parents Strongly Cautioned (as Batman was).[21] Depending on its targets, plus available information on consumption habits and Batman, manufacturers could license the line of images that seemed more likely to trigger purchases in tandem with the film's much advertised opening.

Having seen *Batman*'s extraordinary box office (a record-breaking $40.49 million in its first three days), it may be hard to believe that manufacturers could question the film's ability to sell merchandise.[22] However, as late as 28 February 1989, surveys showed low response from consumers to Batman as a character in general.[23] Consultants 'in the know' counselled potential licensees to stick with the old images. While hindsight may set heads wagging, WCI's own merchandising suggests an attempt to hedge its bets. WCI's product mix included merchandise using the film images as well as the old comics images. Importantly, the company's entire line of Bat-products was energetically promoted in theatres, where a positive reaction to the film could be conveniently translated into purchases. Besides offering a limited line of Bat-products for sale in theatres, WCI provided two major theatre chains with special forms to mail-order Bat-products. Offering each theatre in the chain a 2 per cent rebate on orders received, WCI reported receiving 1,000 forms per day for the first eleven days of *Batman*'s run, with an average order of $75 per form. This practice fostered the interests of all licensees by cultivating demand for Bat-products, thus promoting WCI's direct and indirect revenues earned by Bat-products.[24]

Licensing can also expand markets for Bat-products beyond the film's targeted audiences to reach consumers who may be blocked by parents attending to the 'PG13/Parents Strongly Cautioned' rating. Interestingly, movie-related products targeted for pre-teens do not necessarily require parental permission. The prices of ToyBiz's Batwing ($16.99) or Batcave set (figures not included, $19.99) may block unsupervised purchases; not so Ertl's Batmobile ($1.99) nor Topps's *Batman: Official Souvenir Magazine* ($2.95) nor Topps's packages of trading cards with sticker and bubblegum, the 132 cards in the series featuring visuals from the film with a running plot summary on the back. Similarly, Topps's magazine mixes visuals from the film with a sketch of the plot and information on special effects. These materials are sandwiched between an article on Batman's history and a closing piece on the joys of collecting Bat-products. The centrefold is Keaton's Batman standing in front of the Batmobile. Five pages are given to advertising: ToyBiz Batman action figures and toys; Data East Batman video games (using comic images); movie T-shirts, jewellery, and posters from DC/WCI and Great Southern Company; DC/WCI Bat-books; DC-authorised Batman role-playing game (an abridged version of the DC heroes game) with Mayfair Games. This intermixture sets the new *Batman* in the context of the old, collectible Batman products and new Bat-products with images from comics, television and film versions of Batman. Not only does the souvenir magazine operate as an advertisement and a revenue earner, but it also functions as a particular system of cross-references, as an intertext. And that particular intertext meshes with the web of cross-references created by WCI's entire promotional campaign.

The commercial intertext that results from this combination of advertising and licensing intermixes old themes with new, camp motifs with grim visages, cartooning with live action, thus generating a rich and often contradictory set of understandings and visions about justice and corruption in America. And it does this because of manufacturers' perceptions about acceptable risk, potential profit and targeted consumers. Simultaneously, the plethora of Bat-products intersects with $10 million of paid advertising and a flood of free promotion ('Batdance', reviews, news stories, interviews) to hype the movie – making *Batman* the 'must see' film of the summer. This brings us to the third market, in which WCI transacted its Bat-business with the moviegoing public.

The last market: show

In this last market, the 'show' in show business finally becomes important as the show itself finally earns revenues directly from people through ticket sales. However, this market has some distinctive features which differentiate it from other media markets; but it is similar to most consumer markets in advanced capitalist economies, since the market for movies depends on advertising to stimulate consumption of products selected by an oligopoly of producers.[25] Like most consumer markets, the market for films is not driven by demand; WCI was not picketed by millions of moviegoers demanding a Bat-film. Quite the opposite: once WCI decided to go ahead with the Bat-project, the company needed to test-market the new Bat-image and to convince people that we wanted to see this particular film of *Batman*. So, while we count in this market, we count as consumers who must be enticed to buy a ticket, thus renting a seat for one viewing of a particular film selected from all movies currently playing. Obvious though this process is, it has some rather subtle consequences: in the market where people consume shows, all shows compete against each other regardless of the manufacturer's identity. So if WCI releases five films, each movie competes with the other four films by WCI as well as with all the other films released into the marketplace.

As a result, it is in the interest of film producers to control the number of releases per year, artificially decreasing the number of films available in order to decrease competition between films.[26] By limiting our choices to a handful of films and by consolidating release dates into two 'seasons' – summer and Christmas – the major film studios create a business cycle that alternates forced choices between a limited number of 'hot films' with stretches of doldrums. This industry-generated business cycle sets up conditions of production that favour the funding and distribution of relatively few films by each major studio. By limiting releases, a studio decreases the amount of competition between its releases. Since every studio follows this policy, the effect is a decrease in competition over all films in each season. To augment each season's line-up, a studio will selectively contract with semi-independent producers for a limited number of additional films. Willingness to accept such product varies inversely with the amount of a studio's own product that it has slated for release. Further, releases within a season are staggered so that most studio product (and the more favoured semi-independent product) shares its opening date with no other major release. Such favoured films are preceded by massive advertising campaigns in an attempt to pack the house for the film's premiere. Taken together, these components create a market in which even 'failures' earn a minimum box office, like the $8 million earned by the WCI flop *Supergirl*. This potential for failure regardless of advertising, business cycle, etc. is rooted in the market itself, as will be discussed later.

This decreased competition among films regardless of studio has decreased competition among studios for screens and ticket-buyers. It also has the effect of channelling money from multiple projects into one or two projects, so that major theatrical releases become increasingly expensive with production costs running into millions of dollars, before millions more are spent on advertising. In fact, the enormous cost of a film can be an impetus for news coverage, producing free publicity that might attract some audience members. For *Batman*, the press reported figures ranging from $30 to $40 million, plus another $10 million for promotion.[27] The sheer size of production costs may well be the source of studios' willingness to pay similarly high costs for promotion. The $10 million figure for *Batman* represents an attempt to hype the film as a 'must see', to fill theatres across the nation for its premiere performances. By releasing *Batman* after most major films had opened, including the sequels (*Indiana Jones and the Last Crusade* [1989], *Star Trek VI* [1991]), and by hyping that release through the radio, television, cable, print and film industries, WCI tried to ensure that its early revenues would be as high as possible. Even if word of mouth damned the movie, the early revenues could carry the film into a respectable slot on *Variety*'s chart of moneymakers.

All this joins together to create a market for theatrical release films that stresses high production costs, limited seasons, limited number of releases, slightly staggered releases within a season and extensive pre-release advertising, as film companies try to cope with the vagaries of this last market.

Where people are the prime purchasers, revenues cannot be completely shielded from the direct responses of consumers. Word of mouth can break a film designed as a blockbuster, or elevate an obscure movie to the status of a cult film or even a sleeper. Thus, expensive films may be box-office bonanzas or big-time disasters. Where some media revenues are protected by the habits of subscription, film remains in direct relationship with an open, unstructured market of potential ticket-buyers. This encourages film producers to cultivate brand loyalties in an attempt to establish purchasing habits so that consumers routinely select a particular genre, personnel (actor or director), recurring characters and continuing stories. For consumers, the decision turns on projected satisfaction: we cannot know if the film is worth the price until after viewing it. Thus, word of mouth and published reviews may shape our willingness to pay. Similarly, genre, personnel, recurring characters or continuing stories can be used to make quick decisions based on past experience when selecting from a season's releases. Sequels and stars can be used to manage demand just as pre-release advertising can be used to inflate revenues from premieres before word of mouth makes its rounds. For WCI, building a Bat-series required both extensive pre-release advertising to produce a 'hit' premiere as well as a sufficiently solid foundation to earn a steady income after the hype subsided. By holding the film until 23–24 June, WCI could count on post-premiere drops in attendance for the early releases. After that, the summer-long success of *Batman* at the box office would depend on the film itself, its ability to resonate with our experiences and visions, and to tap into the conflicting ideologies through which we make sense of social life.

From cultural economics to economic culture

That leads us back to the audience for *Batman* and to *Batman* as text and intertext. However, as we again approach *Batman*, Batmania and Bat-audiences, our discussion of economics reminds us that text, intertext and audiences are simultaneously commodity, product line and consumer. Separating reader from text/intertext is the complex structure of interpenetrating cultural industries and the corporate interests of media conglomerates. This complex structure is generally invisible to us. Our personal and shared experience of media – including *Batman* – is emotional, imagistic, interpretive and pleasurable. Thus, the commodification of text, the commodity fetishism of intertext and the management of consumption are obscured behind the 'soft and fuzzies' feeling of experience. The economic logics of profit and cost efficiency suggest that *Batman* is best understood as a multimedia, multimarket sales campaign. Yet, although that campaign's primary purpose is to earn revenues and decrease production costs, it also 'sells' ideologies – visions of the good, the true, the beautiful. Herein lies the contradiction of capitalist media: to understand our mass media, we must be able to understand them as always and simultaneously text and commodity, intertext and product line. This contradiction is well captured in the phrase 'show business'. In our fascination with the highly visible show, let us not overlook the less visible business that ultimately shapes, constructs, recycles, breaks out and distributes the show for a profit. No business means no show and doing business means constructing shows according to business needs. These are the ground rules, recoverable through critical analysis, from which we can safely approach the analysis of a commodified culture and the products of show business. One might well exclaim: 'Holy commodity fetish, Batman!'

Postscript

Much has changed in the worlds of mediated culture, media industries and media scholarship since the 1991 publication of *The Many Lives of the Batman*. Perhaps most notably, our access to computerised, networked technologies has reshaped how we use media artefacts, how corporations advertise to us and track us, and how media scholars conduct research. Despite such changes, continuities persist, particularly in terms of the neoliberal restructuring of media economics, beginning with the Reagan administration in 1981 and continuing to this day. Much that was done and argued in 'Holy Commodity Fetish, Batman!' was shaped by research documenting the transition from quasi-Keynesian regulation to neoliberal deregulation – and contextualising that transition within the larger frame of American capitalism. Here, I will focus first on the essay's methodological issues and then on theoretical concerns.

My task in the original essay was to document and understand the unprecedented outpouring of name-brand products associated with the film *Batman* (Burton, 1989) produced by Warner Communications Incorporated (WCI). My first step was to build a corporate profile for WCI. Critical political economists have long built profiles of major corporations in order to document the extent of their operations within and across industries. Relevant sources include governmental investigations and economic reports, corporate documents filed with the Securities Exchange Commission, in-depth reports by investigative journalists, self-promotional materials produced by corporations and celebratory accounts produced by journalists, commentators, trade publications, etc. We read such documents with *and* against the grain in order to distil embedded assumptions, inherent positions, claims of fact and arguments both manifest and latent.

To build a profile for WCI, I used 10-K reports for WCI, American Express, TCI, Time Incorporated and Time Warner as well as coverage in such financial publications as *Standard & Poor Corporations Descriptions*, Dun & Bradstreet's *Who Owns Whom: 1989 North America*. I also used accounts published in *The Economist, Wall Street Journal, Business Week, New York Times, Los Angeles Times, Variety, Hollywood Reporter, Advertising Age, Billboard* and *Editor and Publisher*. My time frame was 1982–9, which I contextualised by reading widely in the history of film studios and the political economy of the film industry.

My profile of WCI traced its development from a diversified conglomerate, with interests in media, cosmetics and retail sales, to a conglomerate where all operations focused on media. That transformation was facilitated by internal challenges as well as pressures from other corporations. As a transindustrial media conglomerate, WCI could use materials from one media operation to feed as many other operations as possible. That structural logic undergirded WCI's strategy to capitalise on Batman's fiftieth birthday and generated a flood of merchandise.

But how did WCI's strategy manifest itself to people in everyday life? My first contact with Bat-merchandise was at a kiosk at the Sycamore Mall in Iowa City, Iowa. On display were T-shirts featuring an image outlined in yellow on a dark blue background. Instead of seeing the Bat-logo, I saw a shark's jaws, wide open and ready to bite. I queried the clerk, who explained that the T-shirt was for the new Batman movie and then pointed out related products. That exchange inspired the second step in my research: I decided to observe Bat-products' presence in local retail outlets.

Besides the Sycamore Mall with the usual national brands, Iowa City had two big grocery stores, a downtown shopping area with local stores and a flea market with a particular vendor who regularly sold fan-related materials. As I went through these venues looking for *Batman* and Batman merchandise, I was impressed by the wide variety of products and by the density of their presence in the marketplace. My notes described each product and identified the date, price, vendor and location offering the product. I also sketched how the product was displayed. The only person to show an interest in my actions was that particular vendor at the flea market. When I explained, he gave me a copy of a trade magazine published by Advance Publications listing all of the Bat-products that WCI made available to retailers in order to promote the film. Checking my findings against the Advance Publications listing, I found that we had a large array of Bat-products, missing only the most expensive ones.

When I mapped my market observation against WCI's corporate structure, I could see how *Batman* fed the company's operations in media and licensing while creating opportunities to repackage and resell older versions of Batman and older Bat-products. My data suggested that WCI had been conducting a complex, multi-year campaign to simultaneously promote and profit from Batman in all his varied forms. Under quasi-Keynesian regulation, WCI would have been constrained by laws separating the major media industries into discrete oligopolies. Under neoliberal deregulation, WCI could accomplish most of the media transactions in-house.

Tracing the web of commercial intertextuality is a fascinating exercise but, unless the dynamics of that web are explained, the exercise is useless. Explaining why corporations use commercial intertextuality and synergy is essential. Throughout the essay, I explain the dynamics and pressures that provided WCI with opportunities to act in its own self-interest, maximise its earnings and feed its operations in ways that are relatively inexpensive yet earn external revenues. Within those contexts, we can see how a media artefact is a commodity, how commercial intertexts are product lines and how audiences are targeted purchasers. This reminds us that, while we may think of media as culture or entertainment, media are primarily business operations. That fact places them squarely within the domain of economics and, in our case, both US and global capitalism. As I argue, the media are indeed a form of show business: no business means no show. The next Bat-product line will undoubtedly utilise new technologies and be distributed over platforms that have yet to be imagined. But it will be rooted in corporate ownership, corporate structure and the corporate search for profits.

Notes

1. The author would like to thank Tim Emmerson for research assistance and Alfred Babbit for word-processing the original text.
2. Jim Robbins, 'Orders for Batstuff Bring 2% to Exhibs; Brochure System Cheered', *Variety*, 5 July 1989, p. 8.
3. Advance Comics is a catalogue listing comic books and fan materials that are scheduled to be distributed to speciality stores in two months' time. Resembling a black-and-white comic book, issues include an order form.
4. See, for example, Charles Higham, *Warner Brothers* (New York: Scribner's, 1975); William R. Meyer, *Warner Brothers Directors* (New Rochelle, NY: Arlington House, 1975); Ted Sennett, *Warner Brothers Presents* (New Rochelle, NY: Arlington House, 1971); Nick Roddick, *A New Deal in Entertainment: Warner Brothers in the 1930s* (London: BFI, 1983). For an analysis of finance capital and C1, see Janet Wasko, *Movies and Money* (Norwood, NJ: Ablex, 1982); and for the structural analysis of WCI, QUBE and MTV, see Eileen R. Meehan, 'Technical Capability Versus Corporate Imperatives', in Vincent Mosco and Janet Wasko (eds), *The Political Economy of Information* (Norwood, NJ: Ablex, 1988), pp. 167–87.
5. For a complete listing of Time's and Warner's holdings, consult *Standard & Poor's Corporation Descriptions* (New York, 1989), and *Who Owns Whom: North America* (London: Dun & Bradstreet International, 1989).

6. *Standard & Poor's Corporation Descriptions*.

7. This collapse elicited considerable commentary in the *Wall Street Journal*, as suggested by representative titles: 'Atari to Idle 1,700 at California Site, Move Jobs to Asia', 13 February 1983, p. 6; Laura Landro, 'Warner's Atari Staff Facing Shake-Up; Merger of Video and Computer Divisions Set', 31 May 1983, p. 5; 'Warner's Atari Unit Reorganizes Its Lines in Bid to Stem Losses', 2 June 1983, p. 20; 'S and P Adds 4 Makers of Home Computers, Games to Credit Watch', 27 June 1983, p. 41; 'Warners Ratings Cut by Standard and Poor's; Atari Troubles Cited', 28 October 1983, p. 48. The effect on Warner was duly chronicled in the *Wall Street Journal* with such headlines as 'Warner Communications Stock Continues to Slide as Analysts' 2nd [sic] Period Loss Estimates Growth', 20 July 1983, p. 55, and 'Warner Lays Off 30% of Its Staff at Headquarters', 14 October 1983, p. 3. Headlines in the *New York Times* were equally grim: 'Warner's Profit Falls by 56.5%', 17 February 1983, p. D14; 'Warner Amex Cable Cuts 57 More Positions', 17 May 1983, p. 2; 'Warner Posts a $283.4 Million Loss', 22 July 1983, pp. D1, D5; '$122.4 Million Loss at Warner', 15 October 1983, p. 37; 'Layoffs Predicted at Warner Amex', 28 December 1983, p. 4.

8. American Express attempted to end the joint ventures by forcing Warner to either buy it out or to let American Express buy out Warner with the understanding that American Express would sell the ventures to either Time or TCI or to a Time-TCI joint venture. Warner was reluctant to exit the cable industry, particularly if its cable, satellite, and programming operations would be absorbed by the two largest operators of multiple cable systems, Time and TCI. The maneuverings of all parties were thoroughly reported in the financial pages of the New York Times (representative titles: "Warner Amex Bid Confirmed," 30 May 1985, pp. D2 and D19; "American Express Bids for All of Warner Amex," 18 July 1985, p. 2; "Warner to Buy Out Amex Unit," 10 August 1985, pp. 31 and 33) as well as in the *Wall Street Journal* (representative titles: "American Express Offers to Purchase Rest of Warner Amex for $450 Million," 18 July 1985; "Meeting Is Delayed Again by Warner Communications," 12 July 1985, p. 15; "Warner to Buy Partner's Stake in Cable Firm," 12 August 1985, p. 31.

9. The *Wall Street Journal*'s 'Heard on the Street' featured items on Murdoch's attempt to take over Warner (30 September 1983, p. 59, and 20 December 1983, p. 55) and covered the story in some detail from the start ('Warner Communications Stake Is Boosted to 7% by Murdoch – Control Isn't Sought', 16 December 1983, p. 10) to finish ('Murdoch Loses Round in Fight for Warner as FCC Approves Chris-Craft Stock Swap', 9 March 1984, p. 6; 'Warner's Plan to Buy Back Shares from Murdoch Boosts Chris-Craft', 19 March 1984, pp. 35–8).

10. Laura Landro, 'Warner to Post $5 Million Net for Quarter but $420 Million Deficit for the Full Year', *Wall Street Journal*, 16 February 1984, p. 4; 'Viacom Gets Its MTV', *Broadcasting*, 2 September 1985, pp. 50–2; Bill Abrams, 'Viacom Will Pay Warner $500 Million for Stakes in MTV Networks, Showtime', *Wall Street Journal*, 27 August 1985, p. 4.

11. Geraldine Fabrikant, 'How Warner Got Back Its Glitter', *New York Times*, 14 December 1983, section 3, p. 1.

12. 'Warner Pact Helps Rescue Cannon', *New York Times*, 24 December 1986, p. 2; Geraldine Fabrikant, 'Warner and Lorimar in "Early" Talks', *New York Times*, 8 March 1988, section 4, p. 1; Richard Gold, 'WCI to Appeal N.Y. Court Ruling against Its Merger with Lorimar', *Variety*, 5 October 1988, p. 3; 'Warner Merges with Lorimar', *New York Times*, 12 January 1989, p. D19; Laura Landro, 'Warner Is Cleared to Buy 50% Stake in Cinema Venture', *Wall Street Journal*, 14 December 1988, p. B6; 'Purchase of Chappell Music from Investors Is Completed', *Wall Street Journal*, 8 October 1987, p. 16.

13. Philip S. Gritis, 'Turning Superheroes into Super Sales', *New York Times*, 6 January 1985, p. 6.

14. Kurt Eichenwald, 'Grown-ups Gather at the Comic Book Stand', *New York Times*, 30 September 1987, p. 1; Richard W. Anderson, 'Biff! Pow! Comic Books Make a Comeback', *Business Week*, 2 September 1985, pp. 59–60.

15. Joe Morgenstern, 'Tim Burton, Batman, and the Joker', *New York Times Magazine*, 9 April 1989, pp. 45, 46, 50, 53, 60.

16. Information on the *Dark Knight Returns*, on circulation, demographics and Robin is taken from Georgia Dullea, 'Holy Bomb Blast! The Real Robin Fights On', *New York Times*, 10 November 1988, p. 23; Alexandra Peers, 'Given His Costume, It's a Wonder He Didn't Die of Embarrassment', *Wall Street Journal*, 26 October 1988, p. B1; Lisa H. Towle, 'What's New in the Comic Book Business', *New York Times*, 31 January 1988, p. 21; 'Growing up into Graphic Novels' and 'America Is Taking Comic Books Seriously', *New York Times*, 31 July 1988, p. 7.

17. Kathleen A. Hughes, 'Batman Fans Fear the Joke's on Them in Hollywood Epic', *Wall Street Journal*, 29 November 1988, pp. 1, 8.

18. Kevin Zimmerman, 'Soundtracks: Not Too Much Noise in '89', *Variety*, 3 January 1990, pp. 49–57.

19. Nelson George, 'Prince Is Back on Wings of Batdance', *Billboard*, 24 June 1989, p. 4.

20. From the start, MTV was targeted at white audiences, aged fourteen to thirty-four, with an average income of $30,000 (Jack Loftus, 'Warner Amex Preps All-Music Cable Channel', *Variety*, 4 March 1981, p. 1; Sally Bedell, 'All Rock Cable-TV Service Is a Hit', *New York Times*, 2 August 1982, p. 15; Ed Levine, 'TV Rocks with Music', *New York Times*, 8 May 1983, pp. 42, 55–6, 61).

21. 'Cape, Mask, Platform Heels', *The Economist*, 14 January 1989, p. 84.

22. Joseph McBride, '"Batman" Swoops to Conquer: WB Pic Sees Hottest B.O. Action in History', *Variety*, 28 June–4 July 1989, p. 1.

23. Bruce Horovitz, 'Holy Tie-In! Batman Bores Consumers Just as Retailers Prepared for Film', *Los Angeles Times*, 28 February 1989, p. 6.

24. Robbins, 'Orders for Batstuff Bring 2% to Exhibs'.

25. Thomas Guback, 'Capital, Labor Power, and the Identity of Film', paper presented at the Conference on Culture and Communication, Philadelphia, March 1983. See also Wasko, *Movies and Money*.

26. This market structure arises from two conditions. The first condition was the divorcement of film production and film exhibition required by the decision rendered in *U.S. v. Paramount Pictures* (334 U.S. 131, 142, 161). This decision resulted in the studios

divesting themselves of their theatre chains, which freed the studios from the necessity of producing B-movies simply to fill screens. Such production became less attractive partly due to the availability of 'free' entertainment from broadcasters, which eroded the guaranteed audience that had once existed for any film (cf. Thomas Guback, 'Theatrical Film', in Benjamin M. Compaine, *Who Owns the Media?* [New York: Harmony Books, 1979], pp. 179–250, and Wasko, *Movies and Money*, pp. 103–47). Currently, WCI and other conglomerates with interests in film studios are reintegrating film production and exhibition, while also pursuing further integration of film as an industry with the once distinct industries of television, cable, recorded music, book publishing, etc. Reintegration may encourage the production of more film product for the screen, since that product can also be recycled across the entire array of distribution channels, including pay cable and video cassette rental. Reintegration may also encourage the current practice of playing a single title on several screens at multiplexes, followed by shortened runs at independent theatres and a quick turnaround to cable and rental. The precise dynamics have yet to be worked out by the relevant companies.

27. The $30 million figure is the most widely reported, generally with $10 million given for advertising costs. The $40 million figure tends to be cited without a separate figure for advertising.

7

BATMAN IN EAST ASIA

Mark Gallagher

Christopher Nolan's *Batman* trilogy of 2005–12 (aka 'the Dark Knight trilogy') has been one of Warner Bros.', and Hollywood's, most successful franchises ever at the global box office. The first reboot of the Batman film franchise (and the first big-screen treatment since 1997's *Batman & Robin*), *Batman Begins*, was the ninth-largest global release of 2005, its sequel, *The Dark Knight*, was famously number one worldwide in 2008, and *The Dark Knight Rises* was the number three film worldwide in 2012. *Batman Begins* earned just under 45 per cent of its over $374 million worldwide gross outside the US, and *The Dark Knight* earned nearly 47 per cent of its $1.004 billion gross overseas.[1] Even more remarkably, over 58 per cent of *The Dark Knight Rises'* $1.084 billion gross came from outside North America.[2] One might reasonably assume that contemporary Hollywood's international hits are hits everywhere, and that the *Batman* films' earnings in particular regions would be commensurate with those territories' share of the global film market. As of 2013, East Asia includes three of the world's ten largest film markets as measured by box-office revenues, including China at number two, Japan in third and South Korea at number seven (with Taiwan also in the top twenty, at number eighteen).[3] Yet in the major markets in East Asia, the films' performances have been surprisingly variable – impressive in South Korea, Hong Kong and Taiwan and progressively stronger there across the series, but consistently weak in Japan, and ranging in China from dominant to not even released. Prevailing discourses in film culture construct Hollywood releases as juggernauts that dominate exhibition in developed countries. In practice, Hollywood films released overseas must contend with strong local film industries, domestic protectionism and unpredictable external events. Pursuing the 'many more lives of the Batman' into East Asia reveals that not only does global Hollywood not necessarily crush everything in its path, sometimes it barely registers.

This chapter seeks to shed some light on the processes and limits of Hollywood globalisation through consideration of a major film series in an increasingly critical release region. To account for the *Batman* series' variable fortunes in East Asian release, I address conditions in the exhibition sector contributing to the films' performances, textual features of the three films that may resonate particularly strongly in East Asian release contexts, and their reception by major publications and popular discourses. The protracted arc of the *Batman* films' production and release makes them compelling case studies through which to track evolving economic, industrial and cinema-infrastructure intersections among US, East Asian and global companies. Their content and reception also indicate how international releases sit in local contexts: how they correspond technically and aesthetically to surrounding releases and whether viewers receive such large-scale Hollywood films as the *Batman* series on a par with, or distinct from, other films in domestic exhibition. Reception discourses within East Asia have both framed the films as Hollywood imports and translated them into works relevant to their own cultural perspectives and viewing protocols. Unlike other major franchises such as *Star Wars* (1977–2005) or *Lord of the Rings* (2001–12) – though like other superhero series – the *Batman* films take place in a recognisable historical reality, enabling references to specific places and cultures, including many within Asia. Curiously, the films performed progressively better at the East Asian box office with each new instalment – even as textual attention to specific East Asian characters and cultural forms evaporates across the series.

The trilogy has distinctive characteristics that inform its engagement with East Asian cultures and audiences. At the same time, the cases reveal a good deal about Hollywood's present interactions with the world at large. Both by default and design, Nolan's *Batman* films include characters, locations, pacing, thematics and other areas of content specifically tied to East Asia or compatible with local viewer expectations.[4] Production and marketing initiatives have attempted to broaden the films' appeal and box-office visibility. Efforts such as *Batman Begins*' Japan premiere at the Nagoya World Expo site, *The Dark Knight*'s Hong Kong location shooting, and *The Dark Knight Rises*' release and partial filming in the IMAX format all indicate a range of strategies designed to cultivate viewerships in specific territories within East Asia. Overall, the cases remind us that while many Hollywood releases travel abroad, that journey is not frictionless. Films such as the *Batman* trilogy face political and cultural obstacles, though their circulation can be stimulated by intertextual resonance with local films and pop culture as well as by audiences' abilities to mould relatively open texts according to their desired consumption practices.

The Bat-numbers

How important are East Asian markets to the *Batman* trilogy's fortunes? An overview of their performance in the major East Asian markets of Japan, South Korea, China, Hong Kong and Taiwan shows how those markets contributed to the films' global receipts. Until recently, Japan represented the world's second-largest market in terms of overall theatrical revenues for both domestic and foreign releases. With a thriving domestic film industry, Japan's market has been somewhat resistant to US and other imports. *Batman Begins*, the number eight film of 2005 in the US, ranked only thirty-fourth in Japan, where it earned just over $12 million despite its high-profile premiere.[5] *The Dark Knight* fared no better, earning $14.5 million in Japan to rank thirty-sixth in 2008. And with just over $24 million in receipts, the third entry, released as *Dark Knight Rising*, ranked twenty-seventh at the Japanese box office in 2012, a year in which only six US films cracked the top twenty.

Batman Begins (2005)

With a smaller, less established domestic film industry than Japan and a corollary openness to imports, South Korea tells a rather different story. *Batman Begins* earned only $6 million in South Korea in 2005.[6] *The Dark Knight* fared somewhat better in 2008, earning $25 million and ranking eleventh for the year, behind five other Hollywood studio releases. And in 2012, while five of the year's top ten films were South Korean productions, Hollywood superhero adaptations filled three of the top seven positions, with *The Dark Knight Rises* grossing nearly $42 million to claim the number five position. The series has thus become exponentially more popular with each successive film, making South Korea the series' most lucrative non-English-language market to date.[7]

China, which in 2011 surpassed Japan as the world's number two release market, offers the most curious statistics. *Batman Begins* earned just over $1 million in China in 2005,[8] but *The Dark Knight* received no mainland release. Warner Bros. declined to submit the film to Chinese regulators owing to content issues, including a scene set in Hong Kong showing criminal activity, Batman's unsanctioned vigilantism on Chinese soil and a cameo from Hong Kong star Edison Chen, at the time embroiled in a sex scandal involving lewd photographs.[9] *The Dark Knight Rises* did earn a Chinese release, grossing over $32 million in its first week of mainland exhibition despite being forced by regulators to open the same day as competing Hollywood release *The Amazing Spider-Man*.[10] Across its Chinese run, *The Dark Knight Rises* earned nearly $53 million, so even though it was only the number twelve film in China in 2012, China was still the film's third-largest market (behind North America and the UK).[11] In the greater Chinese region, the *Batman* films have performed increasingly well in Hong Kong and Taiwan. In Hong Kong, *Batman Begins* ranked nineteenth for 2005 with just under $1.8 million in receipts, *The Dark Knight* ranked first for 2008 with a gross over $7.5 million, and *The Dark Knight Rises* was at number two in 2012 with earnings of over $10 million.[12] In Taiwan, *Batman Begins* grossed $1.3 million in 2005, *The Dark Knight* ranked third for 2008 with $6.7 million, and *The Dark Knight Rises* was at number two for 2012.[13]

In many cases, clearly, the *Batman* films have been less dominant in East Asian territories than in English-language markets and in continental Europe. Still, as for major Hollywood releases generally, East Asian markets such as China and South Korea have become proportionately more important to the *Batman* series' overall revenues. Benefiting from the continued expansion of overseas markets compared to the relatively flat North American market, the *Batman* trilogy's performance has been progressively stronger in the aggregated East Asian region.[14] The five East Asian territories brought in combined revenues of over $22 million for *Batman Begins*, $54 million for *The Dark Knight* and a remarkable $129 million for *The Dark Knight Rises*.[15] As a proportion of the series' grosses, the five territories accounted for just under 6 per cent of *Batman Begins'* overall global revenue and, with no income from China, for just over 5 per cent of *The Dark Knight's* earnings. For *The Dark Knight Rises*, though, these five territories provided over 10 per cent of the film's global takings. Such figures are particularly notable given the strength of the domestic film industries in the largest of these markets. Emilie Yueh-yu Yeh observes that 'since 2009, domestic films in Japan, South Korea and China have enjoyed 50 percent of overall market share'.[16] Yeh notes further that China uses unofficial protections to limit imports to a 50 per cent market share. Japan and South Korea do not resort to such measures, though, and for the latter, Kyung Hyun Kim notes that 'Korea boasts the best rate among advanced nations (excluding the United States) of local consumption of domestic film products – a rate far better than that of any European country or Japan'.[17]

The *Batman* films' fortunes attest to the significance of key production and exhibition technologies in China and other East Asian markets. Among other factors, the series' rising proportion of revenue from East Asia can be attributed to the support for and incentivisation of speciality formats such as IMAX shown by the emerging markets (particularly China's). Internationally, IMAX screenings of the 2008 and 2012 *Dark Knight* films have boosted revenues thanks to higher ticket prices than for standard exhibition. (*Batman Begins*, shot in 35mm, was also up-converted for selective IMAX exhibition.) While the films do not follow industry trends towards 3-D production and exhibition, their release (and partial shooting) in IMAX format underlines the parallel growth of large-format exhibition. Construction of IMAX theatres has outstripped that of conventional-sized screens in recent years. In 2012, China also announced expansions of its import quota, with fourteen new slots (in addition to the existing twenty) available specifically for IMAX as well as 3-D releases.[18] Meanwhile, the *Batman* series' producers have sought a greater footprint within China, particularly to circumvent quotas restricting imports of overseas films. Production company Legendary Pictures, producer of the *Batman* trilogy and beneficiary of a standing distribution deal with Warner Bros., announced in 2011 the formation of Legendary East, initially partnering with China/Hong Kong producer Huayi Brothers and then with the major mainland producer China Film Co.[19] While not linked to the completed *Batman* series, the initiative shows Warner's and Legendary's substantial interest in East Asian markets.

Caped crusades and East Asian cinema

While blockbuster Hollywood movies might appear to offer viewing experiences substantively different from those supplied by more modestly scaled domestic releases, many features of the Nolan *Batman* films make them compatible with local exhibition practices and releases. The three films' lengthy running times – 140 minutes, 152 minutes and 165 minutes, respectively – help position them as prestige films competitive with, or preferable to, local productions. In China in particular, where historical epics of two and a half hours or more dominate the domestic box office, the lengthy *The Dark Knight Rises* fits easily alongside the durations of domestic releases.[20] Long running times also allow for dense plotting, and here too *The Dark Knight Rises*' multiple plots and array of central characters compares well to the dizzying multitude of characters and subplots in Chinese and Hong Kong releases. Also at the level of content, the *Batman* films' mixture of action and exposition, and in particular the provision of repeated caesuras that allow viewers to pause and reflect, match in part the textual address of prestige domestic productions in China and Japan (and, to an extent, in Korean film as well).

A brief gloss of some popular East Asian releases from the same time period serves to situate the films in a regional context. For example, the Chinese historical epic *Red Cliff*, released in two parts in 2008 and 2009, includes not only extended battle scenes and dense exposition, but also numerous static scenes in which its protagonists silently weigh their responsibilities. (Both films were hits in China, Hong Kong, Taiwan and Japan, and performed strongly in South Korea.) In Japan, the box office in recent years has been dominated by animated films, live-action manga adaptations and sequels, most with dense plotting and ensembles of main characters. Its most successful non-animated film of 2008 was *Departures*, the 130-minute drama of a depressed cellist who turns to the funerary art of 'encoffinment'. With few characters and no kinetic action, it addresses viewers with a slow pace and an emphasis on interiorised emotions. To cite another contemporaneous example, South Korea's top film of 2010, *The Man from Nowhere*, tells a, by turns, languid and violent story of a skilled loner drawn into a criminal plot; it too weaves together complicated plotting, action and many scenes of quiet interiority. Such broad textual similarities arise in part from diffuse intercultural influences. As Stephen Teo argues, 'In the Asian context, Hollywood also exerts a cultural push factor on Asian cinemas inasmuch as there is a commercialised, populist "Hollywood style" that Asian film industries adopt for their own.'[21]

However we perceive the direction of cultural influence (west to east, or vice versa, or both), the *Batman* films echo aspects of popular East Asian dramas in their length, pacing and tone. In addition, the series' fantastic subject matter offers appeals for viewers in regions where specifically 'American' content carries no special value. In Japan, the series joins the many other fantasy and science-fiction films that dominate the domestic box office. China, in comparison, lacks a generic science-fiction film tradition, but the comic book subject matter of films such as the *Batman* series enables much of their content – aside from that with specifically Chinese settings and stars –

to avoid the pitfalls of domestic censorship. The films' vigilante content, if not enacted by costumed fantasy figures who team up with local law enforcement, would likely cause problems with censors. In this respect, Batman's extralegal exploits in Hong Kong in *The Dark Knight* would seem to be a major industrial miscalculation, or alternatively a sign that Warner did not view mainland China as a significant release market in 2008. Numerous news accounts have also testified to Chinese audiences' adeptness at reading films in imaginative, allegorical terms – witness reports of *Avatar* (2009)'s reception in China as, among other things, an anti-totalitarian message film.[22] In contrast to the overtly propagandistic content of many Chinese domestic productions – from the Communist-history pageants *The Founding of a Republic* (2009) and *Beginning of the Great Revival* (2011) to the nationalist, Japan-demonising *Ip Man* (2008) and *Ip Man 2* (2010) – the *Batman* films offer spectacular action and individual and group heroism not tied to a discrete state ideology.

The *Batman* trilogy's characters, storylines, settings and dispositions may harken back to US origins, but the elasticity of the costumed vigilante Batman, and the wide range of settings and subplots across the films, helps the series intersect with East Asian generic and cultural traditions. Hong Kong has a rich history of fantasy and action films featuring soaring hand-to-hand combat, as more recently does China. Hong Kong cinema history includes abundant vigilante fighters as well. South Korean cinema has also evolved in the shadow of the country's long US military presence,[23] and its contemporary cinema (after the end of the military dictatorship in 1987) features science-fiction and monster movies, as well as the occasional costumed vigilante (such as in the 2003 parody *Save the Green Planet!*). Discussing Japan, critic Mark Schilling observes that 'Japanese pop culture, by and large, doesn't do human superheroes.'[24] Still, its cinema does include costumed characters in films such as *K-20: The Fiend with Twenty Faces* (2008) and in superhero parodies such as *Zebraman* (2004). Meanwhile, its long traditions of science fiction, robots, monsters and the supernatural in live-action cinema, anime and manga all make it a favourable reception climate for the *Batman* series – though we should not overlook the films' very modest box-office performance there.

Overall, the elasticity of the narrative universes of Batman and DC Comics in general can be easily manipulated (continuity aside) to suit many industrial agendas and audience expectations. Nolan's *Batman* films echo this process in what may appear an expressly commercial calculation, given Hollywood's history of and continued reputation for absorbing other nations' film styles and talent pools. Reimaginings and adornments to encompass East Asian locations, cultures and performers (and occasionally, industry workers such as location managers, casting teams and animators) can also be regarded, however, as dynamic forms of cultural intertextuality.[25] These sometimes compelling efforts towards interculturalisation merge characters and storyworlds originating in one creative economy with the actual or anticipated sensibilities of cultural agents in other regions. A detailed look at the series' textual innovations casts light on the ways intercultural dialogues take shape in screen texts and on the polyglot landscapes that emerge.

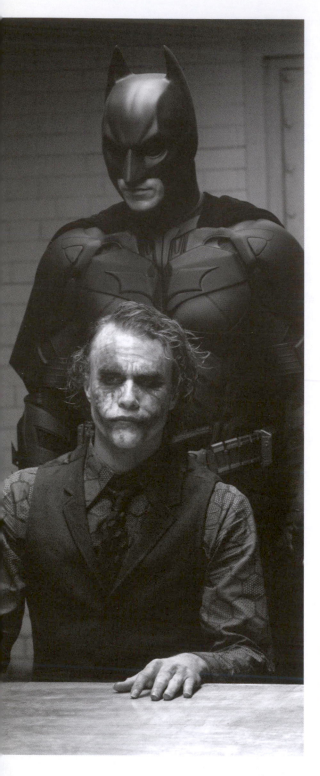

Batman goes to Bhutan

The *Batman* trilogy shows efforts both at acculturation – making its characters citizens of the world, or at least international travellers who interact with aspects of specific cultures – and at what Francis L. F. Lee terms 'de-culturation' – fashioning scenarios with suggestive but vague cultural referents.[26] In the former category, the films explicitly address Asian audiences through representations of Asian settings, characters and cultural traditions. East Asia earns a place in the contemporary *Batman* film series far beyond any other territory besides the US. All three films are set largely in the fictional Gotham City, played by Chicago in the first two films and Pittsburgh and other cities in the third. When the films (or their title character) do travel, Asia is the destination. After a brief scene set in troubled billionaire Bruce Wayne's childhood, *Batman Begins* takes viewers immediately to the adult Wayne (Christian Bale) in a Bhutanese prison. Much of the film's first act occurs in the Himalayan mountain headquarters of martial artist and eventual villain Ra's Al Ghul, whose League of Shadows trains in Japanese ninjitsu fighting, among other styles. In a brief appearance, Japan's Ken Watanabe plays the character first identified as Ra's (though a plot device later reveals him to have been a decoy for the 'real' Ra's, played by Liam Neeson).

The Dark Knight (2008)

The extensive Asia scenes, shot in the UK and at exterior locations in Iceland, are pointedly set adjacent to but not in China, given their depiction of Ra's Al Ghul conspiring with prison guards and then training for vigilante action. The film thus hails Asian audiences without risking Chinese censorship based on specific references to China.

With location filming in Hong Kong, *The Dark Knight* travels to a more recognisable, verifiable East Asia, though in doing so it sacrifices part of its potential theatrical audience. Suspicious of a potential business deal, Wayne, Batman costume in tow, trails Chinese businessman Lau (Chin Han) to Hong Kong, where action scenes ensue. Like the other films, *The Dark Knight*'s key events occur in the noirish, borderline dystopian Gotham City, so the detour here to a specific, contemporary urban area strongly indicates producers' interests in bringing East Asia into the pop Batman milieu. Director Nolan claims that the choice to film in Hong Kong was not an attempt to Asianise the series further but to provide a novel backdrop for Batman's exploits. In one of its numerous articles on the production, Hong Kong's *South China Morning Post* reports that 'Nolan said he had the idea to take Batman out of Gotham City and bring him to Hong Kong to capitalise on the spectacular skyline. "Hong Kong is really an extraordinary place to take this character out of his ordinary environment."'[27] Unsurprisingly, given film-makers' reluctance to claim that market considerations motivate production decisions, Nolan frames the location choice as conducive to characterisation and narrative. Still, Hong Kong's status as the only non-fictional city named across the trilogy indicates producers' cognisance of the East Asian market. Nolan's explanation of this creative decision is particularly notable given that the Batman character is himself extraordinary, a costumed superhero whose 'ordinary environment' is a fictional metropolis imagined as a cartoon-Expressionist dystopia in the 1980s and 90s *Batman* films and in the first two films of the Nolan trilogy. The cognitive challenge in accepting Hong Kong as 'extraordinary' relative to the fantastic Batman/Gotham milieu suggests the unusual juxtaposition of the spectacular and the quotidian *The Dark Knight*'s Hong Kong sequence provides. One objectively extraordinary setting (the fictional Gotham City) is framed as 'ordinary' within the world of the film, while an ordinary one (Hong Kong, exotic to many but also a place where millions of people live and work) is positioned as 'extraordinary' relative to Gotham. As with the Bhutan and Himalayan settings of *Batman Begins*, the Hong Kong visit here denotes both the character's and series' global perspective and awareness of difference.

Somewhat ironically, the film's presentation of Hong Kong criminality made it, as noted, unsuitable for release in mainland China. In this respect, the film continues the pattern of Hollywood studios stumbling in their moves to claim a share of the Chinese market. In preceding years, for example, Shanghai sequences in Paramount's *Mission: Impossible III* (2006) required digital alterations to shots showing laundry hanging outdoors, a routine city sight that did not fit censors' vision of an idealised Chinese metropolis. The following year, Disney's *Pirates of the Caribbean: At World's End* (2007) cast Chinese megastar Chow Yun-Fat but cut his screen time in half for the Chinese release following censors' claims that his character vilified China.[28] With its own mis-

reading of the Chinese region, *The Dark Knight* may stand as the last film to dominate the global box office without benefit of the China market.[29] As mentioned, it did solid but not quite global-blockbuster business in countries such as Japan and South Korea, suggesting that Bruce Wayne's working vacation in Hong Kong did not amount to a wholesale engagement on the film's part with East Asian markets and cultures.

The Dark Knight Rises takes a different international view, on one level thematising the anti-corporate or anti-government sentiment of the Occupy movement that began in 2011, on another conjuring a generically hellish Third World in the form of a primitive superprison, The Pit (its surrounding landscape filmed though not set in Jodhpur, in India). The film is at once the most topical entry in the series and its most abstracted from historical reality. It includes no references to countries other than the US, and while Wayne/Batman again finds himself in a secluded prison, its location is not named – Wayne's butler, Alfred (Michael Caine), coyly refers to it as 'in the more ancient part of the world'. The prison houses brown, black and white inmates of no specific origin: Britain's Tom Conti and Israeli actor Uri Gavriel, for example, play Wayne's main interlocutors there. Thus, the film's depiction of a hugely inhumane carceral colony does not risk offending any specific release market. The prison's most storied inmate turns out to be Marion Cotillard's love interest turned villainess Miranda Tate (aka Talia al Ghul), who also lacks a geographic origin, her accented speech marking her only as a generically *haute* femme-fatale figure.

In limiting specific geographic and ethnic signifiers, *The Dark Knight Rises* makes efforts to overcome the so-called 'cultural discount' that accompanies cultural commodities as they move away from their region of production.[30] For example, most viewers outside North America may disregard the series' expedient decision to reshape Gotham's skyline with each film. *The Dark Knight Rises* not only eliminates the first two films' Chicago locations but also presents a composite Gotham City built from various parts of Pittsburgh, New York City, Newark, Los Angeles and Greater London. Apart from taking advantage of particular regional production incentives, this recasting of Gotham helps transform it from the noirish, nocturnal city of the first two films into a generic municipality under siege, wintry but with abundant sunshine. Indeed, *The Dark Knight Rises*' Gotham appears mostly in daylight (making it more 'rising' than 'dark'). Director Nolan remarks that 'I made that decision [to shoot in daytime] because I thought it was the last barrier to reality we hadn't yet jumped over. [...] It's a lot easier to disguise the fanciful nature of the characters and the story when you're working in the dark.'[31] The appeal to realism fits a prevailing industrial discourse within Hollywood – where film-makers describe even physics-defying superhero films such as *Spider-Man* (2002) as 'heightened reality'[32] – but also translates to other release environments where realist dramas predominate in film and popular culture.

The noir Gotham of *Batman Begins* and *The Dark Knight* slots well into the cultural imagery of Japan, with its long tradition of noir thrillers in cinema and manifold dystopias in manga and anime, but may not register strongly elsewhere in East Asia.

The Dark Knight Rises (2012)

For example, Li Zhang notes of Chinese audiences that aside from the generation now entering adulthood, 'The majority of Chinese viewers [...] do not find the cinema genre based on [...] sci-fi images of dystopia appealing, perhaps because of the absence of such a literary tradition.'[33] Gotham City in The Dark Knight Rises instead functions as a generic urban environment, at most a surrogate New York akin to the conception of the city in the Batman comic book series.[34] The film's key action conflict involves an Occupy-like insurgency spearheaded by the monstrous Svengali Bane (Tom Hardy). Bane's legion of the dispossessed prowls the tunnels beneath the city, creating a paranoid fantasy of a subterranean urban underclass poised to cause anarchy at the expense first of the wealthy, then of the citizenry at large. Arguably, this pulpy appropriation of the global political and economic protests of 2011 and 2012 (and beyond in some places) translates as well in East Asia as in markets such as the US and UK. Moreover, The Dark Knight Rises cannily adds to its roster a virtuous young policeman, Blake (played by Joseph Gordon-Levitt), who both ties together some of the film's complicated plot strands and by association defines the masked superhero as a prosocial, law-respecting figure. Such a figure carries particular value in China, where, as Zhang observes, 'any creative works that accentuate the dark aspects of social life or even allude to the idea of dystopia become especially discordant'.[35] In the censorial Chinese market in particular, then, the addition of a straightforward representative of local authority helps shape the series' fairly confused politics towards ends unthreatening to centralised power structures.

Paradoxically, the series instalment that does not include specific East Asian characters, settings or cultural references proves the most successful in the region. In his study of the performance of Hollywood films in East Asia, Francis L. F. Lee identifies genres such as adventure and romance (broadly defined) with proven cross-cultural appeal, then suggests a tendency for successful international Hollywood releases to include not 'universal' features but 'de-culturated' ones, stripped of any cultural specificity and consequently 'not so much culturally universal as culturally empty'.[36] At one level, the Batman films' global receipts demonstrate the continued success of an industrial logic based on fantasy content with few references to social reality. The Dark Knight Rises invokes the Occupy movement's grass-roots activism chiefly to decorative and thematic ends. The allusion to the extratextual Occupy protests offers a plausible explanation for the enthusiasm of Bane's followers and provides a counterpoint to Batman's mostly solitary vigilantism, contributing to the film's thematic opposition of reflexive mob populism and legitimate consensus. (Rather than leading a cult of personality as Bane does, Batman must team up with law enforcement and government.) Superficial or not, such broad oppositions enable many interpretations, from the most abstracted to the culturally specific, and available for both pro-state and politically oppositional ends. While The Dark Knight Rises lacks the specific hailing of East Asian people and cultures of the first two films, it consolidates the representation of Gotham City as a generic global metropolis and Batman as its generic protector, aligned with the most esteemed representatives of state authority (policeman Blake in the final film, and Gary Oldman's police detective and then Commissioner James Gordon across the series). Though the textual trajectory suggests a scrubbing away of culturally specific material over the course of the series, we may also regard the case in total as indicative of Hollywood's often contradictory appeals to overseas markets. *Batman Begins* offers a suggestive jumble of East Asian content; *The Dark Knight* moves directly to a recognisable East Asia, to the distaste of major player China; and *The Dark Knight Rises* takes us to a 'more ancient part of the world' that is a showpiece of production design but emphatically not anywhere close to a real place.

The Dark Knight received

The *Batman* films' textual elements and their reception in East Asia reveal the efforts of producers and critics to articulate a cosmopolitan sensibility. Nolan and his collaborators craft a fantastic storyworld that stitches together components of the real world, including sites as remote as Bhutan, as alluring as Hong Kong or as prosaic as Pittsburgh. Correspondingly, international critics approach the films from the vantage point of cosmopolitan viewers, not as de facto provincials or even, for the most part, as cheerleaders for cities in which filming occurred. My sampling of reception material indicates that in responding to the *Batman* trilogy, professional reviewers for newspapers and entertainment publications adopt a discourse in which entertainment value rather than relevance to a particular viewing constituency is the key criterion. Exceptional cases such as editorials in propaganda outlets notwithstanding, East Asian newspapers' reviews of the films evidence consensual likes and dislikes rather than culturally divergent responses.

The somewhat delayed East Asian releases of films in the series also means that reviewers joined a cultural conversation already in progress, and begun in the US and Europe. *Batman Begins*, for example, opened in the US in mid-May 2005; then a month later, in mid-June, in Taiwan, Hong Kong and Japan; and in late June in Japan and China. In 2008, *The Dark Knight* opened in Taiwan and Hong Kong a few days after the mid-July US premiere, and in South Korea followed by Japan in early August. *The Dark Knight Rises* opened in Taiwan, Hong Kong and South Korea the same time as in the US, in mid-July 2012, then a week later in Japan, followed by China in late August. Consequently, reviews in East Asian publications tended to echo the prevailing discourse on the films in other countries rather than issuing novel, regionally focused judgments. Unprecedented extratextual events also accompanied the release of two of the three films – *The Dark Knight*, with the death of co-star Heath Ledger from a prescription-drug overdose in late January 2008, nearly six months before the film's US premiere but well into its pre-release marketing campaign; and *The Dark Knight Rises*, with the shooting of eighty-two people (twelve of whom died) at an opening-night screening in Aurora, Colorado. Commentators gave extensive coverage to Ledger's death and the mass shooting, powerfully colouring the films' reception environment worldwide.

With the notion of shared evaluative criteria in mind, the limited international variation in reviews of films in the *Batman* trilogy appears unsurprising. Reviewers for major publications – whether writing for English-language editions of those publications, or in translation[37] – responded to each of the three films in fairly consistent

ways, assessing them in culturally unspecific terms as large-scale industrial enter-
tainments. Reviews often cite the appearance of local stars and locations, though in
a chiefly descriptive rather than analytical way. For example, *Yahoo! Japan*'s short
review of *Batman Begins* notes Ken Watanabe's role in passing, and the two reviews of
The Dark Knight in Hong Kong's *South China Morning Post* mention the sequence set in
Hong Kong.[38] The second Hong Kong reviewer, James Whittle, does inject local pride
into his review by suggesting that 'Perhaps the most exciting thing is the cameo role
played by our very own city', thus hailing a specifically Hong Kong readership and
viewership. Most reviews from East Asia I sampled, however, do not discuss the films
from culturally specific vantage points or as foreign works that demand particular
translation strategies.

Still, reviewers build on the discourse of prior commentators. Even in the era of
'day-and-date' global releases, major Hollywood films often earn domestic US release
before circulating worldwide, so it is often US critics (and, of course, amateur reviewers
online) who initiate conversations about new releases. In this respect, release cycles
partly condition East Asian critics to receive Hollywood films as American exports, to
be approached with a putatively American mindset. Like many such releases, the
Batman films often premiered in East Asian territories weeks or months after their
initial US releases, so an abundance of critical commentary had already circulated
prior to the published judgments of the region's critics. In China, for example, English
editions of the dual-language *China Daily* and *Global Times* covered *The Dark Knight Rises*
repeatedly in the five-week interval between its US and Chinese releases, reporting on
the shootings in Colorado on its opening night, the film's box-office performance outside China, and more. Narratives surrounding the film had thus taken shape in print
journalism well in advance of its release in China, encouraging reception in terms of
US events and sometimes even prompting a referendum on perceived American values.
On the eve of *The Dark Knight Rises*' Chinese release, for example, the state-controlled
Xinhua News Agency circulated an article entitled 'Hollywood Blockbusters Trigger
Reflections on Heroism in China', quoting numerous Beijing filmgoers on the subjects
of heroism and justice.[39] Filmgoers may have had no special interest in such subjects,
but prompted by interviewers, their remarks nonetheless form part of the Chinese
press discourse on the film. Perhaps in response, China's Communist Party organ, the
People's Daily, invoked the film and its competitor *The Amazing Spider-Man* later in 2012
in a short editorial comparing value systems. The unnamed author asserts that 'Chinese heroes usually pursue self-improvement, which reflect [sic] Chinese values. The
over-confidence of Hollywood heroes leads to self-conceit.'[40] Notably, though, the
film's review in the *Global Times*, a sister publication of the *People's Daily*, shows no
explicit ideological preference. The review could easily appear in a US publication,
with claims such as 'if you are usually a couch-potato DVD movie watcher, you may
want to consider getting down to your local Imax to appreciate this film in all its full
technicolor [sic], CGI glory' betraying little cultural or geographic specificity.[41] Many
reviewers frame the series in terms of Hollywood's expected high production values
rather than as ideologically freighted intercultural transmissions.[42] As such, reviews

bear out Francis L. F. Lee's tentative conclusion that 'American movies have also lost some of their capability to serve as sites where intercultural communication proceeds'.[43]

Despite producers' efforts to incorporate specifically Asian characters and cultural traditions into the series, reviewers in East Asia often address the films' most generalisable content: themes of vigilantism and authority, the appeal and implications of a hero's psychological conflict, some aspects of the workings of capitalism and social class, and perhaps most prominently, aesthetic and narrative considerations of tone, pacing and the quality of action sequences and special effects. While reviewers in Japan, South Korea, Hong Kong and China all have established or burgeoning national cinemas they might use for comparison, I found no reviews from the region that judged the films alongside anything but other large-scale Hollywood releases (with preceding films in the series the most frequent point of reference, in the few cases where any comparisons appeared).[44] As in any region with a thriving film culture, reviewers in East Asia periodically use their platform to identify trends in local and international production. However, the *Batman* films engender conversations chiefly about Hollywood blockbusters, generic attributes of superhero films, and depictions of action and violence. One may be dismayed by the 'cultural emptiness' of these discussions, by their lack of cultural specificity or their largely consumerist tenor. At the same time, taking up Lee's argument, we might say that the *Batman* films' reception shows intercultural communication proceeding not through the exchange of local cultural references but through a shared cosmopolitan outlook. At the poles of cultural specificity, after all, members of different cultures have no basis for communication. The generalised discourse around the trilogy's content may lack cultural specificity but enables functional dialogue, with less lost in translation.

I conclude with anecdotal reflections on the films' local reception in one country, South Korea. Speaking broadly of the films' appeals to Korean viewers, one commentator remarks on audiences' fondness for realist dramas over films with fantasy content, and another asserts local preferences for stories of families or groups.[45] Perhaps most significantly, commentators note preferences for upbeat films and characters,[46] hardly the trilogy's chief asset, though *The Dark Knight Rises'* concluding view of a peaceful Gotham City presided over by likeable policemen may cater to such preferences. The move towards visual realism in the third film, the trilogy's narrative arc of Wayne and Batman's retreat from and then re-entry into the social fabric, and the overall emphasis not just on action set pieces but on psychological conflict and interpersonal drama, all suggest ways the films' producers attempt to engage audiences beyond delivering high production values.[47]

Overall, while these efforts have been inconsistently successful, they show how a major production will hail regional viewerships through a strategic combination of specific geographic and cultural references, generalisable narrative elements such as characters tied to families and other social groups, and abstracted themes such as hope, will and conviction. At the beginning of the trilogy, the future Batman seeks discipline and purpose in East Asia, but his film series gains traction there only when he turns away from character-building tourist excursions to act out his devotion to his friends and his fictional city. Ending with the arguably risible cliché of Wayne turning his mansion into a home for wayward orphans, the series may be faulted for its narrative simplifications and focus-grouped emotions, but across its nearly eight hours it demonstrates a range of significant strategies to address viewers in East Asia and worldwide.

Notes

1. All box-office data comes from statistics at *Box Office Mojo*. See 'Batman Begins', *Box Office Mojo*. Available at: <http://www.boxofficemojo.com/movies/?id= batmanbegins.htm>; and 'The Dark Knight', *Box Office Mojo*. Available at: <http://www.boxofficemojo.com/movies/?id=darkknight.htm>.

2. See 'The Dark Knight Rises', *Box Office Mojo*. Available at: <http://www.boxofficemojo.com/movies/?id=batman3.htm>.

3. See Motion Picture Association of America, 'Theatrical Market Statistics 2013', March 2014. Available at: <http://www.mpaa.org/wp-content/uploads/2014/03/MPAA -Theatrical-Market-Statistics-2013_032514-v2.pdf>.

4. I do not contend that the appearance of East Asian characters, locations and cultural elements in the films represents producers' deliberate efforts to exploit East Asian markets. Even if this were the case, producer and other industry discourse tends not to frame creative choices in such terms. Instead, as I partly explore in what follows, producers routinely make claims for elements seen to serve storytelling or to engage audiences in general.

5. For yearly totals for Japan, see 'Japan Yearly Box Office', *Box Office Mojo*. Available at: <http://boxofficemojo.com/intl/japan/yearly/>. Regarding the premiere at Expo 2005, see Rebecca Murray, '"Batman Begins" Premieres in Japan at the US Pavilion of the 2005 World's Fair', *About.com*, 17 February 2005. Available at: <http://movies.about.com/od/batman/a/batmanjap022005.htm>.

6. For figures for South Korea, see 'South Korea Yearly Box Office', *Box Office Mojo*. Available at: <http://boxofficemojo.com/intl/korea/yearly/>. The 2005 listing does not include a box-office ranking.

7. For example, South Korea's $42 million gross for *The Dark Knight Rises* compares to nearly $36 million in France, about $35.5 million in Germany and just under $32 million in Mexico. Among English-language markets outside the US and Canada, top performers are the UK, with over $90 million in receipts, and Australia, with over $44 million ('Dark Knight Rises', *Box Office Mojo*).

8. See country-specific data at 'Batman Begins', *Box Office Mojo*. Available at: <http://boxofficemojo.com/movies/?page=intl&country=CH&id=batmanbegins.htm>.

9. See Jacques Steinberg, 'No "Dark Knight" for China', *New York Times*, 25 December 2008. Available at: <http://www.nytimes.com/2008/12/26/movies/26arts -NODARKKNIGHT_BRF.html>. Relatedly, Jeremy Blum notes that the presence of a corrupt Chinese businessman 'as well as the depiction of Batman forcibly entering and exiting Chinese soil to apprehend a Chinese native [...] prevented the film from

being theatrically released on the mainland'. Jeremy Blum, 'The Dark Knight Rises in Hong Kong', *South China Morning Post*, 25 June 2014. Available at: <http://www.scmp.com/comment/blogs/article/1539756/dark-knight-rises-hong-kong>.

10. On the film's initial receipts, see Frank Segers, '"Dark Knight Rises" Re-Emerges No. 1 Overseas with Strong China Push', *Hollywood Reporter*, 2 September 2012. Available at: <http://www.hollywoodreporter.com/news/dark-knight-rises-china-amazing-spider-man-expendables-367485>; Stephen Cremin, 'Spider-Man Wins First Round of Superhero Duel', *Film Business Asia*, 29 August 2012. Available at: <http://www.film biz.asia/news/spider-man-wins-first-round-of-superhero-duel>; and Robert Cain, 'Spider-Man, Dark Knight Power China's 2nd Best Ever Box Office Week', *China Film Biz* (blog), 4 September 2012. Available at: <http://chinafilmbiz.wordpress.com/>. On the China Film Group's control of release dates and the duelling *Dark Knight Rises/Amazing Spider-Man* releases, see Liz Shackleton, 'DKR, Amazing Spider-Man to Open on Same Day in China', *Screen Daily*, 23 August 2012. Available at: <http://www.screendaily.com/news/asia-pacific/dkr-amazing-spider-man-to-open -on-same-date-in-china/5045601.article>; and Ben Fritz and John Horn, 'Warner, China Film Clash on "Dark Knight" Debut against "Spider-Man" (Los Angeles Times)', *China Screen News*, 12 July 2012. Available at: <http://china-screen-news.com/2012 /07/warner-china-film-clash-on-dark-knight-debut-against-spider-man-la-times/>.

11. Revenue arrangements heavily disadvantage foreign distributors, so Warner's likely received only a small share of the film's theatrical revenues.

12. For Hong Kong numbers, see 'Hong Kong Yearly Box Office', *Box Office Mojo*. Available at: <http://www.boxofficemojo.com/intl/hongkong/yearly/>.

13. For Taiwan data, see 'Taiwan Yearly Box Office', *Box Office Mojo*. Available at: <http://www.boxofficemojo.com/intl/taiwan/yearly/>. *Box Office Mojo* does not provide annual data for Taiwan after 2011, and 2005 figures do not include overall rankings. For a report on 2012 box-office leaders, see '"Life of Pi" Reaches $129.4 Million Overseas', *BoxOffice.com*, 16 December 2012. Available at: <http://www. boxoffice.com/latest-news/2012-11-25-life-of-pi-delivers-promising-overseas-debut>. *The Dark Knight Rises* was the number one film on its opening weekend in Taiwan, with more than $1 million in receipts. See Amy Kaufman, '"The Dark Knight Rises" Sends a Box Office Reminder', *Los Angeles Times*, 5 August 2012. Available at: <http://articles.latimes.com/2012/aug/05/entertainment/la-et-mn-boxoffice-20120806>.

14. In North America, the final film performed well below its predecessor: *The Dark Knight Rises* earned $448 million domestically, compared to *The Dark Knight*'s $533 million. (The disparity widens when accounting for higher ticket prices in 2012 than 2008.) The mass shootings in Aurora, Colorado, on *The Dark Knight Rises*' opening weekend in the US created intense negative publicity, but no industry analysts strongly suggested that those events depressed the film's long-term US box-office receipts.

15. On sites such as *Box Office Mojo*, the other East Asian market, Macau, does not receive individual statistics.

16. Emilie Yueh-yu Yeh, 'Home Is Where Hollywood Isn't: Recasting East Asian Film Industries', *Media Industries* vol. 1 no. 2 (2014), p. 60.

17. Kyung Hyun Kim, *Virtual Hallyu: Korean Cinema of the Global Era* (Durham, NC: Duke University Press, 2011), p. 27.

18. See Patrick Frater, 'China Confirms Unchanged Import Quota System', *Variety*, 12 February 2014. Available at: <http://variety.com/2014/biz/news/china-confirms-unchanged-import-quota-system-1201099541/>.

19. See Marc Graser, 'Legendary East Finds Key Partner in China Film Co.', *Variety*, 30 May 2013. Available at: <http://variety.com/2013/film/news/legendary-east-finds-key-partner-in-china-film-co-1200489836/>.

20. China's top films of 2010, for example, were the 135-minute *Aftershock* and the 132-minute *Let the Bullets Fly*. The top domestic releases of 2011 were the 146-minute *The Flowers of War*, the 122-minute *Flying Swords of Dragon Gate* and the 124-minute *Beginning of the Great Revival*. The mid-length comedy *Lost in Thailand* topped the box office in 2012 but was trailed by the 3-D upgrade of the 194-minute *Titanic* (1997) and the 131-minute *Painted Skin: The Resurrection*.

21. Stephen Teo, *The Asian Cinema Experience: Styles, Spaces, Theory* (London: Routledge, 2013), p. 233.

22. On *Avatar* in China, see Lifang He, '*Avatar* and Chinese Fan Culture', in Henry Jenkins, 'What the Chinese Are Making of *Avatar*', *henryjenkins.org*, 12 March 2010. Available at: <http://henryjenkins.org/2010/03/avatar_and_chinese_fan_culture.html>. Lifang He cites, for example, blogger Chengpeng Li's comparison of Na'vi characters forced off their land with the real-world Chinese equivalent.

23. For an examination of US pop culture's inroads into South Korea thanks to the US military's TV network, see Christina Klein, 'The AFKN Nexus: US Military Broadcasting and New Korean Cinema', *Transnational Cinemas* vol. 3 no. 1 (May 2012), pp. 19–39.

24. Mark Schilling, 'Dueling with a Rare Japanese Superhero', *Japan Times*, 25 December 2008. Available at: <http://www.japantimes.co.jp/culture/2008/12/25/films/dueling-with-a-rare-japanese-superhero/>.

25. For more on global film appropriations of figures such as Batman, see Iain Robert Smith, *The Hollywood Meme* (Edinburgh: Edinburgh University Press, 2015), as well as Smith's chapter in this book.

26. See Francis L. F. Lee, 'Hollywood Movies in East Asia: Examining Cultural Discount and Performance Predictability at the Box Office', *Asian Journal of Communication*, vol. 18 no. 2 (June 2008), p. 133.

27. Barclay Crawford and Kelly Chan, 'Crowds Flock to Greet Batman', *South China Morning Post*, 10 November 2007. Available at: <http://www.scmp.com/article/615071/crowds-flock-greet-batman>.

28. On the *Pirates* cuts, see Clifford Coonan, '"Pirates" Edited for China Release', *Variety*, 11 June 2007. Available at: <http://variety.com/2007/film/news/pirates-edited-for-china-release-1117966663/>; and Chris V. Thangham, 'China Censors "Pirates of the Caribbean 3" for "Vilifying Chinese"', *Digital Journal*, 15 June 2007. Available at: <http://digitaljournal.com/article/196046>.

29. As I have noted, *The Dark Knight* was a hit in Hong Kong, though its returns there were on a par with receipts in small countries such as Denmark, Sweden and Holland, places not often viewed as central to Hollywood studios' global strategies.

30. On the notion of cultural discount, see Colin Hoskins and Rolf Mirus, 'Reasons for the US Dominance of the International Trade in Television Programmes', *Media, Culture and Society*, vol. 10 (October 1988), pp. 499–515.

31. Quoted in Iain Stasukevich, 'Batman to the Max', *American Cinematographer* vol. 93 no. 8 (August 2012), p. 38.

32. Interviewed in 2002, *Spider-Man* cinematographer Don Burgess described the film's aesthetic in these terms. Jay Holben, 'Spider's Stratagem', *American Cinematographer* vol. 83 no. 6 (June 2002), p. 35.

33. Li Zhang, 'Postsocialist Urban Dystopia?', in Gyan Prakash (ed.), *Noir Urbanisms* (Princeton, NJ: Princeton University Press, 2010), p. 146.

34. The DC Comics Universe has historically used New York City as the model for both Batman's Gotham City and Superman's Metropolis.

35. Zhang, 'Postsocialist Urban Dystopia?', p. 144.

36. Lee, 'Hollywood Movies in East Asia', p. 133. Leaving others to probe the specifics of 'de-culturation', Lee offers a largely macroeconomic analysis, not naming individual films.

37. For overseas reviews, I turn to regional English-language newspapers such as the Tokyo-based *Japan Times* and Hong Kong's *South China Morning Post*, and to English-language blogs with Asian perspectives such as the Japan-centred *Mochi Bytes* (www.mochibytes.com). I also use the admittedly imperfect Google Translate tool to scan reviews and commentary in foreign-language publications online.

38. See, respectively, Orita Chizuko, '*Batman Begins*' (film review), *Yahoo! Japan*, 14 June 2005. Available at: <http://info.movies.yahoo.co.jp/detail/tydt/id321232/>; Clarence Tsui, '*The Dark Knight*' (film review), *South China Morning Post*, 17 July 2008. Available at: <http://www.scmp.com/article/645568/darkknight>; and James Whittle, 'Out of the Bat Cave' (film review), *South China Morning Post*, 20 July 2008. Available at: <http://www.scmp.com/article/645961/out-bat-cave>. Whittle says, for example, that 'Perhaps the most exciting thing is the cameo role played by our very own city: yes, Batman comes to Hong Kong. The beautiful Central skyline is a brilliant backdrop as Batman glides in and out of the shadows of the IFC towers.'

39. See Xinhua News Agency, 'Hollywood Blockbusters Trigger Reflections on Heroism in China', *Global Times*, 27 August 2012. Available at: <http://www.globaltimes.cn/content/729367.shtml>.

40. *China Daily* offers excerpts from the editorial; see 'What Makes a True Hero?', *China Daily*, 11 October 2012. Available at: <http://europe.chinadaily.com.cn/opinion/2012-10/11/content_15812055.htm>.

41. Miranda Shek, 'Bat's All Folks!' (film review), *Global Times*, 29 August 2012. Available at: <http://www.globaltimes.cn/content/729838.shtml>.

42. I recognise that by focusing my search on English-language publications, I do not offer the full picture of what East Asian reviewers communicate to readers in their

own languages. Some English-language papers in East Asia, such as Taiwan's *Taipei Times*, simply gather reviews from American newspapers and English-language wire services. Still, English editions of East Asian publications give some sense of how official or professional voices in those territories frame the films for international readerships.

43. Lee, 'Hollywood Movies in East Asia', p. 133.

44. Though not a film review as such, a *HanCinema* commentary article does offer textual comparisons (mostly around genre attributes) of US and Korean films competing for box-office dominance in 2012. See '"The Dark Knight Rises" vs. "The Avengers": What Does It Take to Be Number One in Korea?', *HanCinema* (online), 21 July 2012. Available at: <http://www.hancinema.net/hancinema-s-film-corner-the-dark-knight-rises-vs-the-avengers-what-does-it-take-to-be-number-one-in-korea-45502.html>.

45. The *HanCinema* website's anonymous writer asserts that 'A quick look at the highest grossing Korean films of 2012 [...] will show that dramas, more specifically melodramas, are what local audiences relate to the most. [...] America [sic] dramas don't do well in Korea because they exist more in realm [sic] of fantasy than a down-to-earth drama.' Commenting on the post, Esther Cotton remarks further that 'the Dark Knight is a lone fighter. In Korean culture, groups/teams/families are a central part to the culture, and so to watch a movie where friends ban [sic] together to fight is key. Likewise, in The Avengers there is some sort of familial presence ... like Thor and Loki as brothers. Family and fighting with or against family is yet another aspect that I think appeals to a Korean audience.' See '"The Dark Knight Rises" vs. "The Avengers"'.

46. A *Cinefantastique* reporter, for example, notes that 'apparently, Korean audiences have a tendancy [sic] to prefer more upbeat characters like Spider-Man and Superman and the recent Iron Man, as opposed to darker anti-heroes like Batman'. See Steve Biodrowski, 'Batman Flies to Korea', *Cinefantastique* (online), 25 August 2008. Available at: <http://cinefantastiqueonline.com/2008/08/clybersurfing-batman-flies-to-korea/>.

47. Film-makers and stars have also used personal appearances and social media to connect with potential viewers. For example, director Nolan participated in an online forum with Korean fans in summer 2012, name-checking recent crime film *The Chaser* (2011) to demonstrate his own investment in South Korean film culture. See 'Batman Director Chats Online with Korean Fans', *The Chosunilbo*, 11 July 2012. Available at: <http://english.chosun.com/site/data/html_dir/2012/07/11/2012071101316.html>.

8

BATSPLOITATION
PARODIES, FAN FILMS AND REMAKES
Iain Robert Smith

On 20 July 2012, a new Batman feature film was released to audiences worldwide. Directed by a film-maker with an established auteur reputation, the film included a number of elements adapted from the 1980s Batman graphic novels and was celebrated by critics for 'having costumes that are often startlingly faithful to the comic book visuals'.[1] Promoted with the tagline 'A Legend Will Rise', the poster for the film featured a low-angle shot of Batman framed by crumbling skyscrapers in the shape of the Bat-logo. In addition, the film presented a noticeably darker and more cynical interpretation of the Batman universe than earlier film adaptations. Reflecting the increased prominence of superhero films within contemporary American cinema, the film was a follow-up to one of the most commercially successful comic book adaptations of all time.

Quick Bat-test: What film am I describing? Despite appearances, I am not referring to the official Warner Bros. Pictures release *The Dark Knight Rises* (2012), the final instalment in Christopher Nolan's trilogy of Batman adaptations. Rather, I am describing the resolutely unofficial Vivid Entertainment release *The Dark Knight XXX: A Porn Parody* (2012), Axel Braun's sequel to his earlier *Batman XXX* (2010), a film that I would contend is just as significant as Nolan's work to an understanding of the Batman intertext within contemporary culture. This is because the film exemplifies a phenomenon that I term Batsploitation – describing the unofficial appropriations of the Batman franchise that circulate freely without any form of licensing from DC Comics.

Since the publication of *The Many Lives of the Batman* in 1991, the academic study of Batman has done much to interrogate the intertextual dynamics of the franchise. In their introduction to that collection, Roberta Pearson and William Uricchio highlight the 'complex synchronic and diachronic intertextual frame'[2] that is formed by the simultaneous presence of a wide variety of differing incarnations of the Batman. Similarly, in his recent book *Hunting the Dark Knight*, Will Brooker outlines the ways in which Christopher Nolan's Batman films combine a number of disparate elements from this 'ongoing, ever-growing, multimedia matrix of Batman stories'.[3] Up till now, however, these intertextual analyses have focused on the officially licensed uses of the character. What is missing from these discussions is an engagement with the many Batman adaptations that were not licensed. From Andy Warhol's *Batman Dracula* (1964) through to René Cardona's *La mujer murciélago* (*The Bat Woman* [1968]), and from Axel

Braun's porn parodies through to Aaron Schoenke's fan films, the character has appeared in a multiplicity of narrative incarnations beyond the control of the intellectual property holders. If we are truly to understand the intertextual frame through which audiences and producers perceive the Batman, we need to move beyond a focus that is limited to official incarnations of the character.

This chapter, therefore, provides a sustained examination of Batsploitation,[4] focusing in particular on three distinct, although interrelated, historical conjunctures. Firstly, the chapter situates these borrowings in relation to traditions of global exploitation cinema, analysing the post-1966 trend for exploitation films that appropriate elements from the Batman franchise, such as Jerry Warren's US feature *The Wild World of Batwoman* (1966) and Artemio Marquez's Filipino spoof *James Batman* (1966). Secondly, the chapter examines the numerous Batman fan films that appeared in the early 2000s, with a focus on Sandy Collora's *Batman: Dead End* (2003) and Aaron Schoenke's *Batman: City of Scars* (2010). Finally, the chapter interrogates the adult parodies of the franchise, including the Seduction Cinema spoof *Batbabe: The Dark Knightie* (2009) and Axel Braun's *Batman XXX*. Paying close attention to the variety of ways that the textual signifiers of the Batman franchise are utilised across these different cultural contexts, the chapter considers what they can each tell us about those processes of adaptation that exist at the fringes of intellectual property law.

Part of what makes this so significant is that Batman is not simply a character, but also the intellectual property of DC Comics Inc., a subsidiary of Warner Bros. Entertainment. Throughout the many official incarnations of the Batman franchise, there is a credit asserting that 'Batman and all related characters and elements are trademarks of and © DC Comics.'[5] Furthermore, the Bat-logo itself functions both diegetically and extradiegetically as a brand marker that serves to unify a diverse range of texts. According to Will Brooker, this means that 'Batman – the character, the concept, the cultural icon – is about strategic branding at every level, in a way and to an extent that escapes all other major superheroes.'[6] Yet, as Paul Grainge has argued, the meaning of a brand

> is not simply determined by those who circulate and co-ordinate mass media representations but is also forged in cultural instances where texts, symbols and images are used by social agents, interpreted by audiences and taken up by fan groups in potentially unforeseen ways.[7]

The Bat-logo may be intended as a consistent and coherent trademark that, as Pearson and Uricchio say, 'carries an unchanging set of meanings across a range of diverse creative interpretations',[8] but, as we will see, the meaning of the Batman is not so easily controlled by the rights holder.

Global Batsploitation from Gotham to Manila

In 1966, at the height of the Batmania surrounding the television series, RCA Victor released a 7" single of Neal Hefti's Batman theme song along with a full album entitled

Batman Theme and 11 Hefti Bat Songs. Meanwhile, actors Adam West, Frank Gorshin and Burgess Meredith all released their own Batman-themed singles to capitalise on the popularity of the show. This was far from the only Batman music released that year, however, as in the following months at least thirty-three unofficial covers of the Batman theme song came out.[9] This was a truly transnational phenomenon, with cover versions being recorded in Denmark by Melvis & His Gentlemen, in Argentina by The Korvals, in the Netherlands by De Maskers and Lions Sound, in Austria by The V-Rangers, in Germany by Orchester Friedel Berlipp and in Italy by Ettore Cenci Guitar Trio, not to mention the numerous American bands who also released their own take on Neal Hefti's iconic composition. In the years following that flurry of releases, many more musicians have recorded their own versions of the Batman theme, including the Sun Ra Arkestra, The Jam, The Who and The Ventures.

The proliferation of the theme song reflects a wider global phenomenon whereby a number of elements borrowed from the Batman TV series were being freely adapted and used in unofficial versions. This was especially true within the world of the exploitation film, an area of cinematic production that has long been associated with a tendency to imitate and adapt popular material in a way that circumnavigates copyright laws. As Ian Hunter has noted in his work on the intertexts surrounding *Jaws* (1975), 'exploitation films often explicitly imitate other movies, cannibalising their titles, concepts and publicity gimmicks'.[10] This has a long history within American cinema, from Irvin Berwick's *The Monster of Piedras Blancas* (1959), which was closely modelled on *The Creature from the Black Lagoon* (1954), through to Roger Corman's production *Galaxy of Terror* (1981), which borrowed much of its plot and iconography from *Alien* (1979). The practice is exemplified today by the studio Asylum Pictures, who are best known for producing low-budget imitations of the latest Hollywood releases, often with near-identical titles such as *Snakes on a Train* (2006), *The Day the Earth Stopped* (2008) and *The Amityville Haunting* (2011). These exploitation versions are usually, although not always, timed to coincide with the major release that they are imitating, and it is this associative relationship that is key to their success.

Within the context of the Batmania of the 1960s, it was the ABC television series that would became the model for subsequent exploitation versions around the world. Most representative of this process was Jerry Warren's *The Wild World of Batwoman*. While not the first unofficial Batman feature film – that credit goes to Andy Warhol's never completed *Batman Dracula*[11] – Warren's film was the first to attempt to capitalise on the popularity of the television show. It is notable, however, that even though critic Fred Beldin may describe *The Wild World of Batwoman* as a 'rip-off hack job no matter how you slice it',[12] the film actually contains very few of the core components from the Batman franchise. In Chapter 13 of this collection, Pearson and Uricchio discuss the strategies used by DC to fix and stabilise the character and identify five key components of the character, without which the Batman 'ceases to be the Batman'.[13] These are the 'events; recurrent supporting characters; setting and iconography'.[14] It is notable, therefore, that: a) the central character played by Katherine Victor displays almost none of the recognised traits of either Batman or Batwoman; b) the film contains no reference to any of the established events from the comic books; c) it does not feature any of the supporting characters from the franchise; and d) it is not even set in Gotham City.

The only one of the core components to appear in this adaptation is the iconography – specifically the Bat-logo. While Victor's costume is notably different from any official incarnation of Batwoman, she does have the Bat-logo drawn on her body above her chest. This feature is displayed on all the posters for the film and implies a clear association with the official franchise. Moreover, the pop art visual style of the TV series is also replicated in the trailer for the film, announcing in blocky comic style text that this is 'Batmania at its battiest!' and that these are 'All new adventures of the greatest, the maddest, evil-fighter in the world!'[15] Warren is not so much producing a Batman film complete with consistent characterisation, setting and events but instead appropriating the iconography of the Batman franchise in order to draw attention to his work through that intertextual relationship. This is representative of a trend within exploitation versions more generally, where the film-maker borrows elements of the iconography from the source text, making explicit use of this in the promotional materials such as posters and trailers, but then showing little interest in utilising further elements from the source in the film itself.

Of course, on a certain level, all forms of adaptation are exploitation in this sense. When *The Dark Knight Rises* was released, it was also capitalising on the established consumer knowledge and interest in the Batman franchise. However, as Ian Hunter observes, the distinction is in the way they relate to copyright law:

> Exploitation and adaptation differ insofar as adaptation typically implies an acknowledged and, if copyright is relevant, legitimately purchased relationship with a prior text usually in another medium. An exploitation film that copies another film, as a short cut to establishing a relationship with an audience, is constrained to play a different intertextual game from a conventional adaptation.[16]

In other words, while traditional adaptations often face pressure to be ostensibly faithful to their sources, exploitation versions instead face pressure to make enough changes to avoid accusations of plagiarism.[17] This means that, although exploitation film-makers may utilise some of the core components of the franchise, they are generally wary of replicating much material beyond that required to establish an association in the minds of the audience.

Copyright is not the only structural factor shaping these decisions, however. Even when we look internationally at film-makers in countries that were much less at risk of being sued by DC, the core components of the character were still rarely utilised. In the years immediately following the 1966 Batman TV series, a number of unofficial Batman films were produced outside of the USA, including films made in Turkey, the Philippines and Mexico. As with *The Wild World of Batwoman*, the Mexican adaptation of the franchise, *La mujer murciélago*, utilised a female Batman and displayed little interest in recreating aspects of the setting, characters or narrative from the official series.

Instead, director René Cardona transplanted the character into a Mexican wrestling format that is more commonly associated with luchadores like Santo and The Blue Demon. As before, the only element of the film that is consistent with the official Batman franchise is the iconography, and here it is the costume, including the distinctive Batman cape and mask that is recreated, albeit now combined with a bikini.

Four years later, the Turkish industry produced its own take on the Batwoman character titled *Uçan kiz* (*Flying Girl* [1972]). While that film is now lost, another Turkish Batman film was released the following year, reflecting the prolific cycle of Turkish reworkings of American film and television that flourished during that period.[18] In common with other Turkish comic book adaptations such as *3 dev adam* (*3 Mighty Men* [1973]), in which Captain America joins forces with Santo the wrestler to battle with an evil Spider-Man, *Yarasa adam* (*Bat Man* [1973]) does not attempt to recreate the core components of the Batman source. Far removed from the depiction of Batman enshrined in DC's Batbible, this incarnation of the character smokes heavily, sleeps around, visits strip clubs and even uses a gun. As with *La mujer murciélago*, in which Batwoman had been adapted to fit with the generic conventions of a Mexican wrestling film, *Yarasa adam* follows the pulpy exploitation format prevalent throughout Turkish cinema of the 1970s, and in which Levent Çakır had already starred as Superman, The Phantom and the Italian comic book hero Zagor.[19]

While both Mexico and Turkey produced their own takes on the Batman mythos, there is no other nation – aside from the United States – that has produced as many Batman films as the Philippines. These adaptations appeared from the 1960s onwards, and include *Batman Fights Dracula* (1966), *Alyas Batman at Robin* (*Alias Batman and Robin*, 1966) and *Fight Batman Fight* (1973). While most of these films have sadly now been lost, one that has survived is *James Batman*, in which the popular screen comedian Dolphy takes on the dual role of both Batman and James Bond. Following our two protagonists as they reluctantly team up to fight crime together, the film is capitalising on the contemporaneous popularity of the Adam West Batman and the Sean Connery James Bond. Indeed, Dolphy had already established himself in the Bond role in the earlier spoofs *Dolpinger* (1965) and *Dr Yes* (1965). While the film is set in Manila and includes none of the other recurrent characters from the Batman franchise aside from Robin, it does feature Dolphy in a relatively close recreation of the TV series costume and also utilises a cover of the Batman TV theme.

As should be clear, it is notable that it is primarily the TV series that is the source text for all of these exploitation versions. Richard Berger has identified in his work on Richard Donner's *Superman* (1978) that 'an adaptation can become canonical, and eventually the central text',[20] and what we see here is that it is the Batman TV series, not the comics or the serials, which has become the central text. Even the exploitation films that appeared in the wake of *Batman* in 1989, such as the Mexican parody *La verdadera historia de Barman y Droguin* (*The True Story of Barman and Droguin* [1991]) and the Filipino spoof *Alyas Batman en Robin* (*Alias Batman and Robin* [1993]), were modelled on the 1960s TV series rather than the contemporaneous Tim Burton film. Moreover, throughout these examples of global Batsploitation, we see how the iconography of the TV series has been unmoored from its relationship with the official canon, and is instead being used primarily as an exploitable element to draw attention to these low-budget feature films.

Henry Jenkins has identified a shift in the 1980s in the way in which the comics industry looked at the superhero genre, 'away from focusing primarily on building up continuity within the fictional universe and towards the development of multiple and contradictory versions of the same characters functioning as it were in parallel universes'.[21] What we find in looking at these exploitation versions is that this multiplicity was evident well before 1980, with Batman appearing as a promiscuous, gun-toting anti-hero in Turkey, as a bikini-clad wrestler in Mexico and as a sidekick to James Bond in the Philippines. The migrations of this shifting signifier point to the fluidity of intertextual processes when we move beyond the officially licensed uses of a character. As we have seen, the one consistent element in these exploitation versions is the iconography, and especially the Bat-logo. This marker of brand identity is therefore less an indicator of consistency and coherence than an exploitable element used to capitalise upon the global popularity of the character.

The rise of the fan film

While a handful of unofficial Batman exploitation films continued to appear in later years, it was the rise of the fan film in the 2000s that marked a shift in the ways the character was being used outside of the official franchise. As I will now outline, while the exploitation films rarely recreated the core elements of the source, the fan films were regularly marked by a self-conscious attempt to be faithful to the comic books – often in implicit contradistinction with the official adaptations. Of course, the word faithful raises theoretical complexities. I should be clear that I am not claiming that these fan films actually were more faithful to the canonical Batman. As Robert Stam, Linda Hutcheon, Thomas Leitch and others have argued,[22] we need to avoid simply replicating reductive value judgments whereby adaptations are judged on their supposed fidelity to their source. Not only do such assessments rest upon problematic notions of originality and literary value, but they also assume the identification of an intangible essence at the heart of a source text that an adaptation can capture. There is no single Batman urtext, but even if there were one, I agree with Leitch that fidelity would be a 'hopelessly fallacious measure of a given adaptation's value'.[23] Nevertheless, it is clear that fidelity is a concept that continues to have currency within the production and reception of fan films, and I am therefore using the term here to refer to the ways in which film-makers and audiences make sense of these intertextual relationships with the official Batman franchise.

In his work on convergence culture, Henry Jenkins has discussed the Star Wars fan films that surrounded the release of the digitally enhanced original Star Wars trilogy in 1997 and the subsequent release of The Phantom Menace in 1999. Focusing on films such as Quentin Tarantino's Star Wars (1998) and Troops (1998) that rework characters, situations and material from George Lucas's series, Jenkins argues that the Star Wars fan films represent an intersection between two significant cultural trends. On the one hand, 'the corporate movement towards media convergence' and, on the other, 'the unleashing of significant new tools which enable the grassroots archiving, annotation, appropriation, and recirculation of media content'.[24] For Jenkins, the fans' appropriation of elements from the *Star Wars* universe therefore illustrates a democratisation of the means of cultural production such that media fans are now 'active participants within the current media revolution'.[25]

It should be noted, however, that these media fans are not necessarily functioning outside of the commercial realm and that there is much overlap between fandom and the commercial film industry. The film that best illustrates this intersection is also the one that kick-started much of the trend for superhero fan films, Sandy Collora's *Batman: Dead End*. While the film has been celebrated for being supposedly faithful to the comic books – director and fan Kevin Smith calling it 'possibly the truest, best Batman movie ever made'[26] – it is important that we recognise the commercial and industrial factors that helped shape this claim to fidelity.

The film was premiered at the San Diego Comic-Con and, despite predating the launch of YouTube, became one of the earliest viral internet videos, being downloaded over 600,000 times in the first week.[27] Part of the reason for the interest in the film was that it envisioned a three-way battle between Batman, the Predator and the Alien – evoking the crossover Dark Horse comic series *Batman/Aliens* (1998). More significantly, however, in generating this flurry of interest, it was seen to be adapting the darker Batman character of the comic books in response to 'Schumacher's overly-cartoony version of the Dark Knight'[28] in *Batman & Robin* (1997). This was a Batman modelled on Alex Ross's vision of the character, complete with the distinctive grey-and-black costume – leading the artist himself to declare that this was 'Batman the way I've always wanted to see him.'[29] Unlike the exploitation versions discussed in the previous section, the fan film was utilising a number of the core components derived from its source, in this case the 1980s comic books.

There was more to this film, however, than a fan producing a tribute to the comic books. Before making the film, director Sandy Collora had been employed for a number of years as a concept artist and sculptor within Hollywood, working on the concept designs for *Predator 2* (1990), *The Crow* (1994), *Men in Black* (1997) and *Dogma* (1999). The film was a highly professional production and contained input from a number of industry practitioners including sculptor Henry Alvarez, who had previously worked on *Predator* (1987), *RoboCop* (1987) and *Total Recall* (1990). For many critics, this meant that the film was less a tribute to Batman and more a promotional video for Collora himself. Eric Campos in *Film Threat*, for example, argued that *Batman: Dead End* may be 'geek eye candy' but 'what we have here is more of a director's reel piece for Sandy Collora, rather than an actual film. It's a commercial made by Sandy Collora to sell Sandy Collora and comic book fans are buying.'[30] Interestingly, this is not actually something that Collora denies, admitting in an interview, 'I made this film as a showcase or calling card for my filmmaking abilities.'[31] In a parallel to exploitation strategies, we can see here the industrial function of Collora's choice to produce a Batman fan film. While it may have been celebrated as a more 'faithful' incarnation of the character than the official adaptations, the film was primarily a strategy to build Collora's profile within the film industry, and capitalised upon the fan interest in the Batman franchise in order to generate this attention.

Batman: Dead End was the first fan film to gain this level of exposure, although Collora's film has subsequently been overshadowed by the work of Aaron Schoenke. Starting in 2003 with Batman Beyond: Year One (2003), Schoenke has produced a series of fan films featuring Batman, including Dark Justice (2003), Patient J (2005) and Batman Legends (2006). By far his most ambitious work, however, was 2010's City of Scars, which was shot on a budget of $27,000 and subsequently built up over 2,100,000 views on YouTube.[32] The film focuses on the psychological relationship between Batman and the Joker, and the traumatic underpinnings of Batman's quest for revenge. For many of the fans, this was a marker of the film's fidelity to the darker, more psychologically complex world of the 1980s comic books. As Mark Reinhart observes,

> City of Scars was certainly not a production that rivalled the overall scope and quality of Warner's best Batman films. But even still, it could be argued that its powerful interpretation of Batman and his world was far closer in look and spirit to the character's best comic adventures than any of Warner's Batman efforts.[33]

The film was followed the next year by the sequel, Seeds of Arkham (2011), and Schoenke was quite self-conscious about catering to this fan interest in fidelity, promising that 'there are a lot of things that fans will appreciate in this one',[34] including the use of an authentic 1989 Batmobile, and the appearance of villains Poison Ivy and Killer Croc. Throughout these fan films, there is an investment in catering to fans of the comic books and claiming a sense of fidelity to the source material – often in an implicit or explicit contrast with the official film adaptations. Nevertheless, we should not forget that these fan films still function within a commercial environment and they are often being used as calling cards to break into the commercial film industry. Both of the fan film-makers I have been discussing are in the process of shifting to feature film-making, with Collora having already directed one feature film, Hunter Prey (2010), and Schoenke in the process of putting together a project with Lions Gate Entertainment.

Aside from this fan-industrial strategy, however, what is striking about these fan films is the emphasis that is placed upon recreating the core components of the Batman character, and especially the 1980s comic book incarnations. While a number of fan films, including Batman Evolution (2014), have attempted to remake the 1960s TV series, and there have even been some (such as Batman: Death Wish [2012]) that pay tribute to the Joel Schumacher films, the majority of the fan films produced in this period have adapted the grittier, darker Batman from the 1980s comic books. Unlike the exploitation versions, which often retained only minimal indicators of the Batman franchise, these fan films were far more invested in reproducing the core traits, events, characters and settings associated with the official Batman texts, and predominantly those established within this specific era of the character.

This Ain't *Batman XXX*

The differences I have outlined between the exploitation versions and the fan films are also reflected in a historical shift within the pornography industry. In 1996, when Peter Lehman published the first academic scholarship on porn parodies, he noted that most of the films 'have little or no iconographic connection with their original and they remain, in effect, one-joke remakes'.[35] He was specifically discussing the *Twin Peaks* (1990) parody *Twin Cheeks* (1990), but this same observation holds true for other examples from that era, including *2069: A Sex Odyssey* (1974), *Backside to the Future* (1986), *Sex Trek: The Next Penetration* (1990), *Edward Penishands* (1991) and *Buffy the Vampire Layer* (1997). Beyond a pun in the title and a limited attempt to recreate some of the recognisable costumes, these films rarely included any of the core components of the source text they were adapting.

This is reflected in the Batman pornography that was produced over this period, including *Bat Pussy* (1973), widely considered by fans to be 'the worst porn film ever made',[36] *Bathman dal pianeta Eros* (*Bathman from Planet Eros* [1982]), an Italian porn film that portrays Batman as an alien from the planet Eros, and *Bat Bitch* (1989), a comparatively generic porn feature that has very little connection to the Batman franchise other than the use of a Bat-mask. As we saw in the exploitation versions of the Batman franchise, these films utilise the iconography of the TV series but retain almost none of the other core components of the character.

In the last decade, however, porn parodies have attempted to recreate much more of their source material. As Bethan Jones has recently discussed in relation to *The Sex Files: A Dark XXX Parody* (2009), porn films no longer ignore the themes, settings and plotlines of their sources; instead films like *The Sex Files*, based on *The X-Files* (1993–), draw 'on both canon and fan fiction'[37] in their adaptations.

Indeed, this link with fan fiction is at the core of this historical development, as I would contend that the current cycle of porn parodies resembles less the exploitation features that I discussed earlier than a commercialised form of fan film. While the current cycle is dominated by hardcore features produced by the major studios Vivid and Hustler, we can identify the beginnings of this shift in the cycle of softcore spoofs produced by Seduction Cinema throughout the 1990s and 2000s. Generally circulated in tandem with the home video releases of the latest Hollywood blockbusters, this cycle of softcore parodies was intended to capitalise on the hype surrounding the mainstream films they remade.[38] While the films were given punning titles such as *Lord of the G-Strings* (2003), *Playmate of the Apes* (2002) or *Kinky Kong* (2006), they also contained a substantial amount of material recreating and spoofing sequences from their sources. *Batbabe: The Dark Knightie*, for example, plays with a number of elements from the franchise, including Christian Bale's distinctive Batman voice, the camp aesthetic of Joel Schumacher's films and even the Boom! Kapow! Sock! fight sequences from the 1960s TV series. Relying on a certain level of knowledge of the official franchise for this spoofing to function, *Batbabe* exemplifies a shift towards the incorporation of recognisable aesthetic elements into the porn remake. While *Batbabe* was the final porn remake from Seduction Cinema, and signalled the end of this particular cycle of softcore parodies, this aspect of the porn remake phenomenon would be taken up by a number of subsequent hardcore features released by the major adult studios. Hustler, for example, launched their 'This Ain't' parody film series that same year with *This Ain't Avatar XXX* (2009) and the series now comprises over forty-nine titles, including *This Ain't Curb Your Enthusiasm XXX* (2010), *This Ain't Fox News XXX* (2011), *This Ain't Game of Thrones XXX* (2014), *This Ain't Happy Days XXX* (2009) and *This Ain't Terminator XXX* (2013). Yet, while Hustler has had a great deal of success with this series, it is Vivid's Superhero label that currently dominates the hardcore feature-film parody market.[39] Responsible for generating much of the interest in this cycle, the film which launched the label was Axel Braun's *Batman XXX: A Porn Parody*, a spoof of the 1960s TV series that went on to become the best-selling adult title of 2010.[40]

Unlike the film-makers behind the earlier hardcore parodies, Braun was very invested in displaying his fidelity to the official franchise, utilising an original Bat-mobile car and even tracking down the same fabric and dyes used in the TV series for the costumes. What we see here is an increasingly blurred division between the commercial and non-commercial uses of the character, with Braun himself claiming that he is 'basically making fan films with boobs ... for people who are fans of the source material'.[41] Reflecting this strategy, the film contains a number of inside jokes aimed at knowledgeable fans, such as having actor Randy Spears cover his moustache with white make-up in a reference to Cesar Romero's refusal to shave in the original series. When Braun was asked how close to the original series he was attempting to get, he responded: 'As close as I can get to the spirit of the characters, and to the look and feel of the source material.'[42] Of course, this is partly a public-facing strategy designed to appeal to a certain segment of the fan market, but nevertheless it does reflect a committed attempt to recreate the core components of the source text. Utilising this fidelity strategy, Braun has quickly established himself as a brand name within the adult industry, and the full title of his latest feature reflects this reputation as an auteur with a distinctive aesthetic: *Snow White XXX: An Axel Braun Parody* (2014).

As we have seen in this section, the line between commercial and non-commercial exploitation of the Batman property is becoming increasingly difficult to define. Porn parodies and fan films, if discussed at all, are usually contrasted along commercial lines. Paul Booth, for example, argues that 'porn parody is overtly commercial and emphasizes a producer-led creation, while slash fandom is overtly non-commercial and has the potential to overturn the producer/consumer dialectic'.[43] Yet, although Axel Braun's decision to produce 'fan films with boobs' may have been a highly successful commercial strategy, we shouldn't neglect the fact that the fan works of Schoenke and Collora also had commercial ambitions within the industry. Fan films do not function entirely outside of a commercial environment, and the pornographic industry itself displays an investment in fidelity that cannot be entirely understood as parasitic and commercial. The myriad uses of the Batman intertext within these forms of Batsploitation point to the increasingly overlapping nature of cultural production in an age of convergence, and it is important that we attend to these nuances in our scholarship.

Conclusion: 'There is only one Batman in the world'

In 2008, Hüseyin Kalkan, the mayor of a city in Turkey named Batman, threatened to sue Warner Bros. for royalties from *The Dark Knight*, since 'The American producers used the name of our city without informing us.'[44] While the legal action did not proceed further, it is telling that his case rested on the argument that 'There is only one Batman in the world',[45] referring to the predominantly Kurdish city in the southeastern Anatolia region of Turkey.

As we have seen in this chapter, in fact, there are many Batmen in the world and they circulate freely beyond the control of any rights holder – neither Hüseyin Kalkan nor DC Comics have been able to maintain control over the Batman intertext. By offering a historical overview of this relatively unexplored phenomenon, this chapter has attempted to complicate prevailing understandings of this intertextual matrix and provide an alternative viewpoint on the migrations of this shifting signifier. Drawing attention to the diverse ways in which these films utilise elements from the Batman franchise, the chapter has mapped out the recurrent tendencies across these myriad adaptations and highlighted the symbiotic relationship between the central franchise and its surrounding unlicensed intertexts.

It is no longer enough simply to discuss the complex web of official intertexts that surrounds a character such as Batman, given that these are dwarfed by the vast number of unofficial intertexts. Moving beyond the limited perspective that positions these borrowings as distinct and separate from the ever-expanding matrix of Batman stories, we need to acknowledge the central importance of Batsploitation to an understanding of the position of Batman within an increasingly interdependent popular culture.

Notes

1. Elliott Serrano, '"Geek Porn" Director Axel Braun on Avengers' Quicksilver, Comic Book Costuming', *Red Eye Chicago*, 8 April 2014. Available at: <http://articles.redeyechicago.com/2014-04-08/entertainment/49007606_1_ultron-joss-whedon-costumes>.
2. 'Introduction', in William Uricchio and Roberta Pearson (eds), *The Many Lives of the Batman: Critical Approaches to a Superhero and His Media* (New York: Routledge, 1991), p. 2.
3. Will Brooker, *Hunting the Dark Knight: Twenty-First Century Batman* (London: I. B. Tauris, 2012), p. 1.
4. My focus here is on screen appropriations of the Batman franchise, although Batsploitation is also present in a number of other media.
5. See, for example, the iTunes listing for *The Dark Knight*. Available at: <https://itunes.apple.com/us/movie/the-dark-knight/id764632601>.
6. Brooker, *Hunting the Dark Knight*, p. 83.
7. Paul Grainge, *Brand Hollywood: Selling Entertainment in a Global Media Age* (London: Routledge, 2007), p. 12.
8. Brooker, *Hunting the Dark Knight*, p. 80.
9. These thirty-three cover versions have been recently collected together in a limited-edition vinyl-only collection entitled *Na Na Na Na Na Na Na Na – Batman Theme*.

10. I. Q. Hunter, 'Exploitation as Adaptation', *Scope: An Online Journal of Film & TV Studies* vol. 15 (2009), p. 9.

11. Produced and directed by Andy Warhol, the 1964 film *Batman Dracula* featured the underground director and star Jack Smith in the roles of Batman and Dracula. Unfinished and thought lost for many years, the rough footage was finally shown at the Andy Warhol Museum in 2011.

12. Fred Beldin, 'The Wild World of Batwoman', *AllMovie*, 26 October 2012. Available at: <http://www.allmovie.com/movie/the-wild-world-of-batwoman-v54601/review>.

13. William Uricchio and Roberta Pearson, '"I'm Not Fooled by That Cheap Disguise"', in this volume, p. 210.

14. Ibid., p. 109.

15. These borrowings from the Batman series were not the only exploitation strategies used by Warren, as he also resorted to reusing clips from *The Mole People* (1956) instead of filming scenes with a new monster.

16. Hunter, 'Exploitation as Adaptation', p. 10.

17. Interestingly, DC did attempt to sue Warren for copyright infringement but the case was resolved in his favour.

18. Iain Robert Smith, '"Beam Me up, Ömer": Transnational Media Flow and the Cultural Politics of the Turkish *Star Trek* Remake', *The Velvet Light Trap* vol. 61 (Spring 2008), pp. 3–13.

19. See *Süper adam* (Superman [1971]), *Kizil maske'nin intikami* (*The Vengeance of the Red Mask* [1971]) and *Zagor kara korsan'in hazineleri* (*Zagor: The Black Pirate's Treasure* [1971]).

20. Richard Berger, 'Are There Any More at Home Like You?: Rewiring Superman', *Journal of Adaptation in Film & Performance* vol. 1 no. 2 (June 2008), p. 87.

21. Henry Jenkins, 'Just Men in Capes?' (Part One), *Confessions of an Aca-Fan: The Official Weblog of Henry Jenkins*, 15 March 2007. Available at: <http://henryjenkins.org/2007/03/just_men_in_capes.html>.

22. See Robert Stam, 'Beyond Fidelity: The Dialogics of Adaptation', in James Naremore (ed.), *Film Adaptation* (New Brunswick, NJ: Rutgers University Press, 2000), pp. 54–76, Linda Hutcheon, *A Theory of Adaptation* (New York and London: Routledge, 2006) and Thomas Leitch, *Film Adaptation and Its Discontents* (Baltimore, MD: Johns Hopkins University Press, 2007), for more on the fidelity debates within scholarship on film adaptation.

23. Thomas Leitch, 'Twelve Fallacies in Contemporary Adaptation Theory', *Criticism* vol. 25 no. 2 (Spring 2003), p. 162.

24. Henry Jenkins, 'Quentin Tarantino's Star Wars? Digital Cinema, Media Convergence and Participatory Culture', in David Thorburn and Henry Jenkins (eds), *Rethinking Media Change: The Aesthetics of Transition* (Cambridge, MA: MIT Press, 2003), p. 283.

25. Ibid., p. 282.

26. Kevin Smith, as cited on the DVD box art for *Batman: Dead End*.

27. Whispers68, 'Fan Film Legend Sandy Collora', *ComicBookMovie*, 11 February 2009. Available at: <http://www.comicbookmovie.com/fansites/Whispers68/news/?a=11494>.

28. Kristin M. Barton, 'Can't Stop the Sequel: How the Serenity-Inspired *Browncoats: Redemption* Is Changing the Future of Fan Films', in Kristin M. Barton and Jonathan

Malcolm Lampley (eds), *Fan Culture: Essays on Participatory Fandom in the 21st Century* (Jefferson, NC: McFarland, 2013), p. 13.

29. Alex Ross, as cited in Eric Campos, 'Batman: Dead End', *Film Threat*, 31 July 2003. Available at: <http://www.filmthreat.com/reviews/4789/>.

30. Campos, 'Batman: Dead End'.

31. Sandy Collora, as cited in Jay Knowles, 'Father Geek Has a Talk with BATMAN: DEAD END Director Sandy Collora ...', *Ain't It Cool News*, 23 July 2003. Available at: <http://www.aintitcool.com/node/15721>.

32. As of 11 March 2015, the YouTube views are at 2,137,448. Available at: <https://www.youtube.com/watch?v=0nCcdec8WdM>.

33. Mark S. Reinhart, *The Batman Filmography*, 2nd edn (Jefferson, NC: McFarland, 2013), p. 269.

34. Aaron Schoenke, as cited in Mark Julian, 'Interview with Bat in the Sun's Aaron Schoenke', *ComicBookMovie*, 10 December 2011. Available at: <http://www.comicbook-movie.com/fansites/GraphicCity/news/?a=47857>.

35. Peter Lehman, 'Twin Cheeks, Twin Peaks and Twin Freaks: Porn's Transgressive Remake Humor', in Bonnie Braendlin and Hans Braendlin (eds), *Authority and Transgression in Literature and Film* (Gainesville: University Press of Florida, 1996), p. 50.

36. Michael Hussey, 'Worst Porn Movie Ever', *Pushing Rope*, 1 May 2008. Available at: <http://pushingrope.blogspot.co.uk/2008/05/worst-porn-movie-ever-i-am-not -kidding.html>.

37. Bethan Jones, 'Slow Evolution: "First Time Fics" and The X-Files Porn Parody', *Journal of Adaptation in Film & Performance* vol. 6 no. 3 (November 2013), p. 380.

38. Iain Robert Smith, 'When Spiderman became Spiderbabe: Pornographic Appropriation and the Political Economy of the Softcore Spoof Genre', in Xavier Mendik (ed.), *Peep Shows: Cult Film and the Cine-Erotic* (New York: Columbia University Press, 2012), pp. 109–18.

39. Titles in the series include XXX adaptations of the DC characters Superman and Batman, but also many Marvel characters, including Captain America, Iron Man, She-Hulk, Spider-Man, The Avengers, Thor, Wolverine and The X-Men.

40. Ironically, given the complicated copyright precedent that allows these porn parodies to flourish, Axel Braun has been remarkably litigious regarding his own intellectual property – filing a federal lawsuit against 7,098 individuals who, he claimed, had illegally shared copies of *Batman XXX*.

41. Axel Braun, as cited in Tessa Stuart, 'When Fanfic Becomes Porn', *BuzzFeed*, 7 June 2013. Available at: <http://www.buzzfeed.com/tessastuart/when-fanfic-becomes-porn>.

42. Axel Braun, as cited in John Riggs, 'Axel Braun from Vivid Talks about His Porno Parody Films', *Rock967online*, 29 August 2012. Available at: <http://rock967online.com/axel -braun-from-vivid-talks-about-his-porno-parody-films-interview/>.

43. Paul Booth, 'Slash and Porn: Media Subversion, Hyper-articulation, and Parody', *Continuum* vol. 28 no. 3 (May 2014), p. 406.

44. Austin Modine, 'Batman sues Batman over Batman', *The Register*, 12 November 2008. Available at: <http://www.theregister.co.uk/2008/11/12/batman_city_sues_batman/>.

45. Ibid.

READING THE BATMAN

9

BATMAN VERSUS SUPERMAN
A CONVERSATION
Philip Bevin

> Still talking— keep talking, Clark ... you've always KNOWN just what to say.
> Batman to Superman, *The Dark Knight Returns* [1]

To date, most analyses of Batman have placed emphasis on the character's own corner of the DC Universe, his allies and, particularly, his enemies. While many of these studies, notably the original *The Many Lives of the Batman* and Will Brooker's two monographs *Batman Unmasked* and *Hunting the Dark Knight*, are invaluable to the study of the hero, they focus primarily upon Batman's traditional habitat of Gotham City and leave open a large area of unexamined possibilities regarding the Caped Crusader's dealings with the broader DC Universe and its inhabitants.[2]

Shared universes have been a feature of superhero comics for many decades and the concept is now receiving added emphasis in big-budget blockbusters; following the success of *The Avengers* (2012), the next cinematic incarnation of the Dark Knight in *Batman v Superman: Dawn of Justice* (2016) will interact with other superheroes, most notably Superman and Wonder Woman.[3] In the light of this significant trend, it is important to acknowledge that while Batman's situation in Gotham City and his dealings with its other inhabitants provides an essential foundation for any understanding of the character, a consideration of his relationships with characters from other areas of the DC Universe is also important. To suggest how this broader investigation into Batman and his surrounding universe might begin, this chapter will examine how the Dark Knight's meaning is shaped by his interactions with Superman, who, apart from sidekicks like Robin, has historically been his most common partner in crime-fighting. It will track the development of Batman and Superman's relationship from their first team-up in the 1950s through to their post-Crisis incarnations to show what the changes in their dynamic reveal to us about the nature of Batman and the broader universe in which he exists.

Other analysts have investigated the relationship between the two characters, often emphasising their differences. Such arguments tend to imply that, even though Batman and Superman both occupy the DC Universe, they preside over oppositional domains, both literally and symbolically.[4] John C. Wright, for example, proposes that the heroes 'are as different as day and night': Superman is a 'white knight' and Batman a 'dark one'.[5] For Wright, the contradictions between the two underscore

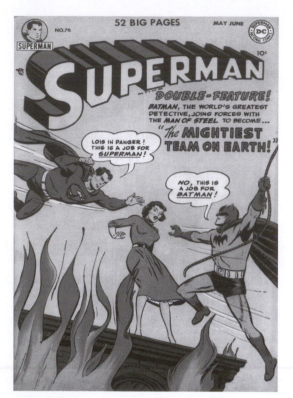

Superman #76 'The Mightiest Team on Earth',
June 1952 (New York: DC Comics)

Batman's 'essential' traits and 'the point of the character', which is 'to scare the villains with greater villainy than theirs while protecting the innocent – to wear the monster's mask but to have the heart of a hero beneath'.[6] Wright's argument implies that the tensions and contrasts present in the relationship between the Dark Knight and the Man of Steel stem from innate, fundamentally oppositional characteristics.[7]

Stories from comics published since 1985, the year DC Comics reset its continuity with the *Crisis on Infinite Earths* event, support Wright's argument.[8] *Superman/Batman: Public Enemies*, for instance, from 2004, opens with a juxtaposition of the two heroes' perspectives.[9] Superman describes his existence in positive terms: 'My parents taught me to side with justice. I came from another planet with powers and abilities far beyond those of other men. I'm known as a hero, an inspiration, a champion. It's been a good life.'[10] Batman's worldview diverges from Superman's positive reflections considerably:

> My parents' killer was never brought to justice. I cloak myself in the very shadows the gunman used to hide his face from me. I'm known as an urban myth, a frightening creature, the bogeyman. It is not a life I would wish on anyone.[11]

The opposition between the two heroes is underscored by the page breakdown, which contrasts an image of Superman soaring confidently through the sunlit skies of Metropolis with a picture of Batman skulking on the ledge of a gothic skyscraper in a shadowy Gotham. As we can see here, Superman has faith in his own role as an unmitigated force for good, leading him to view the values of law and order that he serves with the same uncomplicated positivity.[12] By contrast, Batman hides in the shadows and lives a maligned, lonely existence so that he can utilise fear as a weapon in his own search for justice.

Malcolm Lampley (eds), *Fan Culture: Essays on Participatory Fandom in the 21st Century* (Jefferson, NC: McFarland, 2013), p. 13.

29. Alex Ross, as cited in Eric Campos, 'Batman: Dead End', *Film Threat*, 31 July 2003. Available at: <http://www.filmthreat.com/reviews/4789/>.

30. Campos, 'Batman: Dead End'.

31. Sandy Collora, as cited in Jay Knowles, 'Father Geek Has a Talk with BATMAN: DEAD END Director Sandy Collora …', *Ain't It Cool News*, 23 July 2003. Available at: <http://www.aintitcool.com/node/15721>.

32. As of 11 March 2015, the YouTube views are at 2,137,448. Available at: <https://www.youtube.com/watch?v=0nCcdec8WdM>.

33. Mark S. Reinhart, *The Batman Filmography*, 2nd edn (Jefferson, NC: McFarland, 2013), p. 269.

34. Aaron Schoenke, as cited in Mark Julian, 'Interview with Bat in the Sun's Aaron Schoenke', *ComicBookMovie*, 10 December 2011. Available at: <http://www.comicbook-movie.com/fansites/GraphicCity/news/?a=47857>.

35. Peter Lehman, 'Twin Cheeks, Twin Peaks and Twin Freaks: Porn's Transgressive Remake Humor', in Bonnie Braendlin and Hans Braendlin (eds), *Authority and Transgression in Literature and Film* (Gainesville: University Press of Florida, 1996), p. 50.

36. Michael Hussey, 'Worst Porn Movie Ever', *Pushing Rope*, 1 May 2008. Available at: <http://pushingrope.blogspot.co.uk/2008/05/worst-porn-movie-ever-i-am-not -kidding.html>.

37. Bethan Jones, 'Slow Evolution: "First Time Fics" and The X-Files Porn Parody', *Journal of Adaptation in Film & Performance* vol. 6 no. 3 (November 2013), p. 380.

38. Iain Robert Smith, 'When Spiderman became Spiderbabe: Pornographic Appropriation and the Political Economy of the Softcore Spoof Genre', in Xavier Mendik (ed.), *Peep Shows: Cult Film and the Cine-Erotic* (New York: Columbia University Press, 2012), pp. 109–18.

39. Titles in the series include XXX adaptations of the DC characters Superman and Batman, but also many Marvel characters, including Captain America, Iron Man, She-Hulk, Spider-Man, The Avengers, Thor, Wolverine and The X-Men.

40. Ironically, given the complicated copyright precedent that allows these porn parodies to flourish, Axel Braun has been remarkably litigious regarding his own intellectual property – filing a federal lawsuit against 7,098 individuals who, he claimed, had illegally shared copies of *Batman XXX*.

41. Axel Braun, as cited in Tessa Stuart, 'When Fanfic Becomes Porn', *BuzzFeed*, 7 June 2013. Available at: <http://www.buzzfeed.com/tessastuart/when-fanfic-becomes-porn>.

42. Axel Braun, as cited in John Riggs, 'Axel Braun from Vivid Talks about His Porno Parody Films', *Rock967online*, 29 August 2012. Available at: <http://rock967online.com/axel -braun-from-vivid-talks-about-his-porno-parody-films-interview/>.

43. Paul Booth, 'Slash and Porn: Media Subversion, Hyper-articulation, and Parody', *Continuum* vol. 28 no. 3 (May 2014), p. 406.

44. Austin Modine, 'Batman sues Batman over Batman', *The Register*, 12 November 2008. Available at: <http://www.theregister.co.uk/2008/11/12/batman_city_sues_batman/>.

45. Ibid.

READING THE BATMAN

This implies that Superman and Batman are fundamentally different in terms of their essential characteristics, and have always occupied different symbolic and geographic territories. In fact, their oppositional perspectives, as seen in John Byrne's 'One Night in Gotham City', Jim Aparo and Jim Starlin's *A Death in the Family* and Michael Green and Rags Morales's *Finest Worlds*, are frequently the source of tension, and sometimes even conflict.[13] However, rather than a relationship set in stone since the early 1940s, this Superman–Batman dynamic can, on closer analysis, be seen to represent only a relatively recent artistic consensus. In fact, it dates from the post-Crisis period of 1985 onwards; stories published in the pre-Crisis period from the 1950s through to the 70s give an entirely different perspective.

In tales from the 1950s, far from being at odds in their personalities and methods, Batman and Superman seem surprisingly in sync. The first account of their meeting in 'The Mightiest Team in the World', from June 1952's *Superman* (#76), emphasises the correspondences rather than the differences between the two heroes.[14] For instance, when Clark Kent and Bruce Wayne are assigned the same cabin on a 'coastal cruise' and both realise that they are needed to deal with a dock fire started by a suspicious villain, their concerns about the possible disclosure of their secret identities are remarkably similar. Bruce exclaims, 'I must switch to *Batman* without this Kent chap seeing me!', and chooses to turn off the room's light so that he can change into his superhero uniform without the reporter noticing.[15] Similarly, Clark is relieved by Bruce's suggestion, thinking 'in the dark I can become *Superman* without him seeing!'[16] Once their secrets are simultaneously revealed, their reactions are once more very similar, with a surprised Batman announcing, 'why – you're Superman!', and Superman retorting, 'and you, Bruce Wayne ... you're Batman!'[17] The tensions that underpin their post-Crisis relationship are simply not present here, and a mood of mutual collaboration and cooperation pervades throughout. The two immediately agree that they can depend upon each other to guard their respective secrets and speedily team up to track down the crook who started the fire.

This willingness to cooperate is not only reprised but further emphasised in later 1950s tales. In the adventure 'Batman – Double for Superman!', the two heroes' compatibility is again showcased when, having been spotted in mid-transformation by Lois, Clark Kent enlists Batman's help to stand in as his perfect double in order to confuse her with the pretence that Bruce Wayne is 'really' Superman, while the Man of Steel continues the Caped Crusader's investigation into a group of thugs.[18] Batman proves to be an adept stand-in: he artificially replicates Superman's powers and, just as significantly, at this point in his history has a cheerful demeanour and a morality that make him a natural match for the Man of Steel. If Lois is suspicious of the authenticity of the powers displayed by the false Superman, she expresses no concern over his behaviour or personality.[19] Here again, there is no division between a shadowy, cynical Dark Knight and an optimistic, sunlit White Knight.

In fact, although it presents some contrast between the abilities of the two heroes, 'Batman – Double for Superman!' contributes to the broader sense conveyed by 1950s tales that they are a 'twin nemesis' of crime, with different abilities but a shared, even interchangeable, approach to criminal justice.[20] Indeed, rather than being defined by oppositions, here Batman's nature is illuminated through his closeness to Superman, both in terms of their friendship and their similar personalities; they are, in a sense, both White Knights. This depiction barely changes as the characters move through the 1960s and 70s. In fact, even when Batman began to be reworked as a 'dark' character by Dennis O'Neil and Neal Adams in his solo adventures during the late 1960s and early 70s, he retained much of his cheerfulness in the pages of *World's Finest*, which continued to depict him and Superman as close friends and where he still referred to the Man of Steel as his 'old super-buddy'.[21]

The representation of this easy-going friendship between Superman and Batman still circulates in reprints and collected editions published since the Crisis, but DC dissuades its readers from seeing these older stories as a 'true' portrait of the heroes and their relationship, particularly as far as Batman is concerned. Editorials from collected editions of comics from the period are often dismissive or even disparaging of the Silver Age adventures. In 'Batman's New Look' from *Batman in the Sixties*, episodes from the early part of the decade are described as 'kiddie fare'.[22] In a similar vein, in his introduction to *Batman in the Seventies*, Dennis O'Neil describes the Batman of the 1950s as 'Batman-lite' and criticises the 'camp' 1966 television series, suggesting that it put the character in 'inappropriate contexts' and 'lampooned' him.[23] To understand DC's seeming keenness to dismiss 1950s and 60s Silver Age portrayals of Batman, we have to reflect upon the possible reasons for introducing conflict into the character's relationship with Superman.

Gerard Jones and Will Jacobs's *The Comic Book Heroes* documents the challenge posed to DC Comics by Marvel's ascension in the 1960s and subsequent decades.[24] Jones and Jacobs note that a key characteristic of Marvel superheroes was their tendency to fight with each other. In contrast to DC's characters, who 'were always chummy as could be', 'nearly every time Marvel heroes met, some plot twist had them pounding each other, often tearing up whole city blocks in the process'.[25] This account implies that the element of interpersonal conflict may have been introduced by Marvel to make the characters more like 'real people' than the superheroes of DC Comics.[26] In contrast to these apparently more nuanced, 'realistic' and troubled heroes, DC's consistently cheerful, self-assured characters began 'to look simplistic and clichéd', to the extent that fans eventually thought of Marvel's rival as 'the boring company'.[27] Marvel's approach was so successful that it resulted in a rapid increase in their sales, leading the company at first to challenge and then overtake DC as the biggest American comic book publisher by the dawn of the 1970s.[28]

There is some evidence of DC's response to Marvel's ascendancy in the *World's Finest* comics – which explored Superman and Batman's relationship – throughout the late 1960s and early 70s. A number of covers from the period, including *World's Finest* #180, #183 and #187, show Batman either arguing with or coming to blows with Superman.[29] However, whereas Marvel heroes' clashing personalities seemed naturally at odds, the conflict between DC's characters during this period is not rooted in fundamental differences in their perspectives and motivation.[30] Rather, the 1970s *World's Finest* adventures which placed Superman and Batman in conflict with one another retained their emphasis on the two heroes' shared values, with disagreements usually resulting from the schemes of a villain. For example, the conflict between Batman and Superman in 'Superman's Perfect Crime!' from *World's Finest* #180 (November 1968) is not triggered by a genuine clash but by a villain controlling Superman with a computer and forcing him to commit crimes. In case any of the story's readers were unsure of Superman's true allegiance, the writer goes out of his way to stress that it is an 'imaginary epic' that did not really happen.[31] Similarly, in 'Superman's Crime of the Ages' from *World's Finest* #183 (March 1969), the conflict between the two characters is the result of a plot by Luthor and Brainiac to frame Superman for a fake future crime, which is itself a pretext for a broader scheme to turn the hero 'into a villain ... permanently'.[32] In *World's Finest* #187's 'The Demon Superman' (September 1969), where Superman arrests Batman for witchcraft, his threatening of his former ally is actually a ruse to free Batman from an evil spirit that has possessed his body. The spirit then transfers itself to Superman, causing him to 'turn against' Batman, resulting in further conflict.[33]

These texts show how DC attempted to imitate Marvel's winning style while retaining what artist Carmine Infantino called the 'DC touch'.[34] As far as Batman and Superman are concerned, we can perhaps consider the 'DC touch' to be their shared, upstanding moral qualities, an approach which kept their characters' reputations and sales secure through Fredric Wertham's anti-comics campaign of 1954 and the publication of *Seduction of the Innocent*.[35] The *World's Finest* stories show DC trying to elicit the excitement provoked by Marvel's approach, while maintaining the traditional respectability that had allowed it to flourish in the 1950s when other companies, like EC, with its controversial line of horror titles, were folding in the aftermath of Wertham's campaign.[36] Other storylines from the 1970s support this theory. For example, 'The Kryptonite Express' (#196, September 1970) seems at pains to emphasise its heroes' respect for governmental authorities like the FBI and the UN, and suggests that Superman and Batman's cooperative and mutually respectful friendship is based on a shared subordination to official institutions of national and international law enforcement.[37] DC may have been afraid that pitting one crime-fighter against the other would introduce an element of moral subjectivity and relativism, undermining the authority of their two primary heroes and leaving them open to public criticism.

The threat of moral censure had diminished by the 1970s, when the Comics Code was relaxed, but it still seems plausible that DC, having survived the challenges of Fredric Wertham's 1954 crusade, may have feared that the less morally objective Marvel heroes might draw negative attention to the industry.[38] Whatever the reason, DC appears to have hedged their bets in response to their competitor's success, tentatively emulating Marvel's tendency to emphasise conflict but falling short of compromising the upstanding, uncomplicated morality of their characters. But this strategy failed to take account of comic books' changing readership during the period. As Jones and Jacobs suggest, the 'rising youth culture' that had facilitated the success of Marvel's troubled, unconventional heroes 'posed a challenge that DC's writers didn't quite seem up to', and DC's attempts to 'leapfrog' Marvel resulted in commercial disappointment.[39] DC did not overcome its hesitancy and fully embrace the Marvel approach until 1985, when they again tried to match their rivals by making their universe more accessible and resetting their continuity to 'year one' following the *Crisis on Infinite Earths*. The reboot occasioned a sharp change in the dynamic between Batman and Superman, which is epitomised by Frank Miller's representation of the two characters in the 1986 story *The Dark Knight Returns*, a non-canon narrative that was nevertheless influential in establishing the characteristics of their post-Crisis relationship.

   The Dark Knight Returns, set in Batman's post-retirement future, significantly rewrote the character's personality and motivations.[40] The story implies that Wayne gave up his role as Batman following the death of Jason Todd, the second Robin, and that he has since then tried to suppress his alter ego.[41] However, the Dark Knight resurfaces when Bruce is reminded of his parents' murder.[42] The interior voice of Batman tells Bruce,

> you cannot *escape* me … you are *puny*, you are *small*— you are *nothing*— a hollow *shell*, a rusty *trap* that *cannot* hold me— smoldering, I *burn* you— burning you, I *flare*, hot and bright and fierce and *beautiful*— you cannot *stop* me— not with *wine* or *vows* or the weight of *age* …[43]

Here, Bruce Wayne's Batman identity, a manifestation of Bruce's trauma, appears as a vengeful, controlling force. Given this emphasis, Miller constructs Batman's mission as primarily a personal one, driven by his sense of dislocation, anger and grief. He asserts that 'the world only makes sense if you force it to', and it follows that if Miller's Batman were to change society, he would shape it according to his own principles, and in a way that 'makes sense' according to his own traumatised worldview.[44] This compulsion to remould the world according to his own priorities and desires contrasts with the agenda of Miller's Superman, who, just like his (and Batman's) 1950s and 60s incarnation, willingly defers to authority, specifically the US President. This causes the key conflict between the two, with Batman chiding Superman for his servility: 'You sold us *out* Clark. You gave them— the power— that should have been *ours*.'[45] In response to Batman's lack of respect, Superman tries to make him bow to governmental authority through physical force.

   The contrasting perspectives of the two heroes in Miller's graphic novel obviously mark a change from pre-Crisis portrayals of their relationship, which had presented both characters as similarly willing to put their trust in the established social order and its institutions. It is also clear that Miller's sympathies rest with Batman. The world of Miller's comic is a place where meaningful action is impossible unless strong-minded individuals with clear vision, like Batman, take charge and change society. By contrast, the authority that Superman somewhat naively serves is a corrupted democratic system embodied by a shallow, inert and aged president who is only interested in his own public image and approval ratings, and who is afraid of any decisive action that might affect his popularity.[46]

Although most post-Crisis Batman and Superman stories do not quite reflect the full extent of Miller's cynicism and his contempt for traditional democratic authority, they nevertheless try to replicate his portrayal of the two characters' relationship. Significantly, in 'One Night in Gotham City', the first tale to document Superman and Batman's initial meeting following *Crisis on Infinite Earths*, the two heroes find themselves at odds over their differing methods in a scene reminiscent of *The Dark Knight Returns*. Initially, Superman, who naively adheres to the strict letter of the law, performs a citizen's arrest on Batman for being an 'outlaw' whom he will not tolerate.[47] Batman tries to convince Superman that his more ruthless and sometimes extralegal crime-fighting methods are necessary in Gotham, which is so saturated with corruption that it resembles 'a garbage pile' of crime 'that reaches from the lowest sewers … to the highest offices of City Hall'.[48] Superman, who continues to express a pre-Crisis faith in the traditional structures of law enforcement, is now, as in Miller's comic, coded as a naive optimist. Batman, by contrast, more closely resembles Miller's interpretation in his cynical pragmatism and belief in the need to break the rules to get things done 'properly', at least according to his own worldview. 'One Night in Gotham City' is particularly significant, since it constituted part of John Byrne's *The Man of Steel* miniseries that rebooted Superman's personal history following the Crisis. As one of the series that established the new 'truth' in DC continuity in the wake of the Crisis, the story establishes the opposition between Batman's and Superman's contrasting values and perspectives as one of the new universe's founding principles.

A fuller understanding of the motivations behind *Crisis on Infinite Earths* helps us better to grasp how the reconfigured relationship between Batman and Superman fits into the wider context of the changes applied to Batman's character after the continuity reboot. Will Brooker has provided an in-depth analysis of the reboot's effect on Batman.

> Bat-Girl was gone, Bat-Mite and Ace the Bat-Hound were gone; and so were the various alternate Batmen from those lighter, more playful science fiction stories, such as Negative Batman, the Zebra Batman and, most notoriously of all, the Rainbow Batman, depicted on the cover of *Detective Comics* #241 (January 1957) in a bright pink costume.

> Although it was *Year One*, released in 1987, that literally took the character back to square one and defined a new hardboiled beginning, *Dark Knight* epitomises the armoured, military toughness that underpinned the *Crisis*.[49]

As a result of DC's removal of all pre-1985 storylines from the official canon of continuity, the friendly, 'chummy' relationship originally enjoyed by Superman and Batman is now designated as a false memory, with the new, troubled formulation of their 'friendship' established as the 'correct', authentic interpretation. With DC's future success riding on the post-Crisis interpretations of their characters, we can speculate that the corporation wanted their readers to forget about Superman and Batman's pre-

Crisis incarnations, whose declining appeal in the face of Marvel's more nuanced, complex and argumentative heroes had helped Marvel to dominate the market. Any suggestion of a cooperative and tension-free friendship between the two heroes might now evoke the supposedly dull comics of DC's pre-Crisis past. Therefore, the Crisis and the reboot were designed to confirm the revised, more interesting and conflicting versions of the heroes not just as the current 'truth', but as their essential and accurate underlying nature.

Michael Billig's argument 'that our thinking, or at least our cogitation about loose palmed matters, may be based on dialogue' and that 'we think to ourselves, as if addressing someone else', helps to explain DC's strategy of differentiating the post-Crisis from the pre-Crisis universe, and the newly cynical post-Crisis Batman from his still optimistic counterpart, Superman.[50] As Billig explains, people's thoughts and opinions are, even internally, formed in reference to an opposing point of view. The existence of a counter-position, or anti-logoi, is therefore the necessary condition for the formation of every position, or logoi. It is through juxtaposition and discussion with another view that an individual's own point of view will be refined, defined and clarified. For Billig, one possible consequence of this is that, in some circumstances, 'the removal of the anti-logoi may lessen the need for the logoi and, consequently, an attitude is dropped when the counter-attitudes likewise fade into oblivion'.[51] In other words, not only does a point of view depend upon its opposite for its own refinement and clarification but, if the contradictory perspective ceases to challenge it and a consensus emerges, the former perspective will cease to be articulated and will ultimately disappear.

I have suggested above that the post-Crisis Superman continues to express the worldview previously held by both heroes in pre-Crisis continuity – that is, deference to the established authorities of the US state – whereas the post-Crisis Batman aggressively rejects this view. Following Billig's logic, we can argue that Superman provides the antithesis against which the 'dark' cynicism of Batman is refined, clarified and confirmed. Batman's arguments with Superman can therefore be seen as DC's attempt to emphasise the disparity between the post-Crisis Dark Knight and his pre-Crisis counterpart. The disagreements between the post-Crisis Batman and Superman keep the DC Universe 'dynamic' and vibrant, preventing it from settling into the dull stability and consensus that supposedly characterised Superman and Batman stories from the 1950s and 60s. However, perhaps more significantly, the relationship seems specifically designed to reinforce the notion that Batman's light-hearted persona of the past is 'incorrect'; it makes the 'true', essentially 'dark' Batman now sanctified in the canon of official continuity completely antithetical to Superman's cheerful optimism, shared by both heroes prior to the Crisis. As a result, every time the superheroes disagree, their argument serves to repeat and confirm their differences. This conflict continuously reinforces the idea that, at least officially, there is one, true, canonical Batman who renders the lighter-hearted, earlier version no longer valid.

John C. Wright suggests that the contrast between the shadowy, pragmatic, cynical Batman and the light, optimistic and naive Superman within post-Crisis continuity represents their innately contradictory essences as 'dark' and 'white' knights. But I have argued that the reboot was designed to give the impression that the characters' 'true' personalities are governed by distinct and innately incompatible worldviews in order to introduce tension and conflict into the DC Universe and make the company more competitive with rival Marvel. The post-Crisis Batman needs Superman as one of the key counterpoints against which his character can be defined and clarified. The troubled, traumatised Batman and the dynamic, edgy DC Universe both require Superman to function as a sunny contrast to their darkness.

This chapter has argued that placing Batman in dialogue with Superman delineates and maintains the character's distinct persona of Dark Knight. But Superman provides just one example of how oppositions to other characters define Batman's meaning and place within the DC Universe. Batman has a long history of team-ups and crossovers with other characters, from Robin to Swamp Thing. An investigation of Batman's relationships with any of these would reveal previously undisclosed aspects of the Dark Knight's significance within the DC Universe. This broader project is now essential if we are to fully understand Batman, both as character and as commercial icon, in an era when superheroes in popular culture – most significantly, in cinema – are increasingly being defined by their roles within shared universes and by their relationships with other key characters.[52]

Notes

1. Frank Miller, *Batman: The Dark Knight Returns* (New York: DC Comics, 1986), p. 190.
2. Will Brooker, *Batman Unmasked: Analyzing a Cultural Icon* (London: Continuum, 2000); Brooker, *Hunting the Dark Knight* (London: I. B. Tauris, 2012); Roberta E. Pearson and William Uricchio (eds), *The Many Lives of the Batman: Critical Approaches to a Superhero and His Media* (New York: Routledge, 1991).
3. Ben Child, 'Fast & Furious Star Gal Gadot to Play Wonder Woman', *Guardian*, 5 December 2013. Available at: <http://www.theguardian.com/film/2013/dec/05/wonder-woman-man-of-steel-2-gal-gadot>.
4. In addition to my discussion of John C. Wright's arguments below, see Daniel P. Malloy, 'World's Finest ... Friends? Batman, Superman, and the Nature of Friendship', in Mark D. White and Robert Arp (eds), *Batman and Philosophy: The Dark Knight of the Soul* (Hoboken, NJ: John Wiley & Sons, 2008), pp. 239–40; Douglas Wolk, *Reading Comics and What They Mean* (Philadelphia, PA: Da Capo Press, 2007), p. 97.
5. John C. Wright, 'Heroes of Darkness and Light', in Dennis O'Neil and Leah Wilson (eds), *Batman Unauthorized* (Dallas, TX: BenBella Books, 2008), pp. 181, 193.
6. Ibid., p. 188.
7. Ibid.
8. Marv Wolfman and George Pérez, *Crisis on Infinite Earths* (New York: DC Comics, 2000 [1985]).
9. Jeph Loeb and Ed McGuinness, *Superman/Batman: Public Enemies* (New York: DC Comics, 2005 [2004]).
10. Ibid., p. 13.

11. Ibid.

12. A comparable juxtaposition can be seen in *Superman/Batman: Finest Worlds*, where the contrast between Superman's 'lightness' and permanent 'good mood' and Batman's 'bleak' attitude is epitomised by the differing characteristics of the cities they inhabit. Michael Green, Mike Johnson, Rags Morales and Rafael Albuquerque, *Superman/Batman: Finest Worlds* (New York: DC Comics, 2009), p. 96.

13. John Byrne, 'One Night in Gotham City', in Robert Greenberger (ed.), *Superman: The Man of Steel*, vol. 1 no. 3 (New York: DC Comics, 2003 [1986]), pp. 65–86; Jim Aparo and Jim Starlin, *A Death in the Family* (New York: DC Comics, 1988); Green *et al.*, *Superman/Batman: Finest Worlds*.

14. Edmond Hamilton and Curt Swan, 'The Mightiest Team in the World', in Scott Nybakken (ed.), *Showcase Presents: World's Finest*, vol. 1 (New York: DC Comics, 2007 [1952]), pp. 6–18.

15. Ibid., p. 10.

16. Ibid.

17. Ibid.

18. Alvin Schwartz and Curt Swan, 'Batman – Double for Superman!', in Nybakken (ed.), *World's Finest*, vol. 1, pp. 22–3.

19. Ibid., p. 28.

20. Edmond Hamilton and Curt Swan, 'Batman and Superman, Swamis, Inc.', in Nybakken (ed.), *World's Finest*, vol. 1, p. 46.

21. Bob Haney and Curt Swan, 'The Kryptonite Express', in Robin Wildman (ed.), *World's Finest*, vol. 4 (New York: DC Comics, 2012 [1970]), p. 382.

22. Carmine Infantino and Murphy Anderson, 'Batman's New Look', in Rick Taylor (ed.), *Batman in the Sixties* (New York: DC Comics, 1999), p. 61.

23. Dennis O'Neil, 'Introduction', in Michael Wright (ed.), *Batman in the Seventies* (New York: DC Comics, 1999), pp. 7–8.

24. Gerard Jones and Will Jacobs, *The Comic Book Heroes: The First History of Modern Comic Books from the Silver Age to the Present* (Rocklin, CA: Prima Publishing, 1997).

25. Ibid., p. 89.

26. Ibid., p. 53.

27. Ibid., pp. 53, 186.

28. Ibid., pp. 120, 169.

29. Cary Bates and Ross Andru, 'Superman's Perfect Crime', in Wildman (ed.), *World's Finest*, vol. 4, pp. 100–16; Leo Dorfman and Ross Andru, 'Superman's Crime of the Ages', in Wildman (ed.), *World's Finest*, vol. 4, pp. 155–73; Robert Kaniger and Ross Andru, 'The Demon Superman', in Wildman (ed.), *World's Finest*, vol. 4, pp. 228–45.

30. The early Spider-Man's life, for instance, is peppered with interpersonal conflicts. Not only does he clash with schoolmates who don't appreciate his interest in science, he also annoys other superheroes like the Fantastic Four with his less than respectful attitude. Stan Lee and Steve Ditko, 'Duel to the Death with the Vulture', in Cory Sedlmeier (ed.), *The Amazing Spider-Man: Marvel Masterworks*, vol. 1 (New York: Marvel

Comics, 2009 [1963]), p. 42; Stan Lee and Steve Ditko, 'The Chameleon!', in Sedlmeier (ed.), *Amazing Spider-Man*, p. 30.

31. Cary Bates, Ross Andru and Mike Esposito, 'Superman's Perfect Crime!', in Wildman (ed.), *World's Finest*, vol. 4, p. 100.

32. Leo Dorfman and Ross Andru, 'Superman's Crime of the Ages', in Wildman (ed.), *World's Finest*, vol. 4, p. 171.

33. Kaniger and Andru, 'The Demon Superman', pp. 244–5.

34. Jones and Jacobs, *Comic Book Heroes*, p. 120.

35. Fredric Wertham, *Seduction of the Innocent* (New York: Rinehart & Co., 1954).

36. Jones and Jacobs, *Comic Book Heroes*, p. 10.

37. Haney and Swan, 'Kryptonite Express', pp. 382–401.

38. Amy Nyberg, *Seal of Approval: History of the Comics Code (Studies in Popular Culture)* (Jackson: University Press of Mississippi, 1998), pp. 141–2.

39. Jones and Jacobs, *Comic Book Heroes*, pp. 77, 123, 221.

40. Miller, *Batman: The Dark Knight Returns*, p. 93; Brooker, *Hunting the Dark Knight*, pp. 114–15.

41. Miller, *Batman: The Dark Knight Returns*, p. 93.

42. Ibid., p. 22.

43. Ibid., p. 25.

44. Ibid., p. 192.

45. Ibid.

46. Ibid., p. 108.

47. Byrne, 'One Night in Gotham City', p. 60.

48. Ibid., p. 76.

49. Brooker, *Batman Unmasked*, p. 115.

50. Michael Billig, *Arguing Thinking*, new edn (Cambridge: Cambridge University Press, 1996 [1987]), p. 142.

51. Ibid., p. 274.

52. See William Uricchio and Roberta Pearson, '"I'm Not Fooled by That Cheap Disguise"', in Chapter 13 of this volume, for an analysis of the relationship between Batman and Robin and Batman and the Joker.

10

BATGIRL
CONTINUITY, CRISIS AND FEMINISM
Will Brooker

Absences

This chapter places Batman in the margins, just as Batgirl has been consistently marginalised within Batman narratives and scholarship – just as, more broadly, female characters have been consistently marginalised within the superhero genre, and, even more fundamentally, as women have been consistently marginalised within the dominant narratives of history and culture. The chapter argues that the narrative patterns of the superhero genre – a continuity punctuated by regular reboots and resets, traumas, deaths and rebirths – acquire distinct connotations when applied to female characters. Again, though my specific case study here is Batgirl – more specifically yet, the Barbara Gordon incarnation – I propose that this dynamic applies to female characters throughout the genre and that it reflects and articulates women's role and representation within contemporary western patriarchy.

'Women must learn their own history,' stated a feminist manifesto from 1968, 'because they have a history to be proud of and a history which will give pride to their daughters ... to keep us from our history is to keep us from each other.'[1] Unlike traditional, male history, though, the history of women has been continually under threat, and constantly marginalised, repressed or never recorded. Bonnie S. Anderson and Judith P. Zinsser's *A History of Their Own* cites a women's liberation hymn from the mid-1970s – 'we who are without a past/without history, outcast' – to illustrate the importance of feminist scholarship in recovering women's archives and narratives. To recover women's history is a political act; it is to rethink history itself and to see 'how the entire narrative changes'.[2] It is a process of salvaging stories from the margins; of recognising, celebrating and learning from the past – enabling women to 'think back through our mothers', in Woolf's phrase – and of inspiring future generations.[3] As Sarah M. Gilbert summarises, Virginia Woolf speaks of 'rewriting history'; Adrienne Rich notes that women's writing must begin with a 're-vision' of the past; Carolyn Heilbrun observes that we must 'reinvent' womanhood', and Joan Kelly declares that we must 'restore women to history and ... restore history to women'.[4]

Without this sense of heritage, of mothers and mentors, women are left alone, always starting anew; 'isolated islands of symbolic significance', in Annette Koldny's phrase, lacking the sense of tradition and canon afforded to men.[5] Part of the value of history, then, is a sense of belonging; in this context, of sisterhood. One of patriarchy's key strategies to retain the status quo is the undermining of female identity through the marginalisation and repression of women's history and the erosion of female solidarity. We can see this dynamic of gendered power struggle – repression and reclaiming, bonding and dissolving, advance and backlash – writ large through the history of female characters in popular culture, like Batgirl. The superhero genre is often stylised, simplistic, exaggerated to extremes, but this means it can explore real-world dynamics starkly and boldly through its bright archetypes and melodramas, like a contemporary folk tale or fable, and reveal the subtle machinations of power more crudely, but also more clearly.

Continuity, canon and crisis: Batgirl's history, 1967–88

Barbara Gordon first made her 'Million Dollar Debut' as Batgirl in *Detective Comics* #359 (January 1967), and her first television appearance shortly afterwards, in *Batman* (ABC, 1966–8); the episode was titled 'Enter Batgirl, Exit Penguin' (3: 1). An unaired, eight-minute pilot, introducing the character and pitching her to executives, was produced in January of that year.[6] Which medium introduced Batgirl first, and what role the creative teams from television and comic books played in her invention, are less important to my discussion here than the year of her debut. Nineteen sixty-seven witnessed the first of the gatherings that would grow into a new women's liberation movement, as 'leftist women in several cities around the [United States] banded together in small, independent groups to discuss gender discrimination and how to combat it'.[7] In Sep-

Adam West and Yvonne Craig, *Batman* (1966–8) (left); *Batgirl* #359, 'The Million Dollar Debut of Batgirl' (New York: DC Comics, January 1967)

tember 1968, an estimated four hundred women threw items representing their oppression into a 'freedom trash can' at the Miss America contest in Atlantic City, an event seen as symbolically marking the beginning of the feminist second wave.[8]

Both the unaired TV clip and the comic book begin by locating Batgirl within dominant contemporary stereotypes, only to subvert them. The comic has Barbara excitedly admitting to herself that appearing in a costume at her father's Policeman's Masquerade Ball will be 'the highlight of my life', surpassing her PhD and brown belt in judo, while the narrative captions warn us that 'unexpected developments ... are soon to shake BATGIRL down to her pretty toes!'[9] Barbara's first televised scene, in turn, introduces her as demure and conservative, flattered by Bruce Wayne's flirtation and playfully affectionate to her father, though, as the voiceover soon observes, there is more to her than meets the eye. Shortly after Barbara's capture by Killer Moth, narrator William Dozier muses, 'strange ... she seems very cool about being locked in. And who's locking whom? And what is this? Her own secret panel ... leading to her own secret closet?' Naturally – in keeping with generic conventions – Batgirl displays physical prowess and proves herself a worthy crime-fighter during her first adventure. Her comic book debut concludes with Batman declaring, 'I'll welcome her aid, Commissioner Gordon ... from what I've seen, she doesn't have to take a back seat to anybody!' Gordon tells his daughter, 'That Batgirl sure is tops in my book! Harrumph! Too bad you couldn't be a little more LIKE her, Babs!', while Barbara, her hair neatly pinned, glasses on and her nose back in a book, smiles, thinking, 'If Dad only knew!'[10] Batgirl's first full TV appearance, screened in September 1967, sees her kidnapped by Penguin and pressured into marrying him. 'He'll threaten her, and force her to consent,' Bruce Wayne grimly realises, while Penguin snarls, 'Obedience! That's the first wifely virtue.' Barbara, of course, has other plans, and rescues not just herself but the two heroes. The story ends on a similar note to the comic book episode, with Batman thanking Batgirl, in her absence –'whoever she is behind that mask of hers, she helped us out of a dire dilemma' – while Barbara only pretends to be the helpless and grateful victim.

The defiance of expectations, the narrative irony, the depiction of clueless, blinkered male authority and the shared, secret knowledge between reader and (in this case, female) character are embedded within superhero genre convention. We can see an identical dynamic in the first Batman story of May 1939, where Gordon believes Bruce Wayne is merely a bored, disengaged socialite. By contrast to Batgirl, however, Julie Madison, Bruce Wayne's fiancée from 1939 to 1941, is genuinely a frail, hapless victim, with no secret identity. 'Poor kid!' Batman remarks as he rescues her in her own debut story.[11] Significantly, in this case the reader shares Bruce Wayne's secret – 'Julie would be surprised to know her Batman is her future husband,' he announces while alone in his bedroom – while Julie has no private thoughts of her own, and the story concludes with her declaring, 'I don't know who you are, but you saved my life and I shall be forever grateful!'[12]

The gentle challenging of gender roles evident in the late-1960s Batgirl stories was taken to another level during the early 70s, as evidenced by a public service announcement broadcast from 1973, five years after the *Batman* TV series had concluded. In this short commercial, Batgirl arrives at a warehouse to save the Dynamic Duo from a ticking time bomb. 'Quick, Batgirl,' Batman orders her. 'Untie us, before it's too late.'

'It's already too late. I've worked with you a long time, and I'm paid less than Robin. Same job, same employer means equal pay for men and women.' 'It's no time for jokes, Batgirl,' Batman warns. 'It's no joke. It's the Federal Equal Pay Law,' Batgirl coolly replies, as the timer goes off. The voiceover tells the viewer to 'tune in tomorrow, or contact the Wage and Hour Division, listed in your phone book under the US Department of Labor.'[13]

Barbara's stories also took on a more political aspect in the comic books of this period, engaging increasingly with social issues – and, in a more laboured manner, with contemporary fashions and slang – while also integrating motifs from the romance genre. In a story from 1972, for instance, Barbara gives an old flame a second chance by sponsoring him for parole. 'Was the least I could do, Gregg,' she assures him, 'believing that "criminals are MADE – not BORN! Plus, the "THING" we had going for each other back in GOTHAM HIGH – but that "torch" went out a long time ago!'[14]

Barbara is now chief librarian, and volunteering at her father's campaign headquarters in her spare time; Jim Gordon is running reluctantly for Congress. Again, of course, the demands of the superhero crime narrative come into play – along with the conventions of the romance comic – and Gregg betrays Babs on both a personal and professional level, using their relationship to rob the library. After slapping Gregg in a panel that combines superhero action with a lover's rejection, Babs reflects despairingly on her dual role: 'what good does it do for BATGIRL to toss them into jail … and BABS GORDON to parole them OUT?' In the climactic final scene, Babs rips off her mask, declaring, 'Dad, I want your job! … I want to RUN for Congress in YOUR place … it's the only way I can really fight crime – PREVENT it – through PRISON REFORM! LEGISLATION – LAW that creates ORDER … not disorder!' At the start of the next episode, Gordon gives Babs his approval – 'you're a "chip off the old block"! I'm PROUD of you … KICK OFF, baby – with my BLESSING!'[15] After a few more twists and turns, combining political intrigue, superhero exploits and duplicitous, handsome men, Barbara wins the election and leaves Gotham for Washington DC.

Although she returned to crime-fighting – teaming up with Superman, Robin, Supergirl and the retired Batwoman (Kathy Kane, first introduced during the 1950s) – Barbara retained her position as Congresswoman and also took a lead role in the new title, *Batman Family*, which launched in 1975. In the first issue, she shuts Robin up with a kiss – 'see you around … KID!' – when he tries to patronise her, and delivers a speech to a packed hall in Congress: 'We must always understand the AMERICAN IDEAL and guard that dream bravely.'[16] In the closing sequence, our perspective moves back dramatically from what in cinema would be a mid-shot of Barbara to a long shot of the chamber, then a reaction shot of male listeners (including Dick Grayson) smiling in approval, and finally an exterior of the Capitol, as anonymous voices chorus 'Bravo', 'Hear, hear!' and 'Give 'em hell, Barbara!'[17]

A 1977 episode, with Babs still a Congresswoman (five years is a long time in comics), confirms her role in the Batman mythos as a representative – in the light-hearted terms allowed by the medium – of popular feminism. In this story, she teams up with Dick Grayson to capture Duela Dent, daughter of Two-Face. 'Much as I'd like to sock it to her,' Robin announces, with a mock bow – 'LADIES FIRST!' Babs responds, again half-seriously, 'I always knew you were a gentleman – but in these days of EQUALITY, I must refuse! Take her, ROBIN – she's all yours!'[18]

In this same year, Batgirl met Batwoman, who – with her niece, Bat-Girl – had worked with Batman in the 1950s comic books. In addition to teaming up against Batgirl's first nemesis, Killer Moth, and the patronisingly debonair Cavalier, the two women find time to bond in civilian clothes. Kathy, closer to Bruce Wayne's age, openly admires the younger woman's successful career – 'look at you – a CONGRESSWOMAN!' – while Barbara pays tribute to her predecessor's achievements, declining the suggestion to rename herself and take Kathy's title.[19] 'It's an honor, Kathy,' she decides, 'but, I think I'll stick with being BATGIRL! There always has been and always will be only one BATWOMAN – and retired or not, it's YOU!'[20] The conversation takes place over the last page, as the two women board and ride a Ferris wheel. We see them in two-shot, then a close-up of Kathy's smiling face, and finally in silhouette against a starry sky. The tropes of traditional romance comics here confirm the bond between these women, of different generations – in career terms at least – in a moment of mutual respect and affection.

It is worth dwelling on these examples from Batgirl's 1970s career as an outspoken, confident, determined and liberated figure – a woman with a respect for her heritage and a sense of the female tradition to which she belongs – to confirm how much was lost when these stories, and this version of the character, were written definitively out of history by the *Crisis on Infinite Earths*' storyline of 1985. The 'Crisis', as it is commonly known, was an ambitious, wide-ranging twelve-issue series explicitly designed to change – to streamline and simplify – the DC Universe by combining several alternate earths into one. Batgirl's role in the Crisis was small, but significant in terms of her character and her subsequent development. She appears at one point with Supergirl, confessing to her friend – using her first (human) name in a moment of intimacy – that she has begun to doubt her role. 'Linda – I feel so useless, so helpless, so worthless – and so very, very scared.' As Supergirl flies off to save more lives, ultimately sacrificing herself, Barbara, wiping tears from her eyes, asks herself, 'What have I become?'[21] This is already a different figure from the Batgirl of the 1970s, and it was only the start of a process that fundamentally undermined the character's identity and history.

Of course, we would expect a comic book character to develop over time. The superhero genre is typified by rewrites, revisions and second thoughts, whether through casual plotting and collaborative authorship – multiple writers making quick, careless decisions in a popular form, without time or inclination to double-check the details – or, more recently, through deliberate, corporate attempts to clarify and streamline continuity. Many superhero characters have undergone substantial change; in the 1985 Crisis alone, Superman's powers were scaled down, Batman's origin was rewritten and Flash was killed. But for Batgirl, as one of the relatively few prominent women in the DC Comics Universe, and as a figure associated with a popular version of feminism, the erasure of history has different connotations.

The Crisis repressed and deleted vital aspects of Batgirl's past. Her political career was minimised and her friendships with other women were destroyed. Barbara had, in this post-Crisis rewrite, never bonded with Supergirl and never met Batwoman; that those characters were now officially dead in this new timeline was devastating enough to the depiction of female solidarity and sisterhood, but the erasure was even more thorough. The relationships were not just wiped off the contemporary comic book page, but wiped out of history, out of Batgirl's memories. Not only was Batwoman no longer alive, but the two women's conversation on the Ferris wheel, with its rare, valuable recognition of heritage, mentorship and a sense of female tradition, had now never officially happened.

The official tweaks to Barbara's backstory after the Crisis may seem minor, but the tone of her character is quite different afterwards, as if the reboot – despite the fact that characters were never meant to remember it – had fundamentally changed her. A new origin, published in 1987, reveals that she is now the daughter of Roger and Thelma Gordon, and is only adopted by her uncle Jim Gordon after both her parents die. She still makes her debut fighting Killer Moth, still works briefly at a library, still runs for Congress, and, 'when I turned out to be too liberal for re-election', takes a job at a humanities research institution.[22] The several years she spent as a Congresswoman are reduced to a single panel in a montage. Her previous friendships with Supergirl and Batwoman are now replaced by a flirtation with Robin, a lifelong obsession with Batman and a constant feeling of self-doubt that epitomised the character's reconfiguration, in stark contrast to her previous, popular-feminist incarnation.[23] By losing a sense of female sisterhood, solidarity and history, Barbara had also lost her sense of identity and purpose.

The Crisis was not just a deletion, but a re-edit. In addition to marginalising or repressing key aspects of character history, it also foregrounded minor elements, placing a new stress on stories that would otherwise have been forgotten. Much of Batgirl's 1987 origin story is, therefore, taken up by a retelling of her encounter with a minor villain named Cormorant, who shot her in a comic book published in 1980.[24] This single event, we are now told, traumatised Babs despite her years of bizarre crime-fighting experiences; she even lists some of those stranger cases here, reminding us that she was 'mindwiped, impersonated, turned into a snake'. Within the new continuity, though, we are asked to believe that it only took one lucky shot from Cormorant to make her 'realise I could die doing this'.[25] Cormorant's role in Batgirl's extended narrative is, ostensibly, minimal. He attempted to assassinate her in *Detective Comics* #491 (June 1980), in an episode that should barely have registered in the character's history – especially when we consider all the events that were wiped off the record by the Crisis. However, post-Crisis, DC's editors clearly decided to rework this event into a formative, traumatic encounter for Batgirl, from which she never fully recovered.

In this rewritten origin, Barbara is explicitly alone, swinging solo through Gotham's skies and confirming her loneliness in narrative captions:

I wish I had a sister or a friend or someone who knew what it was like to do this, why I was compelled to be here to protect others. I used to pretend I had a friend, but it hurt much more when I realised I was talking to myself.

She stands on a rooftop, with the ghostly heads of imaginary friends and possible sisters floating around her, an echo of the fading alternate earths from the Crisis storyline. 'Someday,' she thinks to herself in the final panel, 'the morning will come when I won't be needed.'[26]

The effects of robbing Batgirl of female solidarity and history are confirmed in her next major appearance, in *Batgirl Special* #1 – titled 'The Last Batgirl Story' – from January 1988. Here she is further reduced to a solitary, hopeless figure with a fragile sense of identity; an entirely different character from the Batgirl of the 1970s. Again, the episode opens with Barbara reliving the trauma of her encounter with Cormorant. 'He'd killed part of me, reduced my world to a haze of pain and self-protection. I'd never been hurt before. I'd been an innocent hero.'[27] The story's secondary villain is Slash, a new masked character who calls herself 'The Women's Champion'. 'All the victims had been unsuccessfully charged with rape and other crimes against women,' a TV presenter explains. 'We asked the following women's rights activists for their opinions.'[28] Batgirl is, in this context, positioned as a reasonable liberal in contrast to Slash's stylised, comic book version of radical feminism. When the two first meet, Bat-

Batgirl #1, 'The Last Batgirl Story' (New York: DC Comics, January 1988)

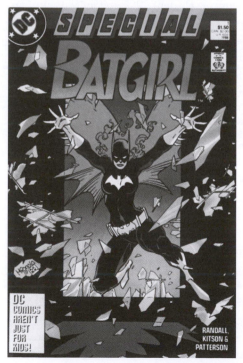

girl tries to save one of the intended male victims. 'Why are you protecting HIM? Don't you know what he's done?' Slash demands. 'How can you, a woman, allow scum like this to go unpunished?' 'I catch them, not kill them,' Babs replies. 'I let the COURTS decide who's guilty.' 'Courts of MEN,' Slash spits back. 'If you can't see the sick truth, you're as guilty as THEM!'[29]

Cormorant's attack on Batgirl at the conclusion of this issue is, in turn, coded as sexual assault and rape threat. 'Just like all women, eh?' he grins. 'Pretend to hate men, then do anything to save us! Now, Batgirl – we're gonna have some fun.'[30] She fights him off, with Slash helping her at the last minute, but the experience has taken its toll. On the final page, Babs gives her folded costume to her friend Marcy. 'I just finished my last case. Batgirl's all finished. There're others out there now who can do this as well or better than me, with less pain.'[31]

Slash's role in the story as an extreme, avenging radical confirms – heavy-handedly, perhaps – that this 'Last Batgirl Story' is intended, in part, as an exploration of contemporary gender roles. Cormorant is a hulking, bare-chested brute; his wife is bruised and bullied, he is accused of 'grave crimes against women' and addresses Batgirl as 'babe'. Her final, fierce attack on him – 'I'm not going to let you scare me anymore! You're a sick, twisted man – I'm just sorry I waited so long!' – can, therefore, be read as a fight back against misogyny.[32] As such, we could see this story as 'progressive' within mainstream superhero terms, except that it concludes with Batgirl's retirement and her admission that she is no longer up to the job.[33] Relegated to the domestic sphere, her superhero outfit becomes 'only a costume', which she says Marcy can hang up with her dresses.

Batgirl was over, beaten by the kind of routine encounter Batman and Robin face, and forget, in each monthly title. In her next appearance, we see her living not with Marcy but with her middle-aged father, Jim, serving him cocoa and acting like a surrogate wife or mother. That next appearance was Alan Moore and Brian Bolland's *The Killing Joke*, and after one page of domestic cosiness, Barbara opened the door to the Joker, and was shot in the spine.

Batgirl and backlash: *The Killing Joke* (1988)

If the 1970s Batgirl can be read as a feminist figure, then the post-Crisis period can, as I have suggested, be seen as an attempt to undermine her in that respect, and *The Killing Joke* as its most vicious strike. As Imelda Whelehan points out, while Susan Faludi's *Backlash* (1991), followed by Marilyn French's *The War against Women* (1992), brought the idea into popular discourse, hostility against feminism – specifically against the achievements of the second wave – had been 'gathering force since the latter half of the eighties'.[34] While Naomi Wolf's *Fire with Fire* (1993) identified a 'genderquake' in which the authority of the white male elite was threatened, the supposed 'crisis of masculinity' – much like the *Crisis on Infinite Earths* – seemed to disrupt existing frameworks and open up new possibilities, only to quickly close them down and impose a familiar structure.[35] The new world was superficially different, perhaps – sensitive guys instead of old-school macho, 'girl power' replacing traditional feminine stereotypes (a new origin and costume for the superheroes and heroines) – but its fundamental power relations were unchanged. Far from threatening male authority, the 'crisis in masculinity' resulted in a backlash that effectively alienated many younger women from second-wave history; in 1990, as Estelle B. Freedman reports in *No Turning Back*, *Newsweek* felt able to announce 'the failure of feminism'.[36] Again, Batgirl's treatment on the bold, simple stage of the superhero genre enacts this process with the force of a Passion play.

Although Barbara had been severely reduced by the Crisis and its aftermath – her confidence shattered, her history simplified, her female friends killed and forgotten, and her resolve, purpose and identity undermined – *The Killing Joke* attacks the character with a new level of graphic, sexualised violence. After being shot by Joker, she is undressed, and photographs of her – in extreme pain, naked and bleeding – are then shown to her father, Jim Gordon, in an attempt to drive him 'crazy' and prove Joker's point that 'one bad day' can change a person irrevocably. Barbara, in this story, is simply a pawn in a larger game between Batman, Joker and, to an extent, Jim; she matters only in terms of what she signifies to the men, and her own trauma – her own 'bad day' – is almost entirely neglected. A later story, from 1996, finally gives her the opportunity to protest:

> Shooting me … kidnapping my dad … it was all just a way to get at you. Do you understand how humiliating, how demeaning, that is?! My life has no importance save in relation to you! Even as Batgirl, I was perceived just as some weaker version of you!

'I caught him, Barbara,' Batman points out. 'Oh, yes. I heard about that. I heard how you two stood there, laughing over some private joke. Tell me – was it me?'[37]

The representation of Barbara's shooting and sexual assault in *The Killing Joke* is explicit for a mainstream superhero comic book of the period; the artwork shows Barbara's naked body, fragmented in a montage of close-up photographs and covered in blood.[38] Batgirl, after a twenty-year career, had not just been retired, killed or defeated in combat, but violated and humiliated as a person and, more particularly, as a woman. Whether or not the creators intended to suggest that she had been raped, there is no question that her experience constituted sexual assault.

The episode takes on an even more misogynistic tone in the context of Alan Moore's conversation with editor Len Wein during the writing process; according to the author, he checked to see whether his plans for the story had DC's approval, and the reply came swiftly. 'Yeah, okay, cripple the bitch.'[39] Moore has subsequently criticised the title as 'clumsy, misjudged' and admitted, 'I don't think it's a very good book'; but while *The Killing Joke* is, on one level, a deeply unpleasant text, it could be argued that it (whatever the creators' intentions) makes explicit, and reveals as unquestionably shocking and horrific, what was only implied by the broader trends and milder examples of the same period.[40] Another of Moore's late-1980s series was a political exposé called *Brought to Light* (1988); *The Killing Joke* – perhaps unwittingly – performs the same act of foregrounding and revealing.

Gail Simone's website *Women in Refrigerators*, launched in 1999, pioneered a campaign within comics fandom to highlight the misogynistic treatment of women within the superhero genre. Drawing her title from the story of Alex DeWitt, who was introduced as Green Lantern's girlfriend and then brutally murdered, Simone lists the names of

> superheroines who have been either depowered, raped, or cut up and stuck in the refrigerator. I know I missed a bunch. Some have been revived, even improved – although the question remains as to why they were thrown in the wood chipper in the first place.[41]

Her project reveals that while Barbara's shooting and sexual assault may have been the best-known and most detailed example of violence against women in the comics of the period, she was one of many victims and survivors, from Batwoman (dead) to Supergirl (dead, brought back and depowered) to Black Canary (tortured, made infertile, depowered) and Wonder Woman (killed, revived without powers). In 2004, a new female Robin, Stephanie Brown, was added to the roster (tortured, apparently killed).

It could be argued that the risk of injury and death are inherent to the genre. To an extent, like the fact that superhero history is regularly wiped and rebooted, this is true; Batman, Robin, Superman and The Flash all died or were seriously disabled between 1985 and 1992. But as with the convention of rebooted history and wiped memory, the rules work differently for women. On an immediate level, the torture of female characters is invariably more sexualised than with their male counterparts, but longer term, the consequences are also more severe. As John Bartol points out in the follow-up to Simone's article, 'Dead Men Defrosting', while male superheroes are also regularly seriously injured, defeated, disabled and killed, 'in cases where male heroes have been altered or appear to die ... they usually come back even better than before, either power-wise or in terms of character development/relevancy to the reader'.[42]

Batman, to take the most obvious example, was crippled by Bane in *Batman* #497 (July 1993). He was in fighting shape again by *Batman* #509 (July 1994), a mere year later. By contrast, it was twenty-three years after *The Killing Joke* before Barbara re-entered continuity as Batgirl, although there were other characters with that title during the intervening period, and flashbacks, time-travel tricks or dream sequences that teasingly returned her to the role. Barbara herself, of course, was still alive, and was reworked into a new role. She first reappeared in a single, enigmatic panel of *Suicide Squad*, a relatively obscure title not directly related to the Batman mythos, in January 1989. 'Hel-lo,' came a disembodied voice from a computer screen. 'I am O-RA-CLE. Is any-one pres-ent?'[43] In February 1990, the voice of Oracle was finally revealed, again in *Suicide Squad* rather than a Batman title; in this issue, again on a single page, we cut from the computer screen to see Barbara, sitting in a wheelchair, in tears, with a Batgirl doll by her side.[44]

There are arguments for and against Barbara's sustained period in a wheelchair and her new role as the information broker Oracle. On the one hand, the idea that her spinal damage could not be cured is absurd within the superhero universe, with its magic and science-fiction technology; and as the description above suggests, Barbara was frequently portrayed as a tragic but brave figure, or, on other occasions, sexualised in her disability.[45] On the other hand, Oracle became a positive, inspiring figure and a role model for many fans, especially when Gail Simone took over authorship of the character in *Birds of Prey* #56 (August 2003). Under Simone, the *Birds of Prey* title, while still embracing the superhero conventions of crimes and costumes, was increasingly centred around female friendship and the relationships between Oracle, Black Canary and Huntress. Barbara had lost the use of her legs, but she'd got her friends back, rebuilt herself from the micro- and macro-aggressions that followed the Crisis, and (re)discovered sisterhood.

As suggested above, the recovery of women's history and the discovery of female community are often interwoven pleasures and processes. The second wave of feminism was formed, in part, through small groups that brought women into contact with other women; as Anderson and Zinsser say, these groups 'confirmed women's perceptions and validated them with other women's experiences ... confirmed that women's personal experiences had important political implications'.[46] 'Since feminism doesn't have an official history, each woman initially rebels in isolation and alone,' wrote two feminists, under pseudonyms, in 1974. 'If she encounters other women who have also thought through and written down what she experienced, then it is to her as if she discovered her origins. She gets back to herself and her life force.'[47] The words of Anja Meulenbelt, discussing her experience of feminism during the period, could almost serve as a caption from *Birds of Prey*: 'I look for women, hesitating at first, just because I need them. Experiences tumble over each other, hardly patience to let each other talk ... Solidarity. I am not alone, I am not alone.'[48]

Although Simone dealt with the aftermath of *The Killing Joke* with intelligence, conscience, wit and compassion, transforming Barbara from an abandoned, isolated victim into the leader of an all-female group and the centre of a community, the broader DC Comics continuity never allowed Barbara to escape the trauma of her shooting. The scene where she opens the apartment door to the Joker became regarded – partly because of Moore and Bolland's celebrated status as creators – as iconic, and was repeated in multiple stories between 1988 and 2014. Some comics made an extended return to the events of *The Killing Joke*, such as *Batman* #511 (September 1994), where Oracle meets a version of herself who can still walk. In *Booster Gold* #5 (February 2008), the eponymous hero attempts to prevent Barbara's shooting, but realises it can't be changed; in *The Brave and the Bold* #3 (April 2010), Wonder Woman and Zatanna have a vision of Barbara's fate, and, again recognising that the event is fixed in time, take her on a 'ladies' night' in a clumsily charitable gesture.

Even the recent video game *Injustice: Gods among Us* (NetherRealm Studios, 2013), which depicts Joker in his distinctive *Killing Joke* outfit of hat, Hawaiian shirt and tourist camera, and the £100 *Killing Joke* figurine – bringing to life 'one of the most famous scenes in the history of comics' – recall and almost celebrate the scene where Batgirl is wounded and violated.[49] Perhaps most insulting, in terms of Batgirl's identity and history, is the fact that Batman now experiences flashbacks to this crucial moment, despite the fact that he was never present.[50] Just as Barbara was used as a possession and pawn between three men in *The Killing Joke*, so her personal, intimate assault has now been co-opted into Batman's memory as one of the traumatic episodes – his parents' death, the loss of various Robins – that forge his character and justify his 'war on crime'.

As noted above, while *The Killing Joke* gave little thought to Barbara after her shooting – a page of her in hospital serves mainly to make the reader, and Batman, worried for Jim Gordon ('What's he doing to my FATHER?') – a 1996 story, 'Oracle Year One: Born of Hope', offered her the opportunity to protest at her treatment by both Batman and Joker ('I heard how you two stood there, laughing over some private joke').[51] This version of events stood in canon for fourteen years, before it was replaced by another. An *Oracle* one-off comic from December 2010, without fanfare or announcement, quietly rewrites the earlier episode and has Barbara recalling:

> I don't know where I'd be right now if Bruce hadn't come to see me that day. I worked harder on getting well than I had ever worked on anything. Mostly for me, but ... I have to admit the thought of letting Bruce down kept me going on more than one occasion ... I was ready to show him all I had accomplished.[52]

Just as the post-Crisis Batgirl origin dismissed her female friendships and replaced them with a lifelong obsession with Batman – and a flirtation with Robin – so this new *Oracle* origin overruled Barbara's righteous anger and independent achievement from the earlier story and replaced them with meek gratitude. As we have seen, comic book continuity, with its constant fluidity and regular quakes in time and history, has the potential to offer liberating possibilities and opportunities for female characters; but in practice, the process and its effects tend to be conservative and reactionary. This would be the last Oracle story. In 2011, another Crisis occurred – an event called 'Flashpoint' – and Oracle was out of the picture, out of history. For better or worse, she had never existed.

New continuity, new opportunities: Gail Simone's *Batgirl* (2011–14)

In September 2011, Barbara Gordon returned to the role of Batgirl – written by Gail Simone – as part of 'The New 52' reboot that, in an attempt to make continuity simpler and more accessible, streamlined and compressed character history once again. Within this new timescale, Barbara had been shot by the Joker after two years as Batgirl, then remained paraplegic before she was restored to full mobility through experimental surgery. *The Killing Joke* is deemed to have taken place three years before the current story events. Again, this can be seen as a wiping of Barbara's history, erasing her twenty-three years within continuity as Oracle, her friendships and relationships, and her gradually earned role as one of the few disabled icons within the superhero genre. These changes were imposed across the DC range of comics – now reduced to fifty-two titles, each recommencing with issue #1 – by (male) senior management, and Gail Simone, as one of the few female writers for the company, was obliged to work creatively within this new framework.

Simone was well aware of the challenge and responsibility involved, speaking from personal involvement and fan investment about her appointment as the new writer:

> Barbara Gordon is pretty much my everything ... Because of the Batman TV show, she was the reason I fell in love with superheroes. Because she was a redhead who could kick ass, she is the reason I fell in love with comics. For a long time, there was simply nothing else like her in comics, and for me and a lot of other readers, her every appearance was joyful and explosive. For many years, I got to write the

character as Oracle, and there is to this day, no character who means more to me. This is classic Barbara as she was originally conceived, with a few big surprises. It's a bit of a shock, to be sure, but we're doing everything we can to be respectful to this character's amazing legacy.[53]

Simone's run on the title was innovative and energetic, redeveloping Barbara and her relationships swiftly and boldly within the structures established by editorial management. In this version, Barbara suffered PTSD from her experience with Joker, and her trauma and recovery were dwelt upon extensively; the shooting, and the personal struggle that followed, were owned fully by Barbara again as a survivor, rather than being treated as a single incident, crucial mainly as a landmark in the Batman/Joker dynamic. Barbara's voice – smart, self-deprecating, sometimes doubting and sometimes determined – dominated the storytelling, through both first-person captions and dialogue. Her family relationships were now central to the ongoing narrative: not just with her father but with her estranged mother, who returned during an early episode, and her criminal brother, James.[54] Beyond her fractured biological family, and her uncertain relationship with Nightwing and Batman, Barbara was sustained by her close friendships with other women, including her roommate Alysia – the first transgender character in mainstream comic books – and her costumed colleagues. Her relationship with Dinah Lance, the Black Canary, provides a particular emotional touchstone throughout the series. Dinah calls her 'sis', and Barbara narrates, 'In this community, this cape thing … I have a lot of people I RESPECT. A smaller handful I TRUST. And a couple I flat-out ADORE. Black Canary is in the centre of all those groups.'[55]

Gail Simone, Ardian Syaf, *Batgirl: The Darkest Reflection* Volume 1 (The New 52) (New York: DC Comics, 2013)

This Batgirl also meets Batwoman again, and while the encounter begins with Batgirl reflecting 'we've never met' – confirming the erasure of previous history – their brief combat is over within two pages, with Batgirl admitting defeat, calling a truce and using Batwoman's handkerchief to mop her bleeding nose.[56] Despite Simone's enthusiastic embrace of superhero convention, her fight scenes are typically emotional and intellectual interactions, loaded with questions of identity, rather than merely physical spectacle; they reintroduce Batgirl to key female figures like Huntress and Poison Ivy, and find possible alliances behind the initial antagonism.

The most fascinating aspect of Simone's run on the title is perhaps also the most subtle. Simone was working creatively within a set of rules specifying that the events of *The Killing Joke* happened, when they happened and what physical effect they had on Batgirl. She and her artists regularly reincorporated the now-iconic image of Joker – in Hawaiian shirt, appearing at Barbara's door with a gun – as a flashback or nightmare. However, through slight tweaks, she changes the attentive reader's understanding of the 1988 story. In a new origin sequence from November 2012, Simone and artist Ed Benes revisit the moment when Barbara opens the door to Joker and his goons, but relocate her alone with a coffee dispenser, rather than in her father's house serving him cocoa while he organises his scrapbooks. Very quietly, in a single panel, they begin to change history. A subsequent issue has Batgirl unmasking a petty thug to discover he is one of the previously anonymous henchmen – now identified as Danny Weaver – who accompanied Joker that night and, within previous continuity, beat her father, then showed him her naked photographs. Barbara's narration rewrites the canon of *The Killing Joke*:

> The Joker and two thugs stepped into my house. I opened the door. That's what kills me. Cop's daughter. Super hero. And I opened the door. I was supposed to die that night. That was his plan. For my father to find me like that. Something went wrong.[57]

Weaver is shot, and confesses his role in the earlier incident:

> I used to work for Mr J himself, THE JOKER. We never asked what was up … there was a young girl at the door, the Commissioner's daughter. We all HATED the Commissioner. So, I guess I hated her too, you know? […] We left her there. Just took off and left. Went drinking.

Barbara interrupts him: 'You called the POLICE. You called and told them exactly which apartment to go to. You saved my life.' The rewrite is minimal in some ways, but radical in others. Barbara was still shot by Joker – Simone presumably had no way of changing that. But she was no longer shot after her resigned retreat to domesticity; she was surprised early in her career. She was no longer part of a plan to drive Gordon crazy, to prove a point in a larger game between Joker and Batman. We can only guess, as Weaver does, at Joker's motivations, but within this new continuity, woven by Simone and her team across a few pages, he intended to leave Barbara dead. At a stroke, the sexual assault and photographs, along with Barbara's role as a pawn in a game between three older men, are seemingly wiped out of history. We see Joker taking photos of Barbara in flashback, but she is still dressed. She remembers Batman coming to her hospital bedside, but in this retelling, she doesn't accuse him of laughing at her, and he doesn't prompt her recovery, as we saw in the two earlier versions of the story. 'He didn't say anything. He just stood there, holding my hand.'[58]

Brendan Fletcher, Cameron Stewart, Babs Tarr, *Batgirl* #36 (The New 52) (New York: DC Comics, 2014)

Inevitably, Simone's run on the title participates in the erasure involved with every narrative reboot. It repeatedly confirms the compression of Batgirl's career into five years, with her time as a Congresswoman finally and decisively cut and deleted. It rules out Oracle's extended career – the story remains ambiguous as to whether Barbara ever took that title, but at best the two decades of stories about Barbara as a paraplegic information broker are reduced to three years. When Bruce whispers 'You were ALWAYS meant to be Batgirl, Barbara,' Simone also closes down the histories of Cassandra Cain and Stephanie Brown, who took the role of Batgirl during her lengthy period as Oracle, between 1988's *Killing Joke* and 2011's *Flashpoint*, and have since been relegated to the margins of continuity.[59]

Her rewriting of *The Killing Joke*, however, remains remarkable. In a few scenes, almost hidden within a larger story – and that story itself operating in the gaps of the higher-profile, higher-status Batman narrative – Simone changes crucial details of a 'landmark' graphic novel, still rated as one of the key Batman tales of all time, by two of the industry's most celebrated male talents. As a fan turned writer, Simone knows the rules of continuity and canon, aware that if one detail changes – Jim was meant to return to the house and find her dead – the whole story is consequently altered. She uses those rules to serve her own agenda and to serve Barbara.

In July 2014, it was announced that Gail Simone was leaving the *Batgirl* title. She had been dropped from it once before in December 2012 and reinstated in response to fan protest; further disagreements with senior editorial staff had finally prompted her to move on. The new creative team – Cameron Stewart, Brenden Fletcher and Babs Tarr – promised a new, lighter tone for the character, ironically something Simone had requested and been denied during her run on the series. As the discussion above has demonstrated, continuity is a double-edged device that can explode a universe or be wielded as a subtle knife; even between massive, Crisis-scale reboots, writers can change a small detail and allow it to alter a character's history, in a domino effect. Simone was able deftly to rewrite Alan Moore's text from twenty-five years ago; now the new writers are able, if they want, to undo everything she wrought.

Consequences

Does any of this matter? Barbara's fate as Oracle and Batgirl matters to Batgirl fans, no doubt; but is this really more than a matter of interest to a niche readership, a case study in representation that, naturally enough, echoes the representation of women in other forms since the 1960s? I think we can argue that it does matter. It is no coincidence that Freedman's book *No Turning Back* has a pop art image of a superheroine on its cover, opening her shirt to reveal the title. As Whelehan discusses, the image of the 'superwoman' – or rather, the failed 'superwoman', who tried to 'have it all' and be 'like men', but (much like Barbara) became depressed, burned out and isolated – was employed during the 1990s to undermine feminism.[60] Our superhero archetypes act out gender dynamics in larger-than-life terms, reflecting and reinforcing changing social patterns. They are more than fictional characters, confined to their own texts; they are popular icons, operating and signifying far outside the niche readership of comic books.

Most obviously, contemporary audiences know the characters through cinema franchises like Joss Whedon's *The Avengers* (2012), which made a box-office total of $1.5 billion. Those global audiences register the representation of women like Black Widow and they will notice the gaps in representation, too. Young, female moviegoers, whether or not they read comic books – whether or not they know that Supergirl has not appeared on film since 1986, and that Batgirl's last big-screen role was limited to a small part in a Joel Schumacher's derided *Batman & Robin* (1997) – will know that a minor figure like Ant-Man was given a film franchise and a comedy character like Rocket Raccoon appeared in a summer blockbuster (James Gunn's *Guardians of the Galaxy* [2014]) long before Wonder Woman earned her own movie.

If we want to claim that superheroes constitute our contemporary mythology, our new folk archetypes, our inspirational figures and role models, we must also recognise that, as Margaret Marshment notes, 'the picture is political': that, 'despite its complexity, there always is a relationship between representation and reality'.[61] Of the millions of women and girls who watched Christopher Nolan's *Dark Knight Trilogy* (2005–12), only a small proportion will have followed the history and ongoing comic book narrative of Barbara Gordon as Batgirl. But if asked, they would register her absence from the franchise. To recover Barbara from the margins, to remember and retell her story – to make this woman and her history more visible – is a small but significant political act of empowerment.

Notes

1. 'The Florida Paper', cited in Beverley Jones, 'Toward a Female Liberation Movement', in Miriam Schneir (ed.), *Feminism in Our Time* (New York: Vintage Books, 1994), p. 123.

2. Bonnie S. Anderson and Judith P. Zinsser, *A History of Their Own: Women in Europe from Prehistory to the Present, Vol II* (Harmondsworth: Penguin, 1990), pp. 248–9.

3. Virginia Woolf, 'A Room of One's Own' (1929), reprinted in Stephen Greenblatt *et al.* (eds), *Norton Anthology of English Literature* (New York: Norton, 2006), p. 2131.

4. Sandra M. Gilbert, 'What Do Feminist Critics Want?', in Elaine Showalter (ed.), *The New Feminist Criticism* (New York: Pantheon, 1985), p. 32.

5. Annette Koldny, 'A Map for Rereading', in Showalter, *New Feminist Criticism*, p. 54.

6. The script is dated 16 January 1967.

7. Jones, 'Toward a Female Liberation Movement', p. 108.

8. See, for instance, Imelda Whelehan, *Overloaded: Popular Culture and the Future of Feminism* (London: The Women's Press, 2000), p. 1.

9. Gardner Fox and Carmine Infantino, 'The Million Dollar Debut of Batgirl', reprinted in *Batgirl: The Greatest Stories Ever Told* (New York: DC Comics, 2000), p. 13.

10. Ibid., p. 21.

11. Bob Kane, Gardner Fox and Bill Finger, *Detective Comics* #31 (September 1939), reprinted in Bob Kane, *Batman Archives Volume 1* (New York: DC Comics, 1990), p. 53.

12. Ibid., p. 64.

13. 1960s unaired Batgirl pilot. Available at: <https://www.youtube.com/watch?v=QCvw90myFBI>.

14. Frank Robbins and Don Heck, 'The Unmasking of Batgirl', *Detective Comics* #422 (April 1972), reprinted in Various, *The Greatest Batgirl Stories Ever Told* (New York: DC Comics, 2010), p. 40.

15. Frank Robbins and Don Heck, 'Candidate for Danger', *Detective Comics* #423 (May 1972), reprinted in Various, *Greatest Batgirl Stories*, p. 48.

16. Elliot S! [sic] Maggin and Mike Grell, 'The Invader from Hell', *Batman Family* #1 (September–October 1975), reprinted in Various, *Greatest Batgirl Stories*, p. 81.

17. Ibid.

18. Bob Rozakis, Irv Novick and Vince Colletta, 'Startling Secret of the Devilish Daughters', *Batman Family* #9 (January–February 1977), reprinted in Various, *Greatest Batgirl Stories*, p. 96.

19. Bob Rozakis, Bob Brown and Vince Coletta, 'Those Were the Bad Old Days!', *Batman Family* #10 (March–April 1977), p. 9.

20. Ibid., p. 24.

21. Marv Wolfman and George Perez, *Crisis on Infinite Earths* #4 (July 1985), p. 2.

22. Barbara Randall Kesel, Rick Leonardi and Dick Giordano, 'Flawed Gems', *Secret Origins* #20 (November 1987), p. 6.

23. In this retelling, young Babs admires Supergirl as a distant idol.

24. Cary Burkett, Jose Delbo and Joe Giella, 'The Assassination of Batgirl!', *Detective Comics* #491 (June 1980).

25. Randall Kesel *et al.*, 'Flawed Gems', p. 16.

26. Ibid., p. 18.

27. Barbara Randall Kesel, Barry Kitson and Bruce D. Patterson, 'The Last Batgirl Story', *Batgirl Special* #1 (1988), p. 1.

28. Ibid., p. 16.

29. Ibid., p. 21.

30. Ibid., p. 34.

31. Ibid., p. 38.

32. Ibid., p. 35.
33. We should note that author Barbara Randall Kesel was first invited to write for DC after she sent a long letter to then editor Dick Giordano, complaining about the company's sexist representation of women. As with Gail Simone, discussed below, it is difficult to know the editorial constraints under which she was working in this case.
34. Whelehan, *Overloaded*, p. 17. See also Susan Faludi, *Backlash: The Undeclared War against Women* (New York: Crown, 1991), and Marilyn French, *The War against Women* (New York: Ballantine Books, 1992).
35. See Naomi Wolf, *Fire with Fire* (New York: Random House, 1993).
36. See Estelle B. Freedman, *No Turning Back: The History of Feminism and the Future of Women* (New York: Random House, 2002), p. 10.
37. John Ostrander, Kim Yale, Brian Stewart and Karl Story, 'Oracle – Year One: Born of Hope', *The Batman Chronicles* #5 (Summer 1996), p. 3.
38. Bolland's original artwork was even more explicit, showing Barbara fully naked, her breasts displayed, with a burst of dark blood covering her pelvis. See 'NSFW Original Artwork from *Batman: The Killing Joke*', *Comics-X-Aminer*, 1 December 2013. Available at: <http://comics-x-aminer.com/2013/12/01/nsfw-original-artwork-from-batman-the-killing-joke/>.
39. Cosmo Felton, 'No Place for a Girl', *Lonely Gods*. Available at: <http://www.lonelygods.com/w/bat4.html>.
40. George Khoury (ed.), *The Extraordinary Works of Alan Moore* (Raleigh, NC: TwoMorrows, 2003), p. 123, and Barry Kavanagh, 'The Alan Moore Interview: *The Killing Joke* and *Brought to Light*', *Blather.net*, 17 October 2000. Available at: <http://blather.net/articles/amoore/brought-to-light1.html>.
41. Gail Simone, *Women in Refrigerators*. Available at: <http://lby3.com/wir/>.
42. John Bartol, 'Dead Men Defrosting', *Women in Refrigerators*. Available at: <http://www.lby3.com/wir/r-jbartol2.html>.
43. John Ostrander, Luke McDonnell and Karl Kesel, *Suicide Squad* #23 (January 1989).
44. John Ostrander, Robert Greenberger, Luke McDonnell, Geof Isherwood, *Suicide Squad* #38 (February 1990).
45. See, for instance, Tony Bedard, Kevin Vanhook *et al.*, *Oracle: The Cure* (New York: DC Comics, 2009).
46. Anderson and Zinsser, *History of Their Own*, p. 410.
47. Quoted in ibid.
48. Ibid., p. 411.
49. *Spacebound Comics and Books*. Available at: <http://www.amazon.co.uk/Kotobukiya-Artfx-Batman-Killing-Statue/dp/B009T6RLD0>.
50. For instance, Grant Morrison, Sandu Florea, Lee Garbett and Trevor Scott, 'What the Butler Saw', *Batman* #683 (January 2009), p. 13.
51. Ostrander *et al.*, 'Oracle – Year One', p. 3.
52. Marc Andreyko and Agustin Padilla, *Bruce Wayne: The Road Home: Oracle* #1 (December 2010), p. 11.

53. Michael Doran, 'Update 7', *Newsarama*, 6 June 2011. Available at:
    <http://www.newsarama.com/7737-update-7-more-dcnu-batman-reveals-batman
    -inc-info.html>.
54. In The New 52, Jim Gordon is once again Barbara's biological, rather than adoptive,
    father.
55. Gail Simone, Robert Gill and Javier Garron, 'When Pamela Gets Blue', *Batgirl Annual #2*
    (June 2014), p. 1.
56. Gail Simone, Ardian Syaf and Vicente Cifuentes, 'Every Time I Fall', *Batgirl* #12 (October
    2012), p. 4.
57. Gail Simone, Alitha Martinez and Vicente Cifuentes, 'No Darker Shadow', *Batgirl* #8
    (June 2012), p. 6.
58. Gail Simone, Ardian Syaf and Vicente Cifuentes, 'A House Made of Spun Glass', *Batgirl*
    #6 (April 2012), p. 6.
59. Ibid., p. 8.
60. Whelehan, *Overloaded*, p. 12.
61. Margaret Marshment, 'The Picture Is Political: Representation of Women in
    Contemporary Popular Culture', in Diane Richardson and Victoria Robinson (eds),
    Introducing Women's Studies: Theory and Practice (New York: New York University Press,
    1997), p. 129.

11

BATMAN: THE MOVIE
NARRATIVE – THE HYPERCONSCIOUS
Jim Collins

Perhaps the best way to introduce the difficulties involved in trying to specify the distinctive features of the Batman narrative in its various incarnations is to begin by relating what occurred when I began my fieldwork for this article.[1] Entering a mall bookstore, I was faced with a massive Batman display that held the following texts: the novelisation of Tim Burton's film *Batman* (1989); the graphic novels of Frank Miller, *The Dark Knight Returns* (1986) and *Batman: Year One* (1987); another graphic novel (in format at least) entitled *Batman's Greatest Adventures*, which promised to be the best of the original comic books; a traditional small-format paperback, *The Further Adventures of Batman* (1989), in which authors such as Isaac Asimov, Max Collins, Robert Silverberg, Joe R. Landsdale and Stuart Kaminsky constructed still more narratives that promised to take Batman into genres hitherto unexplored; and the *Batman Role-Playing Game* (Mayfair Games, 1989), which allows individual readers/players to assume Bat-identities and construct their own narrative adventures as 'participants'. At the local comic shop, I found the current Batman comic books (standard format), as well as a compilation of one of the most popular of the recent series of comics, bound as the graphic novel *A Death in the Family* (1988), and Alan Moore's special-format comic, *Batman: The Killing Joke* (1988).

The array presented multiple narrativisations of the same figure produced over a fifty-year period, appearing as simultaneous options, a simultaneity made more complicated by the fact that these narratives were not just continuations of an urtext, but, in the case of the *Batman* film and *Batman: Year One*, very ambitious attempts to reconstruct the beginnings of the Batman story, reinventing, as it were, the point of origin for the seemingly endless rearticulations. This array of texts could obviously generate any number of narrative analyses that might concentrate on consistent or inconsistent plot functions, significant alterations in the configuration of characters, the use and abuse of certain topoi, etc. I cannot hope to do justice to all these possibilities in an essay of this length, so I will concentrate on what I consider the distinguishing feature of recent popular narrative,[2] namely its increasing hyperconsciousness about both the history of popular culture and the shifting status of popular culture in the current context.

That popular texts demonstrate an awareness of their antecedents and their rivals in the marketplace is itself not a new development. John Cawelti, in his overview of the genre films of the 1960s and 70s, focused on their 'generic transformation' of the mythology of popular culture according to four different perspectives: the burlesque, demythologisation, the evocation of nostalgia, and affirmation of myth for its own sake.[3] I have argued elsewhere[4] that popular texts construct quite elaborate intertextual arenas at every stage of their development, not just in a post-classical decadent stage – for example, even within the classic period of British detective fiction in the 1930s, texts were already situating themselves very self-consciously in relation to earlier forms of the detective novel, as well as the Great Tradition of the British novel. The hypercon-sciousness of popular narrative in the 1980s is not a matter of popular culture 'suddenly' becoming self-reflexive. Like their forebears, popular texts in the 1980s acknowledge the force of what Umberto Eco calls 'the already said',[5] but rather than simply rework con-ventions within the confines of a specific genre (as do, say, *Chinatown* [1974], *The Wild Bunch* [1969], *All That Jazz* [1979], etc.), texts like Tim Burton's *Batman* (1989), Frank Miller's *The Dark Knight Returns* (1986) and Alan Moore's *Watchmen* (1986) reconfigure that 'already said' by moving across genres, mixing different forms of discourse as well as different media, which by extension alters their traditional modes of circulation.

This reconfiguration involves the inversion of specific generic conventions, but more importantly, it depends upon the amalgamation of disparate narrative and visual codes. Joe R. Landsdale's short story 'Subway Jack: A Batman Adventure',[6] for example, is constructed from a number of fragments that feature different narrative modes – journal entries, case files from the Bat-computer, first-person narration from Batman and Commissioner Gordon's perspectives, third-person narration from the authorial voice, and so forth. This combination of fragments is not especially new or unique, since epistolary novels like Bram Stoker's *Dracula* (1895), for instance, feature exactly such a mixture. Landsdale's story is set apart by the introduction of comic book panels into this series of fragments, at which point the prose of the 'short story' gives way to the visual narration of the comic book. In these panels, Landsdale describes in minute detail not the action as such, but the representation of the action within the panel. For example:

Series of Panels, Rich in Shadow and Movement

1) Batcave – Interior

Background: Blue black with stalactites hanging down from the cave roof like witch fingers. There's enough light that we can see the wink of glass trophy cases. Their interiors, except for two – one containing a sampling of the Penguin's umbrellas and another containing Robin's retired uniform – are too dark for us to make out their contents. But we can see the larger ...[7]

The juxtaposition of different media underscores the inseparability of the action from its codified representation; it acknowledges, very explicitly, the complexity of current popular culture in which the negotiation of the array (of the 'already said') forms an essential part of the 'action' of the narrative for both author and audience.

In a recent *Dr. Strange* comic,[8] for example, the cover appears to be that of a tabloid rather than a comic, entitled *Now*, self-consciously modelled after the *National Inquirer*. This cover promises 'A Special Bound-to-be-Controversial New-Book Excerpt about Dr. Strange – The Man – The Myth – the Magic', as well as a 'Startling Interview with Dr. Strange Author Morgana Blessing', and another story in which Janet Van Dyne (aka The Wasp of *Avengers* fame) tells Princess Di to 'Keep your hands off my man, Princess!' The first page of the comic shows an enraged Dr Strange throwing down this copy of *Now* in disgust, followed by two pages of comic book panels in which Strange discusses this outrage with his colleagues. On the following page, the comic gives way to the tabloid excerpt, an extended prose section featuring 'photographs' of Dr Strange (his high school graduation picture – 'Portrait of the Sorcerer as a Young Man' – his mansion on Bleeker Street, his meeting with Moebius on a recent trip to Paris), file photos of the actual locations of his adventures, artists' conceptions of the author Blessing's description of those adventures, stills from a short-lived TV show, a series of photos and drawings of 'the Drac Pack', a vampires-through-the-ages composite. This section is followed by the interview with the author, after which the comic panels return and then give way to a 'Guest Editorial' by J. Jonah Jameson (editor of *The Daily Bugle*, featured in *Spider-Man* and other Marvel comics), 'reprinted' from *Now* magazine, in which Jameson questions the validity of the excerpts and discusses plans for their publication and circulation.

This hybridisation of popular narrative does not destabilise the already said as much as it reveals its fluidity, the absence of any kind of unseen hand or unitary hierarchy that might still delimit the appropriate subject matter, function and audience for different forms of cultural production. In their seminal study of the Bond phenomenon,[9] Tony Bennett and Janet Woollacott make the key point that Bond is a 'mobile signifier', subject to 'multiple activations' which adhere to the texts like so many encrustations, thereby undermining any notion of the 'text itself' or the 'original' text. The figure of the superhero, especially Batman, has clearly become such a mobile signifier, but the activations of Batman by Burton, Miller and company in the later 1980s are differentiated from the redefinitions of Bond in the 60s and 70s by the degree of hyperconsciousness the former display concerning their own status as mobile signifiers, subject to further rearticulation as they circulate throughout disparate cultures, or, more accurately, different micro-cultures. The focus of this essay will be this hybridisation, this narration by amalgamation that is a response to the ways that the superhero has been already activated, an attempt to retell the story of Batman that recognises full well that retelling the story is impossible without reconfiguring the encrustations that have become as inseparable from the 'text' as any generic convention or plot function.

Gaudi Knight: calling up and cutting up the past

Just as we can no longer imagine popular narratives to be so ignorant of their intertextual dimensions and cultural significance, we can no longer presuppose that the attitude towards their antecedents, their very 'retro' quality, will be in any way univocal.

Divergent strategies of rearticulation can be discerned not only between different 'retro' texts but, even more importantly, within individual texts that adopt shifting, ambivalent attitudes towards these antecedents. Burton's *Batman* depends on two such conflicting strategies, and the differences between them are perhaps best understood by comparing the scenes in which Batman and the Joker actively play with images. Throughout the film, we see both figures watching television and manipulating images. That the struggle between them is in large part a televisual one becomes most obvious when the Joker, seeing that Batman has gained greater coverage on the local news programme, asks what kind of world he lives in 'when a guy in a Bat suit can steal my press', then smashes his set in disgust. The destruction of the image here is part of a series of image deformations that the Joker engages in throughout the film. In his hideout, we see the Joker producing 'cut-ups' out of the photographic images which surround him, and then in the later scene at the museum, he defaces one masterpiece after another, either by painting over the original or writing his name across its surface. This hijacking of signs is most obvious in his seizure of the television signal and his replacement of scheduled programming with his own gruesomely parodic advertisements.

Batman's manipulation of images, on the other hand, operates according to an altogether different dynamic. Like the Joker, Batman is shown watching television a number of times in the film, and, like his adversary, he appears to be surrounded by images that he controls for his own purposes. Just as the Joker appears to be practically engulfed by the images he cuts up, the first shots of Batman in the Batcave show him seated before a bank of video monitors, surrounded on all sides by the images of his guests that his hidden cameras have been recording, and which he *calls up* rather than *cuts up* in order to bring back a reality that he has somehow missed. Where the Joker's manipulation of images is a process of deformation, Batman engages in a process of retrieval, drawing from that reservoir of images which constitutes 'the past'. This tension between abduction and retrieval epitomises the conflicting strategies at work in this film, a text which alternately hijacks and 'accesses' the traditional Batman topoi.

The tension between these two opposing yet intermingled strategies of rearticulation is especially prominent in the climactic confrontation between the pair atop the cathedral. The scene's function within the plot could hardly be more traditional – Batman and arch-villain face off in a final battle conducted in an outrageously oversized, artificially isolated location, with Batman using his physical prowess and his utility belt to conquer his opponent. In providing the expected narrative closure, the film unproblematically calls up the appropriate narrative topoi. But the work of the narration here is not restricted to completing the plot, the syntagmatic axis of the narrative. The layering of intertexts that occurs simultaneously deforms those same topoi by resituating them along a paradigmatic axis of antecedent representations of suspense, horror, etc., making explicit connections that were traditionally unstated, as well as introducing juxtapositions that are 'foreign' to the Batman myth. As for the former, the choice of the cathedral, complete with gargoyles, is the culmination of the gothic citations that pervade the text, citations which represent the medieval, Roman-tic, modernist and postmodernist incarnations simultaneously – for example, the explicitly gothic dimension of the cathedral's ornamentation and interior, as well as the Wayne Mansion and the chemical plant that resembles a gothic castle more than a factory; the *mise en scène* that visualises Batman as a menacing figure from 'the dark-ness'; the suggestion that he is a blood-drinking vampire; the doppelgänger relation-ship between the hero-villain; the use of the woman (specifically the control of the woman's body) as the embodiment of their conflict; the very self-conscious invocation of Gaudi's Sagrada Familia cathedral in Barcelona.

But the cathedral scene in *Batman* is not simply a filmic equivalent of Gaudi's design. The former is differentiated from the latter by both the simultaneous presence of the multiplicity of gothic incarnations as well as the introduction of other citations not so explicitly associated with the gothic. The narration of the film, the very forma-tion of the *mise en scène*, depends upon a process of calling up the gothic, but it also 'steals' specific shots from classical Hollywood films just as self-consciously. The high-angle shots of the seemingly endless flights of stairs is reminiscent of *Vertigo* (1958) (as is the basic deployment of characters – woman at the top of the stairs, hero working his way up to save her), and the alternation of high- and low-angle shots between the Joker and Batman and Vicky Vale as they hang from the side of the cathedral is explicitly taken from the conclusion of *North by Northwest* (1959) (as well as the climac-tic confrontation scene in *Blade Runner* [1982]). The invocation of texts as different as *Dracula*, Notre Dame de Paris, the Sagrada Familia and *Vertigo*, as well as all the antecedent comic and graphic-novel versions of Batman, produces an eclecticism that is in many ways even more complicated than Gaudi's cathedral, which postmodernist architects consider one of the high temples of eclecticism. Where Gaudi's cathedral is a repertoire of architectural styles, the narrative structure of *Batman* is founded on a hybrid repertoire, calling up and/or abducting motifs from cinematic and non-cinematic texts alike – comic books, Hollywood films, nineteenth-century novels, medieval architecture, etc.

In his article 'Casablanca: Cult Movies and Intertextual Collage' (written well before Burton's *Batman* went into production), Umberto Eco argues that *Casablanca* (1942) remains a cult favourite because

> Forced to improvise a plot, the authors mixed a little of everything, and everything they chose came from a repertoire that had stood the test of time. When only a few of these formulas are used, the result is kitsch. But when the repertoire of stock formulas is used wholesale, then the result is architecture like Gaudi's Sagrada Familia: the same vertigo, the same stroke of genius.[10]

The relevance of the quote to this scene in *Batman* is obviously uncanny, but I intro-duce it here in order to distinguish between the intertextual narration of *Casablanca* and *Batman*. Although both rely on repertoires of what Eco has referred to as 'the already said', the uses of that repertoire reflect quite different negotiations of their semiotic environments. Where the former might well be a surplus that suggests pastiche, the latter reflects a meticulously constructed *intertextual arena* in which the text positions itself within its own invented array.[11] Eco himself acknowledges that *Casablanca* and a film like *Raiders of the Lost Ark* (1981) involve different contexts regarding both their production and reception, insisting that

> It would be semiotically uninteresting to look for quotations of archetypes in *Raiders* or in *Indiana Jones*. They were conceived within a meta-semiotic culture, and what the semiotician can find in them is exactly what the directors put there. Spielberg and Lucas are semiotically nourished authors working for a culture of instinctive semioticians.[12]

One could easily add Tim Burton, Anton Furst and company to that list of artists, and *Batman*'s audience must certainly be as instinctively semiotic in their orientation. But Eco seriously underestimates the 'interestingness' of meta-semiotic cultures, and his preference for the naiveté of *Casablanca* (and its authors and audiences) seems like badly misplaced nostalgia that fails to specify when a semiotic sophistication somehow corrupted the innocent pleasures of popular culture. What Eco fails to pursue here is just when this semiotic nourishment began, or when audiences became 'instinctively' something other than they were before. What factors produced such awesome and all-pervasive changes in just four decades?

Answering that question has everything to do with specifying the distinctive features of contemporary popular narrative, but it is answerable only if we begin by rejecting the notion that texts are 'interesting' semiotically only when they can be decoded/re-encoded by an analyst capable of exposing the hidden textual mechanisms. The foregrounding of the citations, the explicitness of the calling-up/cutting-up process, reflects a different dynamic in the exchange between producer and audience, one based on the sophistication of both parties, each possessing knowledge formerly (and allegedly) accessible only to the semiotician. The hyperconsciousness of both sides of the 'communication exchange' results from the persistence of the repertoire of antecedent representations, which continue to live in both the various institutionalised reservoirs of images (the comics industry, television, etc.), and by extension in the cultural memory of the audiences that have refused to treat popular texts as disposable commodities. The intertextual narration in a film like *Batman* does indeed depend on a kind of meta-semiotic environment, and as such it is a shining example of meta-popular culture. The emergence of this 'meta-pop'[13] in the 1980s is due to a number of interconnected factors, but its all-pervasiveness in so many different media cannot be fully accounted for by the usual explanation that 'retro' culture is simply 'late' capitalism's way of recycling old merchandise as new for guaranteed audiences, an explanation that carries with it the usual one-dimensional indictment of nostalgia. This explanation has its obvious merits: the Batman 'phenomenon' that began to gather force even before the release of the film represents contemporary capitalism at its most sophisticated. (Eileen Meehan's essay in this collection effectively details these operations.) But to attribute the growing popularity of Batman in the past few years to the force of advertising doesn't explain its attraction to quite diverse audiences, especially the audiences of the comic and graphic novels, which until quite recently enjoyed virtually no advertising support, and were seldom seen in the mall bookstores where they are now so prominently displayed. The fact that Miller's *Batman: Year One* is now offered by the Quality Paperback Book Club as part of a full-page advertisement in the *New York Times Book Review* suggests that the popularity of Batman goes well beyond the sort of people who will use Batman lunch boxes.

The meta-pop phenomenon of the 1980s may be unimaginable outside of corporate capitalism, but its emergence and continuing popularity is attributable to another set of factors in which nostalgia is conceived not in terms of merchandising, but cultural memory. The hyperconsciousness of contemporary popular narrative depends upon a simple realisation on the part of both the producer and the audience: popular culture has a *history*; earlier texts do not simply disappear or become kitsch, but persist in their original forms as well as diverse reactivations that continue to be a source of fascination for audiences, providing pleasure in the present and forming a fundamental part of cultural memory (which has everything to do with that current pleasure for some audiences). The relationship between any text and its audience may of course be said to depend on the appeal to a shared body of assumptions, values, etc., which may be maintained or violated by senders or receivers of a given text. What characterises the meta-pop texts of the 1980s is their appeal to a body of popular texts which are now seen as inseparable from those cultural values, since those texts have been the most forceful vehicles for their transmission and/or contestation.

Eco's apparent dismissal of this meta-semiotic environment is perhaps due to his belief that the mass media may be 'genealogical', in that 'every new intention sets off a chain reaction of inventions, produces a sort of common language'. But they 'have no memory because, when the chain of imitations has been produced, no one can remember who started it, and the head of the clan is confused with the latest great grandson'. Eco goes on to compare Wim Wenders's *Hammett* (1982) to John Huston's *The Maltese Falcon* (1941), arguing that despite the technical sophistication of the former, the latter 'will always enjoy a certain ingenuousness that in Wenders is already lost'.[14] The issue of ingenuousness hides the crucial question: why did Wenders want to make a film about Hammett in the first place? The fascination for the antecedent/originary text is part of a complicated process that distinguishes meta-pop culture – the ad hoc construction of 'traditions' within popular culture, operating outside the realm of the academy (and the traditional mechanism responsible for the canonisation of privileged works). Do the various Batman narratives in their various formats really indicate a lack of memory, a purposeful confusion of themselves and their antecedents as somehow indistinguishable from each other? Alan Moore's *The Killing Joke* and Frank Miller's *Batman: Year One* both attempt to invent new origins for stock characters of the Batman saga, but in so doing they reintroduce the original comics and invest them with the power of any originary narrative. In Moore's work, we learn the origin of the Joker, a failed stand-up comic who turns to a life of crime only after the tragic accidental death of his adoring wife. While Moore 'invents' this aspect of the Batman narrative, he also depends heavily on the original comic book version of the Joker's origins as the infamous Red Hood who jumps into a vat of toxic waste. The end result is both an acknowledgment and an extension, reintroducing the Red Hood narrative while inventing a still earlier backstory.

How many ways do we watch the Watchmen?

The graphic novels of Frank Miller and Alan Moore epitomise the hyperconsciousness of contemporary popular culture in their sophisticated invocation/rearticulation of the historical tradition of the comic book, and the forms of visual narration they have developed (along with artists Klaus Janson, Lynn Varley and Dave Gibbons) represent a meta-semiotic re-envisioning not only of the world of the superhero, but also of the cultures which consume those narratives. What differentiates this visual narration from earlier comics is their extension of the spatial and temporal dimensions of the narrative well beyond the 'action' of the diegesis. The producers of Dark Knight[15] and Watchmen[16] orchestrate textual space and time, but in doing so they also emphasise (through different, but related means) that to envision textual space is to envision at the same time the cultural space surrounding it, specifically the conflicting visual traditions that constitute those semiotic environments.

The most striking feature of Dark Knight, for example, is the radical heterogeneity of its images in regard to their scale, framing and stylistic tradition. Miller's work is often labelled 'cinematic', and in many ways the alternation of image scale does resemble the shift between establishing shots and close-ups in a film narrative. But such analogies are also potentially misleading, because they fail to do justice to the juxtaposition of the disparate images that appear within the single page or two-page unit that constitutes the 'tableaux' of the graphic novel. Mise en scène in film depends upon sequential replacement of one image with another, but the mise en scène of the comic depends upon simultaneous co-presence on the page. In the traditional comic form, from classical Batman back to the Images d'Épinal broadsheet narratives of fairy tales, the consistency of the size and arrangement of the images (respecting the same left-to-right arrangement of print narratives) de-emphasised simultaneity, the chronological succession of narrative incident producing a sequential processing of the images in which the preceding images did not disappear, but were pushed back by the forward thrust of the narrative. But the juxtaposition of different-sized frames on the same page, deployed in constantly changing configurations, intensifies their co-presence, so that the entire page becomes the narrative unit, and the conflictive relationship among the individual images becomes a primary feature of the 'narration' of the text, a narration that details the progression of the plot, but also the transgression of one image by another. The end result is a narration that proceeds syntagmatically across and down the page, but also forces a paradigmatic reading of interrelationships among images on the same page or adjacent pages, so that the tableaux move the plot forward but encourage the eye to move in continually shifting trajectories as it tries to make sense of the overall pattern of fragmentary images.

A number of different visual strategies are used throughout *Dark Knight* to intensify this double movement that projects the story forward frame by frame at a relentless pace, but also arrests the strict linear movement of the image (and the eye) through the invention of the fragmented tableaux that draw relationships between images that are non-successive, but co-present. In the concluding two pages of Book I, the top third of each page is a single image with a cluster of smaller images composing the middle third, and another single image filling out the bottom third. The similarity in configuration makes the two pages read as three bands of images, the spatial continuity intensified in the top band by the use of lighting and angles in the background, so that the two images which follow each other in time appear to form the same spatial/temporal unit, the lines of the venetian blinds seeming to lead back to the same vanishing point. The middle band develops in a more linear fashion on each page, since contiguous images constitute a spatial and temporal continuity, but only up to a certain point. The contiguous clusters of images in the left-hand side of the middle band follow the action in a continuous fashion, but they differ drastically in image size and scale, 'cutting' between long shots and extreme close-ups, followed by a page-wide image in the bottom-third band, which breaks this pattern in reference to size and in the sudden introduction of colour. The right-hand side of the bottom-third panel resembles only the top panel, so that the top and bottom bands of the tableau appear to form one unit, and the middle bands two more. While this subdivision of tableaux into units moves the eye in different rhythms and trajectories all over these pages, the resulting fragmentation is counterbalanced by the use of other visual paradigms which serve to interrelate the disparate units so they might still be conceived as an overall tableau. The consistency in regard to colour – the stark contrasts between dark and white, with yellow introduced only in the images of a massive explosion, the symbolic face of the bat, and the balloons of one dialogue exchange – serves to coordinate (rather than unify) the fragments, just as the top and bottom bands provide a frame for the conflictive relationships within. The construction of tableaux as units of visual narration, then, operates according to two sets of opposing imperatives, to move forward and sideways, to fragment and coordinate the pieces at the same time.

The conflictive relationships among images in *Dark Knight* are further sharpened by the combination of images that reflect very different discursive/institutional sources. In addition to the traditional comic, complete with balloons and panels of written text, the individual images in *Dark Knight* at times take on the function of the Eisensteinian 'montage cell', especially in Batman's flashback to the murder of his parents on pages 14–16 of Book I, where the size and scale are both extremely regular and the sequence is 'done silent'. But at other points in the narrative, this regularity is not only broken, but very self-consciously 'shattered'. After three pages of these regularised cells, the pattern is internalised and foregrounded within the first image at the top of the next page, in which a window frame in the foreground splits the plane in exactly the same pattern as the top three bands of images on the page, a pattern reiterated by the shadow of that window frame pattern on the floor of the first frame and in the foreground of the fourth image. The framing of those window frames begins to change in the second and third row of images, with close-ups of the intersection of the frame bars now set off-kilter, emphasising their 'cross' formation, which are then seen in shadows 'across' the close-ups of Batman's face. This movement away from symmetry is further emphasised by the appearance of the bat, first within the window frame and then in extreme close-up across the frame bars, forming a strong diagonal slash across the image, so that the diagonal slashes across Batman's face in the next frame appear to be the shadows of the bat wings more than the window frame. The progression towards increasingly tighter close-ups within symmetrical frames is then literally and metaphorically smashed in the bottom quarter of the page, where the bat crashes through the window, shattering its frames as well as the symmetrical grid of the page itself. This shattering process could hardly be more self-conscious, and it epitomises this text's determination not only to invoke/rearticulate the figure of the superhero, but also the conventions of visual narrative through which those figures were envisioned – the content of the myth being inseparable from its 'framing'.

Where the use and misuse of traditional comic cells and montage techniques represent one aspect of the narration of *Dark Knight*, at other points in the narrative individual images become television images in bevelled frames, deployed in successive but not contiguous frames usually on a white background with 'voices' appearing below the image. These television images are ubiquitous throughout the narrative, providing a visual and ideological counterpart to the images of the 'real world' that surround them. At other points in *Dark Knight*, we are presented with full-page images resembling classic book illustrations or posters that dwarf the adjacent ones. These oversized illustrations (often referred to as 'splash' pages) function as a sequence of composite images, forming their own paradigm of Batman as Cultural Icon, alternately depicted as muscle-bound superhero or old, demonic-looking pall-bearer of the psychotic American military, or the crazed cowboy on horseback leading his private army of street punks. The latter typifies the composite nature of these images, which feature the same kind of layering of iconography characteristic of different genres and periods (the costumed superhero of the modern comic book, the cowboy of the nineteenth century and the punk costumes of the postmodern city) that was prevalent throughout Burton's *Batman*. Throughout the text, these different image functions/conventions are combined within the same tableau. On pages 14–15 of Book II, for example, the tableau consists of a full-page unframed 'illustration' on the left, and a combination of comic and television frames on the right-hand page (the former including dialogue and interior monologue in balloons or boxes within the frame, the latter accompanied by text below the set). The juxtaposition of these different types of images, each with their own narrational function, bringing with them their respective conventionalised contexts and associations, produces a hybrid tableau which accentuates the different discursive registers of those images by their very proximity. This sort of juxtaposition separates *Dark Knight* from earlier experiments in frame variation like those of Winsor McCay and George Herriman. Where the radical variation of frame size and placement in *Little Nemo* and *Krazy Kat* were tableau-oriented, the discursive framework of each image remained consistent, resulting in visually dazzling, but homogeneous tableaux. *Dark Knight*'s juxtapositions of disparate forms of visual discourse constitute heterogeneous tableaux which may be considered chaotic according to traditional notions of the well-made plane, but nevertheless operate systematically, according to their own logic – i.e. that textual space, like the actual space it depicts (and through which it will circulate as a text), is envisioned according to different institutionalised modes of image-making that were formerly separate, but are now thoroughly intertangled, a world of fragmentary images that might produce some kind of provisional 'big picture', but only when read in aggregate in all their simultaneity.

In Alan Moore's and Dave Gibbon's graphic novel *Watchmen*, the narration by amalgamation is made still more heterogeneous by the inclusion not only of other visual discourses, but also an entire range of non-visual discourses representing different articulations of the superhero as cultural artefact. At the level of the individual page, the development of images in *Watchmen* follows a standard grid with only slight alteration until the series of oversized splash pages at the beginning of Chapter XII. The profoundly intertextual nature of the narration is elaborated on a frame-by-frame basis within that grid, its very regularity emphasising the coexistence of antecedent text and current incarnation. Beginning in Chapter II, *Tales of the Black Freighter*, a comic from the early 1960s, is introduced into the narrative of *Watchmen*. It begins rather simply as a comic-within-a-comic conceit, with a young man reading this comic as he sits next to the news-stand operator. After the initial establishing shots of this figure, with the rolled 'parchment' text panel from *Freighter* appearing over his image as a kind of misplaced 'voiceover' narration, an over-the-shoulder shot shows the actual pages from the comic he is reading, then gives way to actual panels from '*Freighter*', now inserted within the grid, replacing the *Watchmen* images, and then set in varying patterns of alternation throughout the next three chapters, the movement between the two narratives usually accomplished through 'graphic matches' (nearly identical compositions with character substitutions). The intertextual frame here could hardly be more explicit, *Freighter* becoming quite literally an intertext of *Watchmen*, with its images interrelated on a frame-by-frame basis, enjoying the same visual status as the *Watchmen* narrative.

The significance of the *Tales of the Black Freighter* is explained by the long excerpt reprinted from the *Treasure Island Treasury of Comics* that appears at the end of Chapter V. This explanation does not comment directly on the insertion of this comic within the diegesis of *Watchmen*, but it does insert *Watchmen* in the history of the comics, contextualising both *Black Freighter* and *Watchmen* in relation to that historical continuum, which is intensified by those intertextual connections. The explanatory 'reprint' is one of several such inserts, placed between the chapters of *Watchmen*, which function as another chain of intertexts. Where the *Black Freighter* images are interrelated within the narrative world of *Watchmen*, the non-comic inserts comment directly on the various ways superhero narratives are contextualised, expanding the intertextual dimensions of the text still further. These inserts include extracts from the published memoirs of a superhero, academic studies on the significance of superheroes and vigilantism, fan letters to superheroes, and letters from a superhero to his employees regarding the successful marketing of himself and his colleagues as Fully Posable Action Figures. Watchmen presents not only a highly sophisticated rearticulation of superhero narrative, but a fully fictionalised set of encrustations that constitute the actual 'text' of Watchmen, which consists of the comic panels, but also the various forms of discourse which it either generates and/or circulates through. This sort of hyperconsciousness, then, is a far more elaborate form of self-reflexivity than that which characterises the meta-fictional texts of the 1960s, because it shifts the focus away from the agonies of personal expression, stressing instead the intertextual dimensions of both textual production and textual circulation. Texts like Watchmen, Batman and The Dark Knight Returns are paradigmatic examples of contemporary popular culture, where texts now evidence a highly sophisticated understanding of their semiotic environments, thereby collapsing the moments of production and eventual circulation so that the former appears inseparable from the latter.

That the cultural terrain of the contemporary crime-fighter can be adequately envisioned or 'imaged' solely by this assemblage of conflicting images suggests a great deal about the nature of that terrain and the narratives that represent it. Kevin Lynch's notion of the 'imageability' of certain environments (that particular cities are more 'legible' than others because they may be more easily imaged by their inhabitants – i.e. that certain urban environments produce strong, holdable images) is especially relevant, but only if we revise his terminology somewhat.[17] The terrain of Dark Knight and Watchmen appears endlessly 'imageable' in that it can be envisioned any number of ways. It becomes legible – comprehensible, manageable – not in one totalising picture, but in a cluster of images that reveal its discursive discontinuity. The imaging of contemporary environments, then, must begin by recognising the ways in which it has already been framed; the terrain consists of a set of physical characteristics as well as a set of frames in which our successful negotiation of the former depends entirely on our developing a 'competence' in understanding the latter.

The hybridisation of popular narrative that is a response to this cultural terrain which comes to us already framed by different genres, different discursive frameworks and the divergent ways of seeing they entail necessitates a reconsideration of 'genre' as a category of narrative. In other words, where 'genre' depends on the relative stability of its distinctive characteristics that make possible its recognisability as a style for both the producers and consumers of those texts, the hybrid texts discussed above are aggressively destabilising, retaining extremely familiar conventions, but juxtaposing them in ways that undermine the purity or integrity of genre as a category. Rick Altman, in his pivotal article on the semantic and syntactic approaches to genre film,[18] argues that the former approach concentrates on primary elements (iconography, location, stock characters, etc.) that define a genre and make it recognisable as such, while the latter defines genericity in regard to the syntactic bonds which set the relationship between those elements. According to Altman, 'Just as individual texts establish new meanings for familiar terms, only by subjecting well known semantic units to a syntactic redetermination, so generic meaning comes into being only through the repeated deployment of substantially the same syntactic strategies.'[19] But hybrid popular narratives are distinguished by their adoption of those well-known semantic units, deployed according to substantially *different* syntactic strategies. More precisely, hyperconscious popular narrative adopts or appropriates diverse semantic units which, by this point in the development of popular culture, are always already encrusted with one or more sets of syntactic associations that are inseparable from those individual units. The composite splash page in *Dark Knight*, where Batman races through the city on horseback, trailed by an army of street punks, involves not just the combination of different semantic elements, different types of iconography, but the juxtaposition of hitherto divergent syntactic relationships between heroism and villainy, civilisation and savagery, order and disorder, etc., which invest those icons with such different semiotic and ideological values.

This hybridisation could be seen as the development of a second-order 'meta-syntax' that sets new relationships between minimal units that are already bundles of syntactic relationships. While such a description might begin to account for the effect of the simultaneity of the 'array' on the structure of genre narrative, it presupposes: a) that such a meta-syntax could be constructed out of the heterogeneous, ever-shifting, ever-rearticulated 'already said'; b) that individual texts like *Dark Knight*, *Watchmen*, *Batman*, *Blade Runner*, *Mad Max: Road Warrior* (1981), *The Adventures of Buckaroo Banzai* (1984), *Earth Girls Are Easy* (1988), etc. are still committed to producing even ad hoc versions of such a meta-syntax, that they have any interest in codifying or 'setting' new relationships that might encourage audiences to interpret them in the same way they do traditional genre works that have been reconfigured by those very texts. In other words, these graphic novels and films resist any kind of easy 're-genrefication'. Though they are composed entirely of generic material that remains clearly marked as such within these texts, their very hybrid nature works at cross-purposes with the accepted notion of genre as a recognisable, coherent set of formulae that audiences may read predictively. Eco, in his own analysis of the Bond phenomenon, contended that the enjoyment of the generic text comes from precisely that stability that allows predictability, comparing the Bond text to a Harlem Globetrotter game. 'We know with absolute confidence that the Globetrotters will win; the pleasure lies in watching the trained virtuosity with which they delay the final moments, with what ingenious deviations they reconfirm the foregone conclusion.'[20] The hybrid texts purposely frustrate both that stability and that predictability through a process of reconfiguration that precludes the construction of new syntax – not only do we no longer know the inevitable outcome (to say that the conclusions of *Dark Knight* and *Watchmen* are not predictable is an understatement of the first order), but we no longer know if it is really the Globetrotters we are watching, or a group of borderline psychotics dressed in the same costumes, playing a similar game, but driven by entirely different motivations that might push them over the edge at any moment.

In their frustration of the homogeneity and predictability considered the prerequisite for 'genericity', these hybrid popular narratives could be considered 'post-generic' insofar as they resist syntactic stabilisation, but are still composed of what, at this point, must be considered generic artefacts. The trendiness of the 'post' prefix makes the choice of the term dubious, but it describes this seemingly paradoxical situation, in which we encounter texts composed entirely of generic materials that contradict, as an assemblage, the function of genre as the coordinator of narrative convention and audience expectation. These texts remain generic, but only if we recognise that 'genericity' is now a matter of rearticulation and appropriation of semiotic categories, no longer just the ritual confirmation of deeply held community beliefs, nor the secret agenda of Hollywood as 'dominant ideology'. 'Genericity' in this context is not a form of myth, but a feature of hyperconscious discourse, which might still present itself as 'myth', but only in quotation marks, as the citation of antecedent texts rather than the innocent, direct expression of transcendent values.

Texts like *Batman: The Movie*, *The Dark Knight Returns* and *Watchmen* that feature narration by amalgamation suggest the emergence of a new type of narrative which is neither a master narrative that might function as a national myth for entire cultures, nor a micro-narrative that targets a specific subculture or a sharply delimited semiotic community. The popularity of these texts depends on their appeal not to a broad general audience, but a series of audiences varying in degrees of sophistication and stored cultural knowledge (i.e. exposure and competence). As *aggregate narratives*, they appeal to disparate but often overlapping audiences, by presenting different incarnations of the superhero simultaneously, so that the text always comes trailing its intertexts and rearticulations. The significance of the superhero can be ascertained, to borrow a phrase from A. J. Greimas, only in terms of an encyclopedia rather than a dictionary, as an assemblage of intertextual representations rather than a set definition. The simultaneity of the array, then, produces a form of narrative which is itself an array of narrative and visual codes that tells the story of the superheroes, but also tells in the process the history of their cultural significance.

In cultures that are incessantly imaged or framed according to conflicting exigencies of different media, genres and institutions, our notion of narrative 'action' can no longer be restricted to character adventure. The rearticulation of the already said, the ways in which narrative conventions are hybridised and forced to account for a quite different cultural terrain become another type of 'action' that has emerged as a central feature of popular entertainment. At this point, distinctions between the telling and the told, the narration and the narrative, the diegetic action and the extradiegetic intertextual references become not only difficult to make, but decidedly misleading. In the hyperconscious narrative, the intertextual arena can no longer be confined to the realm of the extradiegetic, nor can the conditions of the narrative's eventual circulation be considered somehow 'outside' the text. Both now form part of the 'action' generated by the text, rendering narrative pleasure a process of negotiating the array for both the creators and audiences of those texts.

Postscript

I began my original essay by describing the tableful of Batman texts I encountered at the mall bookstore, but that seems like a paltry list compared to the array of *Batman* narratives available at Amazon. The sort of meta-pop phenomenon I was trying to account for then we might now call a transmediated metaverse with multiple points of entry, and the accumulation of knowledge about that metaverse that fans acquired from comics, graphic novels, films and games could easily be described as a process of additive comprehension with its own very particular architecture of participation. But as useful as those terminological distinctions might be, if I wanted to update my argument to include the most recent incarnations of Batman, I'd need to account for both the quantitative and qualitative changes that have occurred within the realm of *media literacy* over the course of the past twenty-five years.

The sort of hyperconscious narrative that I was describing in my essay was only the initial phase of what would become ubiquitous over the next two decades. The exuberant intertextuality that distinguished films such as Tim Burton's *Batman*, Kathryn Bigelow's *Near Dark* (1987), David Lynch's *Blue Velvet* (1986) and then *Twin Peaks* (1992) is now commonplace, a textual feature of superhero films as well as an astonishingly wide range of popular entertainment. We now live in a post-*Simpsons'* universe; take all of the intertextual references out of *Family Guy* (Fox, 1998–2001, 2005–) and there'd be no there *there*, he said intertextually. But if I were going to account for the fact that what I then referred to as meta-pop has become omnipresent, I'd have to introduce a parallel history of another of type of textuality, namely paratextuality. Paratextuality, the permutations of which Jonathan Gray has rigorously documented, has become an industry unto itself within the past two decades, making the line between primary and ancillary text ever harder to draw. Where, for example, would we locate the elaborate viral marketing campaign for *Dark Knight* crafted by 42 Entertainment which was, in effect, an especially artful alternate reality game incorporating a wide range of old and new media forms of textuality, from websites, to graffiti, to scavenger hunts, to cellphones hidden in cakes, to campaign buses. The commercial intent – to advertise the film and generate greater return for it and all of its related merchandise – is indisputable. On the other hand, to categorise this viral campaign as pure commodification and not to recognise the virtuosity of the paratextual manoeuvres would be to impose procrustean distinctions that would only misrepresent the intricate relationships between studio and fan production, and, more broadly, between culture and commerce, which are intrinsic to popular entertainment in the twenty-first century.

While tracing the historical arc of paratextuality would be central to updating my essay, ultimately, I'd have to explore another aspect of the Batman metaverse if I hoped to define the operative media literacy which now serves as the baseline for the production and enjoyment of popular narrative – how have new digital technologies transformed the delights of that metaverse, not just quantitatively but qualitatively? My essay devoted a significant amount of attention to the scenes in which we see both

Batman and the Joker playing with images in order to explore the media literacy that had become such a vital component of the cultural landscape of the film. We see Batman manipulating images drawn from his video bank archives and the Joker making 'cut-ups' out of his own reservoir of newspaper images. Their war for the hearts and minds of Gotham City was, to a great extent, a war of images. If we fast-forward through the Nolan trilogy, we find comparable scenes, perhaps none more explicit than the episode in *The Dark Knight* where Batman meets Lucius Fox in a cavernous surveillance room filled with what appears to be an endless array of monitors that represents the entirety of Gotham City in aggregate cellphone transmission made visual through sonar. As Fox tells him, 'With half the city feeding you sonar, you can image all of Gotham.'

Nolan's Batman standing before the screens echoes Burton's Batman sitting before his video monitors, tempting me to use that scene as a hinge-point to construct a kind of 'Bat-palimpsest', the perpetuation of certain patterns across what has become an ever more sophisticated digital landscape. But there is a more effective way to address the kind of media literacy that now decodes the imaginative landscape of the Batman metaverse. Imagine the Bat-fan in front of their screen of choice, whether it be their laptop or digital device, navigating through that metaverse, watching the films, reading the comics, playing the games, going to sites, all of which can be called up on the same screen. The multi-functionality of the digital device as screen/private archive/portal to the internet allows the Bat-fan to enjoy the pleasures of media manipulation formerly reserved for superheroes and arch-villains, as well as auteurs, conceptual artists and literary novelists of first-wave postmodernism. The determination to actually include the archive within the text is omnipresent in countless texts inside the Batman metaverse, an impulse nowhere more explicit than in the Deluxe Edition box set of the *Batman Begins* DVD, which included within the accompanying booklet copies of the original *Batman* comic as well as the two comics Nolan cited as his primary inspirations, *The Man Who Falls* (1989) and *The Long Halloween* (1996–7).

This box is a pristine example of one kind of archival textuality. Batman fans are now able to enjoy the adventures of their favourite hero in their narrative format of choice and, at the same time, enjoy the curatorial pleasures within their own archives. The need for an 'archive' of stored textual knowledge to fully savour the permutations of a given metaverse was obviously present long before the advent of digital culture in the form of that hodgepodge of screen memories, stacks of comics, VHS tapes and whatever else became meaningful in the ad hoc, ragtag form of additive comprehension. That archive is now also included in the box – not the boxed set of the DVD release, but the box that is the digital device. When I wrote my essay way back in 1989, creative manipulation of the archive was something that directors of blockbusters and writers of comic books were doing as well as bona fide artists, and that activity had significant entertainment value for mass audiences who took delight in watching that intertextual play. If we fast-forward twenty-five years, the creative play within the Batman archive of our digital devices involves not just a quantitative increase in the number of Batman texts that can be accessed on the same screen or downloaded into the same private archives. The navigational and curatorial capabilities of the device generate another kind of entertainment value in which we no longer just watch various Batmen in front of their screens, but sit before our own screens as Viewer-Reader-Gamer-Listener-Users and play the game called Batman.

Notes

1. I would like to thank Greg McCue for his invaluable suggestions while I was completing the original chapter.
2. Given the conflicted nature of the term 'popular' culture, I should explain why I chose it. I use popular here, first because my argument is that while the hyperconsciousness that I attribute to these texts has been all-pervasive in the 'high arts' of the modernist/postmodernist era, we now encounter it in texts found most often in multiplex cinemas and grocery-store book racks. Here I opt for 'popular' as opposed to 'mass' because of the Frankfurt School presuppositions surrounding the latter (i.e. the Culture Industry cranks out homogeneous texts and subjects). For a more detailed explanation of why I find these presuppositions ideologically repugnant (as well as quaint), see Chapter 1 of my *Uncommon Cultures: Popular Culture and Post-Modernism* (New York: Routledge, 1989).
3. John Cawelti, '*Chinatown* and Generic Transformation in Recent American Films', in Gerald Mast and Marshall Cohen (eds), *Film Theory and Criticism* (New York: Oxford University Press, 1985), pp. 503–20.
4. Collins, *Uncommon Cultures*.
5. Umberto Eco, *Postscript to The Name of the Rose* (New York: Harcourt Brace, 1984).
6. Joe R. Landsdale, 'Subway Jack: A Batman Adventure', in Martin H. Greenberg (ed.), *The Further Adventures of Batman* (New York: Bantam, 1989), pp. 103–38.
7. Ibid., p. 109.
8. Roy Thomas, Dann Thomas and Jackson Guice, *Dr. Strange, Sorcerer Supreme*, vol. 1 #9 (November 1989).
9. Tony Bennett and Janet Woollacott, *Bond and Beyond: The Political Career of a Popular Hero* (New York: Methuen, 1987).
10. Umberto Eco, '*Casablanca*: Cult Movies and Intertextual Collage', in *Travels in Hyperreality* (New York: Harcourt Brace, 1987), p. 202.
11. For a more detailed explanation of this term, see Collins, *Uncommon Cultures*, pp. 43–64.
12. Eco, '*Casablanca*', p. 210.
13. For further discussion of this term, see Jim Collins, 'Appropriating Like *Krazy*: From Pop-Art to Meta-Pop', in James Naremore and Patrick Brantlinger (eds), *Modernity and Mass Culture* (Bloomington: Indiana University Press, 1991), pp. 203–23.
14. Eco, '*Casablanca*', p. 146.
15. Frank Miller, *Batman: The Dark Knight Returns* (New York: DC Comics, 1986).
16. Alan Moore and Dave Gibbons, *Watchmen* (New York: DC Comics, 1986).
17. Kevin Lynch, *The Image of the City* (Cambridge, MA: MIT Press, 1960).

18. Rick Altman, 'A Semantic/Syntactic Approach to Film Genre', *Cinema Journal* vol. 23 no. 3 (Spring 1984), pp. 6–17.

19. Ibid., p. 16.

20. Umberto Eco, 'Narrative Structures in Fleming', in Glenn W. Most and William W. Stowe (eds), *The Poetics of Murder: Detective Fiction and Literary Theory* (New York: Harcourt Brace, 1983), p. 113.

12

SAME BAT CHANNEL, DIFFERENT BAT TIMES
MASS CULTURE AND POPULAR MEMORY
Lynn Spigel and Henry Jenkins

I don't know about the rest of you,
but I feel the cruellest
nostalgia – not for the past –
but nostalgia for the present.

Andrei Voznesensky, 'Nostalgia for the Present'

Batmania hit hard in the summer of 1989, bringing with it a wave of nostalgia that superseded the dark postmodern text projected on the nation's cinema screens.[1] As the truly hysterical Joker danced with the Devil in the pale moonlight, Batmania sparked memories of a better world where good guys always finished first, if only through a camp sensibility. *Batman* and the gift-shop craze of high-ticket memorabilia provoked fond longings for an innocent world of childish play where kids once gathered on back porches, imitating their favourite TV heroes. This super-commercialised comic book text gave rise to a potent historical fantasy as people reappropriated the past to restructure the present.

Looking backwards is a major preoccupation of historians, but it is also something that people do in personal daydreams and everyday contexts as a way to understand their present-day lives. History and memory have traditionally remained separate projects – one highly objective and rational, the other highly subjective and playful. In relatively recent years, historians have questioned this set of 'common sense' oppositions by thinking about the interplay between memory and history in a variety of ways. Intellectual and cultural historians, most notably David Lowenthal, have examined how the idea of memory has been used in various historical and cultural contexts, linking the concept of memory to the ways in which historical consciousness has functioned throughout time.[2] Lowenthal's wide-reaching arguments consider literary and historiographical texts as well as recent research in cognitive psychology that studies 'real uses of memory in humanly understandable situations'.[3] Other historians have examined popular conceptions of the past by using methods of oral history. For example, working within the fields of folklore, anthropology and history, ethnohistorians have tied historical methods to anthropological models in an attempt to explain how people from non-literate cultures use oral traditions and storytelling

practices in their everyday life.[4] Other historians have concentrated on modern western cultures, typically using oral sources as a way to do social history or 'history from
below'. These studies incorporate voices of everyday people into the historical narrative, and, in a dialogical manner, often give community members opportunities to use
their own historical consciousness in politically relevant ways. The community activist
work of Britain's History Workshop and America's Massachusetts History Workshop
are exemplary of this use of oral sources within an explicitly political activist agenda.[5]

Important as oral history is, it tends to sidestep the question of exactly what these
oral utterances represent. Although these histories often ask how oral testimony functions as evidence in an empirical sense (are these memories true or false representations of the past?), they say little about the larger theoretical and historiographical
problems entailed. What do oral testimonies tell us about the nature of historical consciousness? How much are these testimonies based on pre-packaged and culturally
agreed-upon notions of the past? Finally, how does the historian give voice to these
memories? Are we simply a transparent medium for other people's speech, or does
the process of history writing itself tailor these remembrances in specific ways?[6]

Indeed, past experiences, whether academic or personal, can never be directly
reclaimed or relived; they can only be comprehended through the construction of narratives that reshape the past in response to current needs, desires and perspectives. As
Hayden White has argued, the craft of the historian involves the 'emplotment' of past
events into familiar narratives that make sense to people in the present. This emplotment
necessarily ensures that the telling of history is bound by discursive conventions that
simplify and reduce the multiplicity of past events.[7] Although accepting White's basic
intervention, Dominick La Capra has offered an important caveat when he claims that

> White's poetics of historiography stem from a neo-idealist and formalist conception
> of the mind of the historian as a free-shaping agent with respect to an inert,
> neutral documentary record. ... This view tended to obscure both the way people in
> the past lived, told, and wrote 'stories' and the way the documentary record is itself
> always textually processed before any given historian comes to it.[8]

La Capra's challenge is one that is necessarily unresolvable in any complete way, but
it does suggest the need to form a dialogue between historical conventions of writing
and the way language is used in everyday life.

For historians interested in the interplay between mass media and audiences, this
is particularly important, since we are involved in writing historical narratives about
people's encounters with storytelling practices of a prior era. Although we will never
be able to recapture subjective experiences of the past in any definitive way, it is possible to provide partial pictures by reconstructing dialogues between audiences and
texts. Along these lines, George Lipsitz, Colin MacCabe, Roy Rosenzweig and others
have considered the way media texts evoke and shape memories of the past.[9] In this
essay, we would like to build upon this work by looking at the way memories have
reshaped the popular myths surrounding a superhero. What interests us particularly

about Batman is the way this comic book hero has retained cultural significance since Bob Kane created him for DC Comics in 1939. Over the past fifty years, the Caped Crusader has battled crime in the Columbia serials of the 1940s, the TV version and feature-length movie of the late 60s, Frank Miller's *Dark Knight Returns* and other graphic novels of the 80s, and the 1989 blockbuster movie. Along the way, his image was licensed to toy companies like Ideal and Mego that produced everything from Bat-action figures to Bat-periscopes. Batman, then, has become part of our culture's popular memory. Why those memories persist and how they function in everyday life presents a fascinating set of questions for cultural historians.

Writing about *Batman* in the summer of 1989, it became difficult to separate the nostalgic memorabilia and TV reruns from the television *Batman* of the 1960s (ABC, 1966–8) that we sought to explain. For us, like many of our generation, the series evoked vivid images: dime-store heroes and vampish heroines, summer nights with the TV flickering pop art images, children dressed for Halloween, Bat-toys we never had. In short, *Batman* seemed a point of entry into children's culture of the 1960s, and it also provided a clue to yuppie culture of the late 80s, because these memories seemed to constitute a common heritage of a particular adult generation.

Rather than seeing these subjective and often emotional memories as an obstacle to overcome, we decided to incorporate them into our study by setting up a dialogue between our own historical writing and current recollections of the TV programme. Unlike academic history, popular memory is integral to everyday experience; it is memory for the public and understood as being contingent and open rather than definitive and closed. Popular memories are part of the living culture; they are adopted in ways that make them useful for and relevant to present-day situations.

In addition, popular memory is grounded in notions of personal identity. Unlike historical writing conventions that demand the mediation of authorial commentary, popular memory is based on the dialectic between autobiography and the description of public events. This autobiographical element continually entwines the past in present-day identities, so that people strive to place themselves in history, using the past as a way to understand their current lives. As John A. Robinson suggests, 'There is a generative dimension to remembering that mediates the matching of past and present. … Autobiographical memory is not only a record, it is a resource.'[10]

The following essay examines how *Batman* was received by television critics and audiences at the time of its initial airing and then focuses on the way that present-day people who were children in the 1960s remember the TV series and use it in their construction of autobiographical history. For this latter section of the essay, we interviewed adults who were children at the time of *Batman*'s first run on network TV. Certainly, these interviews will not reflect directly how people interpreted *Batman* in their youth; rather they will suggest how individuals use *Batman* as adults to reconstruct their childhood memories and personal histories. Taken as a whole, the study begins to reveal how the initial critical response to *Batman* differs from long-range memories of the series, and more generally it suggests how the reactivation of television in everyday memory might intersect with academic histories of popular culture.

Commercial into pop into art into camp

In 1966, *Mad* magazine asked, 'Would a typical red-blooded teenage boy really be happy dressing in some far-out costume and spending all his free time chasing crooks?' In standard parodic prose, the magazine showed the 'Boy Wonderful', driven 'batty' by his association with the Caped Crusader, trying to overcome public ridicule by plotting his superior's death. Forced to recognise his ward's embarrassment, the more TV-literate 'Bats-man' reminds his earnest sidekick:

> What difference does it make if they laugh, as long as they watch the program! For years TV tried to reach the so-called sophisticates with 'Playhouse 90,' 'The Defenders,' etc. But they wouldn't even turn on their sets. Then along came 'Bats-man' and the industry made a revolutionary discovery. Give the 'in' group garbage – make the show bad enough and they'll call it 'camp' and stay glued to their sets!

Grasping the logic of this industry rhetoric, the 'Boy Wonderful' shouts, 'Holy Nielsen! You mean the swingers are really squarer than the squares?'[11]

This exchange encapsulates the contradictory reception of *Batman* in the 1960s. Like the 'Boy Wonderful', some critics saw the series as an embarrassing blight on their good taste and cultural standing. Savvy ABC executives were likely to identify with the slick and supercilious attitudes of the jaded 'Bats-man', who is willing to sacrifice critical dignity for big-money profits. Still others, less idealistic or cynical than either of *Mad*'s two extremes, entered the fray and battled, often with ambivalent attitudes, over the series' uncomfortable position within the traditional canon of television art.

Upon its initial premiere in 1966, *Batman* evoked a series of critical disputes. Influential East Coast critics, who had typically derided Hollywood's half-hour series, were undecided about how to place the programme in existing cultural hierarchies. For many of these critics, *Batman* appeared to be an emblematic example of commercial trash, with its childish heroes, melodramatic plots and formulaic structure. *Batman* thus defied the golden rules of Golden Age critics who elevated programmes that perpetuated TV's 'hyperrealism', its complete simulation of real-life events.

Indeed, Golden Age newspaper and magazine critics like Jack Gould, Gilbert Seldes and John Crosby claimed that television was best when it presented a heightened sense of reality, when it made viewers feel as if they were actually on the scene, watching a performance in a theatre. For this reason, critics typically elevated the live broadcast over and above filmed presentations. As Seldes told prospective television writers in 1952,

> The essence of television techniques is their contribution to the sense of immediacy ... they [audiences] feel that what they see and hear [on television] is happening in the present and is therefore more real than anything taken and cut and dried which has the feel of the past.

Similarly in 1956, Gould claimed in the *New York Times Magazine* that live television was better than film, because it 'unites the individual at home with the event afar. The viewer has a chance to be in two places at once. Physically, he may be at his own hearthside but intellectually, and above all, emotionally, he is at the cameraman's side.'[12] Critics argued that the immediacy of live presentation was enhanced by slice-of-life stories, characterisations that were drawn with psychological depth, naturalistic acting styles, and shooting strategies that gave the home audience an intimate 'box seat' view of the performance.[13] Indeed, for television's first critics, this hyperrealist aesthetic, with its stress on intimacy, immediacy and presence, was the preferred form for television programmes. Within this hierarchy, the live anthology drama and reality-based news series like *See It Now* (CBS, 1951–8) reigned supreme.

By the time of *Batman*'s appearance in 1966, the number of programmes that met these criteria had dwindled considerably. After 1955, the networks increasingly replaced their expensive live formats with relatively cheap filmed Westerns, sitcoms and adventure shows produced by Hollywood studios. Critics lashed out against these 'degraded' texts, often attacking the regulatory and industrial system that allowed television to be invaded by inferior product.[14] In 1961, in response to these developments, Federal Communications Commission (FCC) Chair Newton Minow told the National Association of Broadcasters that television was a 'vast wasteland' in need of cultural reform. Minow's reform plans centred around the aesthetic hierarchies of the Golden Age critics, calling for more reality-based, educational programmes and fewer game shows, sitcoms and Westerns. Meanwhile, the critics adopted Minow's phrase, applying it to the commercially successful and highly popular series that failed to capture the sense of presence and intimacy so crucial to their notions of TV art. From this perspective, the decidedly unrealistic elements of *Batman* placed it in the outer limits of the critical canon. However, in the mid-1960s, this kind of criticism was disrupted by the new aesthetic of popism, which challenged the aesthetic categories of Golden Age discourses. Andy Warhol's pop creations valorised mass art by appropriating commercial practices for use in high art circles.[15] Beginning in the early 1960s, Warhol used the techniques of slide-screen projection and stencilling to paint over the comic book outlines of Batman and Superman. He applied similar techniques of photo-screen processing to real-life celebrities ranging from movie queens such as Elizabeth Taylor to political leaders such as Chairman Mao, and also used it to mass-produce lifelike replicas of consumer goods, most notably his Campbell soup cans. By applying mass-production techniques to portraiture and by using popular icons as artists' models, Warhol flattened out distinctions between 'good' and 'bad' art. Art was no longer defined by subjective states of talent, greatness and beauty. Instead, pop revelled in cartoonish characters, cheap industrial tools, gimmicky special effects, a flattened-out and exaggerated sense of colour, repetitious imagery and factory-like production.

Not incidentally, all of these aesthetic principles were also part of television's dominant practice, and the striking similarities between popism and television style were not lost on the East Coast TV critics. However, while Warhol and his haute-

Life Magazine Inc., March 1966

couture followers rejoiced in recycling the low for higher pleasures, the TV critics were uneasy about assigning value to what they traditionally viewed as cultural debris. Indeed, popism completely disrupted the typical criteria for judging television. Whereas TV critics valorised programmes that simulated reality and invited viewers to participate intimately with the 'real' event represented on the TV screen, pop denied this illusionary social relationship between viewer and text. In pop, the image was the image and the viewer was the consumer, pure and simple. Pop replaced TV's hyperrealism with hypercommercialism. For TV critics who lived through the sponsor boycotts of McCarthyism and the histrionics of the quiz show scandals, this valorisation of commercialism must have been particularly hard to take. However, since these critics also travelled in New York art circles, they had trouble ignoring the fact that popism was the latest thing in museums, fashion magazines and even in the New York theatre, where Superman and Mad were both adapted for theatrical presentation.

In this context, Batman precipitated a questioning of critical hierarchies, because it self-consciously placed itself within the pop art scene. While shows like Bewitched (ABC, 1964–72), Mr Ed (CBS, 1958–66) and My Favorite Martian (CBS, 1963–6) stretched the limits of TV's realist aesthetic, Batman laughed in the face of realism, making it difficult for critics to dismiss the programme as one more example of TV's puerile content. Batman presented these critics with the particularly chilling possibility that this childish text was really the ultimate in art circle chic. As Life claimed in 1966, 'Pop art and the cult of Camp have turned Superman and Batman into members of the intellectual community, and what the kids used to devour in comic books has become a staple in avant-garde art.'[16]

ABC used the pop aesthetic as a promotional and publicity vehicle, giving the show cultural status by hyperbolically referring to its Warholian aspects. For the premier episode, the network scheduled a 'cocktail and frug' party at the fashionable New York discotheque Harlow's, with Andy Warhol, Harold Prince (director of the League of New York Theaters) and other celebrities attending the event. (Jackie Kennedy, already immortalised in pop iconography on Warhol's canvas, rejected ABC's invitation.) After cocktails, ABC invited the group to see a special screening of Batman at the York Theater, whose lobby was adorned with Batman drawings and stickers that sported slogans proclaiming their status as 'authentic pop art'. Guests at the York were reportedly unexcited about the show, but in true pop style, they cheered when a commercial for cornflakes came on the screen. *Batman* was thus promoted as being part of a larger pop art scene, where unlikely mixtures of social elites gathered to celebrate their own celebrity-hood while getting high on mass culture. As one person at the York Theater said, 'The real pop art ... are the people who are attending this party.'[17]

Television critics often had trouble reconciling popism with their own cultural hierarchies and expressed highly ambivalent sentiments. Jack Gould, the veteran television critic for the *New York Times*, admitted that the programme was 'a belated extension of the phenomenon of pop art to the television medium', and as such might 'be an unforeseen blessing in major proportions'. But with an intonation of sly irony and an acknowledgment of his dubious role as television critic in this case, he also cautioned that pop art had its own inverted standards and that *Batman* 'might not be adequately bad' when compared to *Green Acres* (CBS, 1965–71) and *Camp Runamuck* (NVC, 1965).[18] Similarly, one reviewer for the *Saturday Evening Post* claimed:

> The pop-art fad, one of whose twitches is an enthusiasm for old comic books, had made *Batman* almost flopproof. As long as the pop fad lasted there could be no such things as *bad* pop art ... *Batman* is a success because it is television doing what television does best: doing things badly. *Batman*, in other words, is so bad, it's good. ... *Batman*, faithfully translated from one junk medium into another junk medium, is junk squared. But it is thoroughly successful and – this troubles critics for whom good and bad are art's only poles – it can be surprisingly likable.[19]

In this case as elsewhere, the TV critic felt obliged to express his chic understanding of the new pop aesthetic, even as he mistrusted its ultimate merits.

If pop presented irresolvable anxieties for the critics, they eased these tensions by shifting their focus to *Batman*'s 'camp' qualities. They typically displaced their confusions about the changing status of good and bad art by proposing cultural splits in terms of reception aesthetics. *Batman*, they argued, had two distinct audience groups – adults who understood the programme through camp reception practices, and children who interpreted *Batman* as a fantasy portrayal of real life. *Time* magazine saw *Batman* as a shift from television's 'single-standard' that demanded 'simple-minded cartoons for kids [and] simple-minded programs ... for adults' towards a style of entertainment open to multiple interpretations. While the kids took *Batman* 'seriously', the grown-ups were 'supposed to see Batman as camp'. Similarly, *Newsweek* reported that 'Adults like him [Batman] as a campy put-on. Children thought of him as a hero.' According to one report in the *Saturday Evening Post*, this dual address even created domestic conflicts: '*Batman*-watching families with eight-year-olds in them are torn with dissention because of the "Daddy, stop laughing" problem.'[20]

The camp sensibility gave adult readers, who had previously displayed disdain for mass culture, a comfortable distance from the show's comic book materials, because it reworked the aesthetics of popism in a way more in line with the firmly entrenched 'wasteland' critique. Having earned a legitimate intellectual status after Susan

Sontag's 1964 essay 'Notes on Camp', camp was particularly high cultural capital for television critics at the time.[21] In its earliest years, popism was virtuous in its appeal to mass culture; the pop sensibility exalted in a commercial sublime where mass art was experienced with a kind of detached exhilaration.[22] Camp, however, was playful. It reread mass culture through irony. Its appeal was based on laughing at the empty ideals of outworn texts and faded stars and, for some oppressed groups, this ironic pose was a particularly liberating reception practice. Gay men, for example, resurrected stars such as Judy Garland, Joan Crawford and Montgomery Clift, stars whose tragic life histories threw their romanticised film images into relief. But if camp provided gay men with viewing strategies that expressed their own marginalisation from dominant modes of representation, it allowed straight readers to reaffirm their superior position within the critical hierarchy even as they began to embrace elements of mass culture previously disdained.

When discussing his own interpretive strategies, William Dozier, producer of the series, suggested that the camp sensibility was structured into the programme for exactly these reasons. By the 1960s, Dozier was firmly entrenched in the canon of Golden Age excellence for having produced *Playhouse 90* (CBS, 1956–61), one of the most prestigious and fondly remembered live anthology dramas. Given his status in the cultural elite, Dozier recognised the potentially degrading results of producing a television show based on a comic book hero. Remembering this conflict in a 1986 interview, Dozier admits, 'I had never read a Batman comic book; I had never read *any* comic book. When I was growing up I read *David Copperfield*, *Great Expectations*, and the things you are supposed to read.' Invited to produce the programme, Dozier initially had to familiarise himself with the comic book mythos, resulting in an embarrassing moment when an old associate saw him reading the comics:

> Now I couldn't tell him why a full grown man was sitting there with a lap full of Batman comic books … I felt a little bit like an idiot. … At first I thought they [ABC] were crazy … if they were going to put this on television. Then I had just the simple idea of overdoing it, of making it so square and so serious that adults would find it amusing. I knew kids would go for the derring-do, the adventure, but the trick would be to find adults who would either watch it with their kids, or to hell with the kids, and watch it anyway.[23]

Dozier's awareness of the polysemic nature of reception worked perfectly for ABC executives seeking to appeal to a cross-section of adults and children who watched TV in the early prime-time hours. By 1966, this was a tried and true strategy for the network, which had already programmed dual-address cartoons like *The Flintstones* (1960–6), *The Jetsons* (1962–88) and *The Bugs Bunny Show* (1960–75) in similar time slots. As one *New York Times* reporter explained about *Batman*, 'ABC could not afford to put the show in an expensive time slot if it only appealed to children; they don't have the buying power.' Thus, Dozier's polysemic approach potentially allowed the network to appeal to 'everyone from the milk to the martini set'.[24]

Bat-brats and innocent children

Not all observers shared the producer's and sponsors' enthusiasm over the programme's dual address. Eda J. LeShan, a child psychologist and New York educator, asked the readers of the *New York Times*'s Sunday magazine to consider what happened when camp confronted childhood innocence: 'If camp involves a wry sophistication, an adult grasp of subtleties in language and point of view, does it matter that children watching this program take it absolutely literally?' LeShan thought that children's literalisation of the programme content had brought 'a new kind of wildness in the children's play' that erupted in elementary schools and day-care centres where Bat-brats, clad in home-made capes and cowls, tried to imitate the series' carefully choreographed slug fests: 'One kid pushes another, and suddenly, there's Batman in the middle, socking both of them and running off triumphantly.'[25] Her article attracted considerable response from concerned parents, who wrote to report similar incidents in their neighbourhoods. 'My six-year-old and three-year-old have been wild since Batman's appearance on the scene. We're plagued by the dynamic duo,' one Massachusetts mother reported. Another mother confirmed that Bat-play was 'rough, disorderly, loud and generally aggressive', expressing her hopes that children would soon 'lose their lust for this aggressive fantasy world' and return to the standard children's classics.[26] In these accounts, *Batman* embodied the brutal threat that popular culture posed to middlebrow sensibilities endorsed by the American educational system. Schoolteachers and concerned parents stood as the last bulwark protecting childhood innocence from the corruption of commercial culture, 'at war with Batman' for control over their youngsters' impressionable minds.

LeShan insisted that the programme's young viewers were 'completely confused' about its moral orientation. More generally, however, the confusion that LeShan ascribes to the child was actually a product of the adult mind that wrestled with ways to understand children's play.[27] Cartoonish illustrations of brawling Bat-bullies competed for space in magazines and newspapers with cute photographs of children in handcrafted costumes dancing and leaping with youthful vitality. A *New York Times* article on the death of a young British boy who accidentally hanged himself while play-acting *Batman* was followed one day later by a report on Adam West and Burt Ward, who were dressed in full costume, presenting Junior Good Citizens' awards to worthy children at a Central Park ceremony.[28]

At the centre of these debates about *Batman*'s effect on children was the more general ambivalence about the programme's status as high or low art. In discussions of children, taste distinctions were transformed into moral dilemmas and social problems. The controversy surrounding the show, of course, was simply a new skirmish in a much older battle to define what constituted appropriate children's entertainment. Mark West has traced this controversy from Anthony Comstock's crusade to regulate the content of dime novels at the turn of the century, to the rise of pressure groups in the 1930s and 40s who were concerned about movies and radio programmes, to 50s attacks on the debased nature of rock and roll, TV and comic books.[29] In all cases, childhood was conceived as a never-never land where sexuality was taboo and violence unwelcome. In accordance with this ideal, social reformers typically prescribed a children's culture of innocence, sweetness and higher morals that conformed to adult aesthetic standards.

As Jacqueline Rose claims, this Peter-Panish version of childhood innocence is so conventionalised in our culture that it has become the reigning fantasy at the heart of children's literature:

> Childhood … serves as a term of universal social reference which conceals all the historical divisions and difficulties of which children, no less than ourselves, form a part. There is no child behind the category 'children's fiction,' other than the one which the category itself sets in place, the one which it needs to believe is there for its own purposes.[30]

For the critics of mass culture, this *tabula rasa* conception of the child was often instrumental in the promotion and enforcement of conventional cultural categories. By evoking the 'threat to children', social reformers typically justified their own position as cultural custodians, linking (either implicitly or explicitly) anxieties about violence, sexuality and morality to the mandates of good taste and artistic merit.

Fredric Wertham's *Seduction of the Innocent*, the cornerstone of the 1950s campaign against crime comic books, is a perfect example. The book provided a number of rationales for reform, including the comics' fostering of racial and sexual antagonisms, anxiety over fascistic 'might makes right' ideologies, hesitancy about violent and morbid imagery, and appeals to anti-Communist and homophobic sentiments.[31] Yet, many of Wertham's frequently repeated claims centred around the low aesthetic status of the comic book and the ways its visual immediacy left children vulnerable to its sordid contents. He described comic books as 'a debasement of the old institution of printing, the corruption of the art of drawing and almost an abolition of literary writing'.[32] The book's final chapter, 'Homicide at Home', placed this antagonism towards comics in a much broader cultural context. Wertham claimed that audiences whose generic expectations were shaped by early and constant exposure to comics demanded similar styles of entertainment from the movies and television. In addition, he feared the commercial success of shows like *Captain Video* (DuMont, 1949–55), *Sky King* (CBS, 1951–62), *The Adventures of Rin Tin Tin* (ABC, 1954–9) and *Adventures of Superman* (syndicated, 1952–8) would lead the networks to model children's programming upon the crime comic's sensationalistic themes and crude content.[33]

Wertham's shift of attention towards children's TV reflected the increasing public interest in the role that the medium played in children's social and cultural development.[34] As early as 1949, PTA members voted at their national convention to keep an eye on 'unwholesome television programmes'. In subsequent years, various school boards across the country surveyed TV's effects on youth,[35] while popular magazines cautioned against the 'parental dilemma' that TV brought to the home.[36] Such concerns were given legislative credence in the 1954 hearings held by Estes Kefauver's Senate Subcommittee on Juvenile Delinquency and in subsequent hearings chaired by

Thomas Dodd, both of which focused on television as one of the major factors contributing to a perceived increase in youth crime. Reform sentiments became even stronger by the end of the 1950s. Ron Goulart's *The Assault on Childhood* (1959) and Jules Henry's *Culture against Man* (1963) directed attention to the ways that advertisers targeted children for commercial exploitation.[37] In 1961, Newton Minow incorporated this view into his 'vast wasteland' campaign, claiming that children's television was 'just as tasteless, just as nourishing as dishwater'.[38]

In the popular press of the 1960s, these reform discourses provided a primary way of thinking about television's relation to young people.[39] Popular magazines like *Saturday Review*, *Reader's Digest* and *Parents* championed a succession of popular programmes (*Ding Dong School* [NBC, 1952–6], *Romper Room* [syndicated, 1953–94], *The Shari Lewis Show* [NBC, 1960–3], *Captain Kangaroo* [CBS, 1955–84], even *The Huckleberry Hound Show* [ABC, 1958–62]) that better adhered to their own aesthetic criteria and which promised to raise the standards of audiences accustomed to the heroics of Roy Rogers and the low comedy of Pinky Lee.[40] *Parents* magazine published annual reports from the National Association for Better Radio and Television (NABRT), evaluating all of the network series according to their suitability for young viewers. The organisation's critiques suggest that aesthetic hierarchies were at the centre of public concerns about media violence and vulgarity. The NABRT promoted the folksy humour and hominess of programmes like *The Andy Griffith Show* (CBS, 1960–8) and *The Patty Duke Show* (ABC, 1963–6), while rejecting the grotesquery of *The Addams Family* (ABC, 1964–6) and *The Munsters* (CBS, 1964–6). It celebrated the educational merits of nature documentaries, while condemning the sensationalism of *Flipper* (NBC, 1964–7), *Lassie* (CBS, 1954–74) and *Gentle Ben* (CBS, 1967–9). More generally, the Association directed protests against larger-than-life adventure programmes such as *Lost in Space* (CBS, 1965–8), *Man from U.N.C.L.E.* (NBC, 1964–8), *The Wild Wild West* (CBS, 1965–9), *Voyage to the Bottom of the Sea* (ABC, 1964–8) and *Johnny Quest* (ABC, 1964–5), whose intensified fascination with crime, suspense and intrigue were 'terrifying to young children' and 'unpleasant' to adults.[41]

Batman emerged, then, at the end of nearly two decades of controversy surrounding the quality of children's television and the suitability of comic book adventure programmes for young viewers. Some of the critics could trace their activism back to earlier participation in Wertham's anti-comic book campaigns, regarding the series as yet another attempt to televise crime comics. Moreover, the series seemed a composite of all the qualities that the NABRT protested about in earlier programmes: an exaggerated style of performance, lurid use of colours and graphics, larger-than-life protagonists, cliffhanger conclusions, the glamorisation of criminals and the ridicule of traditional authority. The merchandising of the series, which amounted to some $75 to $80 million in sales in 1966, fuelled concerns about the commercial exploitation of child consumers. Not surprisingly, reform organisations expressed scepticism and dismay over the premiere of *Batman*. PTA magazine, for example, warned that children 'should not be permitted to watch' *Batman* unless they have 'developed antibodies to nightmares by previous exposure to crime-and-horror comics and television programs'.[42]

Indeed, the regulation of children was particularly important for those critics who were confused about their own cultural authority at a time when critical hierarchies were shifting ground. Popism blurred distinctions between high and low art, but, even more importantly, it suggested that the whole enterprise of assigning value to art was itself undemocratic and 'unpopular'. For TV critics worried about their public appeal, allusions to the innocent child worked to justify their position as cultural custodians. By evoking the 'threat to children', they secured (at least temporarily) their own position as arbiters of good taste, giving moral purpose to their tirades against mass culture.

But moral condemnation wasn't the only strategy by which critics positioned themselves as mediators of cultural change. Robert E. Terwilliger, an Episcopal minister, countered this position, arguing in *Catholic World* that *Batman* provided 'an American fantasy of salvation for spiritually frustrated people'. Similarly, a critic for the *Christian Century* argued that while

> here is a danger that this type of parody might lead to a complete cynicism concerning moral judgment and action, a TV series such as *Batman* performs the necessary function in society of profaning the holy. ... If we do not laugh at ourselves, others will – which, after all, is the moral of the story.[43]

Such commentary recognised the changing tides of mass culture and popular taste, embracing, if only by default, the new camp aesthetic as a vehicle for spiritual enlightenment within the more traditional confines of the clergy.

Batman also elicited reactions that were based less on moral-ethical norms than on deeply personalised ideals. These commentators still evoked childhood innocence, but this time they did so by remembering a better mass culture, located somewhere in their autobiographical past. Here, nostalgia worked to transform Minow's dirty dishwater into a sparkling fountain of youth as popular icons disparaged in bygone decades were filtered and purified through romanticised memories. As one writer for the *New York Times* argued, 'For the adult viewer dipping into his reservoir of nostalgia it [*Batman*] was probably the best therapy since Lawrence Welk's Champagne Music.'[44]

Fredric Wertham had predicted that American teenagers of the 1950s would discard their comic books with shame and revulsion as soon as they reached maturity. Instead, in the 1960s, many critics celebrated the revival of Bat-culture as 'a deliberate evocation of juvenile fantasy',[45] an invitation to turn the present into a childhood playground. In this respect, Batman's television incarnation tapped into a wider revival of interest in comic book heroes of the previous decades. In 1965, Jules Feiffer published a book-length elegy to superheroes[46] and, in that same year, college-town theatres revived the 1943 Batman movie serial. One man attending a marathon screening in Illinois confessed, 'I saw one episode when I was eleven and wanted to know how it came out.'[47] Here, as elsewhere, *Batman* reintroduced childhood enigmas, opening a space for childish play and fantasy to re-enter adult life. Upon *Batman*'s TV premiere, this kind of childish play found another expressive outlet. *Life*'s 11 March 1966 cover story played on the desire to return to innocence by juxtaposing images of dancing children dressed in Bat-capes with adults out for the night at Wayne Manor, San Francisco's Bat-motif discotheque.[48] College students at a Connecticut university capered around campus dressed as the daring duo. Even the FCC Chair, E. William Henry, succumbed to childish fun when he appeared at a Washington benefit dressed as the Caped Crusader.[49]

If these examples present somewhat liminal celebrations of the past, others used nostalgic readings in ways that valorised their adult authority in the present. Here, the once 'noxious' comic books were trumpeted as good objects against which the ills of the more contemporary commercial culture could be evaluated. Batman was rejected by these critics not because it failed to measure up to 'high' TV art, but rather because it betrayed the pulp traditions by turning the larger-than-life Detective Comics hero into a campy clown. When reviewing Batman for the New York Times, Russell Baker used Feiffer's idealised memories as a vehicle through which to deride contemporary mass art. He compared the 'dim-witted stooges' and 'social carnage' of the TV show to the more heroic comic book figure who offered earlier readers the utopian possibility of escaping 'the humdrum prison of teachers, parents and block bullies'. A Saturday Review commentator sounded a similar note, contrasting the new camp crusader with his own boyhood spent leaping from garage rooftops imitating a Batman who 'burned with belief'.[50] Thus, quite paradoxically, the degraded forms of their childhood days provided the content for satisfying visions of a more perfect world. Indeed, for these critics and their readers, the process of remembering was more important than the actual objects upon which memory was fixed. For it was their romantic fantasies of the past that empowered them to police the present.

Nostalgia for the present

This history of Batman's critical reception in the 1960s is clearly laced with personal memories, evocations of earlier and simpler times. In this respect, our own historiographical account is founded on a series of fantasies about the personal past that permeate the written documents we cite. If traditional historiographers see this as an obstacle to a full objective account of the past, our interest lies precisely in this overlapping between subjective memories and academic history writing. From our point of view, the goal is not to obliterate the 'distorted' memories from the historical record, but to account for their construction of historical consciousness. By examining memories of past events, we might better understand the processes by which people shape their past and understand the present.

During the height of this summer's Batman nostalgia wave, we interviewed four groups of adults who were schoolchildren at the time of Batman's TV premiere. The groups ranged from two to four participants, mixed by gender, income levels and occupations. Two groups were interviewed in Madison, Wisconsin; one in Santa Barbara, California; and the last in Cambridge, Massachusetts. Obviously, we did not attempt to gather a statistically representative sample, but rather we sought to provide what Clifford Geertz calls a 'thick description' of localised conditions of reception.[51] We tried to get to know the interview participants through a relatively unstructured and lengthy interaction, allowing their interests and memories to determine the direction that the session took. We were as interested in the associative logic by which *Batman* was linked to other aspects of their lives as we were with their interpretations of the programme itself.

The interview participants were not compensated for their time; when asked why they had come to the group, they provided various personal interests for talking about *Batman* with others. The *Batman* series gave these individuals a shared set of references and experiences that facilitated warm and animated communication, even among people who had little else in common. As Connie, a Cambridge computer technician, exclaimed at the end of one session, 'I get a big smile on my face just thinking about it all.' Memories of *Batman* opened up a floodgate of television references as people recalled encounters with TV shows and other popular texts of the late 1960s. *Batman* was also a catalyst for a far-reaching exploration of the 1960s, as people remembered political and social struggles, moving fluidly between memories of a personal and a public past.

It is wise to be cautious about the types of generalisations that we can draw from this data. Memories that are discussed in a group situation are not necessarily the same as internalised memories; the act of telling already involves a restructuring of the remembered material. Despite the interviews' relatively unstructured and undirected approach, the research process and researcher's goals always affect the type of information gathered and the nature of the responses elicited. In addition, as other studies have shown, people's lived experiences, their cultural and social environment, impact upon the way they interpret texts. Despite our attempt to conduct interviews in distinctive geographical regions and to talk to people from different walks of life, much of this everyday context was not retrievable in the interview situation. Finally, since psychological and historical studies of memory are still at an early and exploratory stage, we do not intend to reach firm conclusions. However, this type of study, especially when coupled with the emerging body of literature on the logic and functions of personal memory, does allow us to pose a series of questions and to speculate about the role that memory plays in the reception of popular media.

Memory of past events is necessarily selective and partial. None of us can recall everything that happens to us. Instead, certain moments are selected based on criteria of personal and public pertinence. In David Lowenthal's words, 'All memory transmutes experience, distils the past rather than simply reflecting it. ... Memory sifts again what perception had already sifted, leaving us only fragments of the fragments of what was initially on view.'[52] Perhaps the most persistent complaint that the interview participants expressed was their inability to recall aspects of their personal and public past. Susan, a Madison law student, jokingly suggested that she suffered 'total amnesia about everything that ever happened to me'. Yet, most people repeatedly resorted to vague descriptions and qualifying terms ('I can't quite recall', 'As far as I can remember', 'I guess', 'It must have been') in order to convey a sense of the forgetting that is inextricably bound to the process of remembering. We might, then, find it productive to direct attention to those aspects of the media past that survive in popular memory, what has been forgotten and what potential criteria govern this selective process of memory and forgetfulness.

Popular memories of *Batman* actively reworked the terms of its original reception, often appealing to a similar logic of nostalgia and cultural custodianship as the 1960s critics did, yet defining the terms of the debate in fundamentally different ways. Our respondents shared few of the earlier critics' anxiety about the programme's aesthetic status. Most insisted that they could not remember a time when television had not played a central role in their lives. So enmeshed had *Batman* become in their personal life histories that they did not feel compelled or even able to judge its merits. Still, some type of evaluative distance is suggested by the consistency with which people denied having ever taken the programme content seriously or literally. All insisted that they, like the adult spectators constructed by the 1960s critical discourse, had always been 'in on the joke', had always read the series as camp.

Similarly, any concerns about the suitability of *Batman* for young viewers had vanished from popular memory. Several people expressed astonishment when learning of the controversy surrounding the programme in the 1960s: 'Really! *Batman* bad for kids. You've got to be kidding,' Lori, a Madison game-shop owner, declared. Instead, the programme had become emblematic of a purer children's culture against which the offensive features of contemporary mass culture might be judged and condemned. Kate, a Madison commercial artist, contrasted her childhood experience of *Batman* with the consumer-oriented programmes preferred by her children: 'I can't remember that there even were Batman figures when the show was first on. ... I don't remember shows at the time being promoted as such a big package deal.' Kate's denial of the series' commercialisation was shared by other interview participants, most of whom claimed no knowledge or access to Batman spin-off products in the 1960s and saw the commodification of children's television as a relatively new development. While we cannot be sure what any of these people might or might not have known about the cultural past, the general pattern of these memories suggests a simplification of historical contradictions in favour of an image of the past as a purer, less complex time, as a place not yet confronted with our contemporary problems. What is remembered works to confirm those suppositions, what is forgotten is often information that might challenge such a picture.

When remembering the *Batman* series, people tended to construct vivid images of themselves watching the programme as children:

DOUG: (a Madison graduate student in psychology) We tended to eat dinner later, 'cause that was when my dad was going to seminary so he would often get back late. I remember several episodes – I mean – incidents where I was upstairs shovelling down my dinner 'cause I wanted to get downstairs to turn on the television by 6:30 or whatever, and I was told that was not to be done. I was not to rush through dinner in order to go see some television show.

LORI: The one scene that stands out in my mind is the third week it was on
             and the backyard cleared, like that, at 6:25. There was not a kid to be
             found in the whole neighbourhood. Everybody went to their respective
             houses to watch. ... In fact, as soon as it was over, we'd go back outside.
             ... One kid in the neighbourhood could laugh like the Riddler on
             command. Someone else did the Joker, I guess, I don't remember. ...
             As far as I recall, we'd just imitate the scenes we liked.

For these and other people, remembering *Batman* brought back a situational context,
a scene that painted a rough sketch of places in the house, times of the day and childhood relationships with family or friends.

As recent work on autobiographical memory has argued, our memory of public
events – the Kennedy assassination, say – includes not only the actual event, but also
our own relationship to it, the circumstances in which we received this news, where
we were, what we were doing, who told us about it.[53] As David C. Rubin and Marc
Kozin have shown, even more personal events (car accidents, school days, deaths in
the family) tend to be described through vivid situational contexts.[54]

The degree to which these remembered episodes are actually photographic
records of an event is, of course, another question.[55] In describing these past situations, the interview participants seem more likely to have been recasting their memories in terms of a set of shared cultural experiences, rather than merely recounting
their own individual past. The degree to which these people relied on shared cultural
and social frameworks – family settings, childhood games, schoolyard contexts – suggests the relational aspects of popular memory, the attempt to use memory in a way
that binds the individual to a larger community of ideas. Indeed, *Batman* and an array
of other media texts served to evoke a collective past that was discussed in remarkably conventionalised ways. These memories may have differed in details, but their
basic narrative form and themes were strikingly shaped by cultural, rather than
simply individuated, codes of storytelling.

The narrative elements of long-term memory have been the subject of study by
cognitive psychologists in recent years. Although more interested in the mental
schemes and paradigms that govern memory, Ulric Neisser has argued that autobiographical memory tends less to be a record of the past than a composite image of
numerous events that occur over time. In his study of John Dean's memory, for
example, Neisser shows how Dean's testimony in the Watergate investigation often
evoked specific episodes in which he met and spoke with Nixon. However, Dean's
memories were rarely accurate in their details; instead they were true to a more generalised conception of the historical past. Neisser thus concludes,

What seems to be specific in his memory actually depends upon repeated episodes,
rehearsed presentations or overall impressions. ... The single clear memories that
we recollect so vividly actually stand for something else; they are 'screen
memories' a little like those Freud discussed long ago. Often their real basis is a set

of repeated experiences, a sequence of related events that the single recollection merely typifies and represents.

Neisser describes such memories as 'repisodic' rather than episodic, suggesting that much of what we think we remember about our past involves an abstraction of lived experience into something more generic or prototypical, something that doesn't necessarily reflect a single incident as it occurs, but rather preserves the truth of a series of related experiences.[56] Popular memory thus tends to be prototypical and constructive, rather than specific and fixed.

Even when interview participants talked about the programme, their accounts tended to be highly generic. Rather than remembering specific episodes, they remembered *Batman* in repisodic ways, expressing fondness for isolated but recurring images (the screeching of the Batmobile's tyres, the heroes sliding down the Batpole, the red glow of the Batphone, Batrope ascents, zany graphics, hyperbolic voiceovers and, especially, exotic deathtraps). Often, however, they could not recount specific plots or point towards concrete examples of broader generic elements. Connie confessed at one point, 'I don't remember a single deathtrap he [King Tut] put them through.' Similarly, particular character traits – the Joker's laugh, the Catwoman's sensuality, Mr Freeze's icy personality – had been abstracted from the text. Even when we showed one group a *Batman* episode, the discussion quickly drifted from reflections on specifics towards more generic commentary. What remained in memory was not the single episode, but rather a prototypical text, a repisodic memory that reflected the generic qualities of the series. These prototypical texts bear the marks of the memory process itself – the necessary simplification of the flux of lived experience into terms that can be more readily recalled and comprehended.

In addition to their repisodic nature, popular memories of *Batman* were often highly intertextual and expansive. Here, people recalled the body of other texts they read during the same period or texts which, at later dates, had become associated with their memories of this primary text. For most people, this intertextual framework was in fact a *necessary condition* of popular memory; these people drew on a matrix of cultural materials in attempts to explain their personal encounters with the series. Our discussions of the Catwoman flowed naturally into considerations of *The Avengers*' (ABC Weekend Television, 1961–9) Emma Peel; recollections of the opening credits merged into memories of *Bonanza*'s (NBC, 1959–73) opening song and map-burning sequence; discussions of *Batman*'s campy and self-conscious qualities repeatedly invited analogies to *Laugh-in* (NBC, 1967–73), *The Monkees* (NBC, 1966–8), *Rocky and Bullwinkle* (ABC, 1959–64) and *Mad* magazine. As Susan confessed, 'I can never keep my series apart.'

For some people, the ability to tap into this intertextual grid became a source of pride among peers. Dan, a Boston man, identified supporting performers who had appeared as henchmen on both *Batman* and *Superman*, and spotted athletes behind the monster make-up on *Lost in Space*. Responding to the game that Dan had initiated, other group members also exhibited their skills at citing the instances in which

Batman villains appeared in other programmes and films. Tom, a night janitor in Madison, continually displayed his knowledge of TV lore, boasting at one point, 'I seem to remember more TV than everybody.' This display of TV literacy was clearly a pleasurable activity, one that seemed to give Tom a sense of personal pride because it marked a difference from his present-day life and otherwise mundane family history. At one point, immediately after recounting his knowledge of stars and programmes, Tom drifted off into a melancholy confession about his personal life, telling us that his 'parents were always busy working, just like me these days'. This admission suggested that his pleasurable TV memories might be a buffer against the more arduous conditions of the work-a-day world. Possibly, as well, since Tom was the only working-class member in this particular discussion group, his display of TV literacy might have provided him with feelings of superiority when talking to white-collar professionals.

More generally, people used memories of *Batman* to evoke their own personal identity and explain their particular relationship to the social world. As Lowenthal notes, memory often 'converts events into idiosyncratic personal experiences', retaining details about a public past insofar as they serve more personal needs: 'Remembering the past is crucial for our sense of identity. ... Recalling past experiences links us with our earlier selves, however different we may since have become.'[57] For our respondents, remembering *Batman* meant remembering themselves, and that dialogue between programme and self continually framed the stories they told about the past.

In many conversations, *Batman* seemed to elicit stories that told of transitional moments, rites of passage, through which people moved from child to adult, from family to larger social meanings.

JIM: (a Santa Barbara computer technician) I remember we used to watch, the whole family did. My dad always watched television, period, when he came home. I can remember watching it and being excited when I first started to tune in the advertisements, seeing the Batmobile come screaming out of the cave and over the fence that falls down. I can remember my sister thought it was really cool ... and she would sit there and watch it with me. She was a young teenager. ... When she went off to college she became a hippy ... and completely stopped watching. I was amazed, because I always loved the show.

Jim's narrative positions *Batman* as a mediator between his family's personal history and the larger social changes of the 1960s, measuring the counterculture's impact upon his sister via her shifting attitudes towards a cultural product that they once enjoyed together. His story allows him to come to terms with his personal past with his sister, while also serving to explain his place in the public past of student protests. Here, as elsewhere, these memories fluidly move from personal to collective consciousness as people weave histories around themselves, while at the same time imbricating themselves into the wider social fabric.

Indeed, this matching of personal and public pasts became a strategy for understanding the relationship of self to society, and within this matching process television memories served a key role. John, a Madison graduate student, summarised his feelings upon reviewing an episode of *Batman*: 'When I go back and see something from that long ago, I tend to remember who I was when I first saw it, how I thought the world was.' As John suggests, these memories aren't simply the residue of earlier times; instead they are a resource people use to think about the world and their position within it.

Memories of *Batman* often evoked tales in which people took on a liminal status – existing somewhere between child and adult. Most of the participants invoked some aspects of the general myth of childhood innocence, constructing children as unknowledgeable and pre-sexual. As Rose suggests, this notion of childhood innocence constitutes a universalised category that erases questions of sexual and cultural difference. Yet, these differences resurface in contradictory ways within personal memories that depend for their vividness upon references to gender, sexuality and resistance to adult authorities. In the interviews, memory entitled people to play with the ideological distinctions between child and adult. Childhood memories evoked a pleasure in liminality as people moved fluidly between imagining themselves as children and recognising their current adult status.

Ambiguities between child and adult surfaced most vividly in discussions of the Catwoman. Several of the male respondents spoke of the Dark Knight's feline foe as one of the first objects of their erotic interest, suggesting that her role in the programme invited a greater awareness of sexual difference. As Jim remarked, 'I can remember not being interested in any of the female characters until halfway through the series, when suddenly I became exceedingly interested in the Catwoman.' Frequently, however, these claims were coupled with a denial of childhood sexuality. Michael, a Santa Barbara computer technician, admitted, 'I appreciated the women right from the start, but to me they looked like really great mother figures. I didn't know what they meant at the time.' In another discussion group, Lori speculated, 'I guess maybe subconsciously I was aware of female–male interactions but they certainly hadn't entered my life yet.' Michael and Lori remember themselves at a time before erotic desire entered their lives. Still, as adults, they find it important to employ categories of sexual difference as they reflect on their narrative pleasure in *Batman*. What emerges is a complex economy of desire where they invoke their own erotic fantasies while still maintaining the culturally defined differences between child (pre-sexual) and adult (sexual). Moreover, the memory of *Batman* seems pleasurable precisely in its ability to maintain this liminal state between knowing adult and innocent child.

For others, Catwoman introduced contradictions surrounding gender. Catwoman's exercise of authority over her gang and her resistance to Batman suggested, for some women, the possibility of feminine power. Yet, simultaneously, many of these same women claimed initial disinterest, ignorance or hostility to what they called 'women's lib attitudes', which were being debated elsewhere in the 1960s. The women often spoke of their initial ignorance of gender roles even as they evoked their youthful pleasure in resisting or redefining those roles. Susan recalled discussing with her play-mates the pleasure they took in Catwoman's antisocial antics:

> The Catwoman was having so much fun, and we were discussing the fact that Batman and Robin never had any fun. ... And, of course, parents would have been appalled hearing this, but we had this discussion. Are we really allowed to draw this moral ... that the bad girls have more fun? Can we do that?

Here, Susan attributes to adult authorities certain attitudes about childhood inno-cence while constructing a memory that celebrates the possibilities of feminine resist-ance to sex-role stereotyping.

As with Susan's account, many of the memories centred around a childhood fan-tasy of resisting the adult culture. Jim recalled an incident when he used Batman and Robin Halloween costumes to confound adult authorities through an elaborate play with secret identities: 'I put on the Batman costume and went trick-or-treating. Then I came home and put on the Robin costume and went trick-or-treating again and hit a lot of the same houses!' While most interview participants remembered their par-ents as exercising only minimal control over their use of television and other media, those moments when entertainment choices faced parental resistance seemed to be particularly charged memories. Dan expressed regret that he saw *Batman* mostly on summer reruns, since his mother refused to allow him to watch television on school nights. He enthusiastically recalled how he and his siblings conspired to thwart his mother's edicts:

> My mother's big thing was she would pull the cord out from behind the back of the TV. ... So we discovered what she was doing and I figured out how to plug it back in. ... I was the one who figured out how to fix the TV. And to this day, they always give me the clicker [at family gatherings]. It's like I'm the master of the TV.

Dan treated this incident of childhood resistance to adult control as an origin myth that explains his own particular placement in his family structure.

But these accounts of childhood resistance often gave way to adult anxieties about control and power over youth. Indeed, people seemed to move between the alternate states of child and adult, at once condemning and embracing the social structure that regulates childhood. Doug, for example, remembered how

> I wanted to stay up and watch George Pal's War of the Worlds [1953] ... and my folks didn't think that would be such a good idea. ... But finally they caved in. In retrospect, I think they were right. I should have listened to them.

Doug's account shifts between two identificatory positions. He identifies with himself as a child controlled by his parents, and then shifts the terms, using memory to accept the rules of the adult culture. In this way, memory works to maintain the ideological construction of adult authority over children, particularly when it comes to policing the media choices of youth. The older Doug now thinks as his parents did ('they were right'), but he still maintains continuity with his own life history by thinking back to when he resisted adult rules. This tenuous balance between child and adult identificatory positions seems to present Doug with a pleasurable equilibrium, giving him a way of explaining his present-day life while still maintaining a sense of his past.

These fluid transfers between different attitudes and cultural positions suggest the political duality of popular memory, the degree to which reflections on the past can be simultaneously a progressive and a conservative force. On the one hand, memory can assume a utopian quality, offering a fantasy of resistance to adult norms that also provides a basis upon which to criticise contemporary social conditions. On the other hand, memory can assume a more conservative quality, denying cultural and social change and justifying the exercise of custodial authority over contemporary children's culture. Memories of *Batman* assumed both dimensions in our discussions, sometimes inviting regret over the 'political apathy' of 1980s culture in contrast to the more activist period when the show was first aired, elsewhere provoking expressions of outrage over the 'poor quality' and 'shabbiness' of more recent children's programmes. Often, the same person expressed both attitudes in the course of the interview, suggesting a range of contradictory emotions and thoughts that emerged when people compared past and present-day worlds. These comparisons were indeed endemic to the memory process itself, as all respondents used their recollections to consider the merits and failures of contemporary life.

Some people used their memories of *Batman* to invoke an image of a more politicised past. Recollections of the series were intertwined with memories of 1960s news events where student protests, civil rights riots and the Vietnam War provoked fond longings for a radical time when the world was full of possibilities. Indeed, since all of the people interviewed were too young to have participated in these events at the time, memories of television broadcasts were the key to historical consciousness. Michael traced his radical political commitments to 1960s television, suggesting that what he learned from *Batman* was 'a strong aversion to injustice', and a distrust of authority: 'If you're fighting injustice, sometimes you're not necessarily working for the police. Sometimes the police obstruct justice.' This fantasy of a more just and more politically righteous past was often compared to the moral confusion and passive acceptance of adult life. Kate confessed, '*Batman* makes me remember the sixties a lot. The confusion, a lot of anger … Suddenly it brings back a lot of those feelings and makes me realise how politically uninvolved I am now.' Responding to this, Susan explained that the reason 'everything has gotten the way it is now' is because people no longer protest social problems the way they did in the 1960s. The ability to remember the 1960s, if only through its media images, authorised these women to evaluate and condemn contemporary political culture: 'There aren't the same kind of questions anymore. … All of those things [reforms] are gone because nobody fought for them anymore.'

Yet, this logic of nostalgia may just as readily be evoked to justify a more repressive attitude towards contemporary culture. Just like the critics of the 1960s who used their romanticised memories of the *Batman* comics to condemn the TV version, many of the people compared the more wholesome texts of their childhood to the degraded media forms of the present. Most saw television as corrupting childhood innocence, producing a generation that is too 'sophisticated' in its understanding of sexual matters, too accepting of media violence and too enamoured with the pleasure of overconsumption. As Jim explained, 'There's just not that much on television any more that I can consider innocent. … I don't want my little kids watching the *A-Team*! It's a lot more violent and a lot less straightforward fun than what we used to watch.' This comparison with the past entitled him to boast about his current role as watchful father, making sure to tell us how he had steered his youngsters away from broadcast television and onto books and 'videotapes of known quality'. Even the acknowledged shortcomings of the 1960s series – the cardboard sets, the flabby Adam West, the squealing Robin – were remembered affectionately by the respondents, who often claimed that these low production values actually enhanced opportunities for imaginative participation in the programme. These responses suggest that children who grew up watching *Batman* had reversed a previous generation's condemnation of the programme, yet had retained the same cultural logic upon which the earlier criticism had been founded. Like the 1960s critics, they appealed to a better past to justify their criticisms of contemporary mass culture, to rationalise their exercise of cultural authority and to motivate their construction of a new aesthetic canon.

This conservative mode of popular memory also shaped their own responses to contemporary media. Many of the respondents expressed lack of interest in and sometimes hostility to the new *Batman* movie, holding open little possibility for the 1989 release to duplicate the pleasures they found in the TV series. In Kate's words, 'I don't think you could make that series now, I don't think you could make an eighties' version and have it come out the same.' Many found the darker tone of the Tim Burton film emblematic of the loss of innocence and playfulness that their childhood texts had once contained. Reflecting on a recent Batman comic book, Connie suggested, 'Gotham City used to be a much more fun place.' Susan, who had yet to see the film at the time of the interview, compared it to the *Star Trek* films, which she liked best when they were 'consistent with a lot of the things in the original series … so you felt like you were in the same place again.' If the merchandising and publicity materials surrounding the film's release invited baby boomers to return to a pre-packaged version of their childhood, it is clear that many rejected this invitation, desiring instead to cling to their more 'authentic' autobiographical memories of the series. Perhaps, in fact, it was this pleasurable reconstruction of a personal past that was really at the heart of their reluctance to accept a new version of Batman.

Conclusion
We would like to end by returning to the problems entailed in writing the history of memory and, more specifically, in using memory as a way to understand people's encounters with mass culture. History, media texts and personal memories all share in

a common project of narrativisation, although the conventions, desires and mechanisms of storytelling differ in each case. By forging connections between these different storytelling practices, we bring into relief not one historical truth, but rather a set of differences, of separate truths, of versions of the past that often contradict each other.

This is especially important when we consider the chameleon-like nature of popular heroes like Batman. These heroes retain their cultural significance precisely because they are open to reinterpretation by different generations. For the critics of the 1960s, the transformation of the comic book hero into a campy clown created a series of disputes around the meanings of *Batman* and, more generally, the status of popular texts. The anxieties that these critics displayed over the series and their attempts to divide audience interpretation along generational lines belie their desire to control cultural change, to stabilise meanings and pleasures in a way that better suits the meanings of the past.

By 1989, the anxieties about the 1960s series had vanished from popular memory. Instead, the programme now presents opportunities for thinking about a decade that is out of focus but still part of our collective and autobiographical past. Remembering our own TV histories evokes powerful, even poignant, moments as we reinvent ourselves and the times from which we came. Here, memory mediates our present-day desires and gives the past an imaginary status that strips away closure, opening it up to personal (although culturally mediated) fantasies. At times, in our interviews, these memories seemed to serve a conservative function, as people used romantic visions of a better past to control and police the often difficult realities of present-day life. At other times, these memories seemed to have a potentially liberating dimension, as people imagined themselves in a liminal state, somewhere in between child and adult, using this indistinction to transgress the rules of normal adult conversations. Memories, in other words, entitled people to think and speak about themselves in opposition to adult authorities and, in more politicised discussions, to imagine a less authoritarian world where peace rallies and Bob Dylan were virtuous and authentic once more.

In all of these discussions, history-making was clearly enjoyable for the group. Indeed, whereas traditional history effaces the pleasure of the text, popular memory is full of self-parody, wit and laughter. In its own historical context, *Batman* was viewed with a high degree of anxiety over its status as high or low art, but in the 1980s this angst had virtually disappeared from historical consciousness and *Batman* instead found resonance in satisfying childhood memories and reflections on contemporary struggles. The interview participants were making *Batman* mean something new, and in the process they drew upon shared cultural myths, actively engaged in collective storytelling and intertwined their own personal histories with the many lives of the Batman.

But within the collective process of making history, where do we, the historians, stand? What function did we serve in this study? Facilitators? Mediators? Authorities? As Alessandro Portelli claims, even while they draw autonomous voices into their texts, oral historians still make 'them [the informants] speak; and the "floor," whether admittedly or not, is still the historian's'. Expanding this, Karl Figlio argues that while the oral historian might have control over the way people express themselves in the interview situation, he or she is always part of a set of relationships that involve at least three groups: 'that on which his or her sample gives testimony; that to which the informants and the historian belong; and that made up of the informants, the historian and the audience for the historical project'. Figlio thus foregrounds the inter-subjective character of history-making and in so doing stresses the collaborative dimension of historical truths.[58]

In the end, perhaps, the historians do still have the floor, but at least the act of speaking about the past has been more of a dialogue than a monologue. The question of how this dialogue with the past can be relevant in the present is one that tortures the texts of modern philosophers and historians, from Marx to Foucault. But rather than look for large-scale political relevance behind the memories of ordinary folks, perhaps we need to start with the idea that memories are themselves relevant in the small-scale politics of everyday life. Memories are one of the rare common grounds upon which people think about the present-day world. If mass-media texts are now part of our historical consciousness, this is no time to bemoan the passing of a truer, more politically acute historical consciousness, one based on wars, class struggle and other more 'authentic' historical experiences. Nor is it useful to fall into a completely nihilistic embrace of postmodern pastiche where history is emptied of all meaning to become pure style, an endless TV re-rerun. Instead, we think, autobiographical memories of media texts can shed light on how people use and reuse media in their daily lives. These memories begin to show how sense is wrestled from the claws of the past, how historical meanings are disengaged and reworked for contemporary purposes.

As the case of Batman so vividly illustrates, we are now encountering popular texts that endure, in transformed states, for multiple generations. These texts provide clues to a shared, collective past that runs parallel to and often intersects with our own life histories. In our study, remembering *Batman* evoked a transitional space where people actively used their previous encounters with mass culture to reshape and understand their relation to larger social practices. Popular memory, then, is the place where private and public pasts meet. At this crossroads, we find a mix of personal and collective fantasies that transform the products of mass culture into the tools of everyday life.

Postscript

In January 2014, DC Entertainment announced plans to release a DVD box set of the 1966 *Batman* television series. Although nearly four decades of legal roadblocks made the 1966–8 TV series far less available to the public, it never really disappeared from the popular imagination. Local TV stations ran syndicated episodes (sometimes in 'Batmania' marathons), while bootleg copies of the full series could be purchased online or under the table at comics and science-fiction conventions. Shows like *The Simpsons* (Fox, 1989–) and *Family Guy* (Fox, 1998–2001, 2005–) feature guest appearances by Adam West (and often include jokes about his fading celebrity or spoofs of the *Batman* TV series). During the 2008 presidential campaign, there were remixes and memes casting John McCain as the Penguin or Sarah Palin as the Catwoman, almost always as they appeared in the 1960s television series. In advance of their DVD announcement, DC Comics launched a new *Batman 66* comic book series, where original stories depict the Caped Crusader and the Boy Wonder battling such dastardly TV villains as Cesar Romero's Joker, Frank Gorshin's Riddler, Vincent Price's Egg Head, and both Julie Newmar's and Eartha Kitt's Catwoman.[59] Rather than fade from memory, TV's *Batman* is even more visible today than it was in 1989 when, inspired by Tim Burton's first film remake, we decided to explore the significance of TV's *Batman* for our (baby-boom) generation.

At the time we wrote 'Same Bat Channel, Different Bat Times', the US broadcast system was just beginning its transformation into the narrowcast television system of contemporary times. In that context, *Batman* (like other 1960s reruns) was already a relic of an earlier industrial formation, and it provoked (both for us and the people we interviewed) childhood memories of television culture and everyday life during the decade. Today, anyone teaching a course on television will immediately notice that very few of the students in the room watch the same TV shows, a situation that has provoked critics to wonder about the fate of collective culture in a niche media environment. Yet despite the fragmentation, students still collectively remember childhood programmes as key to the formation of their identity as a 'generation'. Nickelodeon cartoons like *As Told by Ginger* (Nickelodeon, 2000–3) (a programme millennials remember for its 'post-feminist' girl power ethos) serve similar 'generation binding' functions that *Batman* did for us. Even TV reruns from the late network era have become memory texts for the post-network millennial generation. (For example, millennials often collectively remember themselves as children watching reruns of *Cosby* [CBS, 1996–2000] and *Friends* [NBC, 1994–2004]. Even if the narrowcast world fragments viewers, media memories still often provoke utopian longings for a collective childhood past.

Since we wrote this essay, there have been many changes – in the media industry, in media technologies, in media cultures and in media scholarship itself. Our essay related the production and reception history of the 1960s ABC series to its lasting resonance with its initial child audiences (that is, people like us who grew up as Bat-fans). When we did the focus group research for the essay, we had to solicit responses from people who recalled watching *Batman* as children. Today, we might locate many online sites where people share their memories of the series with each other, and memories that might have seemed personal and idiosyncratic have become public and collective. The dynamics of popular memory that our original essay described still hold, we think, despite the changes. Just as they did in the past, people now turn TV's *Batman* into a usable past – a past that functions as a resource for the present. Today, however, the TV past is often imagined and creatively revised through participations within online platforms. On Wikipedia, Bat-fans pool knowledge; on ebay, they exchange collectables; on multiple fan forums, they are still debating their favourite deathtraps; and on YouTube, they share meaningful clips from the programme, often curated around the same generic/iconic elements that ran through our interviews two decades before. On YouTube, you'll find fan-produced video montages that feature clips of all the Bat-villains (from the Archer to Zelda the Great); 'Biff, Bam, Pow' fights season by season; cameos of stars who pop out of windows during beloved 'Bat Climb' segments; or Batgirl's best and worst moments.

Beyond the case of *Batman*, scholarship on memory has proliferated in recent decades. In 1989, very few scholars were thinking about popular TV programmes as source for collective memory.[60] At that time, we were reacting against the then widespread notion that TV was a medium of postmodern amnesia. Today, the archive, memory and nostalgia are prominent scholarly issues and people interested in television have produced important work on such varied topics as reruns, collector's cultures, bootleg videos, ephemeral and residual media, and the nostalgia industry.[61] Meanwhile, post-network programmes such as *Mad Men* (AMC, 2007–), *The Hour* (BBC, 2011–12), *Pan Am* (ABC, 2011–12), *The Americans* (FX, 2013–), *Masters of Sex* (Showtime, 2013–) and *Vegas* (CBS, 2012–13) revisit post-war culture, often transforming the look of baby-boom nostalgia from *Batman*'s pop art borrowings to *Mad Men*'s penchant for the more high-end look of mid-century modern design. Streaming services like Hulu and Netflix go way beyond the logic of reruns, giving viewers a fantasy of total recall on demand. We stress the word fantasy here because these services are not a transparent window onto the past, but rather often offer content that is edited and repackaged according to marketing logics.

But there is something more to *Batman*'s legacy than the routine commodification and regressive recycling of the culture industry. In memory, the 1960s *Batman* series affords adult viewers a chance to narrate (and often creatively revise) a story about their childhood past. And, as we discuss in our essay, because *Batman* evokes memories of growing up in the 1960s, the reruns also allow viewers – and creators alike – to play with the socially constructed (and often policed) categories of adult and child. In the contemporary context, reruns, remixes and remakes continue to provoke childhood wonder. When film-maker Kevin Smith was commissioned to write a new *Batman 66* graphic novel (which paired the Dynamic Duo with the Green Hornet and Kato), he enthused: 'It's like getting to be five years old again and tell stories that you would have made up while watching the show as a kid.' Or, when considering the recent reissue of a collection of Silver Age Batman stories, Michael Uslan (producer of the Christopher Nolan Batman films) confessed his childhood ambivalence about the TV series, 'I was thrilled that Batman was on TV ... in colour ... with no expense spared ... driving a very cool Batmobile ... BUT ... I was horrified that the whole world was laughing at Batman.'[62] Sooner or later, every creative involved in these new DC projects has authenticated their participation through reference to childhood memories.

Given that more than two decades have passed since our 1989 account, it would be foolish to assume that everything we said in our essay is directly transferable to *Batman* as it circulates today. Batman's meanings shift across its many textual incarnations and reception contexts. For example, when we wrote our essay, the status of the 1960s *Batman* TV series was still very much in dispute: fans of the series often saw the darker Batman that emerged in the graphic novels and films as a backlash against the camp and pop aesthetics of the original series. Yet, today, with its new TV-inspired comic book series, DC clearly has learned to stop worrying and rekindle its love for a character who can pull Bat Shark Repellent out of his utility belt or who ends up imprisoned in a giant snow cone. *Batman*, in other words, is always about the 'Different Bat Times' evoked by our chapter's title. But even while things have changed, we hope that our chapter will serve as a guidepost for thinking through the history and memory of the television series and its relation to today's Bat-fans.

Notes

1. We are grateful to Janet Bergstrom, Michael Curtin, Bill Forman and Cindy Jenkins for reading and improving upon the original version of this essay. We also extend thanks to David Bordwell and George Lipsitz for their extremely helpful bibliographical suggestions; to Kevin Glynn, Shelly Happy and Paul Seale for their research assistance; and to Mike Lord and Tom Patterson for watching *Batman* with so much pleasure. Most importantly, to all the people who participated in the interview sessions, thanks for the memories. The authors collaborated equally in the writing of this essay.

2. David Lowenthal, *The Past Is a Foreign Country* (Cambridge and New York: Cambridge University Press, 1985).

3. Ulric Neisser, *Memory Observed: Remembering in Natural Contexts* (San Francisco: Freeman, 1982), p. 12.

4. For an introduction, see Jan Vansina, *Oral Tradition as History* (Madison: Wisconsin University Press, 1985).

5. For good introductions to oral history and the wider implications that it has for engaging people in the process of history-making, see James Green, 'Engaging in People's History: The Massachusetts History Workshop', in Susan Porter Benson *et al.* (eds), *Presenting the Past: Essays on History and the Public* (Philadelphia, PA: Temple University Press, 1986), pp. 339–59; and Linda Shopes, 'Oral History and Community Involvement: The Baltimore Neighborhood Heritage Project', *Radical History Review* no. 25 (October 1981), pp. 27–44, reprinted in Porter Benson *et al.* (eds), *Presenting the Past*, pp. 249–63.

6. For interesting considerations of these problems, see Michael H. Frisch, 'The Memory of History', *Radical History Review* no. 25 (October 1981), pp. 9–23; Philippe Lejeune, *On Autobiography* (Minneapolis: Minnesota University Press, 1989), especially pp. 185–215.

7. Hayden White, *Tropics of Discourse: Essays in Cultural Criticism* (Baltimore and London: Johns Hopkins University Press, 1978).

8. Dominick La Capra, *History and Criticism* (Ithaca, NY, and London: Cornell University Press, 1985), pp. 34–5.

9. See George Lipsitz, 'The Meaning of Memory: Family, Class and Ethnicity in Early Network Television Programs', *Camera Obscura* vol. 16 (January 1988), pp. 79–117. Also see his *Time Passages: Collective Memory and American Popular Culture* (Minneapolis: Minnesota University Press, 1989); Colin MacCabe, 'Memory, Phantasy, Identity: "Days of Hope" and the Politics of the Past', *Edinburgh Magazine* no. 2 (1977), pp. 13–17; Roy Rosenzweig, 'American Heritage and Popular History in the United States', in Porter Benson *et al.* (eds), *Presenting the Past*, pp. 21–49; Eric Breitbart, 'Historical

Recreation from the Panorama to the Docudrama', in Porter Benson et al. (eds), *Presenting the Past*, pp. 105–17; Henry Jenkins, 'Reading Popular History: *The Atlanta Child Murders', Journal of Communication Inquiry* vol. 11 no. 2 (Summer 1987), pp. 60–78.

10. John A. Robinson, 'Autobiographical Memory: A Historical Prologue', in David C. Rubin (ed.), *Autobiographical Memory* (Cambridge: Cambridge University Press, 1986), p. 23.

11. Mort Drucker and Lou Silverstone, 'Bats-Man', *Mad*, September 1966, pp. 7–12.

12. Gilbert Seldes, *Writing for Television* (Garden City, NY: Doubleday, 1952), p. 32; Jack Gould, '"Live" vs "Canned"', *New York Times Magazine*, 5 February 1956, p. 27.

13. For more on Golden Age aesthetics, see William Boddy's important account of Golden Age critical discourses in 'From the "Golden Age" to the "Vast Wasteland": 'The Struggles over Market Power and Dramatic Formats in 1950s Television', PhD dissertation (New York University, 1984), pp. 104–15; for more on hyperrealism and TV aesthetic ideals in the 1950s, see Lynn Spigel's 'Installing the Television Set: The Social Construction of Television's Place in the American Home', PhD dissertation (University of California, Los Angeles, 1988), pp. 293–352.

14. For more on the critics' response to the telefilm, see Boddy, 'From the "Golden Age" to the "Vast Wasteland"'. For an analysis of critical discourses in relation to industrial and regulatory reforms, see James L. Baughman, *Television's Guardians: The FCC and the Politics of Programming, 1958–1967* (Knoxville: Tennessee University Press, 1985), and Baughman, 'The National Purpose and the Newest Medium: Liberal Critics of Television, 1958–60', *Mid-America* vol. 64 no. 2 (April–July 1982), pp. 41–55.

15. Note that we have focused on Andy Warhol in our discussion of popism because the television critics of the 1960s saw him as being synonymous with the pop movement. Indeed, the critics continually referenced Warhol's work to the exclusion of other pop artists.

16. 'The Whole Country Goes Supermad', *Life*, 11 March 1966, p. 23.

17. 'Discotheque Frug Party Heralds Batman's Film and TV Premiere', *New York Times*, 13 January 1966, p. 79.

18. Jack Gould, 'Too Good to Be Camp', *New York Times*, 23 January 1966, section 1, p. 17.

19. John Skow, 'Has TV Gasp Gone Batty?', *Saturday Evening Post*, 7 May 1966, p. 95.

20. *Time*, 28 January 1966, p. 61; 'Holy Cancellation!', *Newsweek*, 5 February 1968, p. 84; Skow, 'Has TV Gasp Gone Batty?', p. 96.

21. Susan Sontag, 'Notes on Camp', in *Against Interpretation* (New York: Farrar, Straus and Giroux, 1966), pp. 275–92.

22. For more on pop and camp, see Andrew Ross, *No Respect: Intellectuals and Popular Culture* (New York and London: Routledge, 1989), pp. 135–70.

23. Joel Eisner, *The Official Batman Batbook* (Chicago, IL: Contemporary, 1986), pp. 5–6.

24. Dozier, quoted in Judy Stone, 'Caped Crusader of Camp', *New York Times*, 4 January 1966, p. 15.

25. Eda J. LeShan, 'At War with Batman', *New York Times Magazine*, 15 May 1966, p. 112.

26. Mrs B. Cloosin, 'What's So Wrong with Batman?', *New York Times Magazine*, 5 June 1966, p. 41; Mrs Helen Heinman, 'Batman: Menace or Hero?', *New York Times Magazine*, 29 May 1966, p. 40.

27. LeShan, 'At War with Batman', p. 122.

28. 'Young Britons Told Not to Copy Batman', *New York Times*, 24 August 1966, p. 38; 'Wow! Bam! Socko! Seven Thousand Children Greet Batman', *New York Times*, 25 August 1966, p. 424.

29. Mark West, *Children, Culture and Controversy* (Hamden, CT: Archon, 1988).

30. Jacqueline Rose, *The Case of Peter Pan, or The Impossibility of Children's Fiction* (London: Macmillan, 1984), p. 10.

31. For a detailed discussion of Wertham's anti-comic book campaign, see James Gilbert, *A Cycle of Outrage: America's Reaction to the Juvenile Delinquent in the 1950s* (New York: Oxford, 1986); William Lloyd Oakley Jr, 'The Destruction of an Industry: Dr Wertham, the Henderickson Committee, William Gaines and the Comic Book Controversy of the 1950s', AB thesis (Harvard University, 1988).

32. Fredric Wertham, *Seduction of the Innocent* (New York: Rinehart, 1953), p. 381. Although he acknowledged, albeit begrudgingly, that the classics often had the same themes of sex and violence, Wertham insisted that their aesthetic qualities and sensitivity more than offset any unsavouriness. Moreover, the effort required in the reading process provided an imaginative buffer for children that protected them from 'merging completely with the story', while the visual immediacy of comic books absorbed children completely, making it impossible to separate violent fantasies from real life. Fredric Wertham, 'How Movie and TV Violence Affects Children', *Ladies' Home Journal*, February 1960, pp. 58–9.

33. Wertham, *Seduction of the Innocent*, pp. 354–97.

34. See, for example, Wertham, 'How Movie and TV Violence Affects Children', pp. 58–9.

35. PTA reform reported in 'Another TV Censor', *Variety*, 5 October 1949, p. 27. For early school board activities, see, for example, 'TV Also Alarms Cleve. Educators', *Variety*, 22 March 1950, p. 29; 'Students Read, Sleep Less in TV Homes, Ohio School Survey Shows', *Variety*, 5 April 1950, p. 38.

36. Lloyd Shearer, 'The Parental Dilemma', *House Beautiful*, October 1951, pp. 220, 222, 224. For other examples from women's home magazines, see Dorothy Diamond and Frances Tenenbaum, 'Should You Tear 'Em Away from TV?', *Better Homes and Gardens*, September 1950, pp. 56, 239–40; William Porter, 'Is Your Child Glued to TV, Radio, Movies, or Comics?', *Better Homes and Gardens*, October 1951, pp. 125, 178–9; Ann Usher, 'TV … Good or Bad for Your Children?', *Better Homes and Gardens*, October 1955, pp. 145, 176, 202. As Spigel has argued elsewhere, the debates over television's effects on youth pivoted on the question of adult authority over children, raising parental anxiety about television's effects on their own everyday lives. See Spigel, 'Installing the Television Set', especially pp. 143–65.

37. Ron Goulart, *The Assault on Childhood* (Los Angeles, CA: Shelbourne, 1959); Jules Henry, *Culture against Man* (New York: Random House, 1963).

38. Newton Minow, 'Is TV Cheating Our Children?', *Parents*, February 1962, pp. 52–3; 'Minow Magic', *Newsweek*, 14 August 1963, p. 66.

39. See, for example, Benjamin Spock, 'Television, Radio, Comics and Movies', *Ladies' Home Journal*, April 1969, p. 61; Eve Merriam, 'We're Teaching Our Children That

Violence Is Fun', *Ladies' Home Journal*, October 1964, p. 44; Anna W. M. Woolfe, 'TV, Movies, Comics … Boon or Bane to Children?', *Parents*, April 1961, pp. 46–8; Bruno Bettelheim, 'Sex and Violence in Television', *Redbook*, May 1964, pp. 60–1.

40. See, for example, Jane Kesner Ardmore, 'Television without Terror', *Parents*, July 1962, pp. 42–3; 'To Improve TV for Children', *America*, 23 April 1955, p. 94; 'Culture for Kids', *Newsweek*, 21 February 1955, p. 62; 'Children's Hour', *Newsweek*, 16 January 1956, p. 78.

41. Frank Orme, 'TV for Children: What's Good? What's Bad?', *Parents*, February 1962, p. 54; 'TV for Children', *Parents*, February 1966, pp. 42–3; 'Report on TV for Children', *Parents*, February 1967, pp. 63–5; 'Best on TV: Choosing Programs for Children', *Parents*, February 1968, pp. 58–9.

42. 'Time out for Television', *PTA*, April 1966, p. 22.

43. Robert E. Terwilliger, 'The Theology of Batman', *Catholic World*, November 1966, p. 127; M. Conrad Hyers, 'Batman and the Comic Profanation of the Sacred', *Christian Century*, 18 October 1967, p. 1323.

44. 'TV: Pow! Zap! It's Batman and Robin', *New York Times*, 13 January 1966, p. 79.

45. Terwilliger, 'Theology of Batman', p. 127.

46. Jules Feiffer (ed.), *The Great Comic Book Heroes* (New York: Dial, 1965).

47. 'The Return of Batman', *Time*, 26 November 1965, p. 60.

48. 'Whole Country Goes Supermad', p. 26.

49. Skow, 'Has TV Gasp Gone Batty?', p. 93.

50. Russell Baker, 'Observer: Television's Bat Burlesque', *New York Times*, 8 February 1966, p. 38; R. L. Shayon, 'All the Way to the Bank: *Batman*', *Saturday Review*, 12 February 1966, p. 46.

51. Clifford Geertz, *The Interpretation of Culture* (New York: Basic, 1973).

52. Lowenthal, *The Past Is a Foreign Country*, p. 204.

53. For an important study on this, see Roger Brown and James Kulik, 'Flashbulb Memories', *Cognition* vol. 5 no. 1 (1977), pp. 73–99.

54. David C. Rubin and Marc Kozin, 'Vivid Memories', *Cognition* vol. 16 no. 1 (1984), pp. 81–95.

55. See Ulric Neisser, 'Snapshots or Benchmarks', in Neisser (ed.), *Memory Observed*, pp. 43–8.

56. Ulric Neisser, 'John Dean's Memory: A Case Study', *Cognition* vol. 9 no. 1 (1981), p. 20.

57. Lowenthal, *The Past Is a Foreign Country*, pp. 195, 197.

58. Alessandro Portelli, 'The Peculiarities of Oral History', *History Workshop* vol. 12 no. 1 (Autumn 1981), p. 105; Karl Figlio, 'Psychoanalysis and Oral History', *History Workshop* vol. 26 no. 1 (Autumn 1988), p. 120.

59. Jeff Parker and Richard Case, *Batman 66*, Vol. 1 (New York: DC Comics, 2014).

60. George Lipsitz's 1986 essay 'The Meaning of Memory: Family, Class, and Ethnicity in Early Network Television Programs' was trailblazing in its consideration of how popular TV series can activate and revise collective memories of the past, and we were indebted to his observations when we wrote our essay. For Lipsitz's essay, see *Cultural Anthropology* vol. 1 no. 4 (November 1986), pp. 355–87.

61. See, for example, Derek Kompare, *Rerun Nation: How Repeats Invented American Television* (New York: Routledge, 2004); Amy Holdsworth, *Television, Memory, and Nostalgia* (Basingstoke, Hants.: Palgrave Macmillan, 2011); Charles Tashiro, 'The Contradictions of Video Collecting', *Film Quarterly* vol. 50 no. 2 (1996), pp. 11–18; Kim Bjarkman, 'To Have and to Hold: The Video Collector's Relationship with an Ethereal Medium', *Television & New Media* vol. 5 no. 3 (2004), pp. 217–46; Lucas Hildebrandt, *Inherent Vice: Bootleg Histories of Videotape and Copyright* (Durham, NC: Duke University Press, 2009); Lisa Gitelman, *Always Already New: Media, History, and the Data of Culture* (Cambridge, MA: MIT, 2008); Craig Robertson (ed.), *Media History and the Archive* (London: Routledge, 2011); Charles Acland (ed.), *Residual Media* (Minneapolis: University of Minnesota Press, 2007); Wolfgang Ernst, *Digital Media and the Archive*, ed. Jussi Parikka (Minneapolis: University of Minnesota Press, 2012); Robin Nelson and Lez Cooke (eds), special issue on archives, *Critical Studies in Television* vol. 5 no. 2 (2010); Paul Grainger (ed.), *Ephemeral Media: Transitory Screen Culture from Television to YouTube* (London: British Film Institute, 2011); Patrick Vondereau, Pelle Snickers and Jean Burgess (eds), *The YouTube Reader* (Stockholm: National Library of Sweden, 2010); Kate Darian-Smith and Sue Turnbull (eds), *Remembering Television: Histories, Technologies, Memories* (Newcastle upon Tyne: Cambridge Scholars Publishing, 2012); Jérôme Bourdon and Berber Hagedoorn (eds), special issue on 'European Television Memories', *View* vol. 2 no. 3 (2013). Available at: <http://journal.euscreen.eu/index.php/view/issue/view/3/showToc>.

    After co-authoring the Batman essay, we each continued to deal with issues of memory, the archive and/or fan cultures in relation to television and digital media. For Spigel's work, see, for example, 'From the Dark Ages to the Golden Age: Women's Memories and Television Reruns', *Screen* vol. 36 no. 1 (Spring 1995), pp. 16–33; 'Our TV Heritage: Television, the Archive, and the Reasons for Preservation', in Janet Wasko (ed.), *The Television Companion* (London: Blackwell, 2005), pp. 67–102; 'Post-Feminist Nostalgia for a Pre-Feminist Future', *Screen* vol. 54 no. 2 (Summer 2013), pp. 270–8; and her forthcoming book, *TV Snapshots: An Archive of Everyday Life* (Durham, NC: Duke University Press). For Jenkins's work, see 'Death-Defying Heroes', in *The Wow Climax: Tracing the Emotional Impact of Popular Culture* (New York: New York University Press, 2006), pp. 65–74; 'Archival, Ephemeral and Residual: The Functions of Early Comics in Art Spiegelman's *In the Shadow of No Towers*', in Daniel Stein and Jan-Noël Thon (eds), *From Comic Strips to Graphic Novels: Contributions to the Theory and History of Graphic Narrative* (Gottingen: Walter de Gruyter, 2013), pp. 301–24; with Sam Ford and Joshua Green, *Spreadable Media: Creating Meaning and Value in a Networked Culture* (New York: New York University Press, 2013).

62. Kevin Smith, as quoted in 'Kevin Smith Returns to Comics for *Batman 66 Meets the Green Hornet*', *Comic Book Resources*, 11 March 2014. Available at: <http://www.comicbookresources.com/?page=article&id=51383>; Michael Uslan, 'Introduction', *Batman: The TV Stories* (New York: DC Comics, 2014), p. 4.

MULTIPLYING THE BATMAN

13

'I'M NOT FOOLED BY THAT CHEAP DISGUISE'

William Uricchio and Roberta Pearson

The floating signifier

A colony of small, bright-yellow, vaguely bat-like objects floats in a pool of white.[1] A spoon dips into the bowl, scooping up more of the 'crunchy bat shapes, with natural flavours of honey-nut'.[2] On the breakfast table stands a black cereal box, a familiar black bat in a yellow oval prominently emblazoned on all six sides.

During the summer of 1989, this Bat-logo permeated American culture, appearing on candy, boxer shorts, leather medallions, earrings, baseball caps, night lights, sterling silver coins – in short, on any item capable of bearing the trademarked image (or unlicensed likenesses thereof). The Bat-logo's omnipresence diffused its meaning, reducing the wearing of a black bat in a yellow oval to a mere gesture of participation in a particular cultural moment. While the intended meaning of that participation may have varied greatly, and while many Bat-logo purchasers might have had very little knowledge of the Batman mythos, the logo, at the very least, carried the connotation 'Batman' and thus indicated the purchaser's acknowledgment, however minimal, of the character.

One of the more bizarre consumable expressions of Batmania, the crunchy Bat-breakfast cereal, pointedly referenced the *character* of the Caped Crusader, the box copy using such terms as 'terrifying', 'obsession', 'death', 'killed' and 'evildoers'. Though these terms may have constituted a potentially distasteful connotative frame for the tasty Bat-shapes, the side panel containing them successfully summarised most of the salient characteristics of the Dark Knight:

> His name was The Batman. A dark, mysterious character of the night, stalking the streets, defying criminals with the intelligence, athletic prowess, and state of the art gadgetry, terrifying enemies who dare cross his path.

> The Batman had a secret identity, that of Bruce Wayne™, wealthy playboy. At a very young age his parents were killed on the streets of Gotham City™. Later, he used his inheritance to travel around the world, seeking masters of justice and the martial arts, honing his body to perfection. A man with an obsession for justice. When he was ready, he returned to Gotham City™ as The Batman, ready to terrorize the evildoers of the city and to avenge the death of his parents.[3]

This copy suggests the minimal components of the Batman character that have circulated for fifty years in various media and among different publics; filmgoers, television viewers, comic book readers, etc. The Dark Knight's identity has fluctuated over time and across media as multiple authors and fan communities competed over his definition.

The tensions in the character's identity became clearly apparent in the Bat-hyped summer of 1989 when a myriad of Batmen simultaneously vied for the cape and cowl – in the blockbuster film and its numerous tie-ins, the syndicated television series, the ongoing runs of *Detective* and *Batman* comics, as well as in graphic novels, with *The Killing Joke* (1988) and *The Dark Knight Returns* (1986) most prominent among them. The highest-profile Batman, the latest site of fifty years of Bat-hype, appeared in the Warner Bros. film. The scriptwriter, Sam Hamm, claimed that the pervasiveness of this particular Batman granted him automatic authenticity:

> What you wind up doing when you're putting an existing character in a major Hollywood film is you're essentially *defining* that character for a whole generation of people; and most people have certainly heard of Batman, but they are probably not that familiar with it. So what you're doing becomes sort of *ipso facto* canonical.[4]

The film's director, Tim Burton, similarly asserted the canonicity of the Warner's Batman, arguing that his leading man, Michael Keaton, possessed the correct attributes for the role. The Batman 'is the one comic book hero who is not a superhero but a human being. Since Michael is hardly a big he-man, but looks just like a regular guy off the street he was perfect for the role.'[5]

Others disagreed. Science-fiction writer Harlan Ellison believed that the choice of Keaton made little sense:

> Michael Keaton truly contravenes the whole point of Batman. Here's the only prominent superhero without special powers; here's one of the very best detectives who ever lived, and he's being played by a scrawny comedian in plastic armor. That, in a capsule, is the kind of erroneous thinking that dooms films.[6]

Indeed, the Keaton casting had produced such widespread disappointment that the *Wall Street Journal* ran a front-page article speculating about the film's financial prospects in the face of fierce Bat-fan disaffection.

The report deeply disturbed Jon Peters, co-producer of the film: 'Every analyst I knew sent that to me the day it came out. It just deflated everybody. … Nobody wanted Keaton. … We were ostracized by the Bat-community. They booed us at the Bat-convention.'[7] Tim Burton seemed less solicitous of fan reaction. 'There might be something that's sacrilege in the movie. … But I can't care about it. … This is too big a budget movie to worry about what a fan of a comic would say.'[8]

This debate over the 'real' Batman replicated that surrounding the 1960s television programme and reflected an ongoing series of character transmutations. Bob Kane, 'creator' of the Batman, described the potential audience for the 1989 film:

Every ten years, [Batman] changes, you see. Right now there are two factions. There are the baby boomers who know the TV show; they *don't* know the dramatic comic book prior to that, so they think the movie is probably going to be a comedy. Then there are readers who *know* the roots from which he came, that he is a vigilante, mysterious, a loner.[9]

The years since the publication of Miller's *The Dark Knight Returns* have seen the greatest array of character transmutations and violations of heretofore sacrosanct canonicity. The 'miscasting' of the Warner's film constituted one of its lesser heresies. Greater transgressions included the establishment of a continuing (sexual) relationship with, and the revealing of his secret identity to, Vicki Vale, as well as making the Joker the killer of Bruce Wayne's parents and then killing him off. *The Dark Knight Returns* featured a fifty-year-old Batman and a female Robin. *Gotham by Gaslight* (1989) set the Batman characters and locations in the late 1880s, where the Batman encountered Jack the Ripper. In *Son of the Demon* (1987), the Batman married the daughter of an arch-villain and even had a son.

This moment in the last decade of the twentieth century, then, represents the most divergent set of refractions of the Batman character. Whereas broad shifts in emphasis had occurred since 1939, these changes had been, for the most part, consecutive and consensual. Now, newly created Batmen, existing simultaneously with the older Batmen of the television series and comic reprints and back issues, all struggled for recognition and a share of the market. But the contradictions among them may threaten both the integrity of the commodity form and the coherence of the fans' lived experience of the character necessary for the Batman's continued success.

Mike. W. Barr and Jerry Bingham, *Batman: Son of the Demon* (New York: DC Comics, 1987)

Who is the Batman?

The very nature of the Batman's textual existence reveals an impulse towards fragmentation. Since his creation in 1939, numerous editors, writers, artists, directors, scriptwriters, performers and licensed manufacturers have continually 'authored' the Batman, with the specificities of various media necessitating the selective emphasis of character qualities. Unlike some fictional characters, the Batman has no primary urtext set in a specific period, but has rather existed in a plethora of equally valid texts constantly appearing over more than five

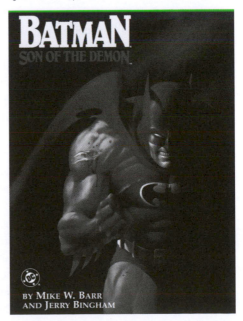

decades. This has freed him from temporal specificity. The Batman remains untouched by the ravages of time, an eternal thirty-year-old, with only a very selective accruing of canonised historical events.[10]

Neither author, nor medium, nor primary text, nor time period defines the Batman. In the absence of these other markers, character – that is, a set of key components – becomes the primary signifier of Batman texts: the key components of the Batman character have constituted the *sine qua non* for any Batman narrative in any medium. This exclusive emphasis on the primacy of key components distinguishes the Batman from other series/serial fictional heroes, where character figures prominently but not exclusively among the defining elements.

Consider, for example, Sherlock Holmes, James Bond and Philip Marlowe. Despite these characters' appearances in films, and even their continuation in literary form beyond their creators' deaths, their central identity resides in a series of literary urtexts penned by single authors and set in single time periods. Hence, were one seeking to define Sherlock Holmes, one would turn not to the latest in a series of numerous pastiches but to the fifty-six short stories and four novels of Sir Arthur Conan Doyle written between 1887 and 1927. Indeed, the fan community in this case tenaciously valorises these texts as the single canonised repository of Holmes's character, extrapolating from them the key components of the Master's identity. While a set of key components centrally identifies the Batman, the Bat-fan has no authoritative repository of these key components to turn to but is faced instead with an ongoing and potentially endless stream of new texts.

By contrast, other fictional characters such as Bugs Bunny and Mickey Mouse, though similar to the Batman in being multiply authored and not bound to a particular medium, urtext or period, differ from the Batman in that they function as actors/celebrities rather than as characters.[11] Bugs Bunny can appear in an opera, a Western, a Sherwood Forest adventure, a science-fiction film or, even, as 'himself' at the Academy Awards. In each case, he plays a role within the narrative as well as constantly remaining Bugs Bunny, in similar fashion to such flesh and blood counterparts as Groucho Marx.

Like Holmes, Bond and Marlowe, and unlike Bugs Bunny and Mickey Mouse, the Batman's set of key components brings with it a particular generic form – in the Batman's case, crime-fighting.[12] The latest Batbible, written by *Batman* and *Detective* editor Dennis O'Neil as a character guide for DC writers, states: '*Everything* with the exception of his friends' welfare is bent to the task he knows he can never accomplish, the elimination of crime. It is this task which imposes meaning on an existence he would otherwise find intolerable.'[13]

What then are the key components of the Batman and how did we go about identifying them, given the lack of authoritative texts and the non-accruing nature of events? Of the many elements that constitute the Batman at any one time, we have privileged the lowest common denominator of long-lasting and recurrent components that often seem to appear in self-conscious and reductionist articulations of the Batman character such as the cereal box side panel. Even at this moment of multiple and competing Batmen, the character remains a rich man who dresses in an icono-graphically specific costume (cape, cowl and Bat-logo). Because of the murder of his parents, he obsessively fights crime, using his superb physical abilities in combination with his deductive capacities. He maintains his secret identity of Bruce Wayne, who lives in Wayne Manor in Gotham City. He is surrounded by a supporting cast of friends and foes.

Five key components constitute the core character of the Batman: traits/attributes; events; recurrent supporting characters; setting and iconography. We briefly adumbrate these components here:

1. TRAITS/ATTRIBUTES

Put most succinctly, the Batman might be said to have four central traits/attributes: wealth; physical prowess; deductive abilities and obsession. The Batbible provides a more detailed breakdown of these central traits/attributes: the Batman is 'tough but not brutal'; 'probably the best martial artist alive, and one of the best gymnasts'; 'strong and athletic'; 'smart with an IQ comfortably in the genius numbers'; 'trained, an autodidact'; 'obsessed … but in the fullest possession of his mental and moral faculties'; 'celibate'; and 'compassionate'. He is also the 'heir to a large fortune, esti-mated at nearly 100 million dollars'.

2. EVENTS

Two different kinds of events constitute this component: fixed and accruing events, such as the origin story, and iterative – that is, repetitive, non-identical and non-accruing events, most of which involve crime-fighting.[14] The central fixed event, the origin story, is the source of many of the Batman's traits/attributes, which play themselves out in the iterative events.

Until recently, the fixed and accruing and hence, canonised, events have been few in number: the origin; the appearance of Robin and a handful of other central characters, and the cases related to the Batcave trophies. In the present moment of extreme character refraction, canonised events seems to be proliferating, with impli-cations for character continuity and containment. The iterative events – that is, inci-dents of obsessive crime-fighting – display the Batman's traits/attributes, constitute the dominant generic form and embody the character's hegemonic function, as we shall discuss later.

3. RECURRENT SUPPORTING CHARACTERS

The Batman's interactions with the good guys and bad guys around him help to define him. Characters such as Commissioner Gordon, Robin I (Dick Grayson), Alfred and the Joker all entered the Batman's world by the early 1940s and have main-tained a constant, though sporadic, presence. Although we use these characters here to define the Batman, they could themselves be defined along many of the same parameters as the Caped Crusader. For example, the Joker has traits/attributes (rhetorical mode and whimsical approach to crime), fixed and iterative events (an origin story and obsessive criminal activities), recurrent characters (Batman and Robin), setting (Gotham City) and iconography (green hair, white face, bright-red mouth set in a permanent grin).

4. SETTING

The Batman/Bruce Wayne lives in Gotham City, which has the same symbiotic relationship with him as the recurrent characters. As the Riddler put it,

> When is a man a city? When it's Batman or when it's Gotham. I'd take either answer. Batman is this city. … That's why we're [the Riddler and other costumed villains] here. That's why we stay. We're trying to survive in the city. It's huge and contradictory and *dark* and funny and threatening.[15]

The fluctuating image of Gotham City relates to the fluctuating nature of crime in the Batman's world and has implications for the playing out of the Batman's hegemonic function.

5. ICONOGRAPHY

The Batman's costume serves him well in his endless war against crime. The colours that permit him to lurk unseen in the shadows and the invocation of a terrifying creature of the night both enable him to seize the psychological element of surprise from Gotham's criminal element.

While various artists have redesigned elements of the costume (shortening the ears or adding a yellow circle to the chest emblem), the basic elements of cape, cowl, gauntlets and logo have remained easily identifiable, as one would expect in primarily visual texts. Taking the cue of costume and cognomen, bat-like shapes, like the Bat-prefix, abound in the Batman's world. The Batmobile, the Batcopter, the Batarang and the Bat-etcs. all serve as repositories of the Bat-look: black, shiny, with a bat-wing design incorporated where possible.

Without the presence of all five key components in some form, the Batman ceases to be the Batman, yet the primarily series nature of the character permits fairly wide variation in the treatment of these components across time and media. The elasticity of the components allows for great stretching, but in this moment of extreme character refraction, the Batman may be stretched thin to the point of invisibility.

Gritty – graphic – grown-up

A DC advertisement in the same issue of *Rolling Stone* which featured a cover story interview with Michael Keaton declared that the company's gritty, graphic and grown-up comics had come of age. 'You outgrew comics, now they've caught up with you.'[16] The advertisement touted the current four most divergent comic book Batmen: *The Killing Joke* by Moore/Bolland, *The Return of the Dark Knight*, *The Greatest Batman Stories Ever Told* and *The Batman Movie Adaptation* (1989) by O'Neil/Ordway. The simultaneous presence of these divergent Batmen, together with the advertising venue, the appeal to adult readership, and the marketing of graphic novels and special-format (high-priced) reprints all signal a major shift in the comic book marketplace.[17]

In the first three decades of the Batman's existence, Bob Kane, now cited in every narrative expression as the character's 'creator', took credit for the production of the majority of Bat-texts. In actuality, a crew of uncredited ghostwriters and ghost-artists – all expected to subordinate their styles to the dominant Kane look – worked on the books. As Kane said, 'I feel a ghost's job is to emulate the cartoonist, as near as you can, instead of recreating what he already did in his own style.'[18] In this period, comic book authorship was not valorised as an expressive act and comic artists had low visibility.

During the mid- to late 1960s, Bat-fans began to exhibit great interest in questions of authorship, using the letter columns as a forum for speculation about the identities of writers, pencillers and inkers, and as a means for communicating with each other about these matters. By 1968, a fan complained, 'Figuring out the authors of stories really isn't much fun now. The fad should soon be dying out because it's getting too easy.' DC, replying to the letter, announced a new policy: 'the author-guessing fad has run its course. From now on we're giving author (and artists) credit along with each story.'[19]

This new crediting of writers and artists reflected increased valorisation of comic book authorship, further encouraging the fans to take an auteurist perspective of the production process. Much as film fan discourse in the 1960s began to revolve around directors, comic fan discourse increasingly centred on the importance of writers and artists. As a letter column correspondent put it in 1980:

> you're going to have to change your entire attitude towards 'putting out' material. Unless you do so, sales will continue to plummet. You will have to produce, on a regular basis, 'special' material by special people that will make your public want to buy your magazines. In the case of BATMAN, this will be like the following: stories by Archie Goodwin, Steve Englehart, and ... artists like: Jim Starlin, Alex Toth, Marshall Rogers, ... and similar talented, but 'different,' 'special' people.[20]

Today, a substantial portion of published fan correspondence concerns authorship issues. The attendance of comic book authors at comic conventions both reflects and enhances their status within the fan community. Those within the industry assert that the names of well-known writers such as Alan Moore, Frank Miller, Dennis O'Neil and John Byrne and well-known illustrators such as Brian Bolland and Bill Sienkiewicz on a cover guarantee greater sales. The emergence of the direct-distribution system, which permitted more accurate tracking of individual title sales, further augmented comic book auteurism by giving rise to a royalty system now used by both the major comic book companies, DC and Marvel. Hence, a system that effaced authorship and insisted upon conformance to the house style has given way to one which relies upon individual authorship as a criterion of quality and marketability.

This economic incentive prompts authors/writers towards maximum differentiation within the standardisation imposed by the key components of the Batman character.

Differential treatment of the key components can identify a writer/artist with a particular version of the Batman. Thus, we refer to Miller's Batman or Moore's Batman, further boosting their stock with fans and industry but also further exacerbating the tendency towards fragmentation of the character's identity.[21]

The language of artistic self-consciousness, however, veils raw economic reality. Since credits, royalties and other recognition have altered the fundamental relationship between the writer/artist and his work, the industry can now, to some extent, accommodate employees' aspirations to create 'art'.[22] This leads to the production of such specialised permutations of the Batman as the recent *Arkham Asylum*, written by Grant Morrison and illustrated by Dave McKean. The hard-cover, 120-page graphic novel self-consciously constructs a fragmented, postmodern narrative relayed by overlapping and conflicting narrative voices and expressed in an evocative melange of artistic styles.

But *Arkham Asylum* and similar books result not only from the artists' economic incentives and creative desires but also from DC's need to expand its market through product differentiation, both from other companies and within its own output. DC now produces standard-format books, new-format books, deluxe-format books, prestige-format books, graphic novels and collected editions, differentiated by price (from $1 to $29.95), length, ink and paper quality, as well as the maturity of the content and the mode of representation. This differentiation not only expands the market, but also gains the industry an unaccustomed measure of respectability. As the Associated Press said about *The Dark Knight Returns*, it 'is not like most comic books. Its printing is deluxe, its artwork is complex, and its mood is nightmarish and somber.'[23]

DC publisher Jenette Kahn addressed the new marketing strategy in her monthly column:

> Of course, no one could be more aware than you, our readers, of the extensive changes in comics during the past six years. We began to publish at different price points in a variety of formats with a wide range of artistic effects and verbal story telling. The diversity in the content of the comics gave rise to an equal diversity in marketing techniques, advertising, and avenues of distribution.[24]

While one might take issue with Kahn's causality, one cannot deny the relationships she draws among marketing, distribution and 'diversity in the content'. The structural incentives for 'diversity' – 'creativity' and an expanding market – speak precisely to the tension between, on the one hand, the essential maintenance of a recognisable set of key character components and, on the other, the increasingly necessary centrifugal dispersion of these components.

'Everything is exactly the same, except for the fact that it's all totally different'

In May 1953, *Detective Comics* #195 ran a story titled 'The Original Batman'. Gotham City suddenly has two Batmen: the familiar Caped Crusader and a competitor, wearing a similar costume – wings instead of cape, no chest logo, Bat-logo on belt.[25] The Batman decides that 'This town isn't big enough for both of us', and it seems as if the Gotham authorities will back him up. After all, Gotham City has passed a law forbidding any-body to pose as the Batman. The competitor, however, turns out to have a prior claim to the name. He had performed as a circus acrobat wearing the Bat-costume and call-ing himself Bat-man. Gotham City attorneys confirm this fact and conclude that the Batman 'no longer has a right to the name'. The competing Bat-man eventually forbids our hero to wear his costume any longer, effectively ending his crime-fighting career. Things look bleak until Robin learns from his old circus friends that Bat-man never performed inside the Gotham City limits, a fact that invalidates his claim to the name and the costume.

The challenging of the Batman's identity threatened Gotham City with the loss of a crime-fighter, but threatens DC with the loss of a profit-maker, a far more trouble-some prospect. The company has good reason to be concerned about the Dark Knight's character, particularly since he has experienced a number of major shifts in emphasis during his fifty-year existence. Mike Gold, in an introduction to *The Greatest Batman Stories Ever Told* (1988), offered a succinct summary:

> The past fifty years of Batman stories could be divided into at least five distinct eras: the earliest days – the creation of the series through the World War II years; the larger-than-life days of big clocks and surrealistic yet existential buildings; the monster days of aliens, gimmick costumes and weirdos; the short-lived 'new look' Batman that stressed the more detective-like aspects of the character; the regrettable and, as far as comic books were concerned equally short-lived television era; and the Darknight Detective era which, oddly, has been the longest and most enduring of them all.[26]

DC's editorial offices form one of the two central bastions of character identity, the other being the legal, licensing and rights departments of both DC and Warner Bros. While the importance of the latter has ebbed and flowed with the Batman's cul-tural currency at a particular moment, the former has served as the main agent of continuity, canonisation and containment throughout the character's entire history.[27] At this current moment of divergent expressions of the Batman in several media, the editor of the main Batman comic books must simultaneously safeguard the key com-ponents of the character and accommodate variant expressions.

The current Batman editor, Dennis O'Neil, ensures consistent depiction of the character in the DC Comics. O'Neil oversees the *Batman* and *Detective* titles and clears the Batman's guest appearances in other titles. The Batbible, quoted above, constitutes the clearest expression of character maintenance through editorial guidelines. The manuscript gives a profile of the character's history, attributes and appropriate behav-iour, ensuring continuity despite turnover in writers. DC has recently decided to impose further continuity on the Batman by linking two of the three Bat-titles more closely. As publisher Kahn explained,

Another concern of Denny's [O'Neil] and mine was to make sure that next year *Detective* and *Batman* reinforced each other. ... We weren't looking for the totally intense continuity that characterizes the Superman books; we just wanted to make sure that if Alfred has a broken arm in *Batman*, he's still nursing that broken arm in *Detective*.[28]

This editorial process has enough flexibility to accommodate some of the most divergent expressions of the Batman, at least, that is, those within the comic book and graphic-novel realm. Recently, this flexibility has manifested itself in the self-consciously ambiguous constructions of some of the supporting cast. As the Joker said of his origin in *The Killing Joke*, 'sometimes I remember it one way, sometimes another ... if I'm going to have a past, I prefer it to be multiple-choice! HA HA HA!'[29] The Riddler, like the Joker, refused to specify his origins, suggesting numerous possibilities:

I've always been the Riddler. I always will be ... maybe it started by cheating in a school history test, photographing a jigsaw puzzle ... maybe I was a carnival barker, E. Nigma, the Puzzle King, Conundrum Champion, Wizard of Quiz ... maybe I decided to turn my talents to crime, maybe I wanted to match wits with ... with Batman, for the glory ... the fame ... the buck$.[30]

This strategy of accommodation delimits the realm of possibilities for character construction: a writer may tinker with aspects of the Joker's origins but a colourist may not give him purple hair.

The strategy of containment that complements the strategy of accommodation derives from DC's editorial offices and from fan response as well. The industry used to assume a total readership turnover every three years, making continuity fairly unimportant.[31] The emergence of the direct-distribution market, the proliferation of comics speciality shops and the targeting of adult audiences have given rise to a more stable readership than in the past. Elements of this new readership exhibit an almost fanatical interest in continuity issues, constantly writing to question, complain or suggest resolutions of apparent contradictions. This fan pressure, coupled with the co-existing divergent expressions of the character, has even necessitated explicit editorial statements about the canonical and non-canonical:

1) By the way, the BATMAN movie (as well as the BATMAN MOVIE ADAPTATION) IS NOT a part of Batman continuity.
2) ... the tale told in BATMAN: THE KILLING JOKE is NOT the definitive origin of the Joker. It's simply one of many POSSIBLE origins. ...
3) Since it is set about 20 years in the future, BATMAN: THE DARK KNIGHT RETURNS is also NOT considered to be a part of normal continuity. It is a POSSIBLE future for Batman, one which may or may not happen. We're NOT saying that it couldn't happen, but it would be a shame to limit the Batman's future to this one story.[32]

Despite the deliberate ambiguity concerning the Joker's origins, a Who's Who entry for the Joker in *Detective Comics Annual #2* incorporated *The Killing Joke* origin, while accompanying illustrations referenced this story as well as *A Death in the Family* and 'The Laughing Fish'.[33] This Who's Who entry again accommodated change yet reveals the containment strategy and self-appointed canonical authority of the DC editorial staff.

While *The Killing Joke* origin may or may not be canonical, the *Batman* film has been declared conclusively non-canonical, indicating that the DC staff, at least, believe that the comic books truly define the character. The explicit disavowal of the Warner Bros. film appears even in the comic book adaptation written by O'Neil, the *Batman* editor, and published by DC. The initial splash page shows a strip of film, bearing key frames drawn from the *Batman* movie, superimposed over an audience in a movie theatre. In the first dialogue balloon on the page, an audience member says, 'It's just a movie, for Heaven's sake.'[34] The back cover also features a filmstrip design with further scenes from the movie. O'Neil said that he intended these filmstrips to bracket the adaptation and distinguish it from DC's continuity.[35]

From a legal perspective, the DC staff is right about their canonical authority – their company and not Warner Bros. holds the trademark for 'Batman and all related characters, the distinctive likenesses thereof and all related indicia', as every *Batman* comic states. DC has gone to great lengths in protecting Bat-expressions through trademarking. *The Batman Role-Playing Game* lists 174 trademarked names for people, devices and places, ranging from Batman specifics such as Batcomputer, Batmobile, Bat-shuriken and Bat-team, to Bat-specific locations and characters such as Gotham City, Gotham Institute of Technology, Gotham Tennis Hall of Fame, to more general locations and names such as Chelsea and Elizabeth Powell. These 174 trademarked names, of course, include only those used in the game, not every DC trademark.[36]

The DC legal department, then, serves to safeguard character identity through trademark and copyright registration and enforcement. The licensing and rights departments also protect character identity, granting permission to use Batman images on products or in other publications. This protection ensures a uniformity of iconographic and narrative depictions of the Batman and prevents dilution of the trademark. While for fans, canonicity and thus character identity reside in the editorial staff's control of the comic books, for the larger public, character identity resides in the legal department's control of commodity circulation of the Batman and related indicia. The floating signifier of the Bat-logo is essentially a legal rather than a narrative evocation of the character.

'I shall become a *bat*!'

Long-term DC artist and editor Dick Giordano explained the importance of the Batman's origin story:

> Let's talk about Batman's origin and why I believe it is intrinsic to his believability, popularity, and longevity. The Batman was born in a few, brief, violent moments in which a young Bruce Wayne was forced to watch the brutal murder of his parents

at the hands of a street thief. ... We can all understand Bruce's grief ... and we all can understand his need to do something to avenge the deaths of his parents. The origin of the Batman is grounded, therefore, in emotion. An emotion that is primal and timeless and dark. The Batman does what he does for himself, for his needs. That society gains from his actions is incidental.[37]

The first recountings of the origin, appearing in *Detective Comics #33* (November 1939) and restaged in *Batman #1* (Spring 1940), set out the minimal elements of a story since subjected to compulsive retellings and variations. In the 1940 version, as Bruce and his parents walked home from a movie, a nameless thug attacked them. Attempting to steal the mother's necklace, the hoodlum shot and killed both mother and father when the latter tried to resist. A traumatised Bruce swore to take vengeance through a war on criminals. He spent several years and some of the family fortune preparing, becoming a master scientist/detective and an amazing athlete. Seeking both disguise and psychological advantage, he decided that 'I shall become a *bat!*' 'And thus is born this weird figure of the dark ... this avenger of evil. The *Batman.*'

Writers have repeatedly returned to the scene of the crime and restaged the origin much as it 'happened' in 1940. Though the basic events remain sacrosanct, certain details have varied. In subsequent expansions and reworkings, the Batman identified the nameless thug as Joe Chill, tracked him down and brought him to justice. A few years later, he discovered that Chill had actually been employed by Lew Moxon, whom he also tracked down and brought to justice. Such details as the film the family had seen and the cause of the mother's death (gunshot or heart attack) may vary from version to version, but the reiteration of the basic origin events holds together otherwise divergent expressions of the Batman.

The fixed events of the origin serve two rather paradoxical functions: 1) they provide the motivation for the endless iterative events necessitated by the character's series nature; and 2) they help to contain the character while also delimiting the traits/attributes that contribute to his elasticity. The origin explains the character's continuous crime-fighting. Though, in elaborations of the origin, the Batman avenges his parents' murder by apprehending the actual perpetrators, the metaphoric perpetrators they represent (the faceless thugs, the brutal hirelings, the crime bosses) still blight the urban landscape. Every encounter with a criminal, then, raises the spectre of that original encounter. Justice-seeking becomes an endless process, with the Batman a Gotham Sisyphus who can never reach the crime-free summit of the mountain. Just as Sisyphus may roll the rock up a different path each time but never achieve the summit, the Batman may combat different criminals with different methods but never eradicate crime. This endless repetition accounts for the non-accruing nature of most of the events.

Sisyphus and the Batman are primarily defined by their iterative actions: Sisyphus is the man who pushes the rock; the Batman is the man who fights crime. The origin thus accounts for the predominant genre of the Batman narratives. Similarly, it accounts for the character's relationship to authority and property rights. His childhood trauma stemmed from an incident in which attempted resistance to a petty violation of property rights (the theft of a necklace) gave rise to a capital crime (murder). Bruce Wayne's father was willing to give his life to defend property and uphold the law. The son followed in his father's footsteps. To compound the irony, the successful theft of the necklace would have deprived the Waynes of a mere fraction of their millions, the inheritance of which enabled Bruce to enter upon his Sisyphean task as the Batman.

Since many of the character's traits/attributes have their origin in the Batman's origin, further examination of the birth of the Dark Knight permits us to explore the primary locus of the character's elasticity. The origin story establishes the four central attributes/traits of the character: obsession; deductive abilities; physical prowess; and wealth. In the 1940 origin, the four-panel sequence following the 'terror and shock' of his parents' death, shows:

1. Young Bruce kneeling by his bedside, saying, 'And I swear by the spirits of my parents to avenge their deaths by spending the rest of my life warring on all criminals.'
2. An older Bruce stands in a smoke-filled laboratory peering into a test tube. The caption reads, 'As the years pass Bruce Wayne prepares himself for his career. He becomes a master scientist.'
3. Bruce holds a massive barbell in one hand. The caption reads, 'Trains his body to physical perfection until he is able to perform amazing athletic feats.'
4. Bruce sits in front of a huge portrait that hangs above a fireplace. He says, 'Dad's estate left me wealthy. I am ready … But first I must have a disguise.'

The sequence is completed when the bat flies in the window and Bruce derives his inspiration.

Over the years, a process of uneven accentuation and development has selectively foregrounded or downplayed certain aspects of the key components. This process accounts for both the character's containment and refraction, the elastic treatment of the key components allowing his narrative undulations and, thus, his longevity. The current divergent forms of the character represent an ever more articulate and conscious reworking of his original capacities rather than the addition or subtraction of key components. This holds true even for that Bat-text most often touted as reconfiguring and thus revitalising the Batman, *The Dark Knight Returns*. Alan Moore realised that Frank Miller had not created a new Batman, but had rather differentially emphasised some of the key traits/attributes. 'Depicted over the years as, alternately, a concerned do-gooder and a revenge-driven psychopath, the character as presented here [*The Dark Knight Returns*] manages to bridge both those interpretations quite easily while integrating them in a much larger and more persuasively realized personality.'[38]

The constant repetition of the basic origin events has turned them into the central touchstone of the character, which can be and frequently are reduced to one-sentence summaries. For example, in *Batman Annual* #13 (1989), the narration states, 'He is a man at war. An intense, obsessed soldier fulfilling an oath he'd made a lifetime ago while standing over his parents' grave.'

Brian Augustyn and Mike Mignola, *Batman: Gotham by Gaslight* (New York: DC Comics, 1989)

The merest reference to the origin events activates an intertextual frame that insists upon the Batman's motivation and key traits/attributes while permitting for variant elaboration, as such recent restagings in *Gotham by Gaslight, Arkham Asylum, Legends of the Dark Knight* #1 and *Batman: The Movie* (all from 1989) attest. *Gotham by Gaslight*, for example, tells a Batman story set in the nineteenth century, but ensures that the reader understands that this Batman is indeed *the* Batman. The first two pages retell the origin with nineteenth-century trappings: the Wayne family rides home in a carriage from an evening in town and is accosted by a highwayman, who murders the parents. This cues the reader to expect the other key components of the Batman character, which are indeed trotted out: Alfred and Commissioner (then Inspector) Gordon; Gotham City, etc. *Arkham Asylum* emphasises young Bruce's subjectivity. Bruce, frightened by the film he has just seen, annoys his mother with his crying. She threatens, 'If you don't stop crying and act like a grown-up, I'm leaving you right here.' She does indeed leave him, as the mugger immediately appears and enacts the ritual murders. This subjective version, foregrounding Bruce's insecurity and terror, and focusing on his mother rather than his father, resonates throughout the highly psychologised narrative.

Ménage à trois

Television static within a blazing white Bat-logo followed by a tracking shot through folds of luminous material to reveal a Bat-costumed dancer. Chorus lines of Batmen and Jokers in choreographed tussles. Prince garbed as half-Batman, half-Joker. Vicki Vale – Batman tattoo on her thigh and a Joker tattoo on her back. Fragments of dialogue sampled from the film.

The multiple Bat-dancers of the Prince 'Batdance' video most clearly epitomise the multiplicity of Batmen currently proliferating in comics and other media. Which of these dancers is the 'real' Batman? Which of the proliferating Batmen is the 'real' Batman? 'Batdance', establishing identity only through iconography and a recurrent character, provides a succinct answer: 'real' Batmen wear Bat-costumes and fight with Jokers. As Tim Burton put it, the movie the Prince video promoted was about 'a man who dresses up like a bat vs. a man who has literally become a clown'.[39]

The video presents us with multiple embodiments of the Batman as well as

Prince's schizophrenic Batman/Joker and constitutes a clear expression of both the current fragmentation of the Batman character and the symbiotic relationship between him and the Joker. Yet the undulations of the character over his fifty-year history have always entailed simultaneous undulations in the presence/absence and depictions of the recurrent characters. In the past few years, the proliferating Batmen in various media present multiple personalities of the Batman, whose psychological make-up crucially relates to the presence/absence and depictions of the two (currently) most important of the recurrent characters: the Joker and Robin.

Both the Joker and Robin characters are defined within many of the same parameters as the Batman, but the parallels between the Batman and the Joker make the Clown Prince of Crime an equal but opposite, an evil doppelgänger, while those between the Batman and Robin make the Boy Wonder a dependent reflection, a son/student. The Joker's crazed opposition to the Batman sets up a narrative tension that pulls the Batman's persona to extremes, driving him to the edge of dissolution, whereas Robin's vulnerable reliance tends to reinforce his more 'human' dimensions, containing him within his traditional bounds. Thus, the tension between do-gooder and revenge-driven psychopath that Alan Moore noted can be seen as a tension between the shifting depictions and the presences/absences of Robin and the Joker.

The Joker, the oldest of the Batman's continuing antagonists, has enjoyed a great deal of popularity. Between his inception in 1940 and the imposition of the Comics Code, he surfaced nearly every month in one of the two Batman titles. Portrayed by Cesar Romero in the 1960s television series, he tied with the Penguin for most guest villain slots (each featured in eighteen episodes). Recently, his popularity has waxed again: the graphic novels *The Dark Knight Returns*, *Arkham Asylum* and *The Killing Joke* all feature him in key roles, as does the Warner's film. DC has recently issued a companion volume to *The Greatest Batman Stories Ever Told* – *The Greatest Joker Stories Ever Told*. The film has generated Joker ephemera to accompany the Batman merchandise – toys, T-shirts, hats, etc.

His longevity and the frequency of his appearances establish his centrality to the Batman mythos, reinforcing the key components of his character. The Joker's origin story, in whatever variation, accounts for his motivation and his iconography. In 'The Man behind the Red Hood' (*Detective* #168, February 1951), the Joker bungles a million-dollar heist from The Monarch Playing Card Company and escapes the clutches of the Batman by diving into a catch basin for noxious chemicals. The chemicals transform him from garden-variety thief into the familiar Clown Prince of Crime. The Joker tells the Batman about looking at himself in the mirror after the accident. Voiceover narration: 'I looked at myself with growing horror.' Panel dialogue: 'That chemical vapor – it turned my hair *green*, my lips *rouge-red*, my skin *chalk-white*! I look like an *evil clown*!' Voiceover: 'Then, I realised my new face could terrify people.'

Both the Batman and the Joker have their origins in cruel twists of fate. Just as the Batman responded to his tragedy by dedicating himself to justice, the Joker responded to his by dedicating himself to perverse, absurdist crime. Both single-mindedly pursue their goals, the Batman striving to impose order on an unjust universe, and the Joker doing his best to enhance the chaos of a meaningless world. Just as the Batman adopts a distinctive costume that enables him to blend with the shadows of the night and to strike terror into cowardly, superstitious criminals, the Joker makes the most of his deformity by adopting a jester-like outfit to strike terror into his victims. Both acquire endless accessories based on their names and costumes, the Joker striving to keep up with the Batman with his Joker-mobile, his own utility belt, etc.

Sometimes the characters themselves address their symbiotic relationship. A panel in *A Death in the Family* alternates medium shots of the Joker and Bruce Wayne, as the latter thinks, 'We've been linked to each other for so long, neither of us truly understanding the bond.' The Joker, too, recognises the bond that links them together, though, typically for him, speaks of it as a game. In a story where the Joker knocks out the Batman, he stands over his unconscious body musing,

> His life is mine. ... I can crush the breath out of him ... *effortlessly!* I can, at last, *triumph!* But such a *hollow* victory—! ... I've always envisioned my winning as a result of *cunning* ... at the end of a *bitter struggle* between *the Batman* and myself – him using his *detective skills* and me employing the divine gift men call *madness!* No! Without the *game* that *the Batman* and I have played for so many years, winning is *nothing!* [40]

DC publisher Kahn agreed with the Joker that his game with the Batman must continue, since the hero and villain complement each other so perfectly:

> The Joker is out of control, and in this way neither Batman's powerful mind or strength can surround him. ... Thus the Batman and the Joker form a Yin/Yang duality, the Joker needing the Batman (for who else could appreciate the bizarre genius of his acts?) and the Batman needing the Joker (for who else, truly, could test him?). It is a world of passionate, binding opposites.[41]

The Batman and the Joker have needed each other throughout their fifty-year relationship, performing a Bat-dance *pas de deux* in which each partner measures his step to the other. The Joker started his career as a smiling killer who murdered for profit, countered by an uncomplicated, no-nonsense, vigilante Batman. In the 1950s and 60s, the Joker became a relatively harmless merry prankster countered by an uncomplicated, good-natured, boy scout Batman.

Today, an increasingly out-of-control Joker is a raging madman who kills 206 people for pleasure (*The Dark Knight Returns*), shoots Commissioner Gordon's daughter and photographs her naked body to drive her father mad (*The Killing Joke*) and eludes justice by becoming the Iranian ambassador to the United Nations, where he tries to gas the entire General Assembly (*A Death in the Family*). The Batman frequently captures the Joker and incarcerates him with the rest of the recurring villains in Gotham City's home for the criminally insane, Arkham Asylum. The graphic novel of that name features the most psychotic Joker of them all, who is so insane he may be sane. A psychotherapist explains the Joker's case to his long-time adversary:

We're not even sure if he can be properly defined as insane ... It's quite possible we may actually be looking at some kind of super-sanity here. A brilliant new modification of human perception. More suited to urban life at the end of the twentieth century. Unlike you and I, the Joker seems to have no control over the sensory information he's receiving from the outside world. He can only cope with that chaotic barrage of input by going with the flow. That's why somedays he's a mischievous clown, others a psychopathic killer. He has no real personality.[42]

While this may make the Joker the ideal postmodern cult figure, it has troubling implications for the more conventional Batman, who continually strives to make sense of that urban chaos which so fundamentally altered his life. If the randomness of late-twentieth-century existence has driven the Joker into the asylum, then the Batman, who shares so much with his adversary, may belong there too, enabling the long-time partners to continue their dance in the proper setting. Indeed, the Joker offers the Batman refuge. 'We want you in here. With us. In the madhouse. Where you belong.' Batman, not thoroughly convinced that he doesn't belong there, admits to Commissioner Gordon:

I'm afraid the Joker may be right about me. Sometimes I ... question the rationality of my actions. And I'm afraid that when I walk through those asylum gates ... when I walk into Arkham and the doors close behind me ... it'll be just like coming home.

While the novelty of a totally obsessed and even crazed Batman may appeal to readers who can afford $24.95 for *Arkham Asylum*, this degree of mental deterioration erodes the character and may threaten his function as the series hero of an ongoing line of comics. The increasing speculation about the character's sanity over the past few years has generated DC insistence upon the Batman's clean bill of health:

It's fashionable these days to claim that the Batman is, in his own way, as crazy as the Joker. ... Everyone whose life has ever been touched by random, tragic chance has come away from it changed, in some way: some transfigured by rage, others by love, some by randomness itself. Bruce Wayne was touched by chance and transfigured by rage; but he's not crazy. And he never has been.[43]

The assertion of the character's sanity forms one of the central premises of the Batbible: 'First, let us agree that Wayne/Batman is not insane. There is a difference between obsession and insanity. Obsessed the man surely is, but he is in the fullest possession of his mental and moral faculties.'

The mental deterioration of the past few years has correlated directly with the comings and goings of various Robins. The first of the Boy Wonders entered the Bat-world in 1940, the writers needing a foil for their hero – a Bat-Watson to serve an expository function.[44] But Robin served another equally important function. No shadowy creature of the night, this lad, his sunny disposition matching his brightly coloured costume. Robin tempered the Batman's grimness, the parallel tragedy of the senseless death of Dick Grayson's parents at the hands of criminals making him, in some respects, a younger version of the Caped Crusader. Robin thus shared with his mentor and surrogate parent not only a bond of sympathy but acted as a continual reminder of the vulnerable youngster Bruce Wayne had himself once been.

With the return to the Dark Knight image in the late 1960s and early 70s, Robin/Dick Grayson, now more of a liability than an asset, was packed off to college. Making occasional guest appearances in his old pal's comics, Dick then went into the superhero business for himself, adopting the disguise of Nightwing and leading the Teen (subsequently the New) Titans. Yet even one of the most divergent articulations of the Batman, *The Dark Knight Returns*, incorporated a (female) Robin. Frank Miller explained why: 'I had always thought that Robin was a real pain-in-the-ass, but I now realize what a brilliant creation it was, because it really does give a human context to Batman's character.'[45] The writers of the regular series also felt the need for a Robin, which Batman himself articulated after the death of Jason Todd (Robin II): 'It's just that I felt so adrift when I lost Dick Grayson as a partner. The Batman needed a Robin.'[46]

The Joker's murder of the second Robin precipitated a severe deterioration of the Batman's mental state, as, wracked by guilt, he refused to come to terms with his grief. Two 1989 serial stories, *Batman: Year Three* and *A Lonely Place of Dying*, centred around the Dark Knight's increasingly bizarre behaviour, as the balance between physical violence and ratiocination which he (and his writers) had maintained shifted in favour of the former. Both Alfred and Dick Grayson express serious doubts about their friend's mental health, constantly reiterating that he has failed to come to terms with Jason's death, and that his violent and brutal responses negate everything that he stood for. As Alfred says,

> I distinctly remember when … you said, 'We're not *brutalizers*. We've got to think with our heads, not with our fists.' Since Master Jason's death you've changed. It seems, sir, that you now do *all* your thinking with those sadly bruised and battered knuckles.[47]

The death of Robin and the subsequent profound psychologisation of the Batman provoked intense fan debate, much centring around his mental state. A typical letter stated:

> His lack of reaction to Jason's death could destroy him. We all need to grieve, and a failure to do so is catastrophic, emotionally and psychologically, for the grieving person. Maybe Dick can heal the rift and, at the same time, help Bruce through this difficult time. But first Bruce must acknowledge these differences. It isn't easy for the Batman to show emotion, as it's a human weakness. If he bottles it all up, however, it will eventually explode, and he himself will suffer most of all.[48]

Only the introduction of yet another Robin could halt the Batman's decline. The mysteriously knowledgeable lad who first appears in *Batman* #440 (October 1989) insists that Dick Grayson revert from Nightwing to Robin and pull his friend back from the brink of psychosis. In *The New Titans* #61 (December 1989), he holds out the old Robin costume to Nightwing. 'Dick, please – take this. It belongs to you! ... He needs a partner again. Someone to care about ... Someone who cares about him.' By *Batman* #442 (December 1989), Tim Drake has inherited Robin's cheery costume and fights crime side by side with the Caped Crusader.

But the last panel of the comic, showcasing the new Robin, contains an extreme close-up of a grinning, bright-red mouth: 'Easy come, easy go! HA HA HA HA.' Evidently, the *ménage à trois* will continue. The Joker has already dispensed with one Robin; the Batman's evil doppelgänger fittingly killing off the sunny presence that ensures the Caped Crusader's psychic balance. How will the newly well-balanced Batman and his new Robin fare when they inevitably encounter the Clown Prince of Crime? We suspect that Robin will survive, for DC has learned a hard-won lesson: as Batman himself said, 'Batman and Robin. Maybe they *have* to be a team.'[49]

'Batman only works if the world really sucks'

Who pays the Batman's salary? Bruce Wayne, of course.[50] And Bruce's money is old money, as the trappings of his existence reaffirm. A recent Diet Coke commercial, at the head of the Warner Bros. video release of the *Batman* movie, features 'stately Wayne Manor', decorated in old-fashioned opulence and serviced by a British butler, the Coca-Cola theme scored for harpsichord reinforcing the dignified ambience. Just as the Coke advertisement juxtaposes 'old world' elegance with a sales pitch, Wayne himself combines his inherited old money with savvy new investment strategies, holding vast amounts of prime Gotham real estate as well as profiting from Wayne Industries and Wayne Tech. He even has a tax shelter, the Wayne Foundation, which makes substantial contributions to charity. He's privileged, he's powerful – and, in recent years, he has increasingly shed his dilettante playboy image for that of good citizen.

Bruce's income as the source of the Batman's salary metaphorically encapsulates several parallels between the daytime millionaire and his night-time alter ego. Bruce Wayne is a pre-eminent citizen, particularly through his charitable works, while the Batman is a pre-eminent state functionary. Wayne's vast inheritance places him largely outside the constraints of capitalist accumulation. The Batman's vigilante brand of justice places him largely outside the constraints of the legal process. Bruce is a super-citizen, the Batman is a super-cop, and both strive to make Gotham City a better place to live – that is, to make it accord with their own values.

While the Batman/Bruce Wayne, like much of popular culture, obviously supports the status quo, not so obvious is the centrality of this support to the character's identity. The particular relationship to property and the state that Bruce/the Batman embodies is embedded in his origins, manifested in the iterative events and reinforced by the other key components. His inheritance and his obsession both stem from an attempt to defend property – a mere necklace – against violation. The obsession causes him to engage in his Sisyphean re-enactment of that original encounter. The recurrent supporting characters of criminal ilk and the setting activate the traits/

attributes and put into play the iterative events which permit him to give rein to his obsession. All these crucially define the nature of crime in the Batman's world, which, in turn, crucially defines the relationship of the Batman to the social order.

Hence, for the Batman to be the Batman, he *must* fight crime, *must* protect property and *must* support the status quo. Other popular heroes such as Sherlock Holmes and Superman may support the status quo, but doing so does not constitute their *sine qua non*. Holmes, for example, dealt with many cases involving no legally defined wrongdoing. But the Batman cannot be the Batman without crime and criminals.

The 'bad' recurrent characters fall into two categories: the highly individualised costumed villains and the endless array of interchangeable criminals in mufti who recur as types, not as individuals. As we have suggested above, one of the narrative functions of the costumed villains is to provide suitable opponents for the Batman. Every crime-fighting hero must have his Moriarty. But the costumed villains do not conform to the psychological profile of ordinary criminality: they steal not because they want the jewels (the money, the gold, etc.) but because the challenge of grappling with the Batman reaffirms their identity. The Batman similarly reaffirms his own identity by grappling with them. Property becomes a kind of McGuffin and both parties – the costumed villains and the Batman – play the game for the game's sake. While the costumed villains do pose a threat to property and the social order, they do so only incidentally – their primary purpose and narrative function being to match wits with the Batman.

When the Batman contests with the costumed villains, his actions to some extent disconnect him from the social order, but his class position remains firmly fixed by his alter ego, while the villains' lack of class position further exacerbates their distance from the social order. Most of their crimes involve grandiose attempts to steal high-visibility items from the wealthy or the state but arise from no political purpose or social need. Instead, the villains are inexorably drawn to capers that provide the greatest challenge and fit their modus operandi. The Penguin, for example, could not resist a Maltese Falcon while Two-Face would have to steal a statue of the Roman god Janus.

The extremely idiosyncratic and personalised nature of the costumed villains' crimes relates to their psychological instability – the villains are always highly abnormal individuals whose crimes result from mental imbalance rather than more systemic social or political causes. Recently, the villains have been written with greater depth, more in accord with the canons of psychological realism. *Secret Origins Special* #1 (1989), for example, grounds the Penguin's compulsive criminal activity in childhood trauma. *The Killing Joke* similarly attributes the Joker's motivation to personal tragedy. The Joker had been an out-of-work comic unable to support his pregnant wife. Driven to desperation, he had agreed to participate in a robbery. Even after his wife's accidental death, the gangsters forced him to go through with the crime, during which he tried to escape into a severely polluted waterway. This 'deglamorisation' of the costumed villains transforms them from flamboyant madmen into pathetic losers but still insists upon the highly personal nature of their criminal activities and connects them no more closely to the social fabric.

Henri Ducard, one of the Batman's former mentors, summed up the relationship between the Caped Crusader and his costumed antagonists:

> [The Batman] … functions as a *lightning rod* for a certain breed of *psychotic*. They specialize in absurdly grandiose *schemes*, and whatever the ostensible rationale – their *true agenda* is always the same: to cast *Batman* in the role of *nemesis*. … He *always triumphs*. If he failed, they'd be *bereft*. The pas de deux would have no *point*. Like naughty children, who tempt the wrath of a stern, demanding *father*, they seek only to *shock* him by the *enormity* of their *transgressions*. It's the moment of *acknowledgement* they crave. Thus 'good' conquers 'evil.' *True* evil seldom *announces* itself so *loudly*.[51]

Does true evil announce itself less loudly through the countless criminals in mufti who plague the great metropolis of Gotham City? Not really. In the universe of the Batman artists, phrenology and allied 'sciences' have never lost their explanatory power. The nameless thugs seem driven to crime by anatomy. To paraphrase Jessica Rabbit, these criminals aren't really bad, they're just drawn bad. This 'badness' extends to their apparel, which classifies them as outside respectable society.

In a very self-conscious restaging of the origin event, the Batman rescues a yuppie couple and their son from three instantly identifiable bad guys, muggers with broken or hooked noses, cauliflower ears and low brows.[52] Each conforms to the stereotype of a different marginalised subculture: Mansonesque biker/hippy; 1950s crew-cutted, leather-jacketed hood and contemporary punk. By contrast, the fair hair and 'clean' good looks of the yuppie family make them suitable models for the jogging outfits they wear. These potential victims, like others throughout the Bat-texts, resemble the Waynes, Graysons, Todds and Drakes, with their blue eyes, firm chins, straight noses, noble brows and Anglo names much more than the nameless, though often clearly ethnic, thugs.

The three street punks who attack the yuppie family typify not only the appearance of their countless colleagues, but also their modus operandi. Most of Gotham City's nameless criminals, the lineal descendants of the initially nameless thief who murdered the Waynes, engage in similar thefts and malefactions. Much like local television newsmen, the Batman expends most of his energy on crimes of violence with visual potential, ignoring the visually boring crimes of political grafters, polluters and slum landlords. In the Batman's universe, those criminals necessarily embodying a critique of the system remain ignored, while the violent criminals whom he fights remain divorced from the social fabric that produces them.

The transiency of these violent criminals usually, of course, prevents any detailed elaboration of their motivation or their social origins. But even one of the most fully elaborated and intermittently reappearing of these bad guys remains largely separate from the social fabric. Boss Anthony Zucco, indirectly responsible for the deaths of Dick Grayson's parents, curiously enough experienced a childhood trauma similar to both the Batman's and Robin's. His father was killed by hoodlums for refusing to pay protection money. Young Anthony grew up in the same orphanage as young Dick

Grayson, but then their paths crucially diverged – Anthony becoming a crime boss and Dick a crime-fighter. The crucial difference: 'Zucco was brought up with hatred, and that's what he returned to the world. Richard Grayson was brought up with love – and not even Zucco's act of murder could change that.'[53] Dick is good because his parents were good, and Zucco is bad because his parents were bad, the explanation for wrongdoing again being cast in highly personal terms.

Despite the fact that the perpetrators of crime have highly personalised motivations which place them outside a socio-economic context, the site of wrongdoing is paradoxically depicted as the very type of urban wasteland which would seem to provide a socio-economic context for crimes of violence. Gotham has in the past been presented as a light and cheery playground (resembling Superman's Metropolis) for the merry pranks of the costumed villains. Of late, the emphasis has been on urban decay. Commissioner Gordon recently said, 'When I first came to Gotham I thought this city couldn't sink any *lower*. Every day proves me wrong!'[54] If Commissioner Gordon knew how the Batbible describes his city, the word lower might take on a whole new meaning for him. 'Gotham is a distillation of everything that's dark, moody and frightening about New York. It is Hell's Kitchen. The Lower East Side. Bed Stuy. The South Bronx. Soho and Tribeca off the main thoroughfares at three in the morning.'

Gotham certainly looks 'dark, moody and frightening', with its deserted warehouse districts, garbage-strewn alleys, lurking shadows, dilapidated buildings, abandoned construction sites and tiny people lost in dark, deserted streets loomed over by grotesquely embellished skyscrapers. As a line from the Batman script, repeated endlessly in the film's publicity, put it, Gotham City looks 'as if hell had erupted through the sidewalks'.[55] This representation of Gotham certainly gives a compelling image of late-twentieth-century urban decay, as any New Yorker can attest, and the astute reader will certainly see these conditions as a causal factor in the high Gotham City crime rate. Yet, like the criminals, Gotham is largely removed from a socio-economic context. The narratives deal with the crime rate, but not the unemployment rate; they deal with criminal brutality, but not brutalising slum landlords; they deal with the greed of petty theft but not poverty and hopelessness – in short, they deal with the transgressions of the under-classes but not the conditions that give rise to these transgressions.

The terrifying reality of the depiction, however, tends to obscure causality while enhancing the Batman's motivation. As Frank Miller said, 'Batman only really works as a character if the world is essentially a malevolent, frightening place.'[56] The depiction of Gotham helps the Batman to work as a character by persuading the reader to empathise uncritically with the hero's actions. Let us return to our yuppie family blithely jogging their way through the urban blight. The polarity between good and evil manifested in the innocent victims and the over-armed, oversized robbers, the dread invoked by the empty, litter-strewn streets, the unfair odds of three armed thugs against one lone, unarmed avenger of the night, all compounded by the deliberate re-invocation of the Batman's own origin/obsession, encourage the reader to urge the Batman to retributive punishment. The final panel leaves the exact nature of this retribution to the reader's imagination.

In this instance, as in any of the iterative events, the Batman fights crime, and thus serves as an agent of political domination, safeguarding property relations and enforcing the law. Extratextually, the character and the Bat-texts serve to gain consent for political authority and the system of property relations it enshrines, and thus support the dominant hegemonic order. Again we ask, who pays the salary of this agent of political domination and this supporter of the hegemonic order? One who has a great stake in the maintenance of the status quo, Bruce Wayne. This may initially appear to be a deconstructive instance of political domination: a rich man devoting his life to vigilante justice. But the Batman's origin/obsession provides an overarching route of emotional identification even for readers who might have qualms about vigilante justice. Young Bruce's witnessing of the violation of property rights – in the fullest sense of human life – both motivates him within the text and, more importantly, wins the reader's consent to a political position: the inviolability of property relations and the justification of their defence by any means necessary (short of death). The divorce of crime from larger social issues and its embodiment in crazed costume villains or brutal gangsters reinforces the acceptance of this political position.

'I'm not fooled by that cheap disguise. I *know* what you are'

The crazed shrink of Arkham Asylum believes the Batman to be the metaphoric bat that has driven him to madness.[57] We harbour no such delusions. We know that the Batman is neither Dr Cavendish's fiendish bat nor the upright defender of the weak and innocent that he himself might claim to be. We know that he functions textually as an agent of political domination and extratextually as both supporter of the hegemonic order and a commodity form. Does the recent fragmentation of his identity that we have discussed threaten any of these functions?

The Batman's hegemonic position seems unassailable, triply reinforced by his definition as an obsessive crime-fighter, his superhero status and the narrative centrality/authority granted him.

1. OBSESSIVE CRIME-FIGHTER

Addressing the recent refractions of the Batman character, novelist Eric Van Lustbader claimed, 'The Batman remains essentially the same, which speaks volumes about his lasting power as a symbol both of elemental fear and of protean protector against the encroachment of night's dread anarchy.'[58] Lustbader here identifies that component we believe most centrally defines and contains the character: protection against night's dread anarchy – that is, against crime as presented in the Bat-texts. For Lustbader, the Batman should symbolise elemental fear only to anarchy's agents. We believe that he may, in fact, symbolise an even greater fear to those whom he might claim to aid and protect. As James Gordon said in *Batman #7* (October/November 1941), 'Yes – he works "outside the law", as you call it, but the legal devices that hamper us are hurdled by this crime-fighter so he may bring these men of evil to justice.'[59] This policeman's willingness to use any means necessary, even 'extralegal' ones, to defend the 'law' provides a particularly clear, if chilling, expression of the Batman's role as an agent of political domination. Nonetheless, his obsession, as we have explained above, serves to disguise his extralegal dimension and gain support for the hegemonic order.

2. SUPERHERO STATUS

Commentators on the Bat-texts constantly refer to that which sets the Batman apart from other superheroes: he has no superpowers. As he himself has said, 'I ... I'm a man.'[60] As editor O'Neil has said, it is the quality of human perfectibility which makes the Batman so attractive to readers, many of whom may secretly believe that they too could become a bat (with sufficient motivation and lots of training).[61] *Christianity Today* (of all publications!) addressed this utopian dimension of the Batman's character:

> But while God is conspicuously absent from this universe, Batman appears to scale the heights to which a mere man can pull himself by his own Bat-boots. It is difficult to believe that, apart from God's grace, personal tragedy and suffering can be turned to such an advantage.[62]

But the Batman deliberately cultivates a non-human image to aid him in his crime-fighting – he became a bat, after all. And the image seems to work. One of the cornered street punks who had attacked the yuppie family, exclaims, 'You're not people! Nothin' like you can be human! You ain't human, so *nothing* can stop you – man, that ain't fair.'[63] This non-human dimension frees him from the standards of evaluation applied to lesser mortals. To quote Frank Miller again:

> I think that in order for the character to work, he has to be a force that in certain ways is beyond good and evil. It can't be judged by the terms we would use to describe something a man would do because we can't think of him as a man.[64]

Though he might be different from his super-colleagues, the Batman is still more superhero than ordinary guy and this status implicitly endorses his actions. Just as superheroes' superpowers transcend those of ordinary individuals, so does their super-morality. The Batman's intertextual construction as superhero reinforces his hegemonic function.

3. NARRATIVE STRUCTURE

While narrative can be construed broadly enough to include the above two points, specific narrative devices may foster further reader acceptance of the Batman's hegemonic function. The Bat-texts clearly focalise around the Batman. *Batman* comics, of course, foreground the hero in the title, but the covers of both *Batman* and *Detective* always feature images of the Batman or at least his distinctive iconography. The stories, in addition to granting him narrative centrality, often cede him narrative authority through point-of-view frames, first-person narration and other devices similar to those film scholars often argue create identification with a character. While we would prefer to deal with actual rather than textually extrapolated readings, dominant cultural constructions of narrative encourage us seriously to consider the implications of these narrative devices.

The Bat-texts' intertextual resonance with the larger genre of detective fiction (very broadly defined) also elicits support for the Batman's activities. Though we earlier differentiated the Batman from such other series heroes as Holmes, Marlowe and Bond, he does, in fact, have a generic affiliation with them, proclaimed by the very title of his longest running comic, *Detective*. Indeed, the cover of the fiftieth-anniversary issue of this title consciously references the Batman's lineage, showing him and Sherlock Holmes together. The detective genre has traditionally privileged the hero and encouraged reader identification with him and his exploits.

Unassailable as the Batman's hegemonic function may seem, given the above three factors, some recent Bat-texts may have widened incipient fissures in the Batman's construction. Miller's *The Dark Knight Returns*, the opening salvo in the Batman's high-end marketing offensive, departed from the Batman mythos by, as we have said, featuring a fifty-year-old Batman with a female Robin. But his outlawing by the Gotham City police force, his resistance of presidential authority and his fighting with Superman severely questioned the Batman's role as an agent of political domination and actually constituted far more significant departures. His new outlaw position caused him to reappraise his analysis of the social order and ultimately to ally with elements of the underclass he had initially struggled to contain. Significantly, however, this alliance took the form of protecting property as the Batman, at the head of the mutant gangs, prevents middle-class rioters from looting a supermarket. *The Dark Knight Returns* problematises the Batman's role within a dominant political order depicted as irredeemably corrupt and bankrupt and challenges a political system which could continually re-elect Reagan president while outlawing the Batman, but reaffirms the Batman's role as lone vigilante striving for a higher justice. Society may be corrupt but the Batman's honour and vision remain above reproach in this libertarian tract.

Significantly, the next texts to exploit potential fissures in the Batman's facade did so not by taking up Miller's political critique but rather by exploring the nature of the character's obsession. *Arkham Asylum* calls the Batman's motivation into question, showing that he himself suffers from serious doubts about his sanity. *The Killing Joke* draws explicit parallels between the Joker's trauma and the Batman's, as the Joker urges his nemesis to succumb to a justifiable madness. *Batman: Year Three* and *A Lonely Place of Dying* show the Batman becoming as brutal as the thugs he fights, ignoring his deductive abilities while relying on his physical prowess to punish malefactors.

While all these texts challenge his motivation, they don't question his role as agent of political domination. Both *Arkham Asylum* and *The Killing Joke* stage confrontations between the Batman and costumed villains in isolated settings – an asylum and an abandoned fairground – environments that reflect and justify the character's extremis and thus serve to contain the broader social implications. And in both narratives, the Batman emerges intact, if not exactly triumphant, from his trial. *Batman: Year Three* and *A Lonely Place of Dying* raise doubts not about his role as agent of political domination, but about his performance of that role. If he becomes too overtly brutal, neither the supporting characters (Alfred and Dick Grayson) nor the reader can continue to give him their consent.

Some recent texts, however – and significantly in the regular titles – have begun to exhibit a certain self-conscious awareness of the Batman's hegemonic function, questioning the most central component of his identity – the nature of crime and his relation to it. 'Anarky™ in Gotham City' (*Detective* #608–9, November–December 1989) potentially redefines crime to include industrial polluters and real-estate speculators. A twelve-year-old boy, calling himself Anarky and dressed in superhero-like garb, kills a chemical manufacturer with the supposedly 'safe' sludge he is dumping into the river, and attempts to demolish a bank being built on the site of a community of homeless persons. The Batman cannot utterly condemn Anarky's actions or his definition of crime, but seeks to distinguish himself from his fellow vigilante. 'His cause may be just – but his methods certainly *aren't*.' Alfred interjects, 'Really, sir?' The Batman responds, 'I know, I know – my own methods aren't always legal, either. But there is a difference, Alfred. ... I only use violence when it's absolutely necessary, not as a form of punishment ... not lately anyway!'[65]

The Batman writers have presented an even blunter reappraisal of their hero's cosmology, permitting Henri Ducard to question the Batman's entire *raison d'être*:

> While Batman busies himself with petty thieves and gaudy *madmen*, an *abyss of rot* yawns ever wider at his feet. He's a *band-aid* on a *cancer patient*. I am of course no *moralist*, but this Batman I think, has a very poor understanding of the *world*.[66]

While this kind of questioning seems to represent a fairly minor component of the Bat-texts and has yet to be valorised by inclusion in a more expensive format, it nonetheless constitutes the gravest threat to the character's identity among the centrifugal forces we have enumerated. But the ™ following the name Anarky raises the issue of whether even this seemingly substantial critique will undermine the character or be incorporated as another marketing technique, for the Batman's circulation in commodity form is as important as his support of the hegemonic order. The contradictions of capitalism would thus permit the commodification of criticisms as long as they resulted in profits.

Yet the endless possibilities of containment and refraction inherent in the Batman character result in tensions, all of which act as potential time bombs. By contrast, the expression of the character that has the widest cultural currency remains unthreatened either by textual challenges to the Batman's role as agent of political domination/supporter of political hegemony or by the centrifugal forces of commodification – valorisation of authorship, market diversification. The Bat-logo constitutes an expression of corporate presence/control, a point of minimal contact with the character for non-Bat-fans and a magnet for discretionary income. Paradoxically, a clearer manifestation of private property and the dominant hegemonic order protecting it than the character it signifies, the Bat-logo floats untouched, above criticism. A resident of Gotham City recently stated, 'I've lived in this city for fifty years and I've never seen any of those creeps [costumed villains]. Or Batman.'[67] But he has surely seen the Bat-logo.

Postscript

This chapter centrally concerned itself with 'the endless possibilities of containment and refraction inherent in the Batman character'; we believed that the 'potential time bombs' of refraction and fragmentation might fatally undermine the sustainability of the character and the franchise. We speculated that the stark contradictions among the Batman's many lives threatened 'both the integrity of the commodity form and the coherence of the fans' lived experience of the character necessary to the Batman's continued success'. Sixteen years after the publication of *The Many Lives of the Batman*, Henry Jenkins provided a somewhat different interpretation of this crucial moment in the character's history: 'Retrospectively, we can see Pearson and Uricchio as describing a moment of transition from continuity to multiplicity.'[68] The continuity strategy catered for the expectations of the core comics readership by maintaining character coherence across multiple narratives. By contrast, the multiplicity strategy caters for a larger and more diverse audience through multiple narratives featuring different versions of the character.

When we wrote our chapter, the comic book industry had not consciously articulated a business model that acknowledged the shift to multiplicity. The strategy was just beginning to emerge in the last decades of the twentieth century in response to the shifts in popular culture and the underlying conditions of production and reception documented by our chapter, together with those by Eileen Meehan and Jim Collins. But, as Jenkins argued in 2007, multiplicity has, in the intervening years, become the industry's prime directive, as the two superpowers, DC and Marvel, frequently reboot their universes and reconfigure their heroes in their ongoing effort to retain old readers and attract new ones, as well as to extend their valuable character brands across multiple platforms. For example, Marvel Comics has just announced the launch of a female Thor and a black Captain America.

Clearly, the question that we posed more than two decades ago concerning containment and refraction has even greater relevance now. As Jenkins says, multiplicity invites 'a search for the core or essence of the character even as [it] encourage[s] us to take pleasure in their many permutations'.[69] The introduction to this new edition discusses the many permutations of the Batman subsequent to our writing this chapter, demonstrating that the character may be even more fragmented and diverse, ever more of a floating signifier, in 2015 than he was in 1991. Nonetheless, those key components of the character we identified in 1991 continue to define the character in 2015. Nolan's Batman may have more psychological depth than Kane's Batman, but still has his wealth, his obsession, his deductive skills and his abnormal physical prowess. He still fights crime as a result of childhood trauma, interacts with a fixed set of recurrent characters, is based in Gotham City and wears a costume and uses accessories that bear a family resemblance to those of the 1939 original.

The multiplicity strategy requires key components as much if not more than did the continuity strategy; readers ignorant of a character's basic building blocks would be unable to take pleasure in their permutations. No doubt the premiere of *Gotham* (Fox, 2014–) was eagerly awaited by Bat-fans in the autumn of 2014, because advance publicity had made it clear that though the television series is set twenty years before the Batman's first appearance, it features the same set of events (murder of the Waynes, crime-fighting), settings (Gotham City) and characters (Bruce Wayne, James Gordon, Alfred and various villains) they have become accustomed to in all the character's multiple iterations. Advance publicity had also made it clear that the television series wouldn't follow the continuity of the feature-film series, thus giving audiences competing large- and small-screen Batmen. The multiplicity strategy perfectly suits a twenty-first-century mediascape characterised by marked industrial and technological convergence (witness Rupert Murdoch's failed attempt to add Time Warner to his Fox empire in 2014). Hence the endless reboots of established properties such as the Batman, Superman, Spider-Man, the Hulk and *Star Trek*. Producers seek to maximise revenue from their intellectual property by creating and spreading new iterations while at the same time continuing to circulate old iterations as widely as possible.

In our chapter, we noted in passing that 'DC's editorial offices form one of the two central bastions of character identity, the other being the legal, licensing and rights departments of both DC and Warner Bros.' Since 1991, intellectual property rights have become increasingly important drivers of content production; they also shape that content's characters and narrative worlds, both encouraging and suppressing multiplicity. In the case of Sherlock Holmes, whose copyright status is now being debated in the US courts, the lack of a strong and coordinating controller of the intellectual property has encouraged multiplicity, resulting in divergent and unconnected representations of the character in film (the Robert Downey/Guy Ritchie *Sherlock Holmes* [2009] and *Sherlock Holmes: A Game of Shadows* [2011], as well as *Mr. Holmes* [2015] starring Sir Ian McKellen as an elderly, Alzheimer's-afflicted version of the detective) and television (*Sherlock* [BBC, 2010–] and *Elementary* [CBS, 2012–]). In the case of *Star Trek*, intellectual property may be suppressing multiplicity. When Viacom split from Paramount in 2005, Paramount retained the rights to *Star Trek* cinema while CBS acquired the rights to *Star Trek* television. There is constant speculation about a new television series, but it seems that the powers that be at both corporations fear that the market may not support multiple new iterations of the *Star Trek* universe, especially while the old iterations and the new films continue to produce so much revenue.[70] But Warner has made precisely the opposite decision, licensing Fox to broadcast a Batman television series while it continues to make Batman films.

The ownership of intellectual property rights can not only encourage or suppress multiplicity in unpredictable fashion, it can also legally mandate the ways in which producers develop their characters and narrative universes. Fox obtained the cinematic rights to *The X-Men* comics prior to the launching of Marvel Studios. After Marvel entered the feature-film business and sought to incorporate X-Men characters into its *Avengers* film series, the potential multiplicity caused legal wrangling between the two studios. As a result, both Fox's *X-Men: Days of Future Past* (2014) and Marvel's *Avengers 2* (2015) feature a minor character called Quicksilver, but he must be conceived entirely differently for each film. Furthermore, Marvel cannot designate the character a mutant or make any reference to Magneto, while Fox cannot make any reference to The Avengers.[71] Although neither of us is familiar with Quicksilver, or indeed, aside from the films, the Marvel Universe, we suppose that his mutant status is most likely one of the character's key components. Rather than different versions of the same character, will the two films actually feature two entirely different characters? Or will viewers acquainted with the Marvel comic universe have no difficulty identifying Quicksilver as a mutant, while the rest of the audience remains baffled? Since Warner continues to be sole owner of the Batman intellectual property, narrative complexities of quite this magnitude are unlikely to arise.

Nonetheless, as the proliferation and permutations of the Batman's many lives continues, from comics to film to television to video games, they will undoubtedly provoke further speculation regarding the character's key components. Indeed, this very volume encompasses divergent opinions. Our original chapter argued for the importance of the Batman's origin story, subsequently 'subjected to compulsive retellings and variations'. But Paul Levitz, in Chapter 1 of this volume, speculates that the Batman's protean nature, what we would term his multiplicity, may stem from his being 'less linked to, and less dependent on, his origin than his peers were'. Contra this, Denny O'Neil, in the interview reprinted in this volume, asserts that 'The origin is the engine that drives Batman.' We tend to agree with O'Neil. Other superheroes' origin stories centre around the acquisition of their superpowers. The Batman, of course, has no superpowers; his origin story provides him instead with the super-motivation that compels his obsessive crime-fighting. It also provides the initial 'darkness', both literal and metaphorical, that has dominated representations of the character in the comics, films and video games since the 1980s and which is an essential element of the new *Gotham*. We therefore stand by our assertion as to the origin story's centrality. We also confidently assert that the key components we identified in 1991 remain key components in 2015. But we are not so confident that they will still be so in 2037, by which time the Batman will have inevitably accrued many more lives.

Notes

1. The title of the chapter is taken from Grant Morrison, *Arkham Asylum* (New York: DC Comics, 1989), n.p.
2. Box side panel, Batman™ Cereal (St Louis, MO: Ralston Purina Co., 1989).
3. Ibid.
4. Quoted in 'Writer: Sam Hamm', *Comics Interview* no. 70 (1989), p. 17.
5. John Marriott, *Batman: The Official Book of the Movie* (London: Bantam Books, 1989), p. 39.
6. Quoted in Howard A. Rodman, 'They Shoot Comic Books, Don't They?', *American Film*, no. 26 (May 1989), p. 38.

7. Bill Barol, 'Batmania', *Newsweek*, 26 June 1989, p. 72.

8. Simon Garfield, 'Batman Versus Hollywood', *Time Out: 20/20*, July 1989, p. 54.

9. Kane, quoted in 'Artist: Bob Kane', *Comics Interview* no. 70 (1989), p. 49.

10. The Batman's mortality, of course, gives him the potential for ageing, though *The Dark Knight Returns* is so far the only text to activate this potential.

11. We are indebted to Henry Jenkins III for this insight.

12. This is not to assert that the Batman has never done anything but fight crime. In *Batman* #156 (June 1963), he even fights a pink space monster, but most fans and writers view this and similar science-fictional episodes as aberrant.

13. Dennis O'Neil, 'A Brief Batbible: Notes on the Dark Knight Detective', unpublished manuscript, April 1989, n.p.

14. We use the term 'iterative' in Umberto Eco's, not Gerard Genette's, sense. Eco defines the iterative as follows: 'a series of events repeated according to a set scheme (… in such a way that each event takes up again from a sort of virtual beginning, ignoring where the preceding event left off)'. Umberto Eco, 'The Myth of Superman', in *The Role of the Reader: Explorations in the Semiotics of Texts* (Bloomington: Indiana University Press, 1979), p. 117.

15. Neil Gaiman, 'When Is a Door. The Secret Origin of the Riddler', *Secret Origins Special* #1 (1989), n.p.

16. *Rolling Stone*, 29 June 1989, p. 43.

17. For a discussion of the rise of the direct-distribution network, we refer the reader to Patrick Parsons's 'Batman and His Audience: The Dialectic of Culture', in Roberta E. Pearson and William Uricchio (eds), *The Many Lives of the Batman: Critical Approaches to a Superhero and His Media* (New York: Routledge, 1991), pp. 66–89.

18. 'Artist: Bob Kane', *Comics Interview* no. 31 (1986), p. 17.

19. *Batman* #206 (November 1968), n.p.

20. Letter from Greg W. Myers, 'Batcave', *Detective Comics* #495 (October 1980), n.p.

21. This recent reconfiguration of authorship in the comics industry accords with the authorship function as described by Michel Foucault. See 'What Is an Author?' in *Language, Counter-Memory, Practice* (Ithaca, NY: Cornell University Press, 1977).

22. The masculine pronoun reflects the current dominance of males at the two major companies.

23. Advertisement for DC Comics in Dennis O'Neil, *The Batman Movie Adaptation* (New York: DC Comics, 1989).

24. Jenette Kahn, 'Don't Call Me Chief!', *The New Titans* #61 (December 1989), n.p.

25. The quotation in the heading of this section is taken from Alan Moore, 'The Mark of Batman', in *The Complete Frank Miller Batman* (Stamford, CT: Longmeadow Press, 1989), n.p.

26. Mike Gold, 'Our Darkest Knight', in Gold (ed.), *The Greatest Batman Stories Ever Told* (New York: DC Comics, 1988), p. 14.

27. For thirty-five of the Caped Crusader's fifty years, two men, Jack Schiff and Julie Schwartz, edited the Batman titles. Most of the editors since Schwartz's retirement had worked with him as writers or artists.

28. Jenette Kahn, 'Don't Call Me Chief!', *Legends of the Dark Knight* #3 (January 1990), n.p.

29. Alan Moore, *Batman: The Killing Joke* (New York: DC Comics, 1988), n.p.

30. Gaiman, 'When Is a Door'.

31. Interview with Dennis O'Neil in this volume.

32. 'Batsignals', *Batman* #442 (December 1989), n.p.

33. 'Who's Who', *Detective Comics Annual* #2 (1989), n.p.

34. Dennis O'Neil, *Batman: The Official Comic Adaptation of the Warner Bros. Motion Picture* (New York: DC Comics, 1989).

35. Personal conversation with Dennis O'Neil, 29 September 1989.

36. *The Batman Role-Playing Game* (Niles, IL: Mayfair Games, 1989).

37. Dick Giordano, 'Growing up with the Greatest', in Gold (ed.), *Greatest Batman Stories Ever Told*, pp. 7–8.

38. Moore, 'The Mark of Batman', n.p.

39. Batman Card #238, second series (The Topps Company, 1989).

40. Dennis O'Neil, 'The Joker's Five-Way Revenge', *Batman* #251 (September 1973), n.p.

41. Jenette Kahn, 'Tribute', *Detective Comics* #599 (April 1989), n.p.

42. Morrison, *Arkham Asylum*.

43. Alan Brennert, 'Tribute', *Detective Comics* #600 (May 1989), n.p.

44. Bob Kane saw both narrative and other reasons for a Robin: 'I think it was a *bad* move to kill Robin off. First of all they were a team – it would be like killing Dr Watson off and leaving Sherlock Holmes by himself or Tonto and the Lone Ranger, Tarzan and Jane. It's the wrong move. And, of course, it kills the merchandizing on Robin.' 'Artist: Bob Kane', *Comics Interview* no. 70 (1989), p. 47.

45. 'Spotlight: Dark Knight', *Comics Interview* no. 31 (1986), p. 32.

46. Jim Starlin, *A Death in the Family* (New York: DC Comics, 1988), n.p.

47. Marv Wolfman, 'A Lonely Place of Dying', part 1, *Batman* #440 (October 1989), n.p.

48. Letter from Malcolm Bourne, *Batman* #440 (October 1989), n.p.

49. Marv Wolfman, 'A Lonely Place of Dying', *Batman* #442 (December 1989), n.p.

50. The quotation in the heading of this section is from 'Frank Miller: Return of the Dark Knight', *The Comics Journal* no. 101 (August 1985), p. 64.

51. Quoted in Sam Hamm, 'Blind Justice (Part III)', *Detective Comics* #600 (May 1989), n.p.

52. Marv Wolfman, 'The Coming of Crimesmith', *Batman* #443 (January 1990).

53. Marv Wolfman, 'Batman: Year Three (Part I)', *Batman* #436 (August 1989), n.p.

54. *Batman* #443, n.p.

55. Sam Hamm and Warren Skaaren, 'BATMAN', unpublished screenplay, 6 October 1988.

56. 'Spotlight: Dark Knight', p. 37.

57. The quotation in the heading of this section is from Morrison, *Arkham Asylum*.

58. Eric Van Lustbader, 'Tribute', *Detective Comics* #600 (May 1989), n.p.

59. *Batman* #7, quoted in Mark Cotta Vaz, *Tales of the Dark Knight: Batman's First Fifty Years, 1939–1989* (New York: Ballantine, 1989), p. 4.

60. Morrison, *Arkham Asylum*.

61. Personal conversation, Dennis O'Neil, 29 September 1989.

62. Dean Husler, 'Gotham Great Grows Grim', *Christianity Today*, 12 May 1989, p. 65.

63. *Batman* #443, n.p.

64. 'Frank Miller: Return of the Dark Knight', p. 61.

65. Alan Grant, 'Anarky in Gotham City', *Detective Comics* #608 (November 1989), n.p.

66. Hamm, 'Blind Justice (Part III)', n.p.

67. Neil Gaiman, 'Original Sins', *Secret Origins* #1 (1989), n.p.

68. Henry Jenkins, 'Just Men in Capes? (Part One)', 15 March 2007. Available at: <http://henryjenkins.org/2007/03/just_men_in_capes.html>.

69. Ibid.

70. See Roberta Pearson and Máire Messenger Davies, *Star Trek and American Television* (Berkeley: University of California Press, 2014), p. 191.

71. Drew McWeeny, 'Why Are Fox and Marvel Having a Showdown over "X-Men" and "The Avengers 2"?', *Hitfix*, 23 May 2013. Available at: <http://www.hitfix.com/motion-captured/why-are-fox-and-marvel-having-a-showdown-over-x-men-and-the-avengers-2#auW0z0pE5MaUM4rY.99>.

INDEX

Page numbers in **bold** indicate detailed analysis; those in *italic* denote illustrations; *n* = endnote.

List of Illustrations

While considerable effort has been made to correctly identify copyright holders this has not been possible in all cases. We apologise for any apparent negligence and any omissions or corrections brought to our attention will be remedied in any future editions.

Batman, Warner Bros./Guber-Peters Company/PolGram Filmed Entertainment; *Superman*, © Film Export A.G.; *Batman Begins*, © Patalex III Productions; *The Dark Knight*, © Warner Bros. Entertainment Inc.; *The Dark Knight Rises*, © Warner Bros. Entertainment Inc./Legendary Pictures Funding LLC; *Batman*, 20th Century-Fox Television/Greenway Productions.